THE COMMUNIST PARTY
OF THE UNITED STATES

THE COMMUNIST PARTY OF THE UNITED STATES

From the Depression to World War II

FRASER M. OTTANELLI

 RUTGERS UNIVERSITY PRESS
New Brunswick and London

Library of Congress Cataloging-in-Publication Data

Ottanelli, Fraser M.
   The Communist party of the United States : from the depression to
world war II / Fraser M. Ottanelli.
     p. cm.
   Includes bibliographical references.
   ISBN 0-8135-1612-9 (cloth)   ISBN 0-8135-1613-7 (pbk.)
   1. Communist Party of the United States of America—History.
2. United States—Politics and government—1929–1933. 3. United
States—Politics and government—1933–1945.   I. Title.
JK2391.C5078 1991
324.273'75'09—dc20   90-34391
                                                               CIP

British Cataloging-in-Publication information available

To my parents

CONTENTS

ACKNOWLEDGMENTS

In the course of researching and writing this book, I have enjoyed help and encouragement from many sources, and I should like to thank them here.

The staff of the George Arents Research Library, Syracuse University; R. W. Woodruff Library, Emory University; Tamiment Library, New York University; and of the New York Public Library, all provided excellent expert assistance. I wish to thank Theodore Draper for allowing me to use his interviews with Earl Browder deposited at the Woodruff Library as well as Paul Buhle for permitting me to cite from the Oral History of the American Left collection housed at the Tamiment Library. I have also benefited greatly from interviews with several persons directly involved in the events described in this work. Gil Green, Saul Wellman, and the late Max Gordon also read several drafts of the manuscript and provided insightful criticism. Over the course of the years I have spent many hours with Steve Nelson discussing and reflecting on his experiences in the communist movement. In the course of these conversations a deep friendship has developed which I greatly cherish.

At Syracuse, William C. Stinchcombe, provided beneficial criticism; Sally Gregory Kohlstedt (now at the University of Minnesota) and John Scott Strickland also supplied many thoughtful comments and suggestions. Based on their impressive knowledge of twentieth-century radicalism, Paul Buhle and Milton Cantor provided penetrating criticism which has contributed greatly to this work. My colleagues at the University of South Florida, Nancy Hewitt, Robert P. Ingalls, and Louis A. Perez Jr., read various versions of the manuscript and made pointed and incisive comments and criticism. This list would not be complete without mention of Giuliano Procacci who first encouraged me to study United States Communists.

I am deeply indebted to Annette Muir for taking the time to read and edit my pre-final draft, improving immeasurably grammar, syntax, and style, and ultimately helping make my ideas clearer.

At every stage of my career I have had the encouragement and support of Giovanna Benadusi. I thank her for this and for much more than words can express.

Our son, Carlo, was born as I was revising the manuscript. His joyful presence has given me an added incentive to finish this book.

Finally, my deepest appreciation goes to my parents, Ann Fraser Ottanelli and Vittorio Ottanelli, to whom I dedicate this book.

THE COMMUNIST PARTY
OF THE UNITED STATES

What the hell is these reds anyways? . . . Well, sir, Hines says, "A red is any son-of-a-bitch that wants thirty cents an hour when we're payin' twenty-five!" Well, this young fella he thinks about her, an' he scratches his head, an' he says, "Well, Jesus, Mr. Hines. I ain't a son-of-a-bitch, but if that's what a red is—why, I want thirty cents an hour. Ever'body does. Hell, Mr. Hines, we're all reds."

JOHN STEINBECK, *The Grapes of Wrath*, 1939

INTRODUCTION

I first became interested in the history of the Communist Party of the United States (CPUSA), as a result of reading Joseph Starobin's *American Communism in Crisis*. What attracted me was Starobin's account of Communists in the United States taking the independent and unprecedented step in 1944 of dissolving their party in order to work within the two-party system. Sensitive to the unique character of both United States society and its political system, Communists chose a course which they believed would help them become a more effective force in their country.

For me the dissolution of the CPUSA, with its broad implications, raised a number of questions. What were the origin, the development, and the forms of the political and cultural process that led Communists in the United States to address the peculiarities of their country's reality? How did the United States experience relate to that of other Communist parties? The pursuit of the answers to these questions led to the present work.

In the most recent general work on the CPUSA, published in 1984, *The Heyday of American Communism*, Harvey Klehr wrote that the Party's changes of policy during the 1930s

> were not in response to any internal changes in American society or the Party itself, but reflected the pull of an external force. If the needs of Russian policy dictated a revolutionary or sectarian Comintern policy, the American Communists swung over to the left. When those needs changed, they swung back to a more reformist or opportunistic line. Within the limits of their knowledge, American Communists always strove to provide what the Comintern wanted, no more, no less.[1]

Klehr's conclusion demonstrates how the study of United States Communism is still strongly influenced by the scholarly studies from the 1950s and early 1960s that examined the Party's history solely from the perspective of establishing the Soviet origins of the Party's policies.

The most significant of these works is Theodore Draper's definitive two-volume history of the Communist party during the 1920s. In *The Roots of American Communism* and *American Communism and Soviet Russia*, Draper describes how American Communism, born from the enthusiastic response of a wide assortment of indigenous radicals to a distant and highly idealized Bolshevik revolution, eventually became subservient to Moscow's control. Draper convincingly argued that Moscow's hand, rather than changing conditions in the United States, directed the Communist party's dizzying succession of conflicting policies during the 1920s. Moreover, Draper generalized this conclusion and applied it to all the subsequent history of the Party. By 1922 he wrote, American Communism, "was transformed from a new expression of radicalism to the American appendage of a Russian revolutionary power. Nothing else so important ever happened to it again."[2] Other works, written in the 1950s that deal with the Party during the depression and the war years have expressed similar conclusions. In his 1952 essay "Marxian Socialism in the United States," Daniel Bell summarized Party history as a series of "twists and 'periods' " reflecting events and concerns within the Soviet Union. A few years later Irving Howe and Lewis Coser described Party members as "malleable objects" completely subordinated to Moscow's directives.[3]

New Left historians also viewed the Party exclusively in its relationship to Moscow. Whereas other historians offered the Moscow connection as their chief evidence that the Communist party was a political organization alien to United States reality, New Left historians utilized the Soviet connection to explain why a mass socialist organization did not develop in the United States during the 1930s. According to this interpretation, the Party's subservience to the Soviet Union privileged the defense of the Socialist State over the creation of a strong revolutionary movement in the United States. Based on this premise, James Weinstein, Stanley Aronowitz, and others concluded that the Communist party did not take advantage of a situation which they considered favorable for the development of a socialist movement and instead subordinated its program of socialist revolution to helping build CIO unions and to collaborating with "New Deal liberalism." In this process the Communist party lost its revolutionary identity and instead actually assisted the capitalist system to overcome some of its major contradictions and strengthen its dominance.[4]

Recent studies have begun to test the limitations of the traditional interpretation. While examining different aspects of the Party's history in the period from the depression through the 1950s, scholars and former Party members have not only written "Party history" but also a social history of American Communism, focusing on Party activities in state and city politics, in ethnic and racial communities, and within the labor movement. These works have examined the motivations that influenced men and women from diverse ethnic and cultural backgrounds to become Communists, the aspirations that carried them through the turbulence of the Party's experience, and the strong sense of community that bound together people working for the same cause. The image that emerges from these studies is one of a diverse and adaptable organization rooted in the social and labor struggles of the time, and capable of adjusting to the complexity and historical peculiarities of the nation's society and the pressures that derived from them. Moreover, these works emphasize that the Party commanded considerable community and labor support.[5]

While balancing the record, the current tendency toward emphasis on the grass roots, however, presents some dangers. Just as sole concentration on the leadership missed the richness and complexity of Communism in the United States, the new history tends to overshadow the fact that the Communist party was a highly centralized Leninist organization with little room for the diversity that characterized, for instance, Populism or the Socialist party. Despite the bitter and at times personal tone of his critique of the new history of the CPUSA, Theodore Draper was correct when he recently warned of the dangers of separating the activities of Communists from the policies of the Party, making it seem, he wrote, "as if there were two Communist parties, one of the leadership and the other of the rank-and-file, each going their own way."[6] In line with his scholarship, Draper contends that the new history distorts the true nature of the CPUSA as it obscures the fact that rank-and-file Communists in the United States were implementing policies originating in Moscow which reflected Soviet priorities of the moment, policies that were filtered down to them through the Communist International and the Party's national leadership.

My criticism of the new history is of a different nature. The exclusive emphasis on the grass roots misses the interaction between local experiences and overall Party policy. In its findings the new history implicitly raises a number of questions concerning the process of policymaking at the leadership level which must be addressed. Specifically, given the Party's authoritarian internal structure and decision-making process which required strict discipline from its members, what was the explanation for the tolerance displayed by its leadership in those numerous instances in which Communist organizers downplayed, modified, and in some cases even defied official policy? Furthermore, did the collective experience of Communist organizers find expression in the elaboration of national policy and, in turn, did this policy encourage and add new insight in the process at the grass roots of following a course better attuned to domestic circumstances?

What follows is a history of the CPUSA from the outset of the depression through the war years. It is a "traditional" account in the sense that it concentrates on the evolution of the Party's policies at a leadership level. However, it uses the new insights of social historians together with published and oral recollections of activists as a vantage point from which to take a fresh look and reinterpret institutional sources such as policy statements, the writings of Party leaders, and the articles that appeared in the Party's press. The present work parts from previous studies in that it avoids a unilateral approach centered exclusively either on the Party's relation with Moscow or on the grassroots activities of Communists. It suggests instead that the two levels be looked at concertedly within the aggregate system of which they were integral component parts in order to understand how together they determined the course of the Communist party in the United States. My research shows that during the Party's period of greatest strength and influence, the origins and the genesis of its overall policies and analysis were quite complex and cannot be viewed simply as being handed down by Moscow. Rather, the policies of the CPUSA were the result of an intricate interaction, and at times struggle among a number of factors: first, the Party's involvement in the great social and labor struggles of the period and the experiences and lessons Communists drew from them; second, the influence these lessons and experiences had on the Party's line nationally; and finally, the Party's relationship with Moscow. In other words, the course of the CPUSA was shaped by a homespun search for policies which would make it an integral part of the country's society as well as by directives from the Communist International.

This approach adds new elements for understanding the sources of the Party's appeal and of its emergence as the foremost expression of left-wing radicalism during the depression and the war years. Scores of Americans embraced the Party's program and ideology to become part of what they considered a national and international revolutionary vanguard, fighting for social justice and already in power in the Soviet Union. Furthermore, the evidence suggests that the success of the CPUSA was also the result of the Party's responsiveness to express, incorporate, and expand upon the desire of Communists to adopt policies relevant to the country's specific circumstances and changing international conditions.

This study emphasizes those events and debates that most heavily weighted and shaped the policies of the CPUSA. In his path-breaking book, Maurice Isserman explained his decision to focus on the activities of the CPUSA during the war years because during that period "for a brief moment, the Communists seemed to be moving toward a more realistic appraisal of their position in American life."[7] While fully agreeing with this assessment, however I believe that it is necessary to expand the breadth of investigation and to place more emphasis on the Party's activities throughout the 1930s. The periodization of this work, starting with the stock market crash and ending with the reconstitution of the CPUSA in 1945, illustrates a continuity in the Party's experience centered around an indigenous quest for policies, organizational forms, language, and overall cultural forms that would adapt the Communists' radicalism to domestic realities and political traditions.

This book is divided into three parts. The first covers the period from 1929 to approximately 1934. Following a chronological development, this section establishes a contrast between the analysis of the Communist International and the day-to-day experiences of scores of Communist activists, leading to tensions between the official Party line and its implementation. The second part, through the end of 1939, shifts from a chronological to a topical organization, and traces the development of the policy and culture of the Popular Front and, particularly, the Party's own redefinition of the latter to make it conform to the singular political reality of the United States. The third part, from 1941 to 1945, examines the attempt by the CPUSA both to repair the loss of prestige and acceptance it had suffered as a result of its shift away from antifascism during the "imperialist war" period and to provide a broad theoretical framework within which to place the evolution of its policies since the early 1930s.

PART ONE

1

DIFFICULT BEGINNINGS, 1919–1929

Looking back upon the nascent Communist movement in the United States, James Cannon, one of its founding members, divided the early years into three distinct periods. During the first, from 1917 to 1919, the left wing of the Socialist party, from which American Communism emerged, strengthened by the First World War and the Bolshevik revolution, battled with the Socialist right-wing along clearly defined lines of political principle. During the second, from 1920 to 1923, the newly formed Communist movement split into factions that agreed on principles but not on tactics in the matter of specific "American" circumstances. In the third period, from 1924 to 1928, factions no longer reflected different views of addressing changing conditions in the United States but rather, Cannon argued, waged a blind power struggle for "supremacy or survival in a form of political gang warfare."[1]

When historians survey the early years of the Communist movement, with its constantly shifting alliances, its apparently inexplicable reversals of positions, and the often abstract character of the issues at the center of discussion, deciphering the Party's history during the 1920s becomes an arduous task. Thus Cannon's three periods, despite the obvious limitations of any participant's attempt to generalize, represent an acceptable synthesis of a very complex decade in the Party's history.[2]

At first the roots of factionalism were indigenous: a clash between the proponents of a sectarian revolutionary orthodoxy and those who wanted an organization with a broad mass following. This clash arose from the diverse legacy of the left-wing elements which founded the Communist movement in the United States: orthodox Marxists, syndicalists, members of the Industrial Workers of the World, and the Socialist party's East European language federations. These left-wing forces were initially united by their common opposition to the World

War and to pro-war Socialists both in Europe and in the United States. As the revolutionary movement began spreading throughout Europe, the Socialist-left predicted that it would soon reach the United States as well. This expectation made the left wing's further coexistence with the advocates of reform and gradual change in the Socialist party impossible.[3]

When it came to determining the nature of the new party the left wing of the Socialist party split into two groups. The language federations, which possessed little understanding of United States reality, dominated the group that wished to abandon the Socialist party to found a tightly knit vanguard organization. The other group, composed of the majority of the English-speaking forces and headed by John Reed and Benjamin Gitlow, sought to exploit the left's strength within the Socialist party to take it over and thus ensure the new Communist organization a large following. Divisions persisted even after John Reed and his followers had failed in their plan to capture the Socialist party. Thus, in early September 1919, not one but two Communist parties were founded. The first, composed mostly of the language federations, was called the Communist party; the second, became the Communist Labor party. Estimates of the combined membership of both parties in 1919 range from 20,000 to 40,000 of whom only 10 percent spoke English.

In 1919, the Communist decision not to participate in the widespread strike wave because its demands were economic rather than revolutionary isolated them from the labor movement.[4] The process of isolation was furthered by the repressive campaign launched by the United States government. The Red Scare of 1920 led to thousands of arrests, the deportation of 550 Communist aliens, and sent the Communist movement underground.[5] While effectively preventing the growth of the movement's political presence, the underground existence also reinforced a mentality and a sense of emulation of the Bolshevik prerevolutionary experience.

Regardless of faction, American Communists acknowledged the preeminence of the Communist International (also referred to as Comintern) which, starting in 1920, began to play an increasingly active role in their affairs. After coming under attack from Lenin and after the Comintern had issued a number of warnings, the two parties finally merged in May 1921.[6] Moscow settled the issue of whether or not United States Communists should reconstitute themselves as a legal organization. While many members of the Party preferred the seemingly more revolutionary underground stance, Moscow sided with those who believed that the changed political climate in the United States made a clandestine organization unnecessary. The process of legalization began in late 1921 with the founding of the Workers party to serve as the Communists' legal extension and was completed sixteen months later when the underground organization was finally disbanded.[7]

In 1921, in the wake of defeat of the revolutionary movement in Europe and in consideration of Lenin's writings on extremism, the Comintern instructed American Communists to abandon their policy of revolutionary isolation and to work instead in defense of workers' immediate demands. This tactic led Communists to work with established unions and opened collaboration with reformist forces around transitional, non-revolutionary programs.[8]

This new line had important implications for American Communists. They abandoned their support for the IWW and their opposition to working within the American Federation of Labor.[9] As a result of this major shift in tactics, William Z. Foster was drawn into the Party and rapidly gained the prominent position which he was to hold for the rest of his life. Tall and lean, Foster's background was impeccably "proletarian." Born in Taunton, Massachusetts, of working class parents, Foster had left school early to go to work and had held an assortment of jobs around the country. As a Populist, Foster supported Bryan in 1896 and in 1901, at the age of twenty, joined the newly formed Socialist party. Expelled eight years later because he was a member of a left-wing faction in the State of Washington, Foster then joined the IWW.[10] In 1910 he traveled to Europe to study French syndicalism first hand. There he acquired a belief in the importance of boring-from-within to capture conservative unions.

Once back in the States Foster found himself at odds with the IWW, which supported dual unionism. Consequently Foster broke with the Wobblies and began his efforts to organize left-wing opposition within the AFL. In 1917 Foster led the AFL's successful drive to organize meat packers in Chicago. During this period he established strong ties with the Chicago Federation of Labor and, in particular, with its leader, John Fitzpatrick, a radical who opposed Samuel Gompers and favored amalgamation.[11] In 1919 Foster led the great steel strike during which 350,000 workers walked off their jobs, virtually shutting down U.S. Steel. Despite the strike's ultimate defeat, Foster's reputation as an extremely capable labor leader had been established. In 1920 he organized the Trade Union Educational League (TUEL), a boring-from-within organization. However, his insistence on working within the AFL brought him much criticism from the left, including the Communists, who referred to him as "E. Z. Foster." The Comintern's new line of working within the AFL changed all of this.[12]

The encounter between Foster and the Communists was mutually beneficial. Foster had been kept at arm's length by the leadership of the AFL and felt increasingly isolated. On the other hand, Communists, by recruiting him, acquired a capable union organizer and a charismatic leader with a national reputation. Through the TUEL, they also gained a foothold within the AFL. Foster was then invited to attend as an observer the first Congress of the Red International of Labor Unions (also known by its Russian abbreviation, Profintern) to be held in Moscow in July. There he readily accepted the International's decision to enter the AFL to create a revolutionary opposition and the TUEL became the Profintern's American section. Upon his return to the States, Foster joined the Communist party, but this decision was not publicly disclosed until 1923, at which time he was put in charge of the Party's labor activities.[13]

The Party's new policy brought Communists notable results. Among labor the TUEL, strengthened by the Party's support and backed by John Fitzpatrick and his Chicago Federation of Labor, together with a number of national, state, and local unions, launched a campaign in favor of industrial unionism and the organization of the unorganized.[14] During 1922 the TUEL was active in the Chicago building trades strike and in the coal strike; in the United Mine Workers' Union it supported the coalition of forces opposing John L. Lewis. The TUEL also succeeded in establishing close ties with the Auto Workers Unions.[15] Because of these activities the TUEL broadened its support and entrenched itself within a number of locals in major unions making it very difficult for the leadership of the AFL to dislodge it.

In electoral politics Communists ran candidates in local elections and in 1922 supported the Socialist candidate for Congress, Meyer London, from New York City's East Side. At the same time they joined those in favor of the formation of a new national farmer-labor party, first by joining with Fitzpatrick in 1923 and later by supporting Robert La Follette's bid for the presidency in 1924. Both attempts, however, led to major setbacks for the Party. In the first case, the Communists' arrogant and clumsy maneuver to take over the leader-

ship of the movement caused a break with Fitzpatrick and his supporters and left the Communist party in control of an empty shell. In the
second, the reasons for the Party's fiasco had nothing to do with
United States Communists but was, rather, the direct consequence of
decisions made in Moscow. Torn by the factional infighting of Trotsky
against Zinoviev-Kamenev and Stalin, the Comintern reversed its position on alliances with organizations such as the farmer-labor movement and forced the Communist party to break with it and run its
own candidate.[16]

The consequences for Communists of their split with the farmer-
labor forces were catastrophic. Communists lost the support of their
progressive allies and their enemies were quick to take full advantage
of the situation. At the AFL's 1923 convention, the TUEL was branded
a dual union and its members expelled from AFL unions. The TUEL
rapidly lost the strength and influence it had gained and found itself
on the defensive and at the margins of organized labor. The Party had
to wait for over ten years before being able to rebuild ties with progressive and labor forces. Consumed by factional infighting, after 1924 the
Party lived on the margins of United States political life. A prominent
Party leader recalled how Communists spent the rest of the 1920s "in
isolation and destructive inner factionalism."[17]

The Party again split into two camps: on one side Charles Ruthenberg, the Party secretary, together with Jay Lovestone, on the other
Foster and Cannon, with intermediate positions arising from time to
time. The former group had its roots in the left wing of the Socialist
party and favored more "political" activities. The latter originated
mostly from trade union experiences and favored expanding the
Party's role into the ranks of labor. As class struggle gave way to
factional strife, political differences between the two became increasingly blurred by personality clashes. Furthermore, increasingly factionalism became nothing more than a reenactment of the struggle for
power being waged within the Communist party of the Soviet
Union.[18] In 1928, Cannon and a number of his followers were expelled
as Trotskyists and subsequently founded the Communist League of
America. The following year the power struggle between Stalin and
Bukharin spilled over to the United States and led to the eventual
expulsion of Lovestone who had taken over as secretary in 1927 after
Ruthenberg's death. Lovestone insisted that the Comintern's analysis
concerning the upcoming breakdown of capitalism and the resulting
mounting revolutionary movement was not applicable to the United

States. He believed instead in the "exceptionalism" of the country's capitalism and claimed that capitalist development had not peaked in the United States; consequently he disagreed with any prediction of imminent economic collapse and of the development of the Communist party into a mass organization. Lovestone's insistence on defending his analysis despite repeated warnings from Moscow ultimately led to his downfall and expulsion from the Party together with 200 of his followers.[19]

Despite his victory over Lovestone, Foster, contrary to his expectations, was not elevated to the position of Party secretary. Instead he was forced to share the post with Earl Browder, a relatively new name for the majority of the rank-and-file.[20] Browder, who was to become the Communist leader most closely associated with the Party's activities during the 1930s through to 1945, contrasted sharply with Foster. Browder was a small man, reserved in manner and conventional in dress, and although he was an effective public speaker, he could hardly have been called a charismatic figure. In later years he would be described as looking "like the popular concept of a professor in a small Midwest college" or as having "the honest face of a clerk in a Kansas feed-and-grain store." Certainly he was far from the stereotyped image of foreign-looking and -sounding Communists. These characteristics served him well.[21]

Browder's roots went back to seventeenth-century Virginia colonists. His father William, a homesteader of Welsh origin, brought the family from Illinois to Kansas in the 1870s. By the time Earl was born in Wichita in 1891, eighth of ten children, his father had become a schoolteacher. Earl had to leave school at the age of nine and take odd jobs to help the family. Most of his education was self-directed. He eventually became an accountant and, in 1915, received a correspondence school degree in law. He joined the Socialist party in 1907 at the age of sixteen, siding with the left wing and leaving in protest after "Big Bill" Haywood's expulsion in 1913. Instead of going into the IWW, like many of the left, he shared Foster's views in favor of building revolutionary opposition within the AFL and joined the Bookkeepers, Stenographers, and Accountants Union, affiliated with the AFL, for which he was a delegate to the AFL's 1916 convention.

With the outbreak of the World War in Europe, Bowder devoted most of his energies to building up opposition to the war. After the United States entered the conflict in April 1917, he opposed the draft, for which he, and his two brothers, Waldo and William, were arrested, and imprisoned for over two years. In January 1921, shortly after his release, Browder joined the Communist party.[22]

Browder entered the Communist movement just as it was abandoning its dual union policy. Since he was one of the few Party members with experience within the AFL, he immediately came to the attention of the Party's leadership. Consequently he was asked by Sen Katayama, one of the Comintern's representatives in the United States, to organize the American delegation to the Profintern congress. Browder put together a group of twenty labor activists, including Mother Bloor as well as Hulan Welles, who had been active in the Seattle general strike of 1919. However, his major catch, was Foster.[23] Once back in the United States Browder continued to concentrate on trade union work. As Foster's lieutenant he edited the TUEL's monthly *Labor Herald*. Back in Moscow in 1926 as American delegate to the Profintern, he was sent to China where he led the Profintern's Pan-Pacific Trade Union Secretariat for two years.[24] Because of his work for Moscow, Browder did not take direct part in the controversy between Foster and Lovestone, although he strongly criticized the latter. Browder's absence during this crucial time and his close ties with Moscow determined his accession in 1930 to a three-man secretariat together with Foster, and William Weinstone. He was hence viewed within the Party as the Comintern's man, selected to prevent new outbursts of factionalism and to ensure adherence to the International's new line. Browder's role within the leadership, however, initially secondary, was obscured by Foster's prestige and personality.[25]

By 1930 the factionalism that had caused havoc in the Party throughout most of its short existence had ended. The Party was united around a new leadership which was to head it for the next fifteen years. This new found unity could not mask the toll of fierce infighting and the erratic alternation between conflicting positions. The Party was reduced to a fraction of its former strength and had lost whatever influence and alliances it had been able to establish. Of the tens of thousands who had joined the Communist movement in 1919 in the wake of the Bolshevik revolution, only a few remained. At the Sixth Convention in 1929, Jack Stachel reported there were 9,300 dues paying members: by the following year the number had dropped to 7,500. Party members were still predominantly foreign born and concentrated in New York City and the Northeast; there were virtually no members in the South or West outside of California. In addition, for a Party that considered itself a proletarian organization, membership among workers in basic industries—steel, mining, textile, construction, transportation, marine, and automobile—was disappointing.[26]

Just as the first phase of the history of American Communism came to an end so did the boom economy of the 1920s and the faith in endless prosperity. The new decade presented Communists with new challenges and opportunities which, having put factional strife behind them, they felt ready to seize.

2

TO THE MASSES!
1929–1933

> The American revolution, when the workers have finally seized power, will develop even more swiftly in all its phases than has the Russian revolution. This is because in the United States objective conditions are more ripe for revolution than they were in old Russia.
>
> William Z. Foster, 1932

> Why is it . . . that at a moment when the immediate needs of the workers are most pressing, that our revolutionary trade unions grow very slowly indeed, and some of them even retrogress? Something must be wrong. Is there something wrong with our general line . . . or is the fault in our methods of work, in our daily practice?
>
> Earl Browder, 1930[1]

On June 20, 1930, between 10,000 and 12,000 spectators filed into Madison Square Garden for the opening session of the Seventh Convention of the Communist Party of the United States.[2] The hall was adorned with banners imperatively proclaiming "Fight Imperialist War—Defend the Soviet Union," "Long Live the Communist International," "Build the Revolutionary Unions," and "Work or Wages for the Unemployed." An illuminated picture of Lenin adorned with a gigantic red star presided over the speakers' podium. As soon as the proceedings were declared open, the delegates elected an honorary presidium of prominent Communist leaders, including Joseph Stalin, Vyacheslav Molotov, Otto Kuusinen, Ernst Thalmann, and Harry Pollitt; the doors of the hall then opened and contingents from the Young Communist League, the Young Pioneers of America, and a number of

Communist fraternal organizations and unions paraded down the aisles chanting and carrying placards and flags.[3]

The energy and enthusiasm that exuded at the Seventh Convention were signs of the optimism with which American Communists looked to the future. They had put behind them the factionalism of the 1920s and for the first time were united. Furthermore, as they surveyed the deepening crisis surrounding them, Communists were certain that capitalism had begun its long slide into oblivion. They were also convinced that the CPUSA would not remain a small and isolated organization for much longer and, ultimately, that economic hardship would lead inevitably to a victorious Bolshevik-style revolution in the United States. Al Richmond, who in the early 1930s was a member of the Young Communist League in the Bronx, recalled the enthusiasm and certainties shared by Communists at the outset of the new decade:

> We had the elan. We had the exhilarating sense of being on the offensive, ideologically and morally. As we carried the offensive into the public arena our elan was heightened by the responses—by the confusion and repressive reflexes among the financial, political, and ideological pillars of society. By the manifestations of sympathy from the deprived and humiliated.[4]

During the first years of the depression, "third period" analysis dominated Communist worldwide strategy. This policy was first defined by the Sixth Congress of the Communist International in 1928 and later expanded by the Tenth Plenum of the Executive Committee, the ECCI. The Comintern's new strategy was based on an evaluation of the development of the world economy since 1918 and its consequent impact on the revolutionary movement. This evaluation divided capitalist economic development of the postwar years into three periods: the first, the postwar crisis that had marked the development of a general revolutionary movement had ended in 1923; the second, a phase of growth during which economies had been restored to prewar levels, and which put the revolutionary movement on the defensive drew to a close in 1928; the third, characterized by an increase in industrial output due to "rapid technological expansion" and by the incapacity of markets to expand accordingly, became known as the "third period" of capitalist development. The Comintern's Sixth Congress predicted that a crisis would arise from the contradictory economic conditions underlying this final period.[5] A year later in July 1929, the Tenth Plenum described the third period as leading to the rapid disintegration of capitalism. The ECCI predicted an acceleration of the "radicalization" of the working class against capitalist rule, a new revolutionary wave creating conditions favorable for Communist parties to win over the majority of the working class.[6]

Despite the fact the Comintern had expected a crisis, the catastrophic magnitude of the 1929 economic crash exceeded even its own prophecy. The Comintern was nonetheless quick to claim credit for an accurate assessment of capitalist trends. In light of the crisis, the Comintern did not doubt that it would also prove right in its second prediction that a new era of revolutionary upheaval would follow. This analysis guided official Comintern policy until 1934.

In retrospect such expectations may seem delusive, but during the depression, poverty and suffering were so widespread in the United States that revolution seemed a distinct possibility to many besides the Communists. In southern textile towns entire families worked in the mills from eleven to twelve hours a day for an average weekly pay of approximately $12.[7] Between 1929 and 1932, average hourly wages in the bituminous coal fields decreased from $.68 to $.50; weekly hours from 38.4 to 27.2, and the average number of days worked a year from 219 to 146.[8] The depression hit the auto industry with ferocity, making Detroit the city with the highest jobless rate in the country. Between March 1929 and August 1931, employment rolls at Ford Motor Company dropped from 128,142 to 37,000. Conditions were strained even for those persons lucky enough to keep their jobs: Briggs Manufacturing Company in Detroit, for example, paid men $.10 and women $.4 an hour, and half of those employed worked only three days a week.[9] As more workers lost their jobs, the number of those applying for relief rose; lacking a federal welfare system, the limited private and public relief funds available were quickly drained. The reality of soup lines, of Hoovervilles that sprang up on the outskirts of countless cities, of families scavenging for food, of an army of young men and women roaming the country in a desperate search for jobs, and of millions living on the edge of starvation while bumper crops rotted in the fields shattered the American dream and the philosophy of self help, and raised for many serious questions about the future of capitalism itself. Given the desperate situation many were willing to adopt radical solutions to their problems.

In 1932, in a book appropriately entitled *Toward Soviet America*, Foster predicted that a revolutionary wave was about to inundate the United States. The book applied the analysis of the third period to the

United States and offered a clear summary of the Party's official policy of the 1929–1933 period. While advancing short-term demands, such as higher wages and better working conditions, the Party would seek to "transform the workers' defensive struggles into a counteroffensive," and "unite the scattered fights of the workers into broad class struggles and to give them more of a political character."[10] The Party's objective was to show workers that the solution to their situation could be achieved "only by the overthrow of the capitalist system and the establishment of a Workers' and Farmers' Government."[11] There was no question in Foster's mind that the small Communist party would soon develop into a mass organization and eventually lead workers in the inevitable forthcoming revolution; once it had taken place, he wrote, "the period of transition from capitalism to Socialism in the United Soviet States will be much shorter and easier than in the USSR," due to its highly developed industrial system.[12]

In a matter-of-fact tone, at the end of the book, Foster went so far as to describe the measures that the "American Soviet Government" would adopt after it had taken power. The book was a parroting of the Bolshevik model with tones reminiscent of Edward Bellamy's utopian novel *Looking Backward*. Foster wrote that the new government was to be based on local Soviets, its decisions enforced by an American Red Guard, and its seat moved either to Chicago "or some other great industrial center."[13] Banks, businesses, and transportation would be nationalized; "large landed estates" confiscated; workers' living and working conditions improved through a vast plan that included the expropriation of the "fleets of automobiles and steam yachts of the rich" to be placed "at the disposition of the workers' organizations," and centralization of industrial planning and collectivization of agriculture into state farms modeled after the Soviet *kolkoz* and *sovkhoz*.[14]

The third-period policy had far reaching consequences for the American party. Considering itself to be in a pre-revolutionary situation, the Communist party believed that labor unions should make political demands that would negate the existing social system. The third-period analysis also led to opposition to any alliance with social-democratic or reform organizations accused of standing in the way of the radicalization of workers. Consequently, to direct labor toward "revolutionary objectives," Communists needed to form their own revolutionary unions. Clearly "boring from within" was no longer an acceptable strategy.[15] In early 1928, Solomon Lozovsky, head of the Profintern, the Red International of Labor Unions (R.I.L.U.), told

American Communists to stop "dancing around the A. F. of L.," and to begin organizing the unorganized into their own industrial unions. Any resistance, he wrote, to forming independent revolutionary unions struck at "the very basis of Bolshevik tactics."[16] Lozovsky's blast was repeated at the RILU's Fourth Congress, which stated that the "TUEL must itself become the basis of organization for the . . . unorganized."[17]

The Party's shift to dual unionism, while originating in Moscow, was not without justification in the United States, nor was it exclusive to Communists. Red baiting in the AFL and other unions had reached such a level that it was objectively difficult for Communists to continue to work within them. Although some within the Party disagreed with the new strategy, they stopped short of actually challenging Moscow's directives. Furthermore, after the defeat of the strike wave of 1919–1922, and given the unwillingness of the AFL to take on the organization of mass production industries, in 1927 A. J. Muste and other progressives associated with the Brookwood Labor College advocated the need to shift away from working within the AFL national unions toward the formation of new industrial unions, thus anticipating the Communist party on this issue by a year.[18]

The first Communist led union was the National Miners Union (NMU) founded on September 9–10, 1928, followed a few days later by the National Textile Workers Union and the Needle Trades Workers Industrial Union on January 1, 1929. At its fourth convention, held August 31–September 1, 1929 in Cleveland, the TUEL was transformed into the Trade Union Unity League (TUUL).[19] The slogan of the new organization was Class Against Class; its program stated its main task as "the organization of the unorganized into industrial unions independent of the A. F. of L."[20] The TUUL made no pretense of being autonomous from the Communist party; leaders of both organizations were interchangeable and red unions openly supported the Party's program. Business and local authorities never had to prove who was behind the TUUL—red unions wore their Communist badge with pride.

Between 1930 and 1933 traditional unions, already weakened during the 1920s, saw their membership decline further due to unemployment and wage cuts. Their treasuries empty and their capacity to provide relief eroded, unions hesitated to mount strikes as a weapon with which to fight management, and resorted to them only as a last measure. Generally these last ditch strikes were lost. Since expansion was out of the question, the main concern of traditional unions was self preservation. They concentrated on defending the interests mostly of skilled, native-born, white workers, with no effort made to organize the unorganized.[21]

In contrast, Communists challenged conventional wisdom and moved to the offensive prompted by the belief that the crisis offered new revolutionary opportunities. The Communist party concentrated its efforts on building unions within basic industries; such selection partially compensated for its limited numbers and resources.[22] Communists' dedication provided them with the fortitude and perseverance to embark on a momentous task, the scope and the physical dangers of which would have scared away most who did not share their ideological commitment. While aware of the risks implicit in their policy, as Browder recalled, the CPUSA still determined that the only way to establish a foothold "was to take it the hard way—go out and be the leader of every economic struggle that would show itself."[23] As spontaneous movements broke out across the country, Communists were among the few eager to provide leadership and support, thus organizing unskilled workers in those industries most heavily hit by the depression who had been shunned by traditional trade unions. So it was that in textile mills, in coal fields, in automobile factories, and in the fields of California's Imperial Valley, Communists led a series of strikes.

Communists were not newcomers to labor organizing. Throughout the 1920s they had campaigned for industrial unionism, for rank-and-file control, as well as for improvements in workers' living and working conditions. In 1926 in Passaic, and again two years later in New Bedford, Communists were in the forefront of strikes among textile workers. In both walk-outs the combination of police violence, intervention on the part of the National Guard, and economic hardships led to defeat.[24] In the coal fields, Communists were among the most active opponents within the miners' union of the autocratic rule of John L. Lewis, UMW president. In 1924 a rank and file Illinois Communist miner, George Voyzey, running on a broad anti-Lewis ticket, was officially credited with 66,000 votes against 136,000 for Lewis in the election for union president. Two years later, in another unsuccessful attempt to unseat Lewis, Communists backed the "Save the Union" ticket headed by John Brophy, president of District 2 in Central Pennsylvania.[25] In 1928 the Party could count on a solid base of between 300 and 400 members working in the mines.[26] Once the

NMU was formed, however, Communists removed themselves as an opposition force within the UMW; rather than attempting to change it from within, Communists were going to replace it with a new union. In the auto industry, while vainly calling for the AFL to organize all auto workers, the Party had continued building its own independent union to fill the vacuum, the Auto Workers Union (AWU), which Communists had taken over from its Socialist leadership in 1927. Throughout the decade Communists maintained a degree of visibility in the industry mostly through the publication of a number of shop papers. In 1928 there were 407 Communist auto workers; the Party had 480 members in Detroit, most of them "proletarians and their wives"; 210 were organized in shop nuclei within the major auto plants. There were also small pockets of Communists in Pontiac, Flint, and Cleveland.[27] Even among agricultural workers, which Communists had ignored during the 1920s despite repeated directives from the Comintern, the Party had a following, albeit a small one, as it was reported that at the founding convention of the TUUL a "handful of agricultural worker delegates from the Far West" founded the Agricultural Workers Industrial League.[28]

By the end of the decade Communists had established a presence within a number of industries from which to spread their activities. With the onset of the depression, as living and working conditions deteriorated, workers who lacked any effective form of union organization to channel their discontent found in Communist-led unions a willing and eager voice.

Rather than initiating their own strikes after careful preparation and planning, with few exceptions Communists found themselves taking over the leadership of ill-timed and poorly organized spontaneous movements. As companies slashed workers' low wages they exacerbated already harsh conditions and ignited strikes. The 1929 textile workers strike in Gastonia, North Carolina, was the first Communist-led walkout under the new union policy. The strike began as a result of the workers' overwhelming willingness to respond to the deterioration of their living conditions and to the anti-union practices of the mill owners in spite of the fact that the local NTWU organizer, Fred Beal, was concerned that it might be premature and that the union was not strong enough to endure a long walk-out.[29] Similarly Communists placed themselves at the head of spontaneous and poorly organized strikes of miners in Illinois in 1929, and two years later of autoworkers in Flint, and again of miners in Western Pennsylvania, eastern Ohio, and northern West Virginia.[30] Both in the case of the 1930 lettuce workers' strike in California, and of the 1931 miners' strike in Harlan county ("Bloody Harlan") and neighboring Bell County, Kentucky, Communists moved in after other unions had been forced out of the area by a combination of vigilante violence, intervention by the National Guard, lack of adequate relief, and judicial attack.[31]

In order to make up for their limited numbers and resources Communists concentrated their available support and organizational capacities behind organizing efforts, even at the cost of depleting their resources in other areas. Through secret meetings, distributing literature, and providing relief for striking workers, the Party and the TUUL broadened their base and created a small but effective cadre of militants. Once a strike had begun, the Party appeared in force with scores of militants as well as with its relief organizations, the Workers International Relief and its legal arm the International Labor Defense (ILD) and top Party and TUUL figures to assist in organizing the movement.

In the attempt to broaden support for strikers the Party publicized their plight nationwide. During the 1933 cotton pickers' strike in the San Joaquin Valley, the exposure of the violence by growers and local police, which left three strikers dead, led to the intervention for the first time of state and federal mediators who won farm workers substantial concessions.[32] Communists were instrumental in making the Harlan miners strike a national cause célèbre by sponsoring the trip to the Kentucky coal fields by a group of prominent intellectuals led by Theodore Dreiser and including John Dos Passos, Charles Rumford Walker, Samuel Ornitz, Lester Cohen, and Bruce Crawford, to investigate reports of starvation, hardship, and violence. They interviewed miners who provided testimony of their shocking living and working conditions. In this case the publicity was insufficient to secure victory but it did ensure that Harlan county would continue to draw national attention, ultimately leading to a Senate investigation.[33]

With few exceptions, from their outset the course of Communist-led strikes followed a common pattern of commitment, violence, and defeat. The same violent tactics used against traditional unions were now also applied against the TUUL, only more so. The image of radical outsiders was more readily applicable to Communists, and employers made communism the issue rather than the workers' living and working conditions. They aroused xenophobia, fueled opposition to all unions, and set the stage for a bloody confrontation. The power of the local business community, combined with the local press, the courts, the police, the clergy, and in many cases of the AFL was mobilized against the union and virtually everywhere doomed the TUUL's organizing efforts.

During the Gastonia strike, inflamed by a number of incendiary appeals, vigilante groups destroyed the strike headquarters together with the relief committee provisions. The heavily armed National Guard, stationed close by, intervened only after the raiding party had left and then only to arrest a number of strikers. Sporadic violence continued, and following a confrontation in which the police chief was killed and three officers and one striker wounded, armed mobs rampaged against unionists and union sympathizers. In one of these attacks vigilantes fired on a truck-load of union members, killing Ella May Wiggins, a twenty-nine-year-old mother of five and a union songwriter. By the time the strike was finally broken, scores of workers had been arrested and eleven sentenced to lengthy prison terms. The Communist union was destroyed.[34]

Although not as heavily marred by violence as in Gastonia, the Party's activity among autoworkers fared no better. In July 1930 the AWU-led strike of 7,400 employees at Fisher Body Plant No. 1 in Flint was broken after state and city police attacked pickets and demonstrators, arrested organizers, and raided the offices of the AWU. Organizers who had not been run out of town were fired.[35] Earlier that same year Communist efforts to revive a flagging walk-out of predominantly Mexican and Filipino lettuce workers in California's Imperial Valley elicited a swift and effective response of local authorities. Three Communist organizers, Harry Harvey, Tsuji Hiriuchi, and Frank Waldron (better known under his letter name, Gene Dennis), were arrested together with several farm workers. All outside shipments of food and other supplies for the strikers were blocked and federal immigration officials in collaboration with Mexican consular authorities deported most strikers. In April 1930 and also in August of the following year, analogous attempts to organize cantaloupe and cannery workers led to violent attacks by police and vigilantes and finally failed after local and state authorities arrested scores of Communist organizers and over 100 militant farm workers and charged them under the state's criminal syndicalism law. Eventually nine Communists were convicted and sentenced to prison terms ranging from two to forty-two years.[36] During the next two years, Communists led similarly ineffective walk-outs of cannery workers in the Santa Clara

Valley, pea pickers in Half Moon Bay, orchard pruners in Solano County, and of beet workers in Colorado.[37]

In 1931 police intervention broke the textile workers' walk-out in Lawrence, Massachusetts. Once the strike committee was arrested and several leaders of the National Textile Workers Union held for deportation, disheartened workers in increasing numbers drifted back to work.[38] In Tampa the Communist Tobacco Workers Industrial Union led the cigar workers' strike to protest arrests made after a meeting celebrating the Bolshevik revolution and the removal of readers from factories. The walkout faltered following police raids against the union, sweeping federal injunctions, and the threat of renewed vigilante activities against strikers in a city with a long record of anti-labor and anti-radical violence.[39] Anti-union violence also doomed the Party's efforts in the mine fields. Steve Nelson, who had been an NMU organizer in southern Illinois, recalled that repression, "a reality that the men of the NMU had to face daily," was the worst aspect of life in the mining areas.[40] During the spring and summer of 1931 the union's activities degenerated into open warfare of police, vigilantes, and mine guards against the miners and their families. By the end of these confrontations a number of strikers and NMU organizers had been killed and scores injured. Once again violence and insufficient strike relief broke the Communist effort. A last attempt to revive the movement in Kentucky by launching a general strike on January 1, 1932, failed to shut down the mines, since most of the NMU's supporters were by then blacklisted, unemployed miners. As Foster later recognized, "this strike lacked force, as it was ill prepared in face of the fierce terrorism prevailing, and it soon frittered away."[41] By 1932 anti-union violence and intimidation had also smashed revolutionary unions among miners and steel workers in Alabama. The inability to overcome such repression induced the local Communist leadership to abandon its efforts toward the formation of red-unions and instead to direct workers back into the AFL.[42] The decision by Alabama Communists to disband the TUUL was not an isolated incident, rather it was an indication of what was becoming a national trend.

Even when, capitalizing on past experience and mistakes, Communists carefully planned and organized their strikes they failed because employers refused to negotiate. After protracted struggle the denouement of the 1931 miners' strike came on June 23, when the Pittsburgh Terminal Company, the second largest coal operator in Pennsylvania, announced an agreement with the UMW, which had not participated in the strike. Mine operators had turned to Lewis in order to avoid dealing with what they considered a greater threat. The NMU had been driven out of the coal fields by a combination of violence, hunger, and John L. Lewis.[43] An article in the *Communist* acknowledged the *"isolation of the union from the masses of miners"*; according to Foster the defeat was a "deadly blow" for the NMU. By 1932, the miners' union was reduced to less than 500 dues-paying members.[44] Similarly, in January 1933 during the Briggs strike, the most important labor confrontation in the industry during the pre-New Deal era, management used the presence of Communists in the strike committee as a pretext for not considering the workers' demands. Once the company, with the help of scab labor, resumed limited deliveries, most of the strike-committee members caved in and expelled the Communists. This purge, however, did not soften management. It succeeded only in dividing the strikers along factional lines and deprived them of the Party organization and support groups, ultimately accelerating the collapse of the strike.[45]

In 1933 in California, through planning and organization, the recently renamed Cannery and Agricultural Workers Industrial Union was able to wrest from growers substantial salary raises for cherry, pear, peach, and cotton pickers.[46] Despite these victories, over the long run the union could do little against a combination of constant, unrestrained violation of the strikers' civil liberties and other hardships. In early 1934, after a new attempt to unionize lettuce workers in the Imperial Valley was broken, the CAWIU's ability to continue its activities state-wide was severely limited, leading to its eventual demise.[47]

These years of commitment, hard work, and participation in the forefront of labor's battles gained Communists considerable national attention, but few tangible results. In 1932, according to Foster the total membership of the TUUL was 40,000.[48] Most TUUL unions, however, never overcame an initial weakness. The common pattern of circumstances—legal and vigilante violence against organizers, strikers, and their families; the diminishing number of employed workers; the material inability to provide relief for protracted strikes; and, in the case of agricultural workers, the seasonal character of their employment—all combined to make the organization and strengthening of unions impossible. After successive defeats, unemployed and blacklisted workers constituted the TUUL's main membership.

Communists failed not because they politicized struggles. Quite the contrary. In spite of official policy, revolutionary rhetoric was not particularly noticeable either at strike meetings nor in the literature distributed. Their grievances stemmed mainly from concerns over low wages, dangerous working conditions, a forty-hour week, and union recognition—the kind of demands that almost any other union would have made in times of prosperity. Employers and local authorities opposed Communist efforts because, like traditional labor organizations, TUUL unions organized workers, made economic demands, and attempted to limit the power of management. The Party's revolutionary ideology was only an added reason for attack. Given the general conditions during the first years of the depression, notwithstanding their political philosophies, those unions that also led strike movements encountered the same strong opposition from management and local authorities, and in the end, they shared the same fate.

The Party did not overlook the importance of organizing the unemployed whose plight dramatically expressed the human suffering of the economic crisis. By March 1930, 5 million workers were unemployed, ten times the number of the previous year. This figure doubled the following year and peaked in March 1933 at 15 million.[49] The growing army of unemployed seemed ready for revolutionary organization; the inadequacy of public relief as well as the worsening of the depression generated a determination among many jobless not to suffer hardship passively but to adopt radical, if not political, solutions to their problems. The reluctance of business, labor, and political leaders to deal with the increasing number of unemployed workers contrasted with the Party's willingness to initiate immediate and concrete actions. In a situation which paralyzed traditional institutions, Communists led activities that attracted many jobless workers.

Communists saw the unemployed as representing the natural vanguard of the revolutionary movement. Their organization and recruitment became one of the Party's top priorities; for Communists the fight against unemployment was "the tactical key to the present state of class struggle."[50] By early 1930 Communists began to form a network of local jobless organizations known either as the Unemployed Councils or the Councils of the Unemployed under the umbrella of the TUUL. The slogans "Fight! Don't Starve" and "Work or Wages" embodied the overall program of the councils.

Councils formed around small groups of Party members and sympathizers, mostly on a block or neighborhood basis. Communist organizers recruited at city parks, bread lines, soup kitchens, flop-houses, relief offices—anywhere jobless workers might gather. Officially dues were $.25 a month, but they were seldom collected. Recounting the origins of the unemployed movement, Steve Nelson described how some organizers had approached a group of workers they heard "complaining about the relief that they were receiving and the discrimination in handling the relief." The workers helped draw up a leaflet, distribute it, and organize a first meeting. The next step was to circulate a petition among the unemployed and their families listing their demands. Soon an unemployed council was organized.[51] Once the council became visible, people turned to it for help in great numbers. Councils concentrated on such immediate issues as more funds for relief, public work programs, moratoriums on mortgages, resistance to evictions, and rent strikes. Their broader objective was a national unemployment insurance paid for by employers and government. Once a Council was established, Communists organized marches and delegations to relief bureaus and open-air meetings. At times delegations refused to leave welfare offices until their demands were met, and the police were called to evict them.[52]

In cities and towns across the country, Communist militants became experts in restoring disconnected gas and electricity with meter jumps. Communists played a leading role in neighborhood protests against evictions. Scores of incidents are recorded of Communists helping move the furniture of evicted tenants back into their homes. In some cities local councils were so strong that landlords would try unsuccessfully to secure their permission before evicting tenants.[53] Unemployed organizers were so forthright and brazen that in some cases they would leave a sign on doors proclaiming "this furniture was moved back by local 23 of the Unemployed Council." An instance is recorded of a black women who upon receiving notice of eviction shouted to her children "Run quick and find the Reds!"[54]

Often these activities led to violence. In Tampa's Latin community of Ybor City, demonstrators protesting evictions were confronted by deputized Anglo vigilantes. In February 1930, crowds of jobless workers, called out to demonstrate by the Councils, battled with police in Cleveland, Philadelphia, Chicago, and Los Angeles while attempting to bring their grievances to local authorities.[55] In August 1931, after Chicago police shot into a crowd of people trying to prevent an eviction, killing three blacks and injuring several demonstrators and bystanders, the Unemployed Councils received 3,000 membership applications, the Party 500, and the Young Communists League 200.[56] The councils became a visible and recognized presence in neighborhoods across the country. On numerous occasions local residents intervened to prevent police from arresting unemployed organizers. Some would go as far as to use deeds on their homes to bail out arrested organizers. Women played a very prominent role in the struggle for organization of the unemployed. One organizer remembered how in Brooklyn after spending the night in jail she and other women returned home to discover that in their absence neighbors had cleaned the house and looked after their children; for one woman whose husband was an orthodox Jew they had prepared a traditional Saturday meal.[57]

As in the case of labor, through daily contact with the problems and the experience that came from them, Communist organizers soon shed much of their ideological rhetoric and concentrated instead on immediate grievances. Only by developing an ability to deal with the immediate needs of the unemployed were Communists able to become a part of the mainstream of depression protest movements. They tried to enlist the support of local legislators, of aldermen, and of ministers; they held meetings of unemployed anywhere—from church basements to pool halls to government buildings. They made use of traditional community fund raisers such as bingo, raffles, dances, and block parties. They learned, moreover, not to force themselves on a community as spokespersons for the grievances of the jobless and their families. As Steve Nelson recounted, "if there were articulate local people in the group, it was better to let them speak up and then support what they said. Even if they didn't express themselves as well as Party members might, they were known to the people and would not be looked upon as outsiders."[58]

The Party's role in the organization of the unemployed movement achieved national attention following nationwide demonstrations on March 6, 1930, the first major organized protest against the human cost of the economic crisis. In mid-January 1930, the political secretariat of the Executive Committee of the Comintern called for an "international day" against unemployment, scheduled at first for February 27 then moved to March 6. In response, the CPUSA mobilized all its available resources to insure a large turnout. In two months time, the Party, the TUUL, and the Young Communist League set out to insure a maximum turnout for the demonstration; one million leaflets were distributed and preparatory meetings were held in many cities. In

Chicago alone Communists handed out 200,000 leaflets, 50,000 stickers, and 50,000 shop papers.[59]

On the morning of March 6 the front-page headline of the *New York Times* read:

HOOVER FORECASTS
EMPLOYMENT GAIN
NO CAUSE FOR ALARM.[60]

Judging from the events of that day, reality was very different. The Party's efforts became evident as workers throughout the country took to the streets in numbers well beyond even the most optimistic predictions of Communist leaders. According to Party sources, over 1 million workers participated and, while this estimate was certainly inflated, there is little doubt that the demonstration was a great success.[61] Marches took place in San Francisco, where a sympathetic mayor addressed 2,000 demonstrators in front of City Hall. In Chicago tens of thousands marched peacefully despite a police raid on an organizational meeting and the arrest and beating of fourteen organizers in an attempt to discourage the demonstration. In Flint, Michigan, where there were only twenty-two Party members, over 15,000 people, by police estimates, turned out to demonstrate. Peaceful demonstrations were the exception, however, since most of them were marked by violent clashes with police. In Washington, D.C., the police used tear gas to disperse a crowd gathered in front of the White House. In Los Angeles hundreds were injured as scores of club-swinging policemen on foot, horseback, and in police cars battled with demonstrators, including a number of Japanese-American Communists skilled in martial arts, who were attempting to reach City Hall. In downtown Detroit, the city's entire police force of 3,600, with the aid of an armored car, fought a crowd for two hours. Similar riots occurred in Boston, Cleveland, and Milwaukee.

The most violent, as well as most publicized demonstration, took place in New York City. Tension had been building in the city for over a month; police and demonstrators had already repeatedly clashed in front of City Hall. On March 6, thousands massed for an authorized rally in Union Square, reputed to be the city's Red Square. William Z. Foster and other speakers on five platforms scattered throughout the square addressed the crowd. Police in great numbers stood by and made no effort to disperse the crowd. At the end of the rally, however, violence broke out when demonstrators tried to march down Broadway toward City Hall to present their demands to Mayor James Walker. Scores of marchers and bystanders were injured, and four of the demonstration's organizers were arrested; Foster, Robert Minor, and Israel Amter served six months in jail and Harry Raymond served ten.[62]

The overall success of those demonstrations led to some important consequences both for Communists and for national awareness of the problems of the unemployed. Nationwide coverage of the demonstrations illuminated the plight of the unemployed, dispelling Hoover's optimistic forecasts and predictions. The inescapable fact that the demonstrations had been organized by the Communist party was a considerable propaganda success. The party as well as many of its opponents saw its accomplishment in rallying the unemployed as proof that there was a real possibility of the CPUSA becoming the focal point of a mass movement and that predictions of the radicalization of American workers had been confirmed. Moissaye Olgin, editor of the Party's Yiddish-language daily paper, *Freiheit*, described the March 6 demonstrations as the "expression of an acceleration of all social processes in this country, a maturing of all conflicts, a crystallization of all forces, a sharpening of all tendencies, an uncovering of qualities hidden under a cloak of phrases." From these accomplishments, Communists gained a new sense of political strength.[63]

In the wake of the demonstrations, the councils were given a national organization. In early July 1930, 1,120 delegates met at the National Unemployment Convention in Chicago to establish the Unemployed Councils of the United States. The convention elected a Party member, Bill Mathieson, as its national secretary while Foster, Minor, and Amter, then still in jail, became honorary members. In an apparent attempt to provide the Councils with a broader base of support, the new organization decided it would not affiliate with the TUUL. The Party would later claim that the Councils gained over 75,000 members.[64]

Following the March 6 demonstrations, Communist activities among the unemployed increased. New councils were founded in Milwaukee, Duluth, Indianapolis, Grand Rapids, and Minneapolis; Chicago had twelve councils with a total membership of 1,000, Philadelphia had seven, while Detroit by 1931 had 15, with 1,500 members.[65] These councils continued to function on a local basis, mainly by resisting evictions and demanding relief from local authorities. At the same time unemployed councils also stepped up national demonstrations to keep attention focused on the plight of the unemployed and to pressure Congress into taking action. On February 10, 1931, the Workers' Unemployment Insurance Delegation arrived in Washington, D.C., to present to Congress the text of the Unemployment Insurance Bill. The bill called for unemployment insurance of $25 a week, with $3 additional for every dependent, to be administered by workers themselves. The necessary funds were to be raised through a levy on all capital and property over $25,000, and a graduated tax on incomes over $5,000. The Party claimed that the bill had been signed or endorsed by 1.5 million workers and a number of AFL unions.[66]

The lack of any initiative from Congress led to the first Hunger March on the nation's capital, organized by the Unemployed Councils. Riding in old cars and trucks, fed and housed along the way by supporters, 1,200 delegates from the Councils, mostly from the East Coast and the Midwest, converged on Washington, D.C., on December 6, 1931. The following day, flanked and outnumbered by scores of policemen and thousands of spectators, they paraded down Pennsylvania Avenue to the Capitol. At their head marched several hundred members of the Workers Ex-Servicemen's League with banners that read "We fought the last war for capitalists; we will fight the next war for the workers." The marchers formed a semi-circle in front of the Capitol, while outside a band played "The International." Inside, a delegation of twelve headed by William Dunne tried unsuccessfully to gain the floor of both the House and the Senate. A group then marched on the White House where President Hoover refused to see them. They went on to the headquarters of the AFL to protest William Green's opposition to unemployment insurance.[67] Although the Party did not obtain any immediate results, its action kept the jobless on the front page of newspapers. Aside from the national demonstration, the Unemployed Councils organized twelve state and scores of city hunger marches to pressure local authorities into providing relief. In early December 1932, 3,000 delegates participated in a second march on Washington, D.C.[68]

Not all hunger marches took place without violence. One march that turned violent occurred in Dearborn, Michigan, on March 7, 1932, and became known as the Ford Massacre. On a cold Monday morning, between 3,000 and 5,000 men and women marched from Detroit to the River Rouge Ford plant in Dearborn to present a list of demands to the company's management. At the gates of the factory marchers were confronted by police, firemen, and Ford's thugs who prevented them from entering the plant. A fight broke out, and suddenly policemen began firing into the crowd. By the time the shooting was over, twenty-three workers had been wounded and four were killed, including a sixteen-year-old boy and Joe York, the Young Communist League district organizer. The bodies of the four men lay in state for several days at the Workers Hall under a huge red flag with a picture of Lenin, and over 30,000 people marched in the funeral procession down Dearborn's Woodward Avenue. The four men were buried together in Woodmere Cemetery overlooking Ford's River Rouge plant.[69]

Despite continued efforts, the demonstrations of March 6, 1930, clearly marked the high point of the Party's activity among the unemployed. In similar nation-wide demonstrations held on February 25, 1931, and again on February 4, 1932, the number of participants decreased sharply from those of March 1930.[70] By the summer of 1930, Party leaders realized that despite a steadily rising number of unemployed the CPUSA had made very little real progress among the jobless and that "despite millions of leaflets and hundreds of meetings, not to speak of the half-dozen demonstrations in every city, organized unemployed councils are almost nonexistent."[71] As the Party acknowledged later, the major problems were the inability of the unemployed councils to retain their membership beyond demonstrations and protests and their total dependence on Communist members to hold the organization together between mass actions. As one of the organization's leaders eventually recognized, the councils "took on the appearance of imitation Communist party units, or appeared to be 'mechanically controlled' and 'dominated' by the Communist party."[72]

Meanwhile, the Party increased efforts, and even resorted to lobbying, to have Congress pass a comprehensive federal unemployment insurance bill. The Party backed a slightly revised version of the Unemployed Bill. In early 1934, when Congressman Ernest Lundeen (Farmer-Labor, Minnesota) introduced the first unemployment insurance bill in the House, the Party organized a National Convention Against Unemployment in Washington, D. C., to coincide with the event and another one a year later in early January.[73] Scores of Communists testified in favor of the Lundeen Act in front of the House Subcommittee on Labor. In his statement to the subcommittee on February 12, 1935, Browder declared that the bill embodied "the principles which alone can provide any measure of 'social insurance' for the workers, and, thereby, also alleviate the condition of impover-

ished farmers, professional, and middle class people." He also added
that the demand for the enactment of the bill was

> the front-line trench today in the battle for preserving a measure of life,
> liberty and the pursuit of happiness in this country. It is the essential
> foundation for preservation of a measure of civil liberties, for resistance to
> fascism and war. It is a fight for all those good things of life, which the
> masses of the people, as distinguished from the professional patriots, mean
> when they speak of "Americanism."[74]

Even as the Party was bringing social insurance to the attention of
the country, it was failing in its objective to create a strong unemployed organization under Communist leadership. What were the
reasons for this failure? As Daniel Leab has argued, the attempt by
Communists to inject into the movement for the unemployed their
own slogans and programs, such as its call for "Defense of Chinese
Soviets" or against "social-fascists," alienated many jobless workers.[75]
It is essential, however, just as with the case of labor, not to exaggerate the extent of this revolutionary posturing nor, most importantly,
to underestimate the difficulties inherent in organizing such a hetero-
geneous group.

The unemployed were a mobile group. They were weakly bonded
to each other and their demands tended to be broad and diverse—
hardly the most favorable circumstances in which to instill class consciousness or to achieve organization. As a group they lacked stability, moving on when the search for a job proved futile. Councils grew
rapidly when they were viewed as the best and most effective way of
solving the grievances of unemployed, but, as hard times persisted,
many unemployed either resorted to other means or resigned themselves to inaction. Furthermore, the new wave of strikes and the
revival of activism among labor in 1933 raised once more for Communists the primacy of shop organization. The Unemployed Councils
survived until April 8, 1936, when they merged with the Socialist-led
Workers Alliance and a number of other smaller groups.[76]

The positive and long-term consequences of the Party's activity
among the unemployed, however, should not be underestimated. Certainly Browder's claim that no one "realized the desperation of the
situation for large masses of the people. . . . We were the only people
in the field," was hyperbolic. But it is also undeniable that Communists
were among the first to unmask the human cost of suffering caused by

the depression and to raise the issue of the need for effective measures to help the unemployed.[77] In many instances Communist-led protests proved successful in obtaining some form of relief for the jobless. For many unemployed their experience in the Councils was their first in any organized social and economic protest. This exposure made many of them more receptive to unionization when they did find a job. Furthermore, through its activities in favor of unemployment insurance, the CPUSA helped overcome the ideological opposition to the concept of pay for no work. By showing that unemployment was not the workers' fault, but rather the consequence of a broader economic situation, Communists helped in opening the way that would lead to the passage of the Social Security Act.[78]

Another cornerstone of the CPUSA's policies during the third period was its campaign against racial discrimination and for black liberation. The Party's emphasis on recruiting blacks, as well as recognizing their specific situation, made a considerable departure from the Left's traditional lack of concern with the specific conditions of blacks. During its early years the Communist movement, in the tradition of the Socialist party, showed no special concern for the problems of black Americans, an attitude shared by the International up to 1928. The problems of blacks were addressed not as those of a race but rather as those of exploited proletarians who would have to wait for socialism to solve their problems. Implicitly, this solution meant that whatever activity existed in the Party among blacks was limited to northern industrial ghettos and did not extend to southern blacks who lived in a semi-feudal status. The Party's presence within the black community remained marginal throughout the 1920s since its emphasis on anti-capitalism isolated it from mainstream black social and political activism. Nonetheless, it did attract a small number of blacks, most of them intellectuals drawn into the Communist movement by the anti-colonial appeal of the Comintern and by Soviet society's apparent freedom from racial prejudice.[79]

The "Negro question" assumed a central importance in Party policy as a direct result of the Sixth Congress of the Communist International. The congress identified blacks as subjected to both racial discrimination and economic hardship. In addition, the Comintern described black Americans as an oppressed separate nation with the right to self-determination in areas, such as the Black Belt counties of the deep South, where they were the majority of the population.[80]

The Comintern made the struggle for equal rights and full citizenship for African Americans essential to the victory of proletarian revolution in the United States. This brought the organization of blacks to the forefront of Communist activity, backed by the Party's available financial, political, and human resources. Furthermore, the new policy required the Party to start operating in the South, an area where it had not been active before. Thus, by the beginning of the depression, the CPUSA was attempting to transform a predominantly white, immigrant organization into an interracial party that could lead black Americans in the fight against discrimination.

During the 1930s, Harlem was one of the Party's major areas of concentration. As unemployment figures soared, reaching between one-and-a-half and three times those of the rest of the city, the Party increased its visibility as scores of young Communists converged uptown to help organize the unemployed movement. The length and magnitude of the depression undermined the self-help activities sponsored by churches or black nationalist groups; charity drives, soup kitchens, campaigns in support of black-owned business or "Don't Buy Where You Can't Work" campaigns no longer sufficed to meet the need for survival of tens of thousands of unemployed. The Communist party took a different approach: it emphasized mass action, organizing resistance against evictions, marches, and pickets on city relief bureaus to demand aid and to protest discrimination in the allocation of relief; it played a leading role in the struggle against deteriorating housing conditions and exorbitant rents. Communists also placed great importance on working-class solidarity as the best and most effective means to help solve the community's economic problems and to fight racial discrimination. An example of this campaign was interracial picketing of stores to force the hiring of blacks without the firing of white employees. A considerable number of blacks took part in the March 6, 1930, demonstration in Union Square and in the clashes with police that followed. Black and white workers rioting together had, to that point, never been seen before. According to the black Communist leader, Cyril Briggs, the events of March 6 were a demonstration of the "successful breaking down of the wall of prejudice between white and Negro workers fostered by the employers and the substitution of working-class solidarity and fraternization."[81] The Party's all-out commitment to the solution of the community's problems helped overcome some of its former isolation, and as blacks became more receptive to its appeals, helped establish it as a recognized force in Harlem.

In line with the creation of an interracial organization in the North, the Party set out to eliminate all racial barriers and to dispel any notion of racism within its own ranks. One way of demonstrating this commitment was by elevating blacks to positions of leadership. Significant in this sense was the nomination of James W. Ford as vice-presidential candidate on the Communist ticket in 1932. The national secretary of the ILD, William L. Patterson and one of the national leaders of the Young Communist League, Henry Winston, were also black, as were a growing number of Party officials. Another aspect of the campaign against "white chauvinism" was the "trials" of Party members accused of racism, the most famous of these was the Yokinen trial on March 1, 1931. August Yokinen, a janitor at the Finnish Workers Club in Harlem, was accused of trying to bar blacks from the club. The Party orchestrated a public trial at the Harlem Casino and over 2,000 spectators attended. After hearing testimony and summations by a black defense attorney and a white prosecutor, a "workers' jury," composed of seven whites and seven blacks, handed down a verdict expelling Yokinen from the CPUSA. The Party received much publicity as a result of the trial, which made the front page of the *New York Times* and was also favorably reported within the black community.[82]

The Party's insistence on assimilation and on the creation of an interracial organization in the North placed the CPUSA at odds with black nationalist organizations. Specifying that black protest could assume a nationalist character only in the South, Moscow cautioned Communists not to associate themselves with the "reactionary Negro separatism," of Marcus Garvey whose "Utopia of an isolated Negro state," according to the Comintern, was aimed at diverting "the Negro masses from the real liberation struggle against American imperialism."[83] In its préss and leaders' speeches the CPUSA repeated these accusations against Garvey. In 1931 Cyril Briggs wrote a lengthy analysis of the Garvey movement in which Garvey was described as a petty bourgeois who was directing black revolutionary national sentiment into "utopian, reactionary, 'Back to Africa' channels."[84] The Party aimed at gathering recruits among the rank and file of the UNIA, considered to be sincere and militant and not reactionary as were its leaders. Here the Party had only limited success. Instead, the growing presence of Communists within the black community and the hostility between the two organizations spilled into the streets and led to a series of clashes, the bloodiest of which occurred on Harlem's Lenox Avenue in which a black Communist died.[85]

By 1930 the Party had also begun to comply with the Comintern's directive concerning expansion of organizational efforts in the South. In the face of violence and intimidations the Party set out to organize southern blacks and whites. As soon as a number of branches were established and a weekly, the *Southern Worker*, began publication in Chattanooga in August 1930, energies were turned to the organization of unemployed councils and revolutionary unions. Communists led unemployed protests throughout the South in Chattanooga, Birmingham, and Grenville, South Carolina. In Atlanta on June 30, 1932, over 1,000 white and black workers and their families marched on the Fulton County Courthouse demanding relief. This event, the largest biracial demonstration the South had seen in decades, frightened local officials, who saw it as a further sign, after Gastonia and the Party's consequent activities, that dangerous outsiders were invading the South. Of particular concern was the Party's advocacy of racial equality and opposition to Jim Crow.

Communists also concentrated their efforts to organize red unions among black dockworkers in ports along the Atlantic coast, the Gulf of Mexico, and the Mississippi river, as well as in various urban and industrial centers such as Birmingham. In 1930 the TUUL distributed a leaflet in Birmingham which spelled out the Party's main demands in the South. These demands included jobs or relief for the unemployed regardless of race and sex; houses for the homeless; a moratorium on rents for the unemployed; a seven hour day, five day week; no night work for women; the abolition of child labor; the end of lynchings, discrimination and Jim Crowism; and the right to organize.[86]

An important aspect of the Party's activities in the South was the organization of mostly black sharecroppers and tenant farmers into the Sharecroppers Union. Founded in 1931, the union was strongest in Tallapoosa, Alabama, and in parts of Louisiana. The union's demands included an increase in the quantity of food allotted to sharecroppers during the winter, the right to sell their crops directly, higher wages for laborers, longer lunch breaks, and better schools for their children. These demands, but mostly the existence of the union itself, led to mob and police violence directed against "Communist agitators" that left several sharecroppers and Ralph Gray, a Party organizer, dead. These events forced the union underground. Despite this situation, the union continued to operate and, in 1934, claimed a membership of almost 6,000 most of them in Alabama.[87]

These activities among southern blacks had little to do with the call for self-determination which became "a Sunday ritual": mentioned in most official statements and resolutions only as a final objective.[88] Everyday struggles made more immediate demands for the livelihood of southern workers and farmers and the fight against discrimination. Party organizers in the field realized that short-term practical demands had a better chance of drawing black support than did other, less tangible, issues. For this attitude they were repeatedly criticized in the Party press. William Weinstone, who since 1929 had been the Party's representative to the Comintern, wrote: "The slogan of the right of self-determination of the Negroes has not at all been taken up by the Party. There is opportunistic resistance to this slogan as well as a lack of clarity both of which must be quickly overcome."[89] Eventually, however, the experiences of local organizers prevailed, and by 1935 the slogan had virtually disappeared from official Party statements. As Earl Browder admitted, southern blacks were willing "to fight against jim-crowism and oppression, for democratic rights and other partial economic and political demands," but not to fight for self-determination.[90]

Nothing helped the Communist party more to break out of its isolation and to gain sympathy and support within the black community nationwide than its role in the Scottsboro case. Throughout the early years of the depression, the Party was involved in a number of legal cases in defense of blacks.[91] In the Spring of 1931 nine young black men, aged from 13 to 21, were charged with having raped two white women on a freight train in northern Alabama. After a speedy trial without adequate counsel, eight were sentenced to die in the electric chair. Upon hearing of the conviction, the Party, acting through the ILD, moved in. The Communist party and the ILD were able to secure the support of most of the defendants' parents and, after a brief fight with the NAACP, to take and retain control of the defense until 1935.[92]

The Communist strategy developed along three parallel lines. In the courtroom it enlisted skilled and experienced lawyers to fight a legal battle which transformed the case into a national and international cause célèbre, the most notorious political case of the 1930s. Secondly, believing that only mass action rather than reliance on prejudiced courts could save the youths, the Party organized demonstrations, fund raising events, petition drives, massive mailings, and countless mass meetings, always insuring a numerous white presence to emphasize the interracial character of the fight against racism. No party document or function was complete without an appeal for the freedom of the "Scottsboro boys." Several of the defendants' mothers were sent on speaking tours across the country, and one was even sent abroad. Because of the Party's role in the Scottsboro case, Communist speakers were allowed for the first time to speak in black churches, fraternal organizations, and clubs. The Party began to enlist the support of black religious and community leaders. Most of the nation's black press reported favorably on the efforts of the Party and the ILD in the case. In the words of the editor of the Oklahoma *Black Dispatch*, the Communist party was the first white organization, since the abolitionist movement, to advocate openly "the economic, political, and social equality of black folks." In the eyes of many blacks the Party's role in the Scottsboro case reinforced an image of Communists as outspoken and committed defenders of the rights and freedoms of black Americans.[93]

Lastly, reflecting the policies of the third period, the Communist party worked on discrediting the NAACP, thus portraying the CPUSA as the only organization sincerely committed to the defense of black Americans.[94] The Party found objectionable the NAACP's faith in the system in general and the judicial system in particular. The Party constantly referred to the NAACP's initial ineptitude in handling the case and hence concluded that the leaders of the NAACP were "allies of the lynchers" and "ardent servants of the system of capitalist and landlord slavery."[95]

The ILD fought the case throughout the ensuing series of trials and appeals all the way to the Supreme Court. In November 1932, the Court's decision to declare a mistrial on the grounds that the defendants had been denied adequate counsel during their first trial, was a major victory. By the summer of 1935, the ILD began to loosen control over the case, realizing that the Party's direct involvement not only antagonized southern juries and jeopardized the young men's position, but also obstructed the support of Southern moderates. The decision was also a consequence of the new Popular Front policy which called for the creation of a broad based defense coalition by enlisting the support of liberals. These factors led to the end of its opposition to working with the NAACP and other reform organizations. In December 1935, the ILD signed an agreement with the

NAACP, the ACLU, the League for Industrial Democracy, and the Methodist Federation of Social Service creating the "Scottsboro Defense Committee."[96] Although the case dragged on for years, there is no doubt that the Party, by giving the Scottsboro case so much national exposure, contributed to keeping the trial in the forefront of national attention and therefore deserved credit for saving the defendants' lives.

Nonetheless as was the case with white workers, the Party, despite all efforts and predictions, did not see its ranks swell with blacks. Indeed, very few blacks joined the Party and those that did joined only for very short periods of time.[97] While certainly not commensurate with the Party's efforts, the overall number of blacks joining the CPUSA did increase from between fifty and 200 in 1929 to around 1,000 at the end of 1931. In 1931, while 24 percent of Party members in Chicago and 16 percent in Cleveland were black, the figure was only 3 percent in New York and 7 percent in Detroit, for a meager total of 74 and 33 black members respectively. After 1934 there was a noticeable increase in the number of black Communists in Harlem but overall the percentage remained low. Turnover among black members was always a problem. However, by 1935 blacks made up 11 percent of the total Communist party membership with strong representation in Alabama where blacks accounted for 90 percent of the total membership. In the North and in the South, Communist organizers soon realized that, like white workers, it was easier to mobilize blacks over specific issues than to recruit them into the Party and expect them to abide by its discipline. There were, of course, exceptions to this rule. A number of blacks, largely intellectuals, drawn by the Party's theoretical and political line, did become members and remained so for a long time.[98]

These figures alone do not tell the whole story, since the Party did become an important force within the black community during the first years of the depression. The Party gained credence because it addressed the economic problems of black Americans by opposing racism and discrimination within its own ranks and in society in general and by fighting against lynchings and southern justice. Blacks responded favorably to the Communist tactics of organizing both mass protests against government agencies and expressions of interracial solidarity to further the interests of blacks among labor in particular. Non-Communist protest movements adopted such tactics as legitimate ways to bring problems to public attention. Communist flexibility, their abandonment of abstract slogans, and their willingness to work with the major organizational forms of black life, gained them acceptance in the black community as credible allies.[99]

Three years into the depression, despite all their efforts, Communists could not fail to see that their predictions concerning the development of class consciousness and the consequent growth of the Party into a mass organization had failed to materialize. The United States was no closer to revolution than it had been before the depression. Symptomatic of the failure of the Party was its disappointing performance in the 1932 presidential elections. The CPUSA devoted considerable energies to the campaign as a vehicle to spread its revolutionary program. Clarence Hathaway predicted: "We shall poll one million votes this coming November."[100] Instead of the support of hundreds of thousands of workers and farmers the Communist candidate for president, Foster, received a scant 102,221 votes, only 20,000 more than the Prohibition party. The Communists' call to take "the first step toward the establishment of a workers' and farmers' government" had thus gone unheeded. This reversal of expectations was all the more painful when the Communist candidate votes were compared to the votes for the candidate of the other left wing organization, the Socialist party. Socialist candidate Norman Thomas received 883,990 votes.[101]

The Party quickly became aware of its failures. As early as 1930, Browder had asked the question that certainly was on the mind of many Communists. How was it, he wrote, that "at a moment when the immediate needs of the workers are more pressing, that our revolutionary trade unions grow very slowly indeed, and some of them even retrogress? Something must be wrong."[102] Among Communist parties in the industrialized countries, the experience of the CPUSA during the third period was not unique. Actually, while most of the parties declined, losing up to half of their membership, the American party increased from 7,545 in 1930, to just over 19,000 three years later, a marked improvement but still hardly enough to be called a mass organization.[103] By mid-1933 only 13 percent of the Party's membership was employed in basic industries (steel, mine, automobile, marine, and railroad); only 7 percent in industries that employed more than 500 workers. Two years later the percentage of Communists who worked in basic industries had climbed to only 16 percent, as opposed to 26 percent in light industries and 19 percent "nonproletarian" and white collar workers. The Party was unsuccessful in its objective of basing its organization mostly on shop nuclei. From 1930 to 1933 the number of shop nuclei grew from 64 to 140, then doubled by 1934 to 338 with a total of 2,355 members, of whom less than half were in basic industries. But the number of Communists who were organized where they worked remained limited. In 1933 only 4 percent of all Party members were organized in factory nuclei; by 1935, while 34 percent of all Communists worked in factories, only 15 percent were organized in shop units. Clearly most Communists preferred to join neighborhood units. Overall, even the TUUL served as a poor avenue to recruitment: of all its members, less than 10 percent joined the Party. A further cause for great concern was the fact that of those recruited most were unemployed who had no connection to the productive process or to other workers in factories. In 1934 Browder estimated that between 60 and 70 percent of the Party's members were unemployed; in May, 1935, of 27,000 Communists nearly half were jobless.[104]

The most serious problem of the Party's growth was not one of recruitment but rather retention. Browder estimated that between 1930 and February 1934, the CPUSA recruited 49,000 new members of whom it retained only one-third.[105] There were a number of reasons for this loss. One was simple incompetence and lack of organization in making sure that all those who applied for membership were in fact received into the Party. In addition, the high number of unemployed and their mobility accounted for some loss of membership.[106] The main reason, however, was inner party life.

Joining and remaining within the CPUSA was an all encompassing experience, one that demanded a total commitment. Communists were to devote a considerable part of their leisure time to Party activities. This commitment required the adoption of a lifestyle that not many could endure and that in most cases limited their effectiveness as organizers and recruiters. Clarence Hathaway warned that in New York all active members spent their time in meetings where "good plans for mass work are made to the exclusion of all possibility of carrying out these plans." He went on to describe a Communist's typical weekly schedule:

> *Monday,* unit buro meetings; *Tuesday,* unit meetings; *Wednesday,* department meetings (Agit-prop, Negro, etc.); *Thursday,* school, union meetings, etc.; *Friday,* section committee meetings, street meetings; *Saturday,* free; and *Sunday,* week-end schools, "Red Sundays" (distributing of *Daily Worker,* and other purely agitational work.)[107]

Party membership placed enormous strains on family life. One Communist recalled that it was impossible to be active in the Party "unless your mate had the same opinion."[108] The existence of Lenin's "professional revolutionary" was not full of action and excitement as some might have thought. Until 1936 dues were collected on a weekly basis at unit meetings, a practice that compelled attendance of all members who wished to remain in good standing. Meetings were particularly burdensome. Routinely lasting late into the night, most of the time was taken up by interminable reports delivered in impenetrable jargon. Reflecting a vertical, essentially undemocratic process of decision making within the CPUSA, discussion habitually centered around day-to-day activities, on how best to apply the line rather than on the line itself. Otis Hood, who later became one of the Party's leaders in Massachusetts, recalled the frustration at his first club meeting in 1934. He observed silently from a corner of the room as members devoted all the time to criticizing each other over issues he did not understand. No doubt many others with a similar experience never gave the Party a second chance.

Exploiting the natural enthusiasm of recruits, the Party immediately burdened them with numerous, mostly menial, tasks, such as collecting signatures door-to-door, selling the *Daily Worker*, distributing literature, running-off and distributing thousands of leaflets a week and many assigned organizational responsibilities. Most capable women were usually placed in charge of the Women's Commission. It was not uncommon to send particularly promising new recruits to Party training schools, set up for organizers at a local, state, and national level, where they would attend classes on Marxism and discuss Party policies. Anna Taffler, an organizer of the unemployed councils in Brooklyn was so impressed by the Communists she had met ("they were not cowards") that when asked to join the Party she was flattered. Yet she recalled, her reticence to join; she had two children and understood the great demands the Party placed on its members.[109] It is certainly easy to understand why many recruits, overwhelmed by such a schedule, chose to leave the party.

However, in spite of and possibly even because of the requirements placed upon Party members, many chose to remain. For many of these Communists the opportunity to distribute leaflets, to walk up flights of stairs carrying bundles of the *Daily Worker*, and to address unfriendly crowds on street corners, meant the difference between being a passive victim or spectator and being a fighter against oppression and injustice. Because Communists were striking out against the power of capitalism, even the most menial and repetitive task took on a larger significance: Communists were remaking the world and this made them feel that they were a part of history.

Throughout the third period, the failure of the Communist Party to establish itself as a strong presence among workers became a constant theme in the declarations of its leaders and in its press.[110] In scores of statements, speeches, and documents, Communists relentlessly chastised themselves, varyingly attributing their failures on an unspecified underestimation of the importance of building red unions, the inability to show workers "the revolutionary consequences of their immediate struggles," the use of Communist jargon, and excessive bureaucratization.[111] Party leaders continued to repeat that the only solution to the economic crisis was "the revolutionary way out."[112] An important acknowledgment of the failure of the Party's initiative was the Extraordinary Conference held in early July 1933, called to discuss an "open letter" addressed to its membership.[113] American Communists were caught in a dilemma. By continuing to consider conditions objectively revolutionary Communists themselves had to be at fault for their lack of success. Furthermore, to blame their failure on the general analysis that guided their activities would have been unthinkable, for such a move would have implied criticism of the Comintern. Although the Extraordinary Conference did not lead to any immediate change of policy, it was an important official acknowledgment of the failure of its initiatives and, as such, opened the way to a revision of the Party's overall policy.

The traditional historiographical assessment of the Party's activities during the early years of the depression has not been favorable. Based on the premise that during the early 1930s conditions in the United States were objectively favorable to the establishment of a strong revolutionary movement, a number of historians have attributed the Party's failure to develop into a mass organization to its dogmatic revolutionary posturing which led Communists to underestimate the importance of addressing and finding solutions to the immediate concerns of workers, concentrating instead on politicizing grievances of an economic nature and injecting into them revolutionary demands directed against the power of the state as well as against employers. Communist activities have been described with adjectives such as "cynical," "irresponsible," "manipulative," and "self-serving." To advance their revolutionary objectives Communists used the desperation and hardship of workers and their families attempting to direct them toward demands that were alien to their immediate needs. A clear example of this view is expressed by Klehr who faulted the unwillingness of Communists "to organize, lead, and conclude strikes over concrete economic issues," for the Party's inability to break out of its isolation, broaden its following, root itself firmly among labor, the unemployed, and the black community.[114] Furthermore, according to Klehr, when Communists did fight for partial demands they did so only upon orders from Moscow.[115]

A closer analysis of the Party's activities during the third period leads to a different conclusion. The Party failed to become a mass organization not because of revolutionary posturing and an underestimation of the importance of the workers' immediate concerns. By looking beyond the official statements of the Party's leading bodies and leaders and concentrating on how official policy was applied, it is evident that Communist organizers pressed in the movements they led for solutions to workers' everyday problems, and the demands they put forth dealt mostly with bread-and-butter issues. Evidence also suggests that in many instances Communist organizers ignored central aspects of Party policy as irrelevant to their efforts or antagonistic to the workers they were organizing. In so doing organizers showed sensitivity to the problems and direct knowledge of the needs of the workers.

The main reason for the Party's continued defeats lay in the premise upon which its policies were based: the belief that a revolutionary movement was the inevitable result of the depression. Contrary to the Party's predictions, in the United States and elsewhere, economic hardship tended to weaken labor's initiative rather than reinforce the revolutionary movement. The economic breakdown of capitalism did not free the way to victory: hunger, poverty, and the threat of unemployment undermined any offensive action undertaken by workers. Based on their experiences, Communists learned that hardship neither necessarily turned workers into Bolsheviks, nor sent them to the Communist party for leadership. Furthermore, Communists concluded that class consciousness was the result of a long process. These lessons, learned at great cost, would have significant influence on Communist policies in the years to come.

Despite all its failures, the Party played an important role in awakening the nation to the plight of the unemployed and in courageously battling against deeply entrenched racial discrimination. Perhaps the

47

single most important contribution was that the Party kept the idea of industrial unionism alive during the first years of the depression and thus prepared the ground for the CIO's unionizing drive once economic conditions improved. In these difficult times, Communists acquired considerable organizational training; they developed strategies of concentration and mass picketing that were to prove essential in the years that followed.

During the early years of the depression a new generation of militants, mostly native born ethnics, joined either the Party or the Young Communist League. As Maurice Isserman has pointed out, while the older mostly foreign born leaders, raised in the factional battles of the 1920s, had limited organizing experiences with people outside the Party's ranks and were more concerned with guarding orthodoxy than leading social struggles, for these young men and women the formative political experience which shaped their development was their activity on the forefront of the struggles of the early 1930s.[116] From the new generation emerged a nucleus of experienced young cadres who knew how to organize strikes, coordinate outside support, and talk and deal with workers. By the mid-1930s, after achieving positions of secondary leadership they became the strongest advocates for adapting the Party's program and language to the country's unique political, social, and cultural environment.

3

THE ORIGINS OF THE PEOPLE'S FRONT, 1933–1935

Every anti-fascist is needed in the united front. There must be no base factional quarrels.

Michael Gold, April 1933

The fascist direction in which the Roosevelt policies are carrying the United States is becoming clear to the whole world.

Earl Browder, December 1933[1]

Chapter two made clear the distinction between the Party's official line and the ways in which it was in fact implemented by Communists active in the social struggles of the early years of the depression. While a number of leading Communists did censure what they perceived as local departures from the Party's revolutionary program, in most cases organizers were allowed to follow tactics that emphasized short term objectives over demands for a Soviet America. Due to the Party's centralized structure, the tolerance to deviations from the Party line indicates that the lessons drawn from the day-to-day activities at the grass roots were not lost on the leadership. Eventually the bitter experiences of the first years of the depression, followed by the eruption of working-class militancy and the ominous expansion of fascism in Europe, exerted pressures on the leadership of the CPUSA to reconsider the Party line. For the Communist party the period from 1933 to mid-1935 was a transition away from the third-period analysis and policies toward what became known as the People's Front; during this time both old and new analyses and policies coexisted, accounting for the CPUSA's uneven and contradictory course.

The Party's policies were most changed in the field of labor. The revision of the Party's policies was hastened by the realization that the

AFL and other traditional unions, and not the Trade Union Unity League, were the main beneficiaries of the unionization drive and strike movement of 1933–1934. Compared to an average of 283,000 workers on strike during the previous three years, 1 million workers took part in the strike movement of 1933–1934, spurred by a brief economic upturn and by the sanction of the employees' right to organize and bargain collectively granted by Section 7(a) of the NRA, which President Roosevelt signed in June 1933. During this time workers went on the offensive: in steel, textile, maritime, and in scores of other industries, workers struck for wage increases and union recognition. In some instances, class conflict turned into open warfare. The dramatic labor awakening generated a new sense of militancy, and its most dramatic outbreaks were the Toledo Auto-Lite strike, the Minneapolis teamsters' strike, and the San Francisco general strike. After an initial period of growth, the AFL leadership's inability to deal with this upsurge in rank-and-file militancy, its concern for the interests of the craft unions, and its fear of direct action led to defeat in the auto, steel, and textile industries.[2]

Those organizations that advocated industrial unionism achieved greater gains in rebuilding unions. The United Mine Workers Union, after a long period of stagnation, committed all of its resources to unionization with exceptional results, regaining much of the strength it had lost during the previous decade. Locals were reorganized in areas from which they had been ejected, while non-union mines in Kentucky and Alabama were won over. The UMW's membership grew from 150,000 to 400,000.[3] Similarly, by the end of 1933, Sidney Hillman's Amalgamated Clothing Workers, following a series of successful strikes for higher wages and for recognition in the Northeast and the Midwest, gained 50,000 new members, bringing the total of union membership to 125,000.[4] David Dubinsky's International Ladies' Garment Workers' Union rebounded from a low of 40,000 members in early 1933 to 200,000 two years later.[5]

In 1933 TUUL-affiliated unions initiated a series of small strikes of their own in steel, coal, textile, and marine industries. However, the influence of the TUUL remained limited in most vital industries, and its strength did not increase noticeably during the depression. By the end of 1933, the TUUL claimed to have recruited 100,000 new members. Even if this figure was accurate, however, it only indicates how far the Communist influence lagged behind that of other unions.[6]

In 1934 as independent struggles broke out, Communists had little to do with the Toledo and Minneapolis strikes. They did become an important force in the rank-in-file coalition headed by Harry Bridges that in San Francisco took over the AFL's International Longshoremen's Association and led the successful West Coast longshoremen's strike. Communists, however, achieved a position of prominence not through their red union, the Maritime Workers Industrial Union, but by concentrating all their forces into the ILA.[7] Speaking to the ECCI in December 1934, Browder acknowledged that the 1934 strike movement had taken place "mainly through the channels of the reformist unions, and the Communists in the main were unable to exercise a decisive influence in the leadership of the workers because we were not entrenched as yet inside the A. F. of L. unions which the masses were entering for the purpose of carrying on struggles for their daily interests." With the West Coast events in mind, Browder added that Communists, had "played a leading and decisive role from first to last" only where they were working within the AFL.[8] This new situation required, Browder said, major changes in the Communist party's trade union policy. It had been necessary "to shift the main emphasis to work within the A. F. of L."[9]

During the period between 1930 and 1933, the Party's activities did not prosper due to the rigors of economic chaos. Although through the early years of the depression the TUUL had singlehandedly led the campaign for the organization of the unorganized and the amalgamation of trade unions, when conditions improved and the process of mass unionization began, workers turned to the more traditional labor unions. This movement occurred not because workers rejected industrial unionism but rather because Communist unions were not sufficiently well known. Workers wished to be part of an organization which, while offering the same program as the Communists, had been around longer, was better recognized, perceived as more stable and effective, and could not be as readily red baited. In short, the TUUL had not gained enough credibility to challenge the dominance of other traditional unions. This left the Communist party with no other alternative but to overcome its sectarian opposition to working with non-Communist labor organizations and to go where the workers were.

The experiences and failures of TUUL unions combined with the growth of the AFL and of independent unions, as well as the strengthening within them of the proindustrial union forces, led the Party to abandon dual-unionism in favor of a return to traditional unions. In

December 1933, Browder told the Executive Bureau of the RILU that events in the United States required a "thorough re-examination" of the Party's labor policy; a month later the CPUSA's politburo directed Party members to give *"the most serious attention"* to working within the AFL's "mass unions."[10] Rather than representing a radical departure from previous policy, this statement merely gave official recognition to what was already being done on a local level where, for some time, Communists had been joining the AFL. This process was not uniform, it developed over a period of time, and took on numerous forms. In some instances it was initiated by local union organizers, in others it was the result of pressure from the rank-and-file. Everywhere, however, it reflected a realization at the grass roots that traditional unions were the appropriate place in which to carry on the Party's campaign for amalgamation and a better vehicle through which to obtain workers' demands. Work within these unions was also viewed as a more effective way to break the Party's isolation and to establish a working-class base.

In the coal fields, in some areas as early as 1930, when the first NMU's strikes were broken the Party began directing its members and supporters back into the United Mine Workers. Communist organizers had the difficult task of mitigating rank-and-file resentment against Lewis and convincing miners to go back into the UMW. In the anthracite region of eastern Pennsylvania, opposition among local NMU members to going back into the UMW ran so high that Jack Stachel, acting secretary of the TUUL, had to be called in from New York to convince them to return. Steve Nelson doubtlessly voiced the feelings of many other Communist organizers when he recalled:

> Emotionally we were with them, but we tried to shake them back to reality. We'd say, "Look, you're not in the mines. There are six hundred men working in your mine, and how many of you are out? Only twenty-five. You've got to get back into the mines where the workers are if there is still time.[11]

This process accelerated in 1933. In December, in an unusually candid statement, Browder admitted to the leadership of the RILU that because the NMU had been the only union active in the coal fields of western Pennsylvania, Communists had erroneously concluded that the United Mine Workers had been permanently "removed from the arena of struggle." However, the Communist leader was forced to

acknowledge that, after the passage of the NRA, the UMW had conducted a major recruiting drive signing up most miners including
those "who for a number of years had struggled under the direct
leadership of the National Miners Union." Miners considered a continued existence of the NMU "schismatic and alien to them," and therefore they "obstructed our work of recruiting to the red union."[12]

Another example of a Communist union disbanding to join the AFL
was the Automobile Workers Union local at the White Motor plant in
Cleveland. In 1933, the local was one of the AWU's strong-holds with
50 percent of the plant unionized. At this point organizers from the
AFL's Metal Trades Council distributed leaflets at the plant's gates;
under the picture of an American flag, they urged workers to "Join the
bonafide AMERICAN labor union." This leaflet was followed by another in which workers were pressed to "choose between Franklin
Delano Roosevelt and Joe Stalin." The AFL's red-baiting action created confusion and division among workers, drawing many toward
the AFL. In an effort to preserve the workers' unity, Wyndham Mortimer, the Communist leader of the AWU local, called a meeting and on
his own initiative suggested that all members join the AFL. Accepting
his proposal, the Communist union at White Motors disbanded and
was replaced by Federal Local Union 18463.[13] Across the country Communists and members of the AWU also began entering either the AFL
or the newly formed auto tool and die makers organization, the Me-
chanics Educational Society of America (MESA), drawn to it by the
militancy of its leadership.[14] Within these unions Communists joined
forces with those advocating the amalgamation of all auto workers
into a single industrial union controlled by the rank-and-file and es-
pousing a more militant policy. In June 1934, William Green called a
National Conference of United Automobile Workers Federal Labor
unions, to curb the growing sentiment for an industrial union. At the
conference Wyndham Mortimer led a small group of delegates in an
unsuccessful battle for the immediate creation of an industrial union
to include AFL unions as well as the AWU and MESA.[15] Despite this
setback, the mood within the AWU continued to be in favor of joining
the AFL. By the time the AWU was disbanded at the end of 1934, most
of the Communists in the auto industry were in the AFL or MESA.[16]

Dual unionism was discarded elsewhere. In the steel industry the
TUUL's Steel and Metal Workers Industrial Union (SMWIU), a relative latecomer founded only in August 1932, led a number of unsuccessful strikes. With the spontaneous labor upsurge of 1933, an old

craft union, the AFL's Amalgamated Association of Iron, Steel, and Tin Workers, saw its ranks swell from 4,801 members in the spring of 1934 to 50,000 a year later. In May 1934 the strong rank-and-file movement within the Amalgamated made a first attempt to establish collaboration, an attempt that failed due to Communist opposition. Eventually this opposition subsided and, by the end of the year, members of the SMWIU went over to the Amalgamated.[17]

By March 1934, 1,431 Communists or 30 percent of the Party's union membership were in federal unions; Communists also claimed that revolutionary elements "directly under our guidance" led approximately 150 local unions with a membership of between 50,000 and 60,000.[18] A month later in Cleveland, the party's Eighth Convention formally approved the process of abandoning dual unionism. In his report Browder recognized that most of the recently organized workers had joined the AFL. Given this situation, he stated that Communists had little choice but to go back into the AFL.[19] Despite some opposition to the new labor policy, the Convention's final resolution endorsed the secretary's speech.[20]

The Party did attempt to gain some bargaining power to negotiate a TUUL merger into the AFL. At the convention, in his evaluation of the growth of labor militancy, Browder dealt at length with the development of independent unions whose membership he estimated at 250,000, twice the membership of TUUL unions. Browder saw independent unions as the "result of the mass revolt against the A. F. of L. betrayals." Consequently the Party called for unification between these unions and the TUUL in one single Independent Federation of Labor.[21] The AFL's silence after the TUUL's National Executive Board sent a letter offering unity to the AFL's 54th Convention dispelled the illusion of possible diminution of its anti-Communist stance.[22] Given the general emphasis on entering the AFL, however, Communist leaders had no other choice but to drop the idea of an independent labor federation; as Foster put it, "with no illusion as to the responsiveness of the A.F. of L.'s moguls . . . [the TUUL] went ahead with its policy of amalgamation from the bottom."[23] The Party released the TUUL unions to enter the AFL on any terms they could negotiate.

The pace of the dissolution of red unions increased by the end of 1934 as TUUL unions in mine, auto, steel, textile, marine, and the needle trades dissolved and their members entered the AFL individually. A few unions were able to negotiate favorable conditions for their merger on a local level; the most successful merger occurred when

Ben Gold's fur workers' union joined the AFL union, which, despite William Green's opposition, elected Gold manager of the New York Joint Board.[24] By the end of 1934 red unions had been effectively discarded. However, in order to formalize its doings and to officially disband the TUUL, the Party needed to secure the approval of the Comintern. Consequently in December 1934, Browder addressed the ECCI in Moscow, claiming that the new situation in the United States required the Communist party "to shift the main emphasis to work within the A. F. of L."[25] At a meeting in mid-January, following Moscow's endorsement, the Party's Central Committee announced the decision to liquidate the TUUL, a step which the Communist union, by then with few members, took unceremoniously in mid-March at a convention in New York City.[26]

Central to the Party's reexamination of its policies after 1933 was a reconsideration of its analysis of fascism and, hence, of its attitude toward the Socialist party. One of the main aspects of the Comintern's policy during the third period was the belief that the bourgeoisie, confronted with the strengthening of the revolutionary movement, would abandon the parliamentary system and turn to fascism as a last resort for the defense of its class rule. Thus, the Comintern saw no substantial difference between democratic and fascist forms of government, since in its view both were expressions of the same bourgeois class rule. In this context, fascism was simply further proof of the crisis of bourgeois domination, a desperate reaction that heralded the imminence of revolution itself. The struggle against fascism, the winning over of the working class, and the destruction of capitalism were seen as simultaneous events all leading to a Soviet-style revolution.

According to the Comintern, social-democratic organizations were accomplices of the process of "fascization" of society. These organizations, in order to weaken the revolutionary fervor of workers, created false distinctions between bourgeois democracy and fascism. The Tenth Plenum of the ECCI not only institutionalized the term "social-fascist" as synonymous with "Social-Democratic" but also decreed that Communists were to concentrate their efforts against Socialists as the main supporters of capitalism and as major obstacles in the path of revolution.[27] Even in the face of Hitler's rise to power and the destruction of the Socialist and Communist parties in Germany, the international Communist movement did not immediately reconsider its analysis. Also without regard to the fact that divisions between the two working class parties had aided Hitler's rise, the international Communist movement officially continued with its anti-Socialist stance through the spring of 1934.[28]

The struggle against broadly defined social-fascists became an essential aspect of the policies of the Communist party. According to Foster, the leadership of the AFL—"the Greens, Wolls, Lewises"— were already "practically open Fascists," as defenders of capitalism they had become "the chief strike breaking agency of the employers."[29] The same fiery language had been directed against other reform groups such as A. J. Muste and his Conference for Progressive Labor Action, and the members of the "Progressive bloc" such as the LaFollettes, William Borah, Fiorello La Guardia, George Norris, and Gifford Pinchot; these men Foster called a "lighting rod to shield the capitalist profit edifice."[30] But the strongest language was reserved for Socialists. During the 1932 presidential campaign, Moissaye Olgin called the Socialist party the "Last Bulwark of Capitalism." Its role, he wrote, was to keep workers from joining the Communist party by swaying them with revolutionary phraseology and ultimately *"to make it easier for the capitalists to prolong the existence of this bankrupt system."*[31] Foster wrote that the Socialist party was "particularly dangerous in that it takes the workers, just breaking the ideological chains of capitalist slavery, and confuses them with a defense of capitalism under the pretense of fighting for Socialism. The Socialist party stabs the working class in the back."[32]

In the CPUSA the persistence of third-period analysis and language endured as late as the spring of 1934. How strongly anti-Socialist policies affected Communists in the United States was clearly shown by the events of February 16, 1934, in New York. That day an estimated 5,000 Communists led by Robert Minor and Clarence Hathaway, the editor of the *Daily Worker*, broke up the Socialist rally at the Madison Square Garden called to protest the slaughter in Austria of Socialist workers by the fascist Chancellor Engelbert Dolfuss. The *Times* reported: "Chairs were flung from the balconies and screams, and shrieks of women, mingled with boos, yells and catcalls, drowned out the voices of speakers on the platform." The Communists' action drew strong criticism from many of its supporters. John Dos Passos together with Edmund Wilson and John Chamberlain all signed an open letter condemning the Party's behavior and J. B. Matthews resigned as president of the American League Against War and

Fascism together with six other ranking Socialist members of the organizations' national executive committee. The Communist action also resulted in a sense of bitterness and suspicion that would weigh heavily on future relations with the Socialist party.[33]

In early April 1934, in his address to the Party's Eighth Convention, Browder once more accused the Socialist party's leadership of being "social-fascist," of holding back, together with those of the AFL, "the workers from revolutionary struggle which alone can defeat and destroy fascism." They tied, he continued, "the working class to the chariot wheels of a capitalist democracy which is being transformed into fascism, paralyze their resistance, deliver them over to fascism bound and helpless."[34] Browder also declared:

> True, fascism is a heavy blow against the working class. True, fascism turns loose every black reactionary force against the working class, and tries to physically exterminate its vanguard, the Communist party. But at the same time it is a sign of deepening crisis of capitalism; it solves not one of the basic problems of the crisis, but intensifies them all; it further disrupts the capitalist world system; it destroys the moral base for capitalist rule, discrediting bourgeois law in the eyes of the masses; it hastens the exposure of all demagogic supporters of capitalism, especially its main support among the workers—the Socialist and trade union leaders. It hastens the revolutionization of the workers, destroys their democratic illusions, and thereby prepares the masses for the revolutionary struggle for power.[35]

Despite the Party's official stance, numerous signs indicated that Communists were beginning to transcend this policy by giving fascism a significance of its own as the main adversary, requiring the unity of all anti-fascist forces regardless of their ideologies. An important factor in this reevaluation was the realization, based on recent German events, that fascism, rather than proletarian revolution, was itself the possible outcome of the economic crisis. In light of this, American Communists began to reconsider their analysis of the nature of fascism, to discover the importance of democracy and accordingly change their policy toward the Socialist party.

An early sign of this changing view occurred shortly after Hitler's rise to power. In the United States, concern with the threat of fascism served to unify the intellectual community. That anti-fascism found fertile ground among intellectuals was not surprising. As Matthew Josephson put it:

Writers (whatever their shortcomings) had been singled out for special attention by the new barbarians as being a dangerous breed because of their attachment to the values of humanistic civilization, and because they were conveyors of such values. The writers felt they should return the compliment by directing their attention to the fascists.[36]

In March 1933, *New Masses,* the Party's literary magazine, addressed a letter to several writers asking them to express their condemnation of German events. In the April issue the answers of fourteen writers were published together with an anti-nazi manifesto written by Joseph Freeman. All agreed that Nazism would "crush out everything that artists and writers value."[37] Furthermore, there was agreement that anti-fascism, not merely another aspect of a broader anti-capitalist struggle, transcended class and political lines. Very significant in this respect was Mike Gold's call for "a united front of all the working class parties and liberal groups . . . Every anti-fascist is needed in this united front. There must be no base factional quarrels."[38] It is important to note that despite the official policy of the CPUSA, these writers' appeals for a broad anti-fascist unity, which distinguished between fascist and bourgeois democratic rule, appeared in a Party publication. Although a similarly broad approach to anti-fascism would not figure in the Party's official declarations for some time, this early appeal to intellectuals showed a receptiveness, one that must have extended as far up as the leadership of the Party, to overcome sectarian policies and herald changes in the Party's line.

The Communists' gradual move toward a broadening of the antifascist coalition necessarily entailed a change of attitude toward Socialists. The Comintern's policy of social-fascism was the product of European conditions where Communists were confronted by powerful and influential social-democratic parties. In the United States the influence of the Socialist party was so limited as to make the titanic efforts Communists used to attack it disproportionate. As early as mid-1933, however, young Socialists and Communists, disregarding their parties' official policies, overcame old antagonisms and effectively collaborated around common goals. In their efforts, they gave one of the few effective examples of united front collaboration in the pre-1935 period, all the more important as its inception predated the Comintern's shift away from social-fascism.

One of the characteristics of the 1930s was a resurgence of student concern and activism over domestic and international issues. The depression and growing world tension overcame political apathy among the students, who just a few years earlier Harold Laski had described in his article "Why Don't Young Men Care?"[39] Furthermore, the Soviet experience, which appeared as a successful alternative to economic depression, war, and rising fascism, increased the radicalization of many students. On the left, students could choose between two organizations: the Socialist Student League for Industrial Democracy (SLID) and the Communist National Student League (NSL). SLID was an outgrowth of the Intercollegiate Socialist Society founded in 1905 by Jack London and Upton Sinclair which during the 1920s had become the League for Industrial Democracy. In 1932 its college branch was renamed SLID and also gained a semi-autonomous status from the Socialist party. The organization's executive secretary was Joseph Lash.[40] In 1931 Communists set up their own student organization headed by Donald Henderson, a young economics instructor at Columbia and former LID member. Other leaders were Joseph Starobin of CCNY, Joseph Clark of Brooklyn College, James Wechsler, and, on the West Coast, Celeste Strack. Both organizations had much in common. Their membership was not limited to the respective Party youth organizations; both combined concern for student affairs, such as demands for financial aid, defense of academic freedom, opposition to segregation and to ROTC, with appeals for student support for labor. The most highly publicized example of student support of labor was the NSL's delegation of 82 students from a number of schools to Harlan County during the miners' strike in March 1932. Without a chance to visit the coal miners, the delegation was turned back at the Kentucky border by an armed mob. After this foray on unfamiliar territory, the NSL concentrated its work in the more congenial and familiar campus environment.[41]

Formally separated by their parties, the two organizations were drawn together by the similarities in their programs. On Armistice Day 1933, the two organizations jointly sponsored an anti-war demonstration at Harvard.[42] In Washington a month later during Christmas vacation, the NSL participated at the National Conference of Students in Politics sponsored by SLID. Although this conference was marked mostly by ideological disputes between the two organizations, it managed to bring them together and also to give voice for the first time to the concern of many youth organizations for social and political issues. Despite the Party's official policy, the NSL participated side by side with such organizations as the YMCA, the YWCA, the National Council of Student Christian Organizations and other groups and liberal personalities such as Eleanor Roosevelt, Henry Wallace, Senator Robert Wagner, Philip La Follette, and Reinhold Niebuhr.[43]

The first major sign of the students' interest in politics expressed itself in the anti-war movement. In the United States the international situation, the growing threat of war, and an increased awareness of the futility of World War I, coupled with disclosures of profiteering by the armament industry, served to fuel anti-war sentiment. A 1933 poll of 21,725 students in 65 colleges nationwide found that a plurality of 8,415 declared themselves pacifists, 7,221 saw an invasion of the United States as the only justifiable reason to bear arms, and only 6,089 declared that they would fight as ordered.[44]

The united front anti-war movement developed around the Oxford Pledge approved by the Oxford Student Union in February 1933. Soon students in other British universities adopted the pledge, in which students swore never to fight "for King and Country."[45] In the United States, the Oxford pledge retained the name but was Americanized reflecting the Marxism of its Socialist and Communist framers. It stated: "We pledge not to support the government of the United States" in any war it might conduct. In fact, far from being a declaration against war, it was directed against the government as the initiator of war and left the possibility open for support of wars not caused by the government. It was a compromise between absolute pacifism and the internationalism of those who, while opposed to "imperialist-wars", believed in class war.[46] Led by Brown University, students in a number of other schools endorsed the pledge.[47] In April 1934, the NSL and SLID, on the basis of the Oxford Pledge, jointly sponsored a Student Strike Against War in which they called students to "lay down their books" for one hour. The strike took place on the anniversary of the United States' entry into World War I and was moderately successful. An estimated 25,000 students took part, over half of these in New York City, although there were strong pockets of participation elsewhere in the country.[48] Following the strike the collaboration between the two organizations increased, also extending to other non-marxist liberal and religious youth organizations.

Concerned over the danger of war provoked by fascist aggression in Europe, Africa, and Asia, students linked the causes of anti-fascism and pacifism together and participated in great numbers to the Second Strike Against War in April of the following year. Estimates of the

The Origins of the People's Front

number of participants vary from 60,000 to 175,000; a total of 130 schools were involved, many in the West and the Midwest, twenty in the South. As one of the leaders of the national strike committee recognized "we did not know our own strength." One of the most impressive aspects of this strike was that it was not limited to left-wing or pacifist organizations, but involved a wide range of groups and individuals from religious organizations, fraternities, high school students, college presidents, and local government officials. This diversity was depicted by their banners proclaiming on the one hand "Down With Imperialist War," and on the other "War Is Un-Christian," all showing that the movement went well beyond Socialists and Communists. Neither NSL nor SLID could absorb such diversity; therefore, the impact of the Second Strike and the successful collaboration between the two organizations achieved in the previous sixteen months led to their unification into the American Student Union.

In 1934, the NSL had initiated talks about unification but nothing had come out of them. Now both sides seriously considered the Communists' appeal for a common front of all democratic forces against fascism. Because of its broad composition, not limited to young Socialists but also including liberals, SLID's national executive committee voted to accept the NSL's offer in June, despite the fact that this would be in violation of the Socialist party's National Executive Committee prohibition against joining in united front with Communists.

In December 1935, 450 delegates from approximately 200 schools met in Columbus, Ohio, to found the American Student Union (ASU). As one of the leaders of the new organization stated, the purpose of the amalgamation of the NSL and SLID was to create an organization "which will enroll far more than their present constituencies." To obtain this goal they had to

combat both factionalism and snobbery which have often characterized left-wing ventures and repelled those not committed to the complete tenets of their position. Today the most imminent and menacing danger is the approach of fascism: to resist it will require more than the isolated protests of the left. There are thousands of students who have begun to sense the peril, who are prepared to act against it. They will do so only to the extent that they are convinced of the sincerity of those who offer them cooperation.

Symbolizing the newfound unity between the two organizations, officers were divided equally among them. Socialist George Edwards, a

Phi Beta Kappa from Southern Methodist University, became president of the ASU; fellow Socialists Joseph Lash and Molly Yard became executive secretary and treasurer. Communist James Wechsler was named editor of the organization's magazine *Student Advocate;* the field secretary Serril Gerber and the high school secretary Celeste Strack were also Communists.[49] Immediately successful in its goal of bringing together into one organization diverse groups of people, the ASU was well received in numerous campuses and grew accordingly: while joint membership of the NSL and SLID had been 8,000, the ASU numbered 20,000 members with the strongest pockets at the University of Chicago, CCNY and Brooklyn College. This figure hardly constituted a mass organization when compared with the total number of college students at the time, but the ASU's influence on the student body was considerable. Its members and leaders were among the brightest and most politically active students and its campus-based activities included students' demands for relief, academic freedom, desegregation, and support of workers' demands. Together with its broader anti-fascist sentiment, this assured the ASU the support of a strong, liberal, non-marxist component.[50]

In 1934, in another important example of united front collaboration, the Communist and Socialist youth organizations, the Young Communist League and the Young People's Socialist League, joined forces to take control of the American Youth Congress (AYC) at its founding convention away from Viola Ilma, an ambiguous figure whom they suspected of having Nazi sympathies.[51] The Communists' decision to participate in the founding of the American Youth Congress was the result of a heated battle within the leadership of the YCL. A number of its leaders, chief among them Max Weiss and the representative of the Young Communist International, who was known as Max Young, opposed participation arguing that the AYC was a social-fascist organization. Gil Green, national secretary of the YCL, instead maintained that, in order to prevent the rise of a reactionary youth organization, it was essential to form the broadest democratic, anti-fascist unity, going beyond class lines including a range of youth organizations of a student or religious character such as the YMCA, the YWCA, and the Methodist youth federation.

Toward the end of October 1934, Green received a cable from the Secretariat of the Young Communist International asking him to attend an important meeting in Moscow. Green did not know the purpose of the meeting. He arrived in Moscow in December and learned the meeting was to discuss the YCL's participation to the AYC. Clearly Max Young, who had gone back to the Soviet Union, had informed Moscow of the course taken by the YCL. As the French Communist Youth had been involved in a similar kind of broad-based youth movement, its leader, Raymond Guyot, was also summoned to Moscow to be reprimanded. Green and Guyot were attacked by the Soviet and the German representatives. They were accused of abandoning the class position and weakening class-consciousness by agreeing to YCL's collaboration with bourgeois organizations. YCL's action was compared to the German Socialists' decision to support Hindenburg to stop Hitler. At the end of the first meeting Green and Guyot each received a typewritten resolution which they were asked to endorse and bring back to their organizations. Meetings continued with both sides defending their positions. Finally after three weeks of discussion, Green was warned that, if by the next meeting he did not accept the proposed resolution it would be adopted over his head accompanied with a recommendation by the Young Communist International to the national committee of the YCL that he be removed from office. Clearly there was no more room for debate: either Green and Guyot reconsidered their views or risk major political consequences.

However, when the committee reconvened a day or two later both the American and the French leader were surprised to hear the Soviet delegate announce not only that the resolution was being withdrawn, but that Green and Guyot had been right all along. Green never received an explanation and could only speculate as to what had brought about such a radical transformation. Apparently before taking drastic action against the two youth leaders, the Young Communist International had reported to its elders in the Comintern where Dimitrov was arguing in favor of abandoning the sectarian policies of the third period. It was Green's good fortune that Dimitrov's views were prevailing. Green was in step with the changes brewing within the Comintern, therefore at its 7th Congress, he was elected to the Executive Committee of the Communist International, and his policies were cited as examples to be followed elsewhere.[52]

The new emphasis on a broad antifascist coalition also appeared in the dissolution of the John Reed Clubs. Founded in 1929 and turned into a national organization in 1932, the Clubs' prime objective had been to promote proletarian culture, but the heavy ideological limitations imposed by the third-period analysis on artistic and aesthetic considerations did not sit well with many intellectuals. Therefore, if intellectuals were to be drawn into a common anti-fascist unity, the emphasis on proletarian art had to end. Rather than furthering proletarian art and having Communists in positions of leadership within the writers' organization, the Party now preferred to establish a new organization to enlist well-known liberals and fellow travelers in its battle against fascism, despite their lesser political reliability. Accordingly, on the occasion of the John Reed Clubs' second national conference held in September 1934 in Chicago, the organization's "sectarianism" and "leftism" came under attack and a resolution was formulated condemning "writing which consists of unconvincing, sloganized tracts disguised as poetry."[53] The most important proposal came from Alexander Trachtenberg, head of the Party's International Publishers and the CPUSA's representative in the organization, who proposed the dissolution of the John Reed Clubs and a substitution of a national congress of writers with a much broader, less sectarian mandate. That Trachtenberg was expressing a new Party line became apparent at the Communist caucus held that same evening in a Chicago hotel. Writers were told that the shift of the Party to a new policy of broader appeal required the dissolution of the John Reed Clubs, symbols of past sectarian policies.[54] The Writers' Congress was directed at older and more established writers; the younger, unknown writers, who had been the mainstay of the John Reed Clubs and the Pen and Hammer groups were to play no role in the new organization. By and large intellectuals responded favorably to the Party's new stand as well as to the abandonment of attempts to turn intellectuals into propagandists.

The following January, the *New Masses* published a call for the first Congress of the League of American Writers, written by Granville Hicks and endorsed by 62 writers. Although echoes of third-period rhetoric persisted, it was clear that the new emphasis was no longer on "proletarian revolution" but, rather, on the defense of culture from fascism. The call stated that writers were confronted by two problems: the first, a political one, was the spread of war and fascism; the second, peculiar to writers, was one of describing American reality on the basis of their participation "in the revolutionary cause." The purpose of the congress was to bring writers together "for fundamental discussion" of these issues and to found the League of American Writers. Even in this case it was clear that opposition to fascism took priority: "This Congress will be devoted to the exposition of all phases of a writer's participation in the struggle against war, the preservation of civil liberties, and the destruction of fascist tendencies everywhere." The call was addressed to writers of "considerable achievement and standing, to all American writers, regardless of their aesthetic or political views," who were willing to "unite on a general program for the defense of culture against the threat of Fascism and war."[55]

On April 26, in his welcoming address at the first session of the Congress at the Mecca Temple in New York City, Browder assured an audience of 4,000 that the Party was not going to interfere with the work of the writers. "The first demand of the Party," he said, "upon its writer-members" is that they shall "be good writers, constantly better writers, for only so can they really serve the Party. We do not want to take good writers and make bad strike leaders out of them."[56] The Communist party could not and would not pass any aesthetic or artistic judgment: the "final authority," he said, would be the writer's audience. The Party was not going to put writers "in uniform," nor impose "any pre-conceived patterns."[57] In this situation of independence writers and Communists would be bound by the need to unite "all progressive forces" in a common alliance against "reaction, against Fascism in the inner life of nations and against imperialist war internationally."[58]

While Communists had begun to modify their opposition to working within traditional unions, their analysis of fascism, and their relationship with Socialists, the CPUSA did not reconsider its opposition to President Roosevelt, the New Deal, and reform movements in general. The Party's position toward the president remained essentially the same as it had been at the time of his election despite the evolution of his policies and, eventually, the opposition they generated from the right.

During the 1932 presidential election the policy of the Communist party had been to group together presidential candidates—Republican or Democratic—as representing the same economic interests. Such policy derived from a strict economic analysis that dismissed any differences among capitalist politicians. Communists concentrated on showing that there was no substantial incongruity between these parties and that a vote for the Democratic candidate was not a valid alternative to a vote for Hoover. While it was no secret, Foster wrote, that the Republican party was "the Party of finance capital," voters were not to be fooled by the Democratic party either. In the forthcoming election the Democratic party was to "play its historic role as the second party of capitalism," presenting itself as the alternative to Hoover in order to channel popular discontent. The task of the Democratic party, Foster wrote, was "with a flood of demagogy, to delude these masses, and to prevent their taking serious steps against the capitalists, by keeping them fettered with the two capitalist party system."[59]

Franklin Delano Roosevelt's nomination as the Democratic party candidate in early July 1932, gave the Communists new fuel for their attacks. As William Leuchtenburg points out, the electoral program of the Democratic party "differed little from that of the Republican on economic questions, although the Democrats espoused somewhat more ambitious welfare programs."[60] During the campaign Roosevelt criticized Hoover, but he did not spell out clear policies that he would follow if elected. He exploited instead the incumbent's unpopularity, which made Hoover's defeat virtually certain anyway and, by avoiding any controversial statement, tried not to antagonize either the left or the right. On the one hand, Roosevelt would call for federal aid to farmers, criticize economic oligarchs, and talks of his concern for the "forgotten man at the bottom of the economic pyramid." On the other hand, on issues such as tariffs, unemployment, fiscal policies, and the general role of the federal government, his views appeared similar to those of Hoover, if indeed not more orthodox. Roosevelt even blamed his opponent for excessive spending and promised a balanced budget. One of the few certainties that emerged from this campaign was that Roosevelt strongly opposed prohibition.[61]

The Communists took both the Democratic program and Roosevelt's elusive stand as confirmation of their view that both parties represented the same economic interests. This analysis was expressed in a declaration of the Party's National Executive Election Campaign Committee: "The bosses know that Roosevelt's talk about the 'forgotten man' is only to fool those workers and farmers who are disgusted with Hoover and to try to get them to support the Democratic candidates, who are also, like Hoover, servants of Wall Street."[62]

Roosevelt's vagueness left the Party no choice but to dig deep into his political past. Hence in reference to his role in sending the Marines to Haiti while undersecretary of the navy under President Wilson, the Party came up with the title of "imperialist butcher."[63] Communists took issue with Roosevelt's record during his tenure as governor of New York. An article in *Labor Unity* held Roosevelt responsible for the failure of the state assembly to approve bills protecting the rights of workers and providing adequate relief for the unemployed. At a rally in Columbus, Ohio, Foster argued that New York State had not done "more than any Republican state in the country" to alleviate the problems of the unemployed.[64]

In the main, the Party concentrated attacks principally against the platform of the Democratic party. The CPUSA took the proposal to abolish prohibition, for instance, as further proof of the Democrats' lack of concern for the country's real problems. Democrats called for repeal of the 18th Amendment only "for the purpose of side-tracking the workers and farmers from the real issue of today—the fight against hunger and war and for jobs and bread."[65] It was Hoover and not Roosevelt, however, who emerged as the CPUSA's main target, a choice that did not indicate the slightest conciliation toward Roosevelt. Within the logic of revolutionary struggle, criticism of Hoover, merely the more vulnerable of the two, at the same time implied the involvement of Roosevelt and his party.

A few days after his inauguration on March 4, 1933, Roosevelt requested greater control over monetary policy and banks which began a period of intense legislative activity during which Congress passed the most sweeping economic program in United States history. By the end of May, the federal budget had been cut by half a billion dollars, reducing funds slated for veterans and federal employees. The Agricultural Adjustment Act had been passed to support farm prices, the Civilian Conservation Corps (CCC) to provide jobs for young men, and the Tennessee Valley authority (TVA) to create jobs and provide cheap electrical power. One of the last laws approved by Congress adjourning in mid-June was to create the National Recovery Administration, the NRA.

In the May issue of the Party's theoretical magazine, the *Communist*, an editorial expressed a first judgment on Roosevelt's policies and the New Deal, an analysis which was to remain unchanged during this period. Returning to what had been the basis of the Party's attack on Roosevelt during the campaign, the editorial charged that the president's policies were nothing more than an attempt staged by finance capital, under a new guise and loaded with demagogic promises, to save the system. The New Deal was described as a momentary "experiment" to gain much needed time for capitalist forces. Through a

smoke-screen of promises, its real purpose was to check the development of the workers' insurgency. The Federal government, in the
Party's view, was playing a central role in helping shift the burden of
the economic crisis onto the shoulders of workers. The Communist
party intended to "unmask" the true nature of Roosevelt's policies
and show that they were no different from Hoover's. To dispel any
notion that Roosevelt was advancing the interests of workers, the
Party set out to prove how every act of the Administration revealed
that Roosevelt's stated concern for the "forgotten man" was only
electioneering. Concerning the bank holiday as well as the Emergency
Banking Bill, the editorial stressed that the resulting inflation would
worsen the living conditions of workers; for them "the rise in domestic prices will act as an indirect wage-cut. The dollar will buy less
goods than before. In this manner, the standards of living of the
masses will be further lowered." The editorial claimed that Roosevelt's duplicity was also revealed in the cuts in benefits for veterans
and wages of federal employees.[66]

The measures to improve the lot of the unemployed were denounced as inadequate, demagogic and serving to hide Roosevelt's
war aims. Proof of this last claim, the editorial charged, could be
found in the CCC and the program calling for federally funded public
works, whose purpose was not to solve the problems of unemployment nor to "eliminate slums, to build hospitals, to establish play-
grounds." Rather both were "direct steps in the preparation of war—
one to establish a vast army and the other to build a Navy second to
none."[67] The view that the CCC was a reservoir for strike breakers
and future soldiers led the YCL to devote considerable energies to
organize young men in the camps, activities that aroused great concern on the part of military authorities.[68]

The Administration's farm program also came under fire. Subsi-
dies of farm products would raise prices for consumers, as well as
increase starvation among the poor. The increase in prices was not
going to benefit "poor farmers" but rather "the kulaks, the bankers
and the mortgage companies."[69] The Party's task was to work with
the workers, to enlighten them as to the "true essence of Roosevelt's
program," and to criticize the AFL and the Socialist party for their
support.[70]

Central to the Party's anti-Roosevelt campaign was the denunciation of the National Industrial Recovery Act. According to the Party,
the NRA codes favored the process of "trustification" of the economy

and involved state support of monopoly capital. The increasing role of the federal government in the economy was a clear move toward fascism.[71] Quite predictably, most of the attacks on the act were directed at its labor provisions, Section 7(a). Roosevelt's labor policy was described as "the most direct and open part of the fascist features of the New Deal," part of a plan aimed at the "militarization of labor," which included government-fixed wages, company unions, and limitations to the right to strike. All of this made the New Deal "the American brother of Mussolini's 'corporate state'."[72]

In a pamphlet entitled *Industrial Slavery: Roosevelt's New Deal*, Israel Amter dealt at length with the National Industrial Recovery Act. "What does the Act mean?" he asked.

> It means the organization of the employers into powerful associations, with monopolistic control of the industries, which with governmental 'sanctions' works out codes. For the workers it means the stagger plan with starvation minimum wages which will be maximum wages, so called collective bargaining, and the settling of disputes by the control of boards. The Roosevelt government, to which the workers have looked to solve the crisis, becomes the policeman backing up the employers and enforcing the dictates of General Johnson.[73]

In concluding he called Roosevelt the "great demagogue. . . . the new Messiah, the great savior—the dictator."[74]

For the Communist party the New Deal was not fascism, but a movement in that direction. A careful distinction was drawn between tendencies and *fait accompli*. Browder warned that to label everything capitalist as fascist would result "in destroying all distinction between the various forms of capitalist rule." Fascism was the last resort of the ruling class when its dominance was in danger, and Roosevelt's policies, although a step in that direction, had not yet gone that far. Repeating the major point of the third period, however, he added, Roosevelt's program was proof that there was

> no Chinese wall between democracy and fascism. Roosevelt operates with all the arts of 'democratic' rule, with an emphasized liberal and social-demagogic cover, quite a contrast with Hoover who was outspokenly reactionary. Yet, behind this smoke screen, Roosevelt is carrying out more thoroughly, more brutally than Hoover, the capitalist attack against the living standards of the masses and the sharpest national chauvinism in foreign relations.[75]

All through 1934 the Party continuously portrayed the New Deal as "the official fascization of government."[76] Alexander Bittelman was particularly outspoken in attacks on the New Deal. In the January issue of the *Communist* he wrote that the New Deal was "a sharper turn of the capitalist dictatorship in the United States to war and fascism in the search of the capitalist solution to the crisis."[77] During the summer of 1933 the *Daily Worker* published cartoons depicting the symbol of the NRA, the Blue Eagle, (or, as it was sometimes called, "Blue Buzzard") holding in its claws a swastika. The Party's view of Roosevelt was best reflected in another cartoon in the *New Masses* which portrayed him as a medicine man hawking bottles labeled CCC, AAA, and NRA.[78]

The Communist International expressed its strong position against Roosevelt at the XIII Plenum of its Executive Committee in late November and early December 1933. In the introductory speech, Otto Kuusinen repeated the International's analysis of the world economic crisis as being the "general crisis" of capitalism. He dealt briefly with the New Deal as another attempt to save the system and therefore doomed to failure, serving only to support capitalism "as the rope supports the hanged man." The International, slow to learn from German events, continued to see fascism where it did not exist, even in the United States. The claim of fascism was not direct. In criticizing social-fascism, Kuusinen stated, "in the USA social-fascists and the AFL support Roosevelt's economic measures which are essentially Fascist in character."[79] Similar opinions on the New Deal were expressed by the British delegate, Rajani Palme Dutt, and the Italian, Palmiro Togliatti. The latter drew a parallel between fascist policies in Italy and the various attempts being made in several countries to resolve the crisis. While stating that there were still some differences between Roosevelt's policies and open fascism, Togliatti said:

Here we find State intervention aimed at bringing about a new capitalistic concentration in the industrial sector, an accentuated offensive against the workers' standard of living, the proclamation of the doctrine of the strong state, a disregard of parliamentary processes and even, to a certain degree, an anti-capitalist demagoguery that is aimed at influencing the average farmer in certain American states. . . . [All these were] characteristic of fascist policy and ideology.[80]

Similar statements concerning the "fascist nature" of the New Deal were made at the plenum by Browder and William Weinstone who spoke on behalf of the CPUSA.[81]

Communists were not the only ones to see analogies between the government-business cooperation of fascist corporatist principles and the NRA codes; while the head of the NRA, Hugh Johnson, made no secret of his sympathy for Italian fascism.[82] Also, there was the Communists' concern for Section 7(a) of the NRA which, while guaranteeing the workers' right to organize and bargain collectively through representatives of their own choice, did not bind employers to negotiate with these organizations. That concern would be proven just by later events. The NRA's ambiguity opened the way for management to form company unions to give the appearance of collective bargaining while preserving and, in many cases, expanding the open shop.

Behind the Party's criticism of Roosevelt's policies lay a deeper concern. The Communist party viewed with alarm the president's growing popularity among labor. Browder emphasized:

> The illusions about the new deal as a road back to prosperity are still strong among broad masses. To expose and disperse these illusions will require more experience and above all requires the active, ceaseless, carefully thought-out intervention of the Communist party.[83]

Addressing the Workers' School of New York on September 17, Browder dedicated an entire speech to demystifying the notion that the NRA supported the workers' interests. Were Roosevelt's policies making things better for workers? Predictably, Browder's answer was "no." All economic figures, he continued, showed that the New Deal, far from improving the livelihood of workers and farmers, made life harder for them. "Under Roosevelt and the N.R.A.," he said, "millions of workers are getting less food, less clothing, less shelter, than they did under Hoover."[84] Reflecting the Party's third-period analysis, he concluded that to be a friend of the workers required

> being against the system of private ownership of the means of production by the capitalist class. It requires building up the organized power of the working class in the struggle against the capitalist class. It requires helping the working class to take governmental power out of the hands of the capitalists, and establishing a Workers' Government, which takes the

means of production away from the capitalists and organizes them on a new socialist basis, as the common property of all.[85]

The CPUSA continued to portray Roosevelt's policies as demagogic attempts to gain the support of workers and the New Deal as bound to fail. While recognizing that Roosevelt's policies had gained workers' backing, Browder's conclusion was optimistic: "the depth and tempo of the economic crisis," he said, "have established favorable conditions for a speedy unmasking of the policy of the parties of the bourgeoisie."[86] The Party warned that upon the predicted failure of this plan, the bourgeoisie would drop the mask and resort to more brutal measures. Communists expected "an intensified drive for new wage cuts, speed-ups, cutting of unemployment relief, and the use of more fascist methods against the struggles and organizations of the workers, the use of force and violence, legal and extra-legal to suppress the rising struggles of the workers."[87] Eight months later the Party was forced to recognize that "workers were still under the influence of illusions about Roosevelt," and "these illusions continue to stand up under repeated blows!"[88] Because of these illusions, the New Deal had succeeded in keeping "workers from general resistance."[89]

Even the establishment of formal diplomatic relations between the United States and the Soviet Union in November 1933 did not mitigate the Party's criticism. Uncertain about how to explain this event within the context of policy but not able to avoid the issue altogether, the Party produced a contorted and quite unlikely analysis of the event. Browder, on the one hand, described recognition as a skillful victory of Soviet diplomatic efforts. On the other hand, renewed relations between the two countries did not indicate a shift away from United States military preparations for war against other imperialist rivals, namely Great Britain and Japan, as well as against the Soviet Union. In the end Browder completely avoided explaining why the United States had decided to recognize the Soviet Government.[90]

The Party's antagonism toward Roosevelt did not change even after the 1934 off-year elections. Reversing a tradition that called for the party that controlled the White House to lose seats in Congress, Democrats gained in both Houses. The election had been more in the nature of a referendum over the president's policies and he had won by a considerable margin over the opposition of the Republican party and its right-wing supporters. The Communist party had difficulty concealing its uneasiness with the result of the elections. While on the one hand the Party repeated that Roosevelt's " 'left' demagogy" served only to conceal his defense of the interests of finance capital, on the other, the consolidation of a right-wing opposition to Roosevelt put the Communist party's analysis under increased strain.[91]

By the summer of 1934 the business community's discontent with Roosevelt's policies, which had been brewing for some time, boiled over. Business and industrial leaders, some of whom had initially supported the president, began to view government regulation of business as a threat to free enterprise. They also objected to the administration's fiscal policies and growing deficit as well as to federal spending for relief and public works. In August 1934, a number of conservative businessmen and anti-Roosevelt Democrats founded the American Liberty League, which was to become a focal point of conservative opposition to the New Deal within both parties. The stated purpose of the League was to educate the nation "to the value of encouraging people to work; encouraging people to get rich"; top officials included DuPont executive and former chairman of the Democratic party, John J. Raskob, as well as Al Smith, and John W. Davis.[92]

In early September 1934, Browder spoke of the conservative attack against the New Deal. The Liberty League and the Hearst press wanted to do away with all the social legislation in New Deal policies and to push "the Roosevelt administration more sharply toward fascism."[93] These divergences within the bourgeois camp were real and effectively prevented "the development of a united bourgeois policy" Browder contended, but they were not to be overestimated. The disagreement did not go "any further than the question of how best to throw the burden of the crisis upon the masses for the benefit of finance capital."[94] Repeatedly Browder tried to establish an analogy between ruling class divisions in the United States and the "pre-fascist atomization of bourgeois parties in Germany" on the eve of the Nazi victory.[95] Roosevelt, he said, like the Bruening Government and contrary to the openly fascist forces, would attempt to "orientate to the Left" to attract and insure workers' support. Given this premise it was easy to understand Roosevelt's backing of social reform legislation.[96]

According to the Party, the only real difference between Roosevelt and the Liberty League was that the president believed that their common objectives could be best obtained by maintaining his mass following through demagogic promises. It is apparent that the Communist party was somewhat uncertain on how to judge the right-wing attack on Roosevelt. To differentiate between the two (the most apparent conclusion), would have meant, if not an endorsement, at least a recognition of the sincerity of Roosevelt's concerns for labor. The core of the Party's argument continued to be that the differences were only in tactics; the economic interests they served were exactly the same.[97] The leadership of the CPUSA, which continued to see these differences as simply a further sign of the general crisis of the capitalist system, totally missed the essence of the clash between two very different ways of dealing with the depression.[98]

The most arduous trial, however, came in late May 1935 with the Supreme Court's decision to declare the NRA unconstitutional. Suddenly the entire structure of the New Deal was threatened and the safeguards for labor written into Section 7(a) were swept away. The Party found itself in the ambiguous position of condemning the Court's action while simultaneously stopping distinctly short of an endorsement of the New Deal. The Party reasoned that in the early days of Roosevelt's presidency big business had supported the New Deal policies out of fear for its power. Feeling more secure once economic conditions had begun to improve, these same groups felt they could do away with even modest concessions, such as the NRA, which they had thrown as a sop to workers to keep them from becoming revolutionaries.[99]

Just a few weeks before the Supreme Court's verdict the Party stressed the importance of the struggle "against the Roosevelt-Wall Street N.R.A. program of hunger, fascist reaction and imperialist war." Now writing in *Communist*, Bittelman defined the Court's action as "infamous," instigated by the "most reactionary and aggressive section" of monopolist bourgeoisie, who were against "any sort of legislation that would favor the masses."[100] Similar views were expressed concerning the invalidation of the AAA. By its destruction "monopoly capitalists hope to close the door against all social legislation and to use the Supreme Court's interpretation of the Constitution as the spearhead of their drive against the living standards of the toiling people."[101] Speaking in Springfield, Illinois, Earl Browder drew a symbolic parallel between the Court's invalidation of New Deal legislation and the Dred Scott case. The Court's decisions, according to Browder, were directed at denying Congress the power "to enact social legislation to relieve the distressed masses of the population."[102] Despite all this the basic premise remained unaltered: the issue dividing the president from his right-wing opponents was one of method, not ultimate objective. Browder accused the president of failing to respond to the Supreme Court, of surrendering "all effective power . . . to that reactionary body."[103] This was seen as proof of Roosevelt's unreliability as a defender against reactionary interests. Bittelman wrote:

> Other sections of the bourgeoisie, while seeking the same thing, (to prevent genuine legislation for the masses), yet believe in doing it with different methods. Roosevelt, and the New Deal generally, stand for these different methods, to carry out the same class aim of the bourgeoisie.[104]

By the summer of 1935, there was some slight moderation in the tone of the Communists' attacks against Roosevelt and the New Deal, but their basic substance remained unchanged from that of the fall of 1933. According to the Party, in its two years of existence the New Deal had done a good job of weakening the resistance of workers to capitalism. Communists explained the motivations for the president's support of Senator Wagner's National Labor Relations Act, which replaced Section 7(a) and strengthened labor's right to organize by forbidding all employer interference, and his backing of the Social Security Act and the Works Progress Administration as attempts to paralyze the resistance of workers. On May 1, an editorial in the *Daily Worker* even referred to the Wagner Act as an "anti-strike" measure.[105]

On the eve of the Seventh Congress of the Communist International, the Party's definition of the forces that played a role in the "fascization" of American society was still very broad. Aside from the openly fascist "representatives of finance capital, the Republican party, the Liberty League," as well as Hearst, Coughlin, and Huey Long, the CPUSA once again included the Roosevelt Administration whose policies, Communists repeated, were "*masked* fascization."[106]

Even though anti-fascist concerns led the CPUSA to differentiate between forces it had previously dismissed as being tools of the same class rule, Communists did not consider the evolution of Roosevelt's policies, nor did they differentiate the president from his opponents on the right. The Party continued to oppose Roosevelt as part of a very broad capitalist camp.

The tension between the sectarian policies of the third period and the Communists' new antifascist priorities appears once more in the Party's position toward farmer-labor organizations. During the early 1930s independent farmer-labor parties had gained considerable prominence with programs to the left of the New Deal. The most publicized of these insurgent political organizations was End Poverty in California (EPIC) founded by muckraker journalist, Upton Sinclair. A former Socialist, Sinclair had won the Democratic nomination for Governor in 1934. His "production-for-use" program, which called for the state to take over farm land and idle factories to provide jobs for the unemployed, gained widespread support but did not save him from defeat in the fall. New political organizations also included the LaFollettes' Progressive party in Wisconsin and similar organizations in Oregon and Washington.[107] However, the most powerful of these independent organizations was the Minnesota Farmer-Labor party. Its program was reformist with strong anti-capitalist as well as socialist overtones. Floyd Olson, the Party's leader and the state governor, called for the replacement of capitalism with a vaguely defined "Cooperative Commonwealth" based on consumer and producer cooperatives and public ownership of utilities and transportation. "I am frank to say," he thundered, "that I am not a liberal . . . I am a radical. I am a radical in the sense that I want a definite change in the system."[108]

The Communist party concluded that farmer-labor tickets drew support from what would otherwise have been a Communist constituency.[109] In 1933 the various farmer-labor parties were called "fascist and semi-fascist organizations" set up by reformists to channel the workers discontent with Democratic and Republican candidates toward "left" bourgeois candidates and away from the Communist party. From this analysis came the definition " 'third' capitalist parties."[110] These themes were to imbue the Party's criticism through the 1934 elections.[111] The role of the Communist party then was to expose the true nature of these organizations as "social-fascist," the same way it had done with Roosevelt. At the 1934 elections these organizations scored some impressive successes and established themselves as a new political force; as a result the Communist party partially revised its attitude toward the formation of a Labor party.[112] Although the Party renewed its accusations about these organizations, hidden behind the Communists' hostile attitude was a tendency to view them as positive indications of an imminent disintegration of the two-party system, of a new political trend in the making.

The huge votes for third-party candidates where they presented themselves to the masses is a definite indication both of the weakening of the two-party system, as well as the beginnings of mass disillusionment in

Roosevelt, which the bourgeoisie is trying to stem through these new third-party illusions. Moved by the desire to secure *immediate* relief from the intolerable misery, still doubtful of the election chances of the C.P. candidates, and in the mistaken belief that the "successful" "Left" bourgeois candidates will do something for them, large masses have given their votes to such candidates.[113]

Convinced that workers were breaking away "from the capitalist parties," the Party determined to find ways to take advantage of the situation in order to lead workers "on the road to independent political action."[114] This meant a reorientation in attitude about the creation of a Labor party based on unions and headed by radicals.

Since its founding the Communist party had gone through various phases in its policy toward the formation of a national farmer-labor party. While in the mid-1920s Communists had briefly supported a farmer-labor party, by the early 1930s the proper arenas of political activity were considered only the streets and shops; elections were dismissed as attempts to reform rather than to revolutionize society. As in the case of the 1932 presidential election, participation in the electoral process was seen only as a vehicle of propaganda for the Party's revolutionary objectives to raise the workers' political consciousness.

The CPUSA's revision of its opposition to coalition labor parties can be linked to the general trend to become part of the growing insurgent movement in labor which led first to the dissolution of the TUUL and then to a change in electoral policy. The revival of labor activism, demonstrated by the strikes of 1934 in Minneapolis, Toledo, and San Francisco, was beginning to manifest itself in electoral politics as well.

Shortly after the 1934 elections, Browder spoke to the Executive Committee of the Communist International in Moscow. Referring to the Democrats' victory, he said that it was not an endorsement of Roosevelt's policies but, rather, the choice of a "lesser evil." Wherever there was a chance of a Republican being elected, workers had "turned out *to defeat the Republicans.*" As proof of this, Browder pointed out that in those cases where workers were given an opportunity to vote for candidates and parties which presented themselves as being "to the Left" of Roosevelt, workers had voted for them.[115] While most workers were not ready yet to join the Communist party, Browder saw the growth of independent parties as an indication of a climate favoring the formation of a new radical labor party, opening the possibility of the formation, by the time of the 1936 elections, of a "mass party in opposition to and to the left of Roosevelt."[116] This new situation required a reconsideration by the Party of its opposition to a "Labor Party." The Communists' main concern was not to allow this new movement to fall under the control of liberals, reformists, and demagogues. According to Browder, a "real" labor party was an organization

> built from below, on a trade union basis but in conflict with the bureaucracy, with a program of demands closely associated with mass struggles, strikes, etc., with a decisive role in the leadership played by militant elements, including the Communists.[117]

Moscow gave its approval to the Labor party idea, and Browder announced the Party's new policy in his speech to the National Conference for Unemployed Insurance in early January 1935.[118]

The Communist party's decision to support the formation of a Labor party did not imply a change in the already expressed criticism of farmer-labor organizations nor the possibility of collaborating with non-revolutionary organizations. By their own admission, Communist leaders looked upon the Labor party as a means of attracting new members to the CPUSA and as a possible expedient in coopting an insurgent third-party movement. Communists, Browder stated bluntly, "enter the movement for the Labor Party only with the purpose of helping the masses to break away from the bourgeois camp, break away from social reformists and find the path to the revolutionary class struggle."[119] Jack Stachel expressed a similar view of the purpose of the Labor party. The Communist party, he said, saw the Labor party

> as a means through which the Communist party can aid in setting masses on the road of independent class political action, on the basis of their immediate interests and understanding, but with the hope and the knowledge that in the course of the struggles and as a result of the experience of struggles, the masses will learn that only the program of the Communist party provides the means for the lasting solutions of the problems of workers.[120]

In fact, despite affirmations to the contrary by Communist leaders, the new party's program was no different from that of the CPUSA. The only difference between the two organizations was their name.[121]

One Communist leader said at the time that the formation of the Labor party was the CPUSA's "greatest single task," a claim repeated in all Party statements.[122] An actual organization, however, was never formed. Communists apparently did not want to risk the embarrassment of forming a nonentity and thus repeatedly warned local activists to avoid premature organization of a Labor party. Although Party leaders acknowledged that conditions could vary from state to state, the general view was that the first step would be the formation of local organizations around common programs. These organizations were to be based on local labor unions and other workers' organizations and centered around common programs for legislative change. If successful, these local groups would join together in a national organization.[123]

The period from 1933 to the summer of 1935 was a transitional phase between two very different sets of priorities. On the one hand, the Communist party reversed its labor policy and also concluded that the emphasis on "dictatorship of the proletariat" as the only alternative to fascism had seriously hindered the mobilization of anti-fascist forces. On the other hand, however, the CPUSA maintained many of the analyses and policies of the third period. The Party's analysis of fascist forces remained quite vague and relations with the Socialist party, while improved, continued to be strained. The mounting right-wing opposition to Roosevelt as well as his pro-labor policies put the Party's position under stress, but did not lead to a reevaluation of the CPUSA's opposition to the New Deal. Similarly, the Party response to the growth of the insurgent farmer-labor movement was to conceive an improbable expedient of coopting it. Gil Green described this period as one in which Communists "moved from one level to another," they had "one foot on one step and one on the other." Still conditioned by the policies of the past, Communists "felt we had to move on but did not know how."[124] There is no doubt, however, that a redefinition of Party policies was taking place, which raised the possibility of collaboration with other reform-oriented organizations on immediate issues. Furthermore, the Communists' concern with fascism and their distinction between fascist and bourgeois rule began to point to the importance of defending bourgeois democratic institutions.

The evolution of CPUSA policies occurred within the context of a broad reconsideration on the part of the international Communist movement of the policies of the third period. By early summer 1934, the Comintern reversed its theory of social-fascism and called for a united front between Communists and Socialists. This move officially sanctioned abandonment of the former sectarian policies which had been developing, often dramatically, within the Communist movement for some time. Crucial in this respect were the events in Paris and, as already mentioned, in Austria in February 1934. In both countries, workers ignored ideological barriers and past accusations that had divided Communists from Socialists and moved to unite against a common fascist threat. In Paris Socialists and Communists had gone into the streets together to defend bourgeois-democratic institutions, an unprecedented event which was to have serious repercussions on the International's policies. This movement, which raised important new priorities and expressed a new-found conscience, ultimately led the Comintern to a radical change of policy. The victory of Nazism in Germany and the strengthening of reactionary forces worldwide had proved the analyses and policies of the third period to be ill suited to reality.[125]

A number of historians have traced the origins of the CPUSA's transition away from the policies it followed during the early years of the depression to orders from Moscow handed down in 1934. According to one interpretation since Communists in the United States depended so much on outside directives, they were not "prepared for the dramatic changes" mandated by the Comintern.[126] The evidence presented in this chapter, however, shows otherwise. By 1933, and in some cases even sooner, American Communists, on the basis of their experiences of the previous years, had begun to take steps toward changing their analysis and tactics in the direction of what would later be known as the Popular Front. Thus, for United States Communists, the Seventh Congress of the Communist International in the Summer of 1935, far from simply reflecting Moscow's order to adopt a new policy, represented an encouragement to pursue and expand the course they had already been following for at least two years.

PART TWO

4

THE PEOPLE'S FRONT

> The accession to power of fascism is not an *ordinary succession* of one bourgeois government by another, but a *substitution* for one state form of class domination of the bourgeoisie—bourgeois democracy—by another form—open terrorist dictatorship.
>
> Georgi Dimitrov, 1935[1]

From July 25 to August 20, 1935, delegates from sixty-five Communist parties met in Moscow in the Hall of Columns of the House of Trade Unions for the Seventh World Congress of the Communist International, an event that marked a turning point in the history of the Communist movement. The Seventh Congress ratified the break by the international Communist movement with the policies followed since 1928 and, in particular, recognized their failure to understand fascism as the greatest threat to the working class and to distinguish between bourgeois democracy and reactionary dictatorship. From this realization came the most significant conclusion of the Congress: the need for all socialist organizations and democratic forces to join together in an anti-fascist alliance to defend bourgeois democracy.[2]

The Comintern's secretary general, Georgi Dimitrov, delivered the keynote report to the Congress.[3] The central theme of the speech was fascism, its nature, and the reasons for its victories. The report signaled an overall important change from the third-period analysis and its concern with the crisis of capitalism and the development of its internal contradiction. Contrary to the Comintern's previous analysis, Dimitrov described fascism as a distinct "state form of class domination of the bourgeoisie" based on mass social participation generated by social demagoguery and chauvinism. In fascism, the bourgeoisie had to redefine relationships with other social classes, in order to retain its power the bourgeoisie had to create a strong popular consensus for its rule and was consequently forced to intervene to mediate those social conflicts that could not be eliminated through force. Dimitrov rejected the view that there was no substantial difference between bourgeois parliamentary democracy and bourgeois rule through fascist dictatorship. While during the third period the Comintern had seen the dictatorship of the proletarist as the only alternative to fascism, now Dimitrov spoke of an anti-fascist alliance of Communists with bourgeois-democratic and socialist forces. No longer were anti-fascism and anti-capitalism viewed as synonymous.

Dimitrov blamed the victory of fascism on divisions within the working class for which he faulted not only Socialists but significantly also Communists. "In our ranks," he proclaimed, "there were people who intolerably underrated the fascist danger, a tendency which has not everywhere been overcome to this day."[4] To defeat fascism required the formation of a united front between Socialists and Communists with no preconditions other than a common program of defending the economic and political interests of the working class and fighting against fascism.[5]

The alliance of Socialists and Communists was only the first step. The working class was to become the center of an alternative, diversified, mass movement to counter the fascist movement. This antifascist coalition was to include the "proletariat," the "toiling peasantry and the basic mass of the urban petty bourgeoisie."[6] From these forces was to develop a "popular front" alliance. This proposal, defined by Kermit McKenzie as the speech's "most daring and novel concept," raised the important issue of the Comintern's changing view of the relation between the working class and bourgeois democratic institutions as well as the more general problem of the transition to socialism. Dimitrov stated:

> If we Communists are asked whether we advocate the united front *only* in the struggle for partial demands, or whether we are prepared to share the responsibility even when it will be a question of forming a *government* on the basis of the united front, then we say with a full sense of our responsibility: Yes, we recognize that a situation may arise in which the formation of a *government of the proletarian united front*, or of the *anti-fascist people's front* will become not only necessary in the interests of the proletariat, and in that case we shall declare for the formation of such a government without the slightest hesitation.[7]

Anti-fascist coalition governments, Dimitrov said, could come into existence "on the eve of and before the victory of the Soviet revolution" formed around a program of *"fundamental revolutionary demands"* such as the "control of production, control of the banks, and disbanding of the police."[8] This definition of "popular front government" was notable because it implied a middle transitional phase between bourgeois democracy and socialism; the proposal's innovative aspect was that it allowed Communists to participate in prerevolutionary governments. As McKenzie pointed out, the objectives of this kind of government were not to eliminate capitalism but to "purge it" of fascism and the "economic basis of fascism."[9]

Despite the innovation of his speech, Dimitrov redefined the tactics of the Communist movement but not its strategy. This led to limited and contradictory definitions of the relationship between capitalism and fascism and also between the defense of bourgeois democracy and socialism. A first contradictory aspect of Dimitrov's speech derived from his definition of popular front government. Dimitrov described this government as temporary, with only limited, defensive objectives, unable to introduce manifest socialist measures into society. These measures, he said, could only be achieved by an openly "Soviet government." Put in these terms, the popular front government, even with its support of the workers' everyday struggles, including the fight against fascism, was not seen as being able to lead a gradual transition to a socialist society. Ultimately its only role was to point out the illusory belief in bourgeois democratic institutions and to prepare for armed revolution. In this sense, popular front governments were simply a step toward an inevitable Soviet solution and not an opening of a possibility for a gradual change in society. Immediate goals and demands, the struggle for democratic rights and popular front government itself, were merely limited short-term objectives, eventually aimed at showing that no true solution to the problems of capitalism could be achieved within the limits of a democratic system. Ultimately the role of the popular front government was reduced to helping

> the *millions* to master as rapidly as possible, through their own experience, what they have to do, where to find a radical solution, what party is worthy of their confidence, these among others are the purposes for which both transitional slogans and special "forms of transition or approach to the proletarian revolution" are necessary.[10]

Because they were not in a position to overthrow the class rule of the exploiters, popular front governments could not hope to "eliminate the danger of fascist counterrevolution . . . Soviet power and *only* Soviet power can bring such salvation."[11] By implicitly assuming that one day Communists would have to turn against even coalition antifascist governments, this conclusion undercut the new and advanced ideas behind the popular front proposal as well as the possibilities of establishing future alliances. Here was a clear contradiction between the objective of defending democracy and the belief in the role played by fascism in destroying the myth of the democratic state.

Secondly, Dimitrov described capitalism as a system unable to renew itself and to provide a new foundation for its power within the bourgeois democratic system. He did not contemplate the possibility of capitalism reforming itself, independent of the fascist solution, by increasing the intervention of the state into the economy, by mediating social conflicts and promoting such reforms as minimum wage, unemployment insurance, and recognition of collective bargaining. Dimitrov insisted instead that the "fascist solution" would be the only one to which the bourgeoisie would turn when it could not maintain power through the traditional democratic system. This analysis led to an incomplete discussion of the "bourgeois mass-state" limited to the German and Italian experience. Dimitrov omitted the New Deal, a non-fascist capitalist solution that did not fit his analysis.

The issues that Dimitrov ignored in his speech were not addressed in the debate that followed. Most speakers limited themselves to descriptive accounts of events in their own countries; no major attempt was made to broaden and elaborate on the issues raised in the report.[12] When the New Deal was mentioned at all, it was described, at best, as a failure or, at worst, according to Foster, as fomenting fascism. Foster's attack, as well as others, spurred the British delegate, Rajani Palme Dutt, to criticize the tendency among Communists to "call practically anything outside the Communist camp fascist."[13]

Referring to this remark in his summation to the Congress, Dimitrov made an important, but still limited, statement which had important implications for Communists in the United States. Referring clearly to the CPUSA, he criticized those political groups that "disoriented" the working class by their insistence on defining Roosevelt's New Deal as a "form of the development of the bourgeoisie toward fascism." Those, he said, who insisted on criticizing the New Deal, failed to see that "the most reactionary circles of American finance capital, which are attacking Roosevelt, are above all the very force which is stimulating and organizing the fascist movement in the United States."[14] While making a significant distinction between Roosevelt and his right-wing adversaries, this statement still left undefined the Comintern's analysis of Roosevelt's policies and thus revealed the Eurocentric character of the Seventh Congress.

Dimitrov's underestimation of the New Deal as an internal reform movement, coupled with the weakness of both the Communist and Socialist parties in the United States, led him to call on the CPUSA, not to support Roosevelt but to participate instead in the formation of a national farmer-labor third party. This party, according to Dimitrov, was the "specific form" of the popular front in the United States. In relation to the United States, Dimitrov did not propose a broad antifascist coalition but, rather, favored the formation of a new party to provide American workers with an autonomous political voice. This party was to be *"neither* Socialist *nor* Communist"*, its program "directed against the banks, trusts and monopolies" in favor of

> social legislation, for unemployment insurance . . . for land for white and black sharecroppers and for their liberation for the burden of debt . . . for the cancellation of the farmers' indebtedness . . . for the equal status of the Negroes . . . for the interests of the members of the liberal professions, the small businessmen, the artisans.[15]

Hence, while representing a step forward in the analysis of fascism and in stressing the importance of preserving democracy, the Seventh Congress did not provide any viable answers to the issues raised by Roosevelt's New Deal nor a definition of the relation between democratic struggle and socialism. These were issues of paramount importance that American Communists had to confront and attempt to define on their own. The CPUSA was left to work for the formation of a Farmer-Labor party, a proposal that it soon concluded was unrealistic.

Unlike any other of the shifts in the history of the CPUSA, the adoption of the new policy expressed at the Seventh Congress, renamed in the United States the "people's front," did not cause significant splits or defections. As the Party's policies of the two previous years had shown, Communists increasingly considered fascism to be the main threat. Although the Party recognized that conditions were not such that fascism would develop as quickly as in Italy and Germany, the Party nevertheless concluded that as class conflict increased "American fascism will mature with it."[16]

Browder returned to New York City from Moscow in mid September. He immediately met with reporters and announced that the Communist party's chief objective was the founding of a nationwide Farmer-Labor party.[17] American Communists set themselves immediately to the task. The objectives and composition of the Farmer-Labor party were substantially different from those of the Labor party envisioned by the CPUSA before the Seventh Congress. The Farmer-Labor party, rather than promoting revolutionary socialist objectives, was to unite workers and middle-class elements around a common program defying fascism and promoting immediate social and economic reforms.[18]

The following November, more than 300 leading Party workers from across the country participated in the meeting of the plenum of the Central Committee in New York to discuss the application of the International's new policy. In his report, Browder dealt at great length with the coming presidential election. Reversing the position the Party had held prior to the Seventh Congress, the Communist leader differentiated between President Roosevelt and his right-wing opponents. The Liberty League and its backers, the Morgans and the DuPonts, as well as William Randolph Hearst, were the forces promoting fascism in the United States; to expose them, Browder said, was "a political task of first importance." Having made this distinction, however, did not mean that the Party was going to support Roosevelt. Once again Browder repeated the old argument that the contrast between Roosevelt and his reactionary opponents was an internal struggle within the bourgeoisie solely over methods rather than goals.[19] Communists then had to lead a two-front battle: one against fascist circles, and one, just as important, to show that Roosevelt did not represent an alternative to the fascist threat.[20]

Several elements weighed heavily in the Communists' unrelenting criticism of the president. First, the Party continued to be conditioned by the policies pursued by Roosevelt during his first year at the White House. Its press and its leaders reiterated past criticism of the president's policies, claiming that they were an attempt to save capitalism by strengthening the power of monopolies while granting meager concessions to some workers. Consequently, the Communist party repeated that Roosevelt was too closely tied to powerful economic interests to be an alternative to reactionary forces. The Party described the president as attempting to steer a middle course between reactionary and democratic forces, trying to please everyone and, in the process, retreating from reactionary attacks. In February 1936, Alexander Bittelman wrote in the *Communist,* that whatever concessions Roosevelt gave or planned "to give to other social groups in order to get their support," he did so for the purpose of serving the class interests of an unspecified "section of finance capital . . . it is they whom he is trying to satisfy most completely."[21]

Another explanation given by the CPUSA to oppose Roosevelt was the strength of conservative elements within the Democratic party. In one of his most extreme statements on the subject, Browder told Communists in Boston that the president "roars like a lion and acts like a rabbit." This happened because

> talk is cheap, but action in the Democratic party is controlled by the Solid South of Scottsboro, by half-fascist Democratic Illinois, by California, where McAdoo works with Republicans to smash the maritime unions, by Indiana where a Democratic governor has had the militia out on duty for six months now, breaking strikes. Roosevelt's promises, the New Deal policies, are all in the ash can already. No new promises he can think up will have any hope in them for the workers and farmers.[22]

Communists were not the only left-wing critics of Roosevelt. Liberal papers such as the *Nation,* the *New Republic,* and *Common Sense,* as well as organizations such as the American Commonwealth Federation, continued to express their belief that the president's policies, while lessening part of the burden of the depression, did not go far enough in permanently eradicating its economic and social causes. Like the Communists they saw the president committed to preserving the existing economic system and, therefore, believed in a coming break-up of the Democratic party and the creation of a strong left-wing alternative. Like the rest of the liberal movement, however, these forces, as they began to fear the possibility of a reactionary-Republican victory, postponed any talk of a new party until after the election.[23]

Not to repeat the same mistakes made in Germany, the CPUSA viewed the formation of a united front with the Socialist party as the first, necessary step toward an anti-fascist alliance. Late in the summer of 1934, in response to the first signs of the new course of the Comintern, the CPUSA made several unsuccessful overtures to Socialists in search of a united front. Following Norman Thomas's speech before the American Youth Congress on August 16, 1934, in which he indicated a willingness to work with the Communist party around specific issues, Browder sent a letter to the Socialist leader urging a united front between the two parties. Thomas's reply was lukewarm as he turned the proposal over to the Socialist National Executive Committee that rejected it in early September. Undaunted, during the following months Communists persevered.[24] Their overtures became more pressing after the Seventh Congress of the Communist International. In October 1935 Browder went so far as to predict that joint action would represent an important first step in the direction of the "organic unity" for the two parties, thus putting an end to the split in the socialist movement brought about by World War I and the Bolshevik revolution.[25]

The CPUSA's willingness to form a united front did not engender similar enthusiasm among Socialists. Several factors determined their position. The legacy of reciprocal accusations and attacks accumulated over the years stood in the way of an effective collaboration between the two organizations; events such as those at Madison Square Garden were too fresh in the minds of Socialists to warrant trust of Communist intentions. Although forces within the Socialist party favored closer ties with the Communists, in early December 1934 its National Committee voted to prohibit any united front action with the Communist party for eighteen months, except in some specific local cases.[26] Norman Thomas, who had backed the resolution, expressed his concerns in response to a Socialist who had urged him to accept the Communist offer. Communists, Thomas wrote, "have repeatedly and continuously made it plain that the united front is for the purpose of destroying the Socialist party."[27] Statements such as Browder's suggesting "organic unity" made Socialist leaders all the more nervous.[28]

The situation within the Socialist party, split since the 1932 presidential elections in factional infighting between left and right, was not conducive to improvement of relations with Communists. The virulently anti-Communist right, the Old Guard, was opposed to any talk of a united-front. Communists, however, did not find a receptive audience even among the Socialist left-wing. This was a loose coalition of radical Militants with more moderate forces, including Norman Thomas, united in opposition to the Old Guard. In June 1934, at the Socialists' National Convention held in Detroit this coalition gained the upper hand. By a vote of ninety-nine to forty-seven, the Old Guard was defeated as the Socialist party adopted a Declaration of Principles which was then ratified by the Party's membership in a referendum.[29]

The Declaration jumbled together the issues close to the heart of the various components of the Left coalition. These ranged from pacifist anti-war sentiments to belief in the use of force to overthrow capitalist rule. The Declaration expressed leftist anti-capitalist views similar to those of Communists during the third period. The defeat of fascism, defined as the last resort of a "crumbling capitalist order," meant ultimately to "carry the revolutionary struggle into the camp of the enemy." In light of this, the document added that the goal of the Socialist party was to replace "the bogus democracy of capitalist parliamentarism" with "a genuine workers' democracy." Furthermore, the Declaration concluded that if the capitalist system was to collapse in "general chaos and confusion," the Socialist party "whether or not in such a case it is a majority, will not shrink from the responsibility of organizing and maintaining a government under the rule of the producing masses."[30]

Thus, as the CPUSA elevated anti-fascism and favored a broad-based coalition in defense of bourgeois democracy, the Socialist party moved in the opposite direction. Socialists viewed that the immediate objective was a victory over capitalism rather than over fascism. Norman Thomas disagreed with Communists on the existence of an imminent fascist threat lurking behind a Republican victory in 1936. He saw no substantial difference between Roosevelt and the Republican candidate Alfred Landon, both representatives of capitalist rule and equally opposed to socialism. The issue at the heart of the election, according to the Socialist leader, was not to support the formation of a broad anti-fascist alliance but, rather, a choice between socialism or capitalism.[31]

Eventually, despite the opposition of the Old Guard, Norman Thomas agreed to debate Earl Browder. The debate took place on November 27 at Madison Square Garden in front of a capacity crowd of 20,000 spectators, presided over by Leo Krzycki, chairman of the Socialist party. A climate of comradeship pervaded the same hall where a year and a half earlier Communists and Socialists had battled each other violently; now they joined together in singing the

"International," the "Red Flag," and "Solidarity Forever." Despite this goodwill the debate did not lead to any constructive conclusion.[32] Norman Thomas mocked Communists for their radical switch from attacking to courting the Socialist party. "As for myself," he noted, "I do not recognize myself any more when I read the 'Daily Worker.' " The main point of his speech, nonetheless, was his disagreement with the CPUSA that "democracy, certainly not bourgeois democracy, is even temporarily a satisfactory alternative to Fascism or a satisfactory defense against it." The alternative, he said, was "Socialism or Fascism" not "Democracy or Fascism."[33] Browder insisted that the threat of fascism in the United States was more of a present issue than Norman Thomas thought and made it imperative for both parties to set aside their differences and unite. Were Communists and Socialists, Browder asked, going to wait before uniting their forces "until fascism is actually victorious in the United States?"[34]

Both sides limited themselves to expressing their differences of opinion, dashing whatever hopes Communists had that this would be the first in a series of encounters between the two parties that would open the way to a united front. The two parties did work together locally. In 1934 in some small communities in the Midwest they ran joint Socialist-Communist Workers' tickets.[35] The following year in several cities, including New York, Communists and Socialists paraded together on May Day; in Reading, Pennsylvania, and Milwaukee, Wisconsin the Communist party withdrew its candidates for office in municipal elections in favor of the Socialists. On the national level Communists and Socialists joined forces on a number of issues such as the Scottsboro case and in the unemployed movement; they also passed joint resolutions calling for the release of Angelo Herndon and the withdrawal of the United States team from the 1936 Berlin Olympics. In addition a number of prominent Socialists, favoring closer ties with the CPUSA, defied the National Executive Committee prohibition to work with Communists. Among these was Meta Berger, the widow of the first Socialist Congressman, Victor Berger. However, these were isolated initiatives: the only instances of united front between the leadership of the two parties.[36]

Notwithstanding the opposition of the Socialist party, the CPUSA continued to send out appeals for bipartisan unity. In May 1936, Browder attended the Socialist convention where he renewed his plea for joint action and urged a joint presidential ticket; the offer was turned down when the convention banned any further united-front negotiation until after the elections. Socialist opposition to a united front did not change even after the Old Guard left the Party to found the Social Democratic Federation.[37]

Progressively, the CPUSA returned to attacking Socialist leaders. An editorial in the *Daily Worker* in mid February criticized Militants for their opposition to unity; it even threatened to go over the head of the Socialist leadership and appeal directly to the rank and file. A month later another editorial charged that Thomas's views were not shared by the majority of the membership of the Socialist party and that soon "the voice of these rank and file Socialists will be heard—heard FOR the united front and AGAINST the dead hand of Old Guardism, which still weighs so heavily on the activities of the left Socialists."[38]

Communist attacks on the Socialist party increased during the summer: Thomas was strongly criticized for underestimating of the possibilities of fascism in the United States, his position deemed an "ostrich-like attitude." By the end of the campaign the tension had escalated so far that the Communist party effectively accused the Socialist leader of supporting a Republican victory.[39]

Already strained relations between Communists and Socialists were made more difficult after Trotskyists of the small Workers party, U.S., headed by James Cannon, joined the Socialist party in the Spring of 1936.[40] Almost as a last gesture acknowledging the impossibility of close ties between the two parties, Browder warned Socialists of the dangers of such a move. "Be careful," he said, "you are about to swallow a deadly poison, which we know from sad experience. Better prepare an emetic, for surely you will soon be in convulsions from severe political disturbances."[41]

The Socialist party was a small organization with shrinking influence, which meant its refusal to join in a united front had a largely symbolic effect for the CPUSA. Of greater concern to Communists was the position of organized labor and of the local farmer-labor organizations which the CPUSA saw as the nucleus around which the national Farmer-Labor party would coalesce.

Although sentiment existed within a number of unions in favor of a new labor party, it was expressed only by a minority. A resolution presented by Francis Gorman, leader of the textile workers union, at the Atlantic City convention of the AFL supporting the formation of a labor party was soundly defeated. In early February 1936 an analogous resolution presented to the national convention of the UMW shared the same fate as the majority of the delegates voted to back Roosevelt.[42] New Deal legislation had strengthened the position of organized labor; faced with an increasingly militant right that threatened labor's recent gains, organized labor, led by the young CIO movement, determined that keeping a president sympathetic to its aspirations was paramount. The major figure behind the movement toward a more active participation in politics, John L. Lewis, said, President Roosevelt had "accomplished more for the workers than any other president in the history of the nation and labor owes him a debt of gratitude that can be liquidated only by casting its solid vote for him at the coming elections."[43] His endorsement of Roosevelt recognized that the federal government's continued support through legislation such as the Wagner Act was crucial to the newly formed CIO in its drive to organize the mass of workers in major industries. Labor's assistance in the president's reelection would be repaid, Lewis believed, by Roosevelt's assistance in future CIO unionizing drives.

In April 1936, in order to secure labor's support for the president's reelection, Lewis joined with Sidney Hillman and George L. Berry, president of the AFL's Printing Pressmen's Union, in founding the Labor's Non-Partisan League. There was no precedent for such an effort, organizing labor into a political coalition behind a presidential candidate. Instead of working within parties, the League provided labor with its own political arm, which threw its influence and finances behind pro-labor candidates, regardless of political affiliation. The formation of this independent political labor organization did not exclude future participation in the political process such as the formation in the United States of a party similar to Britain's Labor party. Organized labor's response was overwhelming: labor's human resources were mobilized to support Roosevelt, and the CIO, through a contribution of $780,000 ($469,000 of which came from the treasury of the UMW), became Roosevelt's strongest financial supporter.[44]

Just as was the case with the CIO, most leaders of state and local farmer-labor parties for the 1936 elections wanted the endorsement of Roosevelt, while at the same time they favored extending the movement to other states and running slates of farmer-labor candidates for state and congressional office. This position was clearly seen in the case of the powerful Minnesota Farmer-Labor party, the strongest and most influential organization of its kind in the country and therefore considered the most likely initiator of a national third-party. Governor Floyd Olson had established close and mutually beneficial ties with the president. In exchange for political support, Olson sidetracked any attempt to create a third-party ticket.[45] In the fall of 1935, at a private meeting in Minneapolis with Browder, Olson had frankly stated his support for Roosevelt.[46]

On the initiative of the Farmer-Labor Association of Minnesota, eighty-five delegates from organizations in twenty-two states met in Chicago at the end of May 1936 to consider the formation of a national third party. A number of unions as well as David Dubinsky, Sidney Hillman, and congressmen Ernest Lundeen and Vito Marcantonio sent congratulatory messages.[47] Even before the delegates met it was apparent that the farmer-labor movement was going to endorse the reelection of Roosevelt. Although too ill to appear in person, Floyd Olson stated the movement's policy and analysis in a brief message to the convention. He affirmed that the country was on the eve of a struggle between reactionary and liberal forces in which both traditional parties would defend the interests of the former. As far as the Democratic party was concerned, had it not been "for the influence wielded today by President Roosevelt, the Democratic majority in both the Senate and the House would have a decidedly reactionary tinge. Once this Roosevelt influence is removed, we can safely predict that the Party will move toward the right."[48] A new party had to be created, he said, to represent "all those who feel no economic security under the present iniquitous system," to change "completely the American political scene" and to institute a government responsive to their material welfare and happiness.[49] While calling for the formation of such a party, he added that the job at hand was to concentrate on electing candidates for Congress and local tickets. Despite this premise, it was clear that Olson's major concern was the movement's support for Roosevelt in the coming presidential elections. Olson maintained that it would have been a mistake to present an independent candidate who would only help "defeat our liberal president" and favor the election of a "Fascist Republican."[50] Most of the other speeches at the conference followed Olson's lead; while criticizing both Democratic and Republican parties and calling for a national Farmer-Labor party, they refrained from pressing for an independent presidential ticket.[51]

As expected, Olson's views prevailed. The conference, while going on record in favor of the formation of a national Farmer-Labor party, left the initiative of founding such a party to the Minnesota Farmer-Labor Association without setting any precise timetable. The conference agreed to present independent farmer-labor candidates only in local and congressional elections; for the presidency, the general understanding was that the movement would back Roosevelt.[52]

A careful reading of the Party's press and of the declarations of its leaders reveals that by the late fall of 1935, the CPUSA had concluded that as far as the forthcoming presidential elections were concerned the people's front policy, as it was outlined for the United States by the Seventh Congress, had few chances of succeeding. The majority of those groups that the Party considered its potential Popular Front allies were either lining up behind Roosevelt, or, as in the case of the Socialist party, did not share the Communists' anti-fascist priority. The CPUSA was forced to mold policies accordingly.

The Party had two closely interrelated concerns. Most immediately it feared the possibility of a Republican victory, which the CPUSA deemed as representing a serious fascist menace. To this effect all declarations and statements issued by the Party and its leaders underscored the priority of defeating the Republican party headed by the "Liberty League–Hearst clique." Moreover, while the Party emphatically continued to claim that Roosevelt was not a legitimate shield against reaction, the CPUSA, mindful of the disaster of 1924, wanted to keep the door open to collaboration with those labor and political organizations that had endorsed the president. Whereas the leadership of the Party continued to state that its goal was to convince labor and left-wing political forces to field an independent Farmer-Labor ticket, however, recognizing that there was going to be no national ticket, it hastened to add that Communists would continue to work with those who, while ready to support and help build the Farmer-Labor movement at a local and state level, endorsed Roosevelt's candidacy. In November 1935 Browder spelled out the Communist line. He instructed Party leaders: "we are not going to break with such workers. We are going to build with them local and state parties, and fight with them for control of local and state government." The Communist party hoped that the 1936 elections would crystallize progressive forces and that a national Farmer-Labor party would emerge as a result.[53]

Having realized that the Farmer-Labor party tactic was not immediately practicable the Communist party set aside differences concerning Roosevelt and continued to work with organized labor and progressive organizations on the basis of a common opposition to the

Republican party. This policy provided a solution to the Party's concerns: Communists could concentrate their efforts against a perceived fascist menace without endorsing Roosevelt, about whom they still had strong reservations. At the same time, they did not stand in the way of his reelection and therefore maintained the possibility of future collaboration with organized labor and the left-wing groups that had supported the president.

So, by the end of 1935, the issue for the CPUSA was no longer whether or not to promote an independent progressive ticket but rather to decide whether the Party was going to endorse the president or, given the refusal of the Socialist party to present a joint ticket, if it was going to run its own candidate. Early in 1936, Browder received a hint that Moscow shared the CPUSA's concern about a possible Republican victory and, consequently, favored the Party's endorsement of Roosevelt's reelection.[54] At the end of March, together with William Z. Foster and Sam Darcy the Party's representative to the Communist International, he met in Moscow with Comintern leaders for the express purpose of discussing the CPUSA's electoral policy and stance toward Roosevelt. According to Browder, Dimitrov proposed that the Party, in view of the danger of a Republican victory, endorse Roosevelt. Foster and Darcy agreed with this proposal, but Browder did not. An explicit endorsement, he said, would cost the president more votes than it would gain and would provide a weapon for those who maintained that the New Deal was a socialist program. Ultimately then, such an endorsement would have facilitated a Republican victory. Browder's counterproposal was that the Party should instead present a candidate of its own and, in the course of the campaign, direct its attacks against the Republican candidate. After a lengthy debate in which Stalin himself was involved, Browder's reasoning prevailed.[55]

Many years later, Browder recalled that when the deliberations in Moscow were over, Dimitrov called him aside and told him that, since he was the only one to have understood the complexity of the situation, he was the best person to carry out the new line and to serve as Party's standard bearer.[56] Although it is difficult to check the accuracy of Browder's recollection, it is consistent with the role he played in defining the contours of the Party's electoral policy, in running as its candidate, and as its spokesman during the campaign.

Harvey Klehr portrayed the Moscow meeting as a turning point in the Party's electoral tactics.[57] A closer analysis shows instead that the

American leaders' conference with the Comintern served to confirm a course which they had already been following independently of directives from abroad. Consistent with the Party's attitude toward Roosevelt and the Farmer-Labor proposal as it had emerged in the fall of 1935, during the remainder of the campaign the Party followed a two-pronged strategy. On the one hand, it reiterated that while Roosevelt was "no barrier to the reactionary forces," Communists shared with those labor and left-wing forces that had endorsed the president a common opposition to the Republican party. On the other hand, Communists continued to express their belief in the break-up of old political alignments and therefore renewed a willingness to collaborate with these same forces for the eventual formation of the Farmer-Labor party.

Communists were clearly looking beyond the presidential elections. Browder summarized the Party's strategy in his speech to the Farmer-Labor conference held in Chicago. Over the opposition of a number of personalities and groups, such as Thomas Amlie, Paul Douglas, Alfred Bingham, the American Commonwealth Federation, and the Wisconsin Progressive party, Floyd Olson had seen to it that an invitation was extended to Browder to attend the conference. The invitation was very important since it represented the first time since the La Follette campaign of 1924 that Communists had been officially allowed back into this movement.[58] The Communist leader was not prepared to endanger this new found acceptance. He told the Farmer-Labor party conference that, despite their differences over the decision to endorse Roosevelt, the CPUSA would continue its support for all efforts aimed at creating a party that would unite "the progressive forces of the country, halt the trends toward fascism, and preserve American democratic liberties."[59] Browder also reassured his listeners that the Communist party would not attempt to take over the Farmer-Labor party. Communists, he said, realized that it was not a revolutionary party. "We do not propose to give it a program of revolution, now or later. . . . Such a Party will not bring socialism, but it will greatly lessen the pains of a later transition to socialism."[60] Browder expressed his hope that the conference would provide the various local and state movements with "national unity, guidance, and stimulation" and would coordinate them "in political actions on national questions and which, without putting forward a presidential ticket this year, will in all other respects serve as the beginning of that national Farmer-Labor party which we have been fighting for."[61]

In line with its strategy, the Party attributed great importance to all statements in favor of a Farmer-Labor party when these came from the ranks of organized labor. Francis Gorman, whom Communists had denounced during the 1934 textile strike, now won their praise and support when he made his strong plea in favor of a labor party at the 1935 AFL convention.[62] While the Party criticized organized labor for supporting the president and thereby giving him a "blank check," Communists hailed any step that they felt would lead to independent political action.[63] In the case of the UMW, while lamenting the union's decision not to support an independent Farmer-Labor ticket, the Party commented positively on the fact that it had not excluded the possibility of its formation in the future.[64] Browder expressed very favorable opinions of the "leaders of the progressive industrial unions bloc,"—Lewis, Hillman and Dubinsky—and called for their organization, the Labor's Non-Partisan League, to join with various local farmer-labor organizations and participate in this unification process. When Sidney Hillman and David Dubinsky founded the American Labor party in July 1936 to channel left-wing and labor support to Roosevelt in New York State, the Communist party applauded its formation.[65]

The Party now also viewed the strengthening of insurgent groups locally within both the Democratic and Republican parties, such as EPIC in California, the Commonwealth Federation in Washington State, and the Non-Partisan League in North Dakota, as proof that a realignment of forces was taking place that made the old party system "meaningless." The CPUSA applauded the joint statement of the Minnesota and Wisconsin Farmer-Labor parties in favor of a unified national party after the elections.[66]

As the campaign progressed, Roosevelt's declarations against "economic royalists," as well as his concern for the third of the nation "ill-housed, ill-clothed, and ill-fed," served to lessen the Party's attacks on the president. In an interview in mid-June, Browder stated that a "Democratic administration with all its evils will not be so bad as the Republican would be."[67] Progressively, the Party's position toward Roosevelt and Landon became so one-sided that Communist leaders sometimes found it difficult to counsel a vote for Browder. Various Party leaders praised Roosevelt openly: Bittelman went so far as to define his nomination as a success for "the progressive and labor elements" in the Democratic party.[68] In his address to the Party's Ninth Convention in New York City at the end of June, Browder stated that the issues had become clear-cut: workers had a vital interest "as to which of the two bourgeois parties shall hold power, when one of them is reactionary, desires to wipe out democratic rights and social legislation, while the other in some degree defends these progressive measures achieved under capitalism."[69]

Communists also commented favorably on Roosevelt's speech at Chautauqua, New York, in mid-August; there his attacks on aggressor nations struck the Party as directed against fascist countries. In a radio speech on August 28, Browder praised Roosevelt by asserting that the latter was "aware of the imminent threat" of war. Bittelman expressed similar views: "The peaceful *intentions* underlying Roosevelt's address and its opposition to the war-making designs of the fascist aggressors, the *sentiments* of opposition, could not be mistaken. The expression of such intentions and sentiments by the president of the United States at this time is in itself a deed of importance."[70]

Based on the distinction between the two "bourgeois parties," following the Republican nominating convention held in Cleveland in June, Bittelman described the GOP as displaying "several characteristics of a fascist party."[71] Landon, a moderate Republican, was painted by the Communist party as a dangerous crypto-fascist whose victory would strengthen reactionary forces and their offensive against the rights and standard of living of workers. The Communist party was going to do everything possible to "shift masses" away from Landon, even if, Browder concluded, they would then "vote for Roosevelt."[72]

Because its anti-Landon stand did not mean overtly supporting Roosevelt, a peculiar situation was created. The Party could not fail to recognize the expanding ambiguity of its position and this recognition led it to convoluted attempts to rationalize its stand. Increasingly, while going all out against Landon, the CPUSA expressed very generic criticism of the president. In an attempt to justify the Party's anti-Roosevelt stance, Browder said that the decision to direct the campaign against Landon did not mean that the Communists were indirectly endorsing the president's candidacy. He stated emphatically that Communists were not following the "policy of the 'lesser evil' "; they continued to warn "against any reliance upon Roosevelt," and to "criticize his surrenders to reaction and the many points in which he fully agrees with reaction." Communists, he said, accepted "no responsibility for Roosevelt."[73] While fighting for "progress under capitalism" together with non-socialist forces, Communists would continue to emphasize that "a consistent struggle for democracy and progress leads inevitably, and not in a distant future, to the socialist revolution."[74]

Despite Browder's justification, it is clear that the Party's decision to concentrate on attacking Landon, even while maintaining a critical attitude toward Roosevelt, represented an important new development and obviously suggested the Party's favored candidate. Eventually, the Party even justified its decision as a way of helping to reelect the president. At the end of the summer Browder, referring to the reasons for not endorsing Roosevelt, made a revealing statement. If the Left unanimously endorsed Roosevelt, this action would "encourage Roosevelt to try to win over the Liberty League, confuse all the issues, and throw the election to Landon." Therefore, he added, "We figure that the only way to defeat Landon is to have strong forces that make no compromises with compromising liberalism, and keep the issues so clearly before the nation that even the compromising liberals may be forced to fight a little against reaction."[75] The Party's statements sounded much like a critical endorsement although they were never clearly stated as such.

In line with the decision to run an independent ticket, the Party's Ninth Convention nominated Browder as its presidential candidate in a setting which dramatized the CPUSA's new face of true blue Americanism. A banner hanging from the balcony of the Manhattan Opera House announced boldly that "Communism is Twentieth Century Americanism." The hall was decorated with pictures of Washington, Jefferson, Lincoln, and Frederick Douglass; "Yankee Doodle" joined the "International" as one of the theme songs. Browder was referred to as the "new John Brown from Osawatomie." His running mate, the black leader James W. Ford, became the "Frederick Douglass of 1936."[76] The Communist party's platform for the election reiterated support for the post-election formation of a Farmer-Labor party as the American version of the Popular Front to defend democratic rights against fascism and reaction. It also expressed the Party's program in favor of the extension of social legislation, relief for the unemployed and poor farmers, and equal rights for blacks.[77]

Throughout the campaign Communists pointed out the dangers represented by William Lemke, Gerald L. K. Smith, Father Coughlin, and the Union party. Bittelman wrote how the purpose of these personalities and organizations was to draw votes away from Roosevelt through social demagoguery and thus favor the election of Landon.[78]

The Party's attitude toward the Townsend movement was different.

Despite disagreement about the financing of its plan, the Communist party saw the movement, which claimed a membership of 2 million, as a potential component of the farmer-labor coalition. Clarence Hathaway met with Francis Townsend to discuss possible common ground between the two organizations for the formation of a Farmer-Labor party. But when the doctor moved close to Gerald Smith and endorsed the Union party ticket, Communists attacked him.[79] In a statement addressed to the convention of the Townsend movement in Cleveland in mid-July, the Communist party warned them that Gerald Smith, Father Coughlin, and their supporters wanted to take advantage of legitimate demands for old-age pension to further their own reactionary plans. They, as well as their spokesmen, "have directed their fire against Roosevelt, giving Landon the tacit approval of silence. They have drummed the slogan of 'anybody but Roosevelt', made him appear as your chief opponent, with the resultant effect of boosting Landon." According to the statement, while Roosevelt, had certainly not done enough for old people, "the Liberty League, Landon, and Lemke would reduce even these meager expenditures to alleviate suffering." In concluding, it called on members of the Townsend movement to join the fight against reaction and fascism.[80]

The attempt to link Roosevelt with Communism was a constant theme of his opposition. From San Simeon, William Randolph Hearst had attacked the "imported, autocratic, Asiatic Socialist party of Karl Marx and Franklin Delano Roosevelt." In 1935 Hoover said that the New Deal was about to run out of letters of the alphabet to name its agencies, "but, of course, the new Russian alphabet has thirty-four letters." Along the same line, Al Smith at a Liberty League banquet thundered for an hour against Roosevelt and New Dealers. "It is all right with me," he said, "if they want to disguise themselves as Karl Marx or Lenin or any of the rest of that bunch, but I won't stand for their allowing them to march under the banner of Jackson or Cleveland."[81] On September 19, a front page editorial in Hearst papers claimed that the Communist party was, following orders from Moscow, working to help Roosevelt's reelection. Similar claims increased as the election got closer.[82] In an effort to substantiate such claims and to embarrass the president, a group of Republicans approached Browder and offered the Communist party $250,000 if he withdrew his candidacy and instead endorsed Roosevelt. In relating this event to a Congressional committee, Browder asserted vigorously that the offer was turned down.[83]

Coming to the president's aid at the end of the campaign, the Communist party disclaimed the accusation of Roosevelt's opponents that his policies were "communistic" and leading the country to socialism. On the eve of the vote, in a speech from Madison Square Garden carried by NBC, Browder reassured his audience of the "absurdity" of such assertions. The Communist leader said, far from being a Communist, Roosevelt was committed to the "maintenance of capitalism." The reason for such attacks from the Right was the president's "insistence upon some measure of restraint" against monopoly capital's "greed for mountainous profits and unlimited exploitation of the people." In concluding, Browder once again repeated that Roosevelt's reelection would be "a rebuke to the worst reactionaries."[84]

The Communist party's presidential vote declined from 1932 despite the fact that its membership and influence had grown considerably since then. At the same time, local Communist tickets ran far ahead of the presidential one. The Communist presidential ticket polled 79,211 votes, with almost half coming from New York City. This was in contrast with the approximately 68,000 votes received in the city by the Party's candidates in local races.[85] Clearly then, aside from the votes of the hard-core Communists, most of the Party's electoral base had voted for Roosevelt, showing that the Party's anti-Landon message had been clearly understood. In contrast, the Socialist party's opposition to Roosevelt, its underestimation of fascism, its revolutionary rhetoric, and its internal divisions, accounted for its disastrous showing at the elections. It polled 187,785 votes, its worst showing since 1900. For the first time Communist candidates in New York received more votes than Socialists. In New York State a great number of Socialists switched their vote to Roosevelt on the American Labor party line, which polled three times as many votes as the Socialists. In states like Wisconsin, one of its strongholds, the Socialist party's membership dropped from 5,500 in 1934 to fewer than 1,000 by the end of 1936, even less than the number of CPUSA members. Furthermore, having lost all labor and progressive support, it virtually disappeared from the country's political scene.[86]

Roosevelt's reelection was a triumph. His 27,476,673 votes to Landon's 16,679,583 constituted the largest presidential vote in history: an increase of almost 5 million over the 1932 results.[87] Labor's vote clearly enabled Roosevelt to sweep the country. The Non-Partisan League was given credit for winning Ohio, Illinois, Indiana, and Pennsylvania. Roosevelt won by a landslide in working class areas such as

Allegheny County, Pennsylvania, and Gary, Indiana, areas which he had barely won or had even lost in 1932.[88] Clearly the forces which Communists believed would form the Popular Front coalition had instead come together around the president.

Undoubtedly the Party had underestimated the president's prestige and overestimated the influence of the Liberty League and the possibility of a Republican victory. It is highly improbable that a Communist endorsement would have put the president's reelection in jeopardy. Nevertheless the Party's stance during the campaign, however ambiguous, was successful in enabling it to maintain close ties with the pro-Roosevelt forces within the farmer-labor and trade-union movement and in helping the Communist party establish itself as a recognized force within the non-Communist left. At the same time, it prevented the isolation that affected other left-wing organizations that had openly opposed the New Deal. Clearly, in light of Roosevelt's triumphal reelection, the Party's policy had paid off.

The election provided an opportunity for the CPUSA to illustrate its policies. Communists campaigned extensively throughout the nation distributing literature, holding numerous public forums and rallies that were well attended and not only by Party members. As the Party's presidential candidate, Earl Browder shared the platform with local Democratic party officials and addressed as diverse an audience as one could find at the Institute of Public Affairs of the University of Virginia, the National Press Club, or at the New York *Herald Tribune*'s Annual Forum of Current Problems.[89] Everywhere he received extensive press coverage and was given time on national radio networks. When mobs in Terre Haute, Tampa, Durham, and Toledo tried to prevent Browder and Ford from campaigning, several newspapers came to their defense.[90] Browder himself acknowledged that the CPUSA's campaign was receiving considerable attention from the national press.

> First of all I must disclaim any particular grievance against the press for the way in which they have treated my campaign, or their reporting of my meetings on my recent tour. In fact I found, strangely enough, that in this year of the greatest political tensions, we have experienced an unusual hospitality in the press of this country.[91]

Finally, the 1936 elections turned Browder into a national public figure and solidified his position as the Party's recognized leader.

Browder's rise to power had been gradual. Since becoming a member of the secretariat in 1930, his power had increased steadily after William Weinstone was sent to Moscow as Party representative and following Foster's heart attack during the 1932 presidential campaign which incapacitated him for the next three years. Browder was elected general secretary at the CPUSA's Eighth Convention in 1934; as the Party's main speaker at the Comintern's Seventh Congress and its presidential candidate in 1936, he gradually eclipsed the better known Foster and came into his own right as the leader of the Communist party.

As Browder began his political ascent, his statements and writings show him to have been, among the Party's top leadership, one of the most receptive to guide the official line away from sectarian policies of the third period toward policies that would reflect the experiences and the lessons of Communists during the early years of the depression. His political ability became more apparent following the Seventh Congress of the Comintern. Within the confines of Soviet priorities, Browder demonstrated a notable measure of independence, tactical skills, and a capacity for original thinking, characteristics that he combined with a growing sense of himself, a detached arrogance, and considerable personal ambition. Browder's temperament, joined with a lack of internal democracy within the Party, did not stimulate collective leadership. This meant that for the remainder of the 1930s and through the war years it was Browder who conceived the definition and the contours of the Party's analysis and policies.

In retrospect it appears that Browder perceived the historical significance of the Dimitrov speech not in its specific directives but rather in its endorsement and encouragement of the pursuit of the new course that had been taking shape in response to the new issues raised by the economic crisis and to the growth of fascism. After the Seventh Congress the preservation and the strengthening of the Party's alliances became Browder's foremost concern, eventually forcing him to independently redefine the form of the People's Front in the United States.

5

THE DEMOCRATIC FRONT

> It was as though a new day had dawned for the American
> movement. We were not only Communists, we were
> Americans again. . . . The primary tie was still ideology.
> The main outlook internationalist. Now, however, it also
> comprised a new consciousness of being American, and
> we were readily convinced that the two were not only
> compatible but inseparable.
>
> George Charney, 1968[1]

Throughout the 1936 election campaign, Communists had continued
to express their confidence in the forthcoming break-up of old political alignments that would lead to the creation of a broad-based independent Farmer-Labor party. Once the votes had been counted, the
leadership of the CPUSA saw the result as confirmation of this tendency. For the Central Committee, the elections were a victory for the
"forces advocating democracy," and a setback "to the Hearst–Liberty
League–Wall Street drive towards fascism and to all extreme reactionaries."[2] Especially noteworthy was the statement that the electorate
had divided along "class lines": on the one hand, the "poor and
downtrodden," on the other, "the rich and the oppressors."[3] According to the Central Committee, Landon had been defeated by the coalition of those labor and political organizations "representing the broad
masses of the people" that the Communist party saw as the necessary
components of a People's Front.[4] This coalition was a revival of the
"people's democracy," which had "backed Jefferson, Jackson, and the
Populist movement of the 90's." In the eyes of the CPUSA, this coalition was

coming to life in a different setting and in a more advanced form to protect
the American people, their liberties and their standards of living, from the

rule of decaying reactionary capitalism and its worst products—fascism and war. The union of workers and farmers is coming to life today not as a silent partner of the capitalist politicians which was its role in the past. It is emerging now as an independent force, led by labor, and increasingly conscious of its role as a barrier to reaction, fascism and war.[5]

Paradoxically this analysis assumed that most Americans had voted to repudiate Landon rather than to endorse Roosevelt. Despite their emphasis on the progressive character of the Roosevelt vote, the Party still cautioned against trusting the president. Communists had supported the president's reelection as the lesser of two evils, a position that they had no apparent intention of changing. They still viewed Roosevelt as unreliable, and felt he used left-wing rhetoric while he consented to the demands of conservative forces and Southern Democrats.[6] For the Communists, if reactionary forces had been momentarily checked, they were still very strong even within the Democratic party; reactionaries, the Central Committee warned, would "do everything within their power to realize, *through the Roosevelt regime*, those policies which they sought to realize through a Landon-Knox victory."[7] The only effective long-term guarantee against reaction continued to be the formation of an independent political organization. In the Party's view people had voted for Roosevelt as a defense against reaction and fascism rather than as an endorsement of the president's policies. Alexander Bittelman pursued this line of thought when he wrote that, although they voted for Roosevelt, large numbers of workers were in fact "looking *through* the election campaign *toward* a Farmer-Labor party."[8] He even spelled out some of the intermediate phases in this direction and added:

> The class forces that go into the making of the People's Front, the Farmer-Labor party, are moving–of this there can be not the slightest doubt. Nor can there be any doubts as to the direction in which they are moving. They are breaking with the traditions of the two-party system and are going toward a Farmer-Labor party.[9]

Contrary to Communist expectations, however, the CIO and progressive political organizations remained firm in their support for the president even after the elections. The CIO concluded that it could better further the workers' interests through the Labor's Non-Partisan League by working through the primary system to support liberal

Democrats. The CIO did continue, however, to work with labor parties where they were strong and in New York even promoted the formation of the American Labor Party. It was evident that a political realignment was taking place, not independently of the two-party system but, rather, within it, with labor supporting the Democratic party.

Communists confronted a choice: they could either continue to campaign for a third party at the risk of isolating themselves from the rest of the progressive movement and jeopardize their growing influence within the CIO, or they could join in support of the president. The second alternative, however, posed a number of problems. Most immediately, the Party continued to have serious reservations about Roosevelt's reliability as an opponent of conservative interests. More importantly, supporting Roosevelt implied abandoning the Farmer-Labor tactic and redefining the Popular Front policy in the United States in a way very different from that enunciated by Dimitrov at the Seventh Congress.

Steadily the Communist party moved away from the Farmer-Labor party tactic. Once again the initiative came from Browder. His address to the Central Committee in December signaled a coming change. The analysis of the results of the elections, concerning the sharp class character of the vote as well as the crisis of the two-party system was similar to that of the November Central Committee. The elections, he said, "strengthened all the progressive tendencies among the voting population," thereby improving the prospects for the building of the People's Front.[10] Given this situation, what were the prospects for the formation of an independent Farmer-Labor party? While pointing out that this movement had gained strength in various parts of the country, Browder, in contrast to the November statement, did not exaggerate its importance, recognizing that it had remained limited.[11] Browder said Communists would do well to face up to this situation; consequently, they had to give the People's Front policy a broader form, not one limited to a Farmer-Labor party. They were to conceive of it on a scale that would "unite the forces in the Farmer-Labor party and other progressives together with those forces crystallized in some form or another but not yet independent of the old parties."[12]

In 1937 the pace of the Party's redefinition of the People's Front policy quickened as a result of the Communists' changing stance toward Roosevelt. The Party first began to reconsider its position toward the president as a result of his attempt to pack the Supreme Court.

Relations between the Court and the president had deteriorated ever since the justices' 1935 decisions holding the NRA and the AAA unconstitutional. Similar rulings against other New Deal legislation strengthened the impression of a political drive by the Supreme Court against the New Deal. Based on these precedents, there was a good chance that the Wagner Act and Social Security Act would also be overturned. Within two weeks of his second inauguration, strengthened by victory, Roosevelt moved against the Court. On February 5, 1937, the president requested that Congress grant him the authority to reorganize the judiciary. He asked for the power to appoint a new justice for every sitting justice who did not retire within six months of his seventieth birthday. This plan would have given Roosevelt the possibility of appointing up to six new justices. Roosevelt had, however, failed in his calculations. Congress' general reaction to the proposal was negative. Conservatives, who had always looked upon the Supreme Court as their last defense against Roosevelt's policies, resisted his proposal. Even some of the president's staunchest supporters in the past, such as Joseph O'Mahoney from Wyoming, Tom Connally from Texas, Burton Wheeler from Montana, Hiram Johnson from California, and George Norris from Nebraska, now opposed him. As the battle raged throughout the spring and summer, the anti-New Deal coalition began to recover from its November defeat. Isolated from those he thought would support him, Roosevelt withdrew his proposal in mid-July.[13]

Communists had been strong opponents of the Court's conservative views. In fact, Roosevelt's seeming unwillingness to confront the Court in 1935 was one of the arguments the CPUSA had used to prove that the president could not be relied upon as a defense against reactionary forces. Once Roosevelt moved against the Court, however, the Communist party revised its attitude toward the president and the New Deal. In early February a *Daily Worker* editoral set the tone of the Party's response. The editorial claimed that Roosevelt's proposal further polarized the country. On one side stood "every thing that is progressive, forward looking, in the best traditions of American democracy"; on the other "reaction, hatred of democracy, bigotry, defense of the biggest vested interests."[14]

Implicitly the Party's increasing support for Roosevelt put in question the farmer-labor policy. At first this incongruity led to contradictory statements. Through the late winter, in a number of articles in the *Daily Worker,* the farmer-labor policy took on a local rather than a national scope. However, in the April issue of the *Communist,* Bittelman once again stated that the only effective way to curb the Court's "usurped powers" was to organize the farmer-labor forces throughout the country "in effective independent political organization."[15] In the same issue Clarence Hathaway expressed a radically different evaluation of the prospects for a Farmer-Labor party. In fact, he discarded it. In his opinion, by attempting to limit the powers of the Supreme Court Roosevelt sided with "the most progressive sections of the population," which had come together around the Democratic party and rejuvenated it. Hathaway concluded that the People's Front would not coalesce into a national Farmer-Labor party but rather "inside and around the Democratic party."[16]

Although some Communist leaders continued to repeat that popular support for Roosevelt was dwindling and to criticize the president for what they termed his "middle-of-the-road" policies, a change was clearly taking place.[17] The backing Roosevelt continued to receive from labor and left-wing political organizations and his manifest challenge to domestic conservative forces boosted the Party's broadening of the People's Front to the Democratic party. Browder traveled to Moscow in April 1937 where he procured the Comintern's support for the Party's new course.[18] Just as had been the case in early 1936, once again the Communist party began redefining its policy toward the president on its own initiative and not as a result of directives from abroad.[19]

Following his return to the United States new lines were clearly drawn. At the end of May, speaking to a capacity crowd at Carnegie Hall on the issue of the Supreme Court, Browder placed the Party solidly behind Roosevelt. The battle over the president's proposal, he said, "has reached an intensity far beyond that of the presidential election last year, unprecedentedly bitter as it was." Reactionary forces, including those that had previously remained "for various reasons in the camp of Roosevelt," were now coming together to oppose him.[20] Since Communists perceived that the battle over the Supreme Court had polarized the nation, with the "lower classes" supporting the president and the rich opposing him, Browder stated there could be no "neutral position" in the struggle between "the forces of reaction, fascism and war" and what he called "the forces of popular democracy, and first of all the labor movement." In such a line-up, he concluded, there was "but one possible place for the Communists, on the side of democracy."[21]

The Party's stance toward Roosevelt was detailed further at the

Central Committee plenum held June 17–20. Browder set out to explain the obvious contradiction between the "growth of the People's Front sentiment in the United States, and the slowing up of organizational realization of a national Farmer-Labor party."[22] The announcement of a new policy did not entail a criticism of the former. In fact, Browder tried to show that no change was taking place, because "of the exceptional breadth and speed of the rise of the Farmer-Labor movement," there had been "a pause in organizing the national Farmer-Labor party."[23]

Remarkably for the first time the articulation of the Party's new policy was based on an acknowledgment and consequent attempt to analyze the uniqueness of the country's political tradition. Communists had promoted the Farmer-Labor party as a challenge to the traditional two-party system in which both parties expressed different regional interests but similar economic aims; now they theorized that the inadequacy of the farmer-labor policy was the consequence of several associated circumstances. Specific American conditions, such as the difficulty of getting new parties on the ballot as well as the primary system itself, made the success of a national third party extremely difficult. This difficulty was a reality that had been "insufficiently considered and studied by the vanguard of political radicalism in the United States. . . . Everyone who wants to influence the political actions of millions in the immediate future will have to take these factors increasingly into account."[24] More notably, however, the depression had shattered the two-party system. The 1936 election was portrayed as a turning point in the nation's political system comparable to the realignment of 1854. The economic crisis had led to the formation of two new parties representing political alignments dominated "not by regional differences among the bourgeoisie" but by "class stratification among the masses of the population."[25] While on the one hand conservative forces, including right-wing Democrats, had gathered around the Republican party, on the other hand, a broad and flexible coalition had come together around Roosevelt. This reshuffling of the traditional parties made a new party unnecessary and called for new tactics. In this altered situation, Browder claimed, as far as the People's Front in the United States was concerned, what "particular name the caprice of history may baptize it is immaterial to us."[26] The development of the People's Front in the United States could proceed only by combining the "existing Farmer-Labor party forms" with the "progressive movements" led by Roosevelt within the Democratic party as well as within the Republican party.[27] Communists would support left-wing candidates running either on the Republican, the Democratic, or local farmer-labor tickets. Only when these candidates were not available would the Communist party run its own.[28] This analysis of the two-party system shaped the policies of the CPUSA during the following years. Beyond this however, the accent on the distinctive U.S. character of the country's political system remained one of the main considerations behind Browder's political and theoretical evolution, eventually culminating in 1944 in his proposal to dissolve the CPUSA.

While the CPUSA had drawn closer to Roosevelt, the endorsement was far from complete. Foster and Bittelman remained the president's most consistent critics. Throughout the summer Bittelman repeated that Roosevelt was no check to the "dark enemies of progress"; he even wrote that labor was "shedding the illusion" that Roosevelt was the "genuine class representative of labor," as well as "the leader of labor and its political spokesman."[29] However, following the Party's shift to collective security, its main criticism to Roosevelt was the Administration's isolationism in foreign policy and particularly its policy in regard to the Spanish Civil War.

Following the outbreak of the war, in mid-July 1936, the CPUSA was very critical of Washington's alignment with the British and French governments' policy of nonintervention. Specifically the Party attacked the Administration for extending the Neutrality Act to Spain, a policy approved by Congress on January 6, with John Bernard, Farmer-Labor party representative from Minnesota, casting the lone dissenting vote.[30] Foster blamed Roosevelt for "twisting" the strong anti-war sentiment in the country to pass the arms embargo against Spanish loyalists.[31] Even Browder, the major advocate of the extention of the People's Front to the pro-Roosevelt forces within the Democratic party, criticized the Administration's "shameful capitulation to the reactionaries on the Spanish question."[32] Browder, however, differentiated between the president, Congress, and "reactionary forces" within the Administration. The Communist leader praised any presidential statement that could be interpreted as an endorsement of collective security. The policy of neutrality was the responsibility of Congress and the State Department who "nullified" the president's efforts.[33] In mid-September, speaking to Massachusetts Communists, Browder affirmed the Party's "practical agreement" with the president's statements in his recent Constitution Day address concerning the responsibility of government to assure a higher standard of living for the masses. Communists, Browder added, would "find an ever-growing basis for common action" with any group or personality that shared this view.[34]

Whatever remaining reservations the CPUSA had toward the president disappeared after Roosevelt's Quarantine speech on October 5, 1937, in Chicago. For some time, Roosevelt had been considering making a strong statement against German, Italian, and Japanese aggression and alerting the country to the dangers of war. Referring to growing world tension, he affirmed that the United States could not hope to remain immune, and he therefore proposed that the country abandon its policy of neutrality in favor of "common action" with other "peace-loving" countries to stop fascist expansion. This was to take the form of a "quarantine" against aggressor nations. The president's statement was dramatic in tone, but unclear in content; he did not specify what forms and through which processes the quarantine was to be implemented, how it differed from sanctions, or what effect it would have on the Neutrality Act. He remained vague and no concrete action followed. In fact the speech did not produce any change in foreign policy. Reactions to it were mixed. On the one hand, pacifist organizations protested; the Chicago *Tribune*, the New York *Herald Tribune*, and the Hearst papers lashed out at the president, while isolationist congressmen threatened Roosevelt with impeachment. In an open letter to the president, Norman Thomas warned that the endorsement of collective security would lead the country to war. Meanwhile, many of the president's traditional supporters remained silent. On the other hand, internationalists strongly endorsed his stand, the Communist party was among them.[35]

Communists enthusiastically interpreted the quarantine declaration as the president's support of the collective security policy they were advocating. On October 6, the *Daily Worker* published the speech in its entirety and followed up the next day with an editorial that defined it as the "greatest speech" of Roosevelt's career. The speech had projected "a powerful ray of hope for peace that penetrated to every nook and corner of the world"; its effect had been "electric"; it had shocked "the war mongers" while "galvanizing the forces of peace." Bittelman wrote that now the Party's task was to "*Rouse and mobilize the masses for the realization of the president's peace program!*"[36] In mid-November the Party's Politburo adopted the president's policy. In his report, Browder described Roosevelt as "the most outstanding anti-fascist spokesman within the capitalist democracies." The president's recent stands in domestic and foreign policy provided *"a rounded-out People's Front program of an advanced type,"* a position also expressed by the Party's Central Committee.[37]

By the end of 1937, the process of redefining the Party's policies, which had begun during the presidential campaign, was completed. The Communist party followed Browder's lead and replaced the Comintern's Farmer-Labor policy with a broader coalition of forces behind Roosevelt and the New Deal as the "specific form of the Popular Front in the United States." Hathaway gave this coalition a new and "Americanized" name, not incidentally he called it "Democratic Front."[38] As a final act the CPUSA's modification of the directives of the Seventh Congress was approved by the leadership of the Communist International at a meeting with Party leaders in January 1938.[39]

The Party's Tenth Convention officially sanctioned the modified definition of People's Front policy and the abandonment of the proposed founding of a Farmer-Labor party as no longer pertinent to reality. On May 26, the convention opened in New York with 1,500 delegates from all over the country gathered together in an atmosphere full of symbols of the Party's new policy and image. The hall where they met was decorated with red flags as well as the Stars and Stripes; behind the speakers' podium hung a map of the United States in blue with the slogans "Jobs," "Security," "Democracy," and "Peace" radiating from it in white and red. Delegates, now sang the "Star Spangled Banner" along with the more customary "International," which had been restored to Eugene Poitier's original version by deleting the word "Soviet" from the last line: "the International Soviet will be the human race." The message was clear: the Party's roots were to be firmly planted in the country's political tradition.[40]

In his May 28 report, Browder praised the new coalition. He spoke of a "New Deal wing of the Democratic party" led by Roosevelt and supported by workers, farmers, and urban middle-classes. It was an essential part of "the developing Democratic Front against monopoly capital."[41] On the basis of this broad coalition could be built what he called a "party of the people."[42] American Communists envisioned the formation of a party based on the coalition of various organizations and interests, conforming to the country's political tradition, and united behind a common program. While the Community party continued to state the need to draw the Socialist party into this coalition, in reality, the rift between both organizations over the issue of collective security and the Socialist party's dwindling membership and shrinking influence among labor made the need for a united front less of a priority from the Communist stand point.[43]

Communists gave up any pretense of leading the People's Front coalition; rather, they were willing to remain in the background of the Democratic Front without any immediate "official recognition" or "formal admittance." The Party was prepared to wait and demonstrate to other forces its sincere commitment to the common goal.[44] Hathaway wrote that this coalition included "progressive elements" within both major parties, together with those other organizations that the CPUSA had wanted to unite in the People's Front: industrial unions, the Labor Non-Partisan League, the farmer-labor parties, and a number of left-wing organizations, including of course the CPUSA.[45] In essence, the Democratic Front was, as Eugene Dennis described it shortly after, the People's Front of workers, farmers, and the middle class combined with "important sections of the upper middle class and certain liberal sections of the bourgeoisie."[46]

The program of the Democratic Front was to increase workers' purchasing power and wages, cut hours, and improve working conditions; to provide relief for the jobless; and to improve and broaden social security laws, farm relief, and a number of other social programs. The Democratic Front would also broaden "the democratic rights of the people," as well as limit "the power of big capital" in government and in the economy. Finally, measures would have to be adopted that would encourage the United States to assume its "responsibility for world leadership in organizing world peace."[47] The slogan "For Jobs, Security, Democracy, and Peace" summed up the platform. In the Party leadership's view, this program did not remove the causes of the economic crisis, but ensured that recovery would improve the masses' living conditions and extend democracy rather than cause hardships and fascism.

The CPUSA found itself in a singular situation. In the United States the economic crisis was being confronted not with fascism or the threat of it, but rather through social and economic reforms within the democratic system and with the support of organized labor and progressive organizations. Furthermore the two organizations that were to form the core of the People's Front, the Communist and Socialist parties, were in no condition to play any major role. The CPUSA had no realistic hope of soon becoming a viable mass organization to lead the country to socialism, while the Socialist party had virtually disappeared as an organized political force after the 1936 elections. Clearly the People's Front policy, as expressed at the Seventh Congress, did not take into consideration the complexity and diverse characteristics of progressive forces in the country, hence its failure to enlist broad support. Following Browder's lead, the Communist party had come to the conclusion that conditions in the United States made it necessary for the CPUSA to adopt tactics different from those used in Europe of which the Farmer-Labor party policy was only a reflection, and that the CPUSA had to align itself with the rest of the progressive and labor movement behind the president.

The policy of the CPUSA centered on the maintenance of social progress, democratic values, and peace. Specifically it supported in domestic policy the New Deal, and in foreign policy the implementation of Roosevelt's verbal commitment to concerted action against fascist nations. The president's speeches were reprinted in their entirety in the *Daily Worker* and hardly a week went by without the publication of an article praising him. The responsibility for the country's recession at the end of 1937 was placed squarely on "big monopolies." Their "sabotage" of the economy was the cause for the rise in unemployment, the closing of factories, and the drop in industrial production. In fact, the CPUSA became the political force which possibly supported the New Deal most consistently even when Roosevelt wavered from its ideas. While Roosevelt was searching for ways to cut spending and slash the budget in order to bolster the confidence of business, the Party absolved him of any wrongdoing and responsibility for the critical economic crisis.[48]

Communists instead noted with satisfaction that Roosevelt and prominent members of the administration had spoken against the power and privileges of small minorities. Assistant Attorney General Robert Jackson, head of the anti-trust division of the Justice Department, accused big business of having engaged in a "strike of capital" against reform. He was followed by Secretary of the Interior Ickes who, taking his cue from Léon Blum's campaign against the *deux cent familles* that controlled France's economy, attacked "America's sixty families." Monopoly, he warned, was threatening the country with "big business fascism."[49] These terms became part of the CPUSA's lexicon: "sixty families" was adopted without change, while "strike of capital" was modified to "sit-down strike of capital" indicating the withholding of capital from production. The president's proposals, such as the wages and hours bill and relief and aid to farmers, were

117

strongly supported by the Party, as was the bill to reorganize the federal bureaucracy. Communists also gave strong support to the president's decision to scrap budget balancing and his request to Congress for a new 3 billion dollar spending program in mid-April 1938.[50] The Party also eventually reversed its opposition to the Civilian Conservation Corps.[51]

The blame for the failure to pass more advanced social and civil rights legislation was shifted to reactionary forces in Congress. In an effort to draw closer to Roosevelt, the Party even attributed to these same forces the total responsibility for isolationism, as well as for torpedoing the anti-lynching bill, regardless of the fact that the president's support for it had been anything but enthusiastic.[52] The CPUSA identified with the New Deal to the point that a Communist leaflet in Wisconsin called voters to elect Communists as "Genuine New Dealers and Liberals," while another proclaimed boldly: "*We Do Not Propose to Let the President Down.*"[53]

Following Roosevelt's "quarantine" speech, the main task in foreign policy was to organize all those who had voted for the president in 1936 "into an effective force supporting the president's peace policy." Communists said this had to be done if America was "to play a role in preventing a second world war."[54] Even Foster, momentarily setting aside his criticism of the president, found something good to say about him. Roosevelt's Good-Neighbor policy toward Latin America, he said, "facilitates the anti-fascist and anti-war ends of the peoples of the Americas."[55] Faced with the failure of the Administration to take any effective action to reverse isolationism and help Spanish loyalists, the Party justified its continuous support for the president by differentiating between him and individual members of the Cabinet. The Party directed its attacks particularly against Cordell Hull and Under Secretary of State Sumner Welles; the *Daily Worker* referred to the latter as a spokesman for "world fascism."[56]

The form of the Democratic Front varied to reflect different circumstances.[57] In some places the Party's shift from independent politics to support of the New Deal wing of the Democratic party led to an increase of activities and presence locally within both the Democratic and even the Republican party. In California, working through the Committee for Political Unity, a coalition of progressives, Communists became an active and firmly entrenched force within the Democratic party. Culbert Olson sought their support for his gubernatorial race; they worked closely with members of his administration and were a sizable force within the state's Young Democrats.[58] In Illinois, Communists were told to vote in the Democratic primaries, even if this meant excluding themselves from signing petitions to put the Communist party on the ballot for two years, in order to build "unity behind those candidates who expressed best the program of the Democratic Front."[59]

In a number of states, however, Communists worked within independent local labor parties. In Minnesota, Party members had started joining the state's Farmer-Labor party (MFLP) in early 1935 and had stepped up this process following the Seventh Congress. The CPUSA sent Clarence Hathaway to Minneapolis to supervise the application of the new policy.[60] In October 1935, when he met with Floyd Olson, Browder promised his party's continued backing to him and to his party.[61] After the meeting, Communists were more readily accepted into the MFLP and their activities within it increased. Dropping their past criticism and pledging support to the Farmer-Labor state administration in the 1936 elections, Communists withdrew their candidates and joined the organization. They quickly gained respect and responsibility and even boasted the seating of forty delegates at the state's Farmer-Labor convention in March.[62] After Olson's death in August 1936, Communists maintained close ties with his successor Elmer Benson. They remained a significant force in the MFLP, attained a number of important leadership positions within the party, and consequently achieved positions in Minnesota politics.[63]

In New York State, after the 1936 elections, Communists and Party sympathizers en masse joined the American Labor Party (ALP), which they saw as the umbrella under which pro-New Deal political and labor forces were coming together in that state. In 1937 the Party withdrew its city-wide slate in favor of the ALP ticket headed by LaGuardia and, according to Earl Browder, the Communist vote accounted for 20 percent of the ALP's vote. Communists provided a dependable voting bloc, diligent and disciplined activists all willing to keep a low profile and to accept the ALP's highly centralized and undemocratic nature, controlled from the top by the CIO's leadership. The CPUSA's willingness to help strengthen the ALP was such that in 1938 it withdrew its state ticket and threw its support behind Herbert Lehman after he said he needed the Party's votes to be elected Governor.[64] While backing the American Labor Party slate, the Party ran Israel Amter for congressman-at-large solely to measure its ballot strength. The Communist candidate received an impressive 105,681 votes, all the more remarkable considering that it was a minor post in a mid-term state election when voter turnout is always low.[65]

In Washington State, the Communist party was an important force behind the strengthening of the Commonwealth Federation.[66] Communists were similarly an active and influential force in Wisconsin where Communists withdrew their candidates and joined that state's Farmer-Labor Progressive Federation. A number of them even ran for state and county office on its ticket.[67] Communists were also active in labor parties in Oregon, Massachusetts, Connecticut, Michigan and Ohio.[68]

Implicit in the Party's new direction was opposition to any attempt at forming national third parties to contest Roosevelt's leadership of the progressive coalition. Hence the Party's Central Committee released a lengthy statement criticizing Philip La Follette, governor of Wisconsin, for his decision to launch a new party, the National Progressives of America, as an alternative to the New Deal. Communists would resist any such attempt since it split the progressive forces and hence favored reactionary interests.[69]

Reflecting the Party's new policies and its increasing acceptance, some politicians, risking possible backlash, openly met and courted Party leaders. By 1938 Communist national and state leaders had contacts and sometimes meetings with senators, congressmen, local and state officials, and even White House intermediaries.[70] Tolerance for Communist activities was such that when the New York State legislature passed a law banning the Party, Governor Lehman vetoed it. A similar attempt to expel Communists from the Minnesota Farmer-Labor party failed because of strong opposition from the CPUSA's liberal allies as well as the fact that it would have been difficult to identify Communists since they did not disclose their affiliation.[71]

The Party's call for a broad unity against fascism and reaction generated a notable positive response across the country opening to the Party traditionally closed doors. The contrast was sharp: "from soapbox in the South Bronx to the Ford Hall Forum; from brickbats to applause." George Charney, while secretary for the New England district, addressed audiences at Phillips Academy in Andover, at Dartmouth, at church congregations on Cape Cod, and local town's people on the Rutland common.[72] In Birmingham, Alabama, Communists held out door meetings, had a downtown office, and even opened a Marxist bookstore. Now in cities and towns across the country Communists had regular weekly radio shows. Party functions and Browder's speeches were broadcast over nationwide hookups by major radio networks, and the secretary's picture was even on the cover of *Time* magazine.[73]

The Party's shift away from an exclusive emphasis on the shop floor to include electoral politics, led to a change in its structure, corresponding with the electoral structure of cities and states. In 1925 the Party's structure had been reorganized to mirror the Russian model, a process termed "bolshevization."[74] Party districts covered various states: for instance, the New England district included all of Massachusetts east of Springfield, Rhode Island, New Hampshire, Vermont, and Maine. Pennsylvania was divided into two regions: east and west. Locally the party's organization rested on local units organized prevalently on a shop rather than a territorial basis. Starting in 1936, however, the Party's internal structure was reorganized in an attempt to make it more responsive to new policies as well as to give it names closer to a more familiar American political lexicon. Starting from the top the Political Bureau was renamed Political Committee; the Central Committee became the National Committee; districts now followed state lines; Sections became County Committees and were shaped along assembly district lines. Finally, the Ninth Convention officially merged shop and street units into branches paralleling new industrial unions and electoral district lines to facilitate Communist electoral activities. Through these changes the Party was better equipped to engage in electoral work and to collaborate with other forces with similar organizational structure.[75]

The CPUSA now perceived the need for a legislative representative in Washington as well as in a number of state capitals.[76] Starting in early 1938 the *Daily Worker* began running a new column "Washington Front" written by the paper's editor, Clarence Hathaway, devoted to legislative activities in the nation's capital. George Charney recalled that Communists began studying assembly district maps analyzing the social, ethnic, and political characteristics of various areas:

Everyone became an expert in election strategy, and predicting results became the favorite indoor pastime of all functionaries . . . the party, which hitherto had been oriented to the naked forms of the class struggle, such as picket lines and relief struggles, now acquired an astonishing flair for election politics as well as a capacity for expert organization and mobility.[77]

This less secretive, more open kind of organization was seen as the best way to connect Communists with the life of the neighborhood. According to Brown, the Party's organizational secretary, by creating an organization that more closely resembled traditional American political organizations, "the neighborhood will recognize us as a political party, because we correspond to their conception of a party."[78]

The Party's shift toward policies and organizational forms that better reflected the country's environment also led to the discovery of the importance of national traditions. This search for a usable past was not a new phenomenon; in his 1918 "Letter to American Workers," Lenin himself reminded United States revolutionaries of their country's rich revolutionary traditions.[79] Through the 1920s the Communist press carried a number of articles proclaiming the importance of establishing a tie between the Party's ideology and program and what was termed the revolutionary and anti-institutional heritage of 1776 and 1861; but it was only during the third period that this process gained speed.[80] In the early 1930s, in tune with the Party's policies at the time, reference to 1776 was used as a justification for revolution to show that the Communist party's revolutionary program drew from the country's tradition. During the 1932 presidential elections Foster declared: "History has shown that the masses of America, when faced with a fundamental crisis, are not afraid of a revolutionary solution. The United States was born of a bloody revolution."[81] In 1934 the manifesto of the Party's Eighth Convention stated that only the CPUSA carried "forward the revolutionary traditions of 1776 and 1861." It added that the "new government" mentioned in the Declaration of Independence was, in the present situation, nothing other than the dictatorship of the proletariat in the form of "workers' and farmers' councils."[82] Communists read avidly Carl Becker, Mary and Charles Beard, and Vernon Parrington. In the mid-1920s, reviews in the Party's theoretical journal of *The Rise of American Civilization* and *Main Currents of American Thought*, criticized them for concentrating on the founding fathers as unscrupulous individuals rather than as representatives of their class interests. A decade later this did not stop Browder from borrowing heavily from these historians when he wrote that the United States was the result of a revolutionary struggle, of the "confiscation of the private property of the feudal landlords." The "good old American tradition of revolution," he concluded, was "kept alive *only* by the Communist party. We are the only true Americans."[83]

Although references to the country's revolutionary past continued, the People's Front changed the emphasis. Now rather than revolution, Communists highlighted the importance of defending democracy and therefore discovered worthwhile elements in the "bourgeois" tradition of the United States. In 1935, Earl Browder set the tone in an article significantly titled "Who are the Americans?" Communists, he prefaced, "like this country very much. . . . If we did not like our country so much, perhaps we would surrender it to Wall Street."[84]

In an attempt to reinforce ties between the country's past and the CPUSA's socialist program for the future, the ideological roots of the Communist party grew beyond Marx, Lenin, and Stalin, who were placed on an equal ideological standing with the founding fathers. The preamble to the Party's new constitution adopted at the Tenth Convention stated that American Communists carried "forward today the traditions of Jefferson, Paine, Jackson, and Lincoln, and of the Declaration of Independence."[85] Also included in the Pantheon of Communist heroes, albeit at a lower level, were Ralph Waldo Emerson, Henry Thoreau, Walt Whitman, and Mark Twain. The Declaration of Independence became the *Communist Manifesto* of the eighteenth century. The Party even had its own "Thomas Paine Day," September 18, 1937, to celebrate the 150th anniversary of the Constitution, and important Party functions were held to coincide with Washington's birthday, a date the Party leadership insisted had to be "politically utilized."[86] Aaron Burr, Alexander Hamilton, and Benedict Arnold were either compared to Trotsky, Hearst, or DuPont (also referred to as Tories), or even, after the Moscow trials, to Bukharin and Tukhachevsky. "It took the United States government," Browder declared, "thirty-eight years before it finally suppressed the treasonable circles that had arisen in the first days of the revolution. . . . The Soviet Union has dug out and liquidated its treasonable sects in only about half that time."[87]

The claim of the continuity of the country's revolutionary past and the Communist program, culminated with Browder's slogan "Communism is the Americanism of the twentieth century." By suggesting a historical link between democracy and communism, this slogan embodied the Party's concern with overcoming the image of an organization whose policies and ideology were foreign to the country's reality and tradition. The slogan caught on, and became very prominent during the following years. Objections to the slogan were raised from within the Party as well as by the Comintern so it was withdrawn at the end of

1938. However, in an article in the *Communist*, Browder reassured any-one concerned that this decision might indicate a return to sectarian policies by stating that the slogan was wrong only because it implied that only Communists were "Good Americans," excluding all other progressive forces.[88]

During the battle over Roosevelt's "packing" of the Supreme Court, Browder's speeches were full of references to the structure and his-tory of the nation's government from 1776.[89] Similarly, in foreign pol-icy, Browder resorted to lengthy citations from Jefferson in support of the French revolution to strengthen the Party's campaign in favor of aiding the Spanish Republican forces. Browder implicitly equated the objectives of Spanish Popular Front government with the principles of the minutemen in 1776, adding principles "we Americans hold dear" such as the separation of Church and State, the end of feudalism, and the suppression of special privileges for democratic rights. Franco and his followers were equated to Tories; like them, the fascist generals had counted on "foreign mercenaries in their ferocious attempt to keep America in chains." Through the same process, the United States volunteers who fought on the side of the Loyalist forces were likened to Thaddeus Kosciusko and Casimir Pulaski, and were also referred to as "American Lafayettes"; their brigade, the XVth, was commonly referred to as the "Lincoln Brigade."[90]

This love for country expressed itself in a variety of ways: the *New Masses* started a contest for the best essay on the theme "I Love Amer-ica." Granville Hicks, who had joined the Party in 1935, combined the Popular Front love for country and need for gradual change in a book by the same name with the subtitle "A Communist Looks at His Country."[91]

The emphasis on Americanism did reach some extremes: the geneal-ogy of the Party secretary was traced back to a Littleberry Browder, a soldier in Washington's Continental Army. In 1937, the Young Com-munist League even outdid the Daughters of the American Revolu-tion who had forgotten to celebrate the 162nd anniversary of Paul Revere's ride: a young Communist, dressed in the appropriate cos-tume, rode horseback up and down Broadway carrying a sign "The DAR Forgets But the YCL Remembers."[92]

The Party's defense of democracy also meant trying to shed a num-ber of familiar Communist images. Browder tried to dispel some of the major ones: repeatedly he stated that Communists did not advocate the use of force and were not conspiring to overthrow the country's government. In fact, he pledged the Party's support to "crush" any group or organization "which conspires or acts to subvert, undermine, weaken or overthrow, any or all institutions of American democracy." Communists, he said, respected the will of the majority and therefore as long as "this majority will is to maintain the present system, we submit ourselves to that decision."[93] In 1938, in a statement to the McNaboe Committee investigating subversive organizations in New York State, Browder upheld the Party's defense of democracy and opposition to the use of violence. He added that most of those recruited into the Party during the previous years had joined "precisely as a result of the Party's publicly proclaimed policies, and would quickly abandon it if they should find a contradiction between its inner convictions and beliefs and those which it publicly proclaims."[94]

Another notion that the Party tried to dispel was that it took its orders from Moscow. Browder even had the temerity to deny any such claim: if the CPUSA received any such orders, he claimed, it would "throw them in the wastebasket."[95] The Party tried to place its relationship with Moscow under a different light: at the end of 1936, the CPUSA declared that it was "affiliated," and no longer a "section" of the Communist International, a minor but indicative change that was officially incorporated into the new 1938 constitution. In a claim that few, in or out of the Party, must have believed, the constitution added that the decisions of the International Congress were no longer seen as supreme and binding; rather they were to be "considered" and "acted upon" by the Party's leadership, the only "supreme authority."[96]

Communists now also saw religious groups as an important component of the Democratic Front. Since the early 1920s the Party had enjoyed a strong Jewish following particularly in the garment trades; much of this support had eroded, however, as a consequence of the dissolution of the Yiddish-language federation in the mid-1920s which had eliminated an important vehicle of ethnic identity, as well as the Party's support for the 1929 Arab uprising in Palestine, and the sectarian policies of the third period.[97] With the depression a new generation of young Jewish recruits, eager for social involvement, spurred by the fascist threat, and attracted by the Party's "American" image, joined the CPUSA. The People's Front policy and the emphasis on democratic values also led to an appreciation of ethnic cultural traditions for which Communists had previously showed little concern. This emphasis produced a flowering of organizations under the umbrella of the Communist-led International Workers Order (IWO), a coalition of language fraternal organizations with a dozen daily and weekly papers, to preserve and spread Jewish culture. Initiatives such as these helped the CPUSA overcome its isolation from the Jewish community, spread the Party's influence as well as provided an important vehicle for recruitment.[98]

The Party's position also applied to other religious communities in the country. A number of Protestant clergymen and groups became active in Communist-sponsored organizations. Significant also was the Party's attitude in the Deep South. During the sectarian third period in Alabama, where many Party members also regularly attended church, local Communist leaders refrained from attacking religion. Religious metaphors were included into the local Communist lexicon to help illustrate the Party's program.[99] With Catholics the issue was more complex because of the Church's strong anti-communism. Communists wanted to enlist Catholics in the struggle against fascism, they also wanted to ease relations with Catholic workers in Communist-led unions such as the Transport Workers Union in New York and the United Electrical Workers in Schenectady. The Party depicted itself as a staunch defender of religious freedom against fascist intolerance. Speaking at the Party's Tenth Convention, Browder outstretched a "hand of brotherly cooperation" to Catholics. Not shying away from quoting the Old and New Testaments, the Communist leader tried to emphasize the common moral and ethnic standards as well as the social concerns shared by Communists and Catholics: "Christian brotherhood and charity," he said, were social virtues "that we of no religion appreciate." Communists and Catholics had to join "hands for our common salvation" against the common fascist foe that threatened "everything progressive and decent in human life."[100]

These statements were more than simple declarations brought forth for political expediency. They represented a further sign of the Party's attempt to sink its roots in its national soil and provided a stimulus for Communists to explore their country's traditions, culture, and institutions and to analyze what transformed and shaped them. This process, together with the shift in the membership base from foreign to native-born, had far-reaching consequences for the CPUSA, modifying its image, policies, and methods of work, as well as how Communists presented themselves and communicated with other Americans. As George Charney wrote in his autobiography,

The proletarian garb favored by functionaries was replaced by the business suit; our professional revolutionaries could hardly be distinguished from office executives; bus travel was replaced by Pullman; having children was no longer frowned upon, though hardly encouraged; and the day Earl Browder stood up in a restaurant to help his wife don her coat initiated a new standard of deportment.[101]

A changed political reality led to a new terminology: "anti-fascist," "progressive," and "democracy" became the new catch-words replacing "proletarian," and "dictatorship of the proletariat." The *Daily Worker* opened its pages to a range of nonpolitical topics including reviews of popular movies and a column on the problems of raising and disciplining children. The paper's sports writer, Lester Rodney, successfully combined first class reporting with the denunciation of racial discrimination in professional sports. The Young Communist League, not to be outdone, sponsored fashion shows complete with models sporting the latest in "new anti-fascist style" women's' clothing, and promoted the boycott of Japanese silk in favor of synthetic substitutes and cotton. A Sunday edition of the paper inaugurated in 1936, the *Worker*, directed by Joseph North, contained less political and more popular journalism with more feature articles; it was aimed at a broad audience of sympathizers and their families. Reaching a peak circulation of 100,000 it alternated from full-page cover photos of Joe Lewis bearing the legend *"Joe Lewis vs. Jim Crow: The Battle of the Century,"* to articles titled *"Al Capone Wouldn't Strike"* or *"The Truth About Shirley Temple."*[102]

When young Communists met in convention they no longer limited themselves to speeches and passing resolutions. They now also rocked Madison Square Garden with jitterbugging and even performed a musical revue, "Socialism in Swing," that, as John Gates remarked, must have struck many old-timers as more appropriate for Broadway rather than a Party affair.[103] To raise money for the Japanese language paper, a Party section in Los Angeles held "Japan nights" complete with chop suey and entertainment featuring Japanese plays and songs, as well as judo and fencing exhibitions.[104] Communists also began promoting Big Band music, more specifically black music such as swing, jazz, and even traditional spirituals as embodiments of the country's national character and popular music. Black artists such as W. C. Handy, Fats Waller, Cab Calloway, Jimmy Lunceford, Count Basie, and boogie-woogie pianists Albert Ammons and Meade Lewis, played at Party-sponsored events.[105]

Mike Gold expressed very clearly what Communists had learned from their experiences of the previous years. In commenting on the decision to introduce a sport's page in the *Daily Worker* as a regular feature in 1936, he wrote:

> When you run the news of a strike alongside the news of a baseball game, you are making American workers feel at home. It gives them the feeling that Communism is nothing strange and foreign, but is as real as baseball . . . let's loosen up. Let's begin to prove that we can be a human being as well as a Communist. It isn't a little sect of bookworms or soapboxers.[106]

In terms of membership the Communist policies paid off; in the period between its Ninth and Tenth conventions, the Party registered its strongest growth. By 1938 the Party's membership had more than doubled from three years before, increasing from 30,000 to 75,000 without including the 20,000 members of the Young Communist League. By the end of the decade the Party was recruiting an average of 30,000 new members a year, moving Browder to predict that it would soon reach and surpass the threshold of 200,000.[107] New York still led all other states in the total and relative number of members and recruits, but other states such as Michigan, Ohio, Illinois, Washington, and California also showed substantial growth.[108] By the end of 1936 an important watershed was crossed when for the first time it was announced that the majority of party members were native born. By 1938 the figure was as high as 65 percent.[109] In order to shed the Party's image as an organization of foreigners Charles Krumbein told the Party's Ninth Convention that it was important to promote "American" leaders; Otis Hood speculated that his Yankee background going back to the Pilgrims, was among the considerations that led the Party to run him for mayor of Boston and governor of Massachusetts.[110]

Another important change was that the CPUSA was no longer an organization of unemployed workers as it had been during the early 1930s. By 1936 the majority of its members were employed. Between 1936 and 1938 the number of Communists organized in units directly involved on the shop floor and within unions increased from 6,000 to

18,000.[111] The highest percentage of recruits, however, was not workers in basic industries but rather composed of professionals and white-collar workers possibly attracted by the Party's militant antifascism.[112] Consequently, most new Party members joined neighborhood branches. Although the shift from shop to neighborhood activities raised some concern among the leadership of the CPUSA, it was also viewed with satisfaction because it made it possible to "establish the individual members of the Party as citizens of the community, and thereby enable the Party to participate more successfully in the political life of the assembly, district, wards or precincts."[113] While the number of black members increased to 5,000 their overall percentage compared to the total membership was still viewed as too low. Better results were achieved in recruiting women, particularly those who were employed: their overall percentage compared to total membership rose from under 10 percent to 26 percent.[114] But traditional barriers, that had kept women on the fringes of the Communist party were not easily overcome. Some joined only to learn with dismay at the first meeting that they were the only women in their club. One organizer's marriage foundered because her husband was "honest" but politically "not developed." Many others like her faced opposition from husbands who "talked revolution very good but did not practice what they talked." In some instances the fact that women were becoming more active and were achieving leadership positions generated so much resistance and prejudice that several male Party members had to be expelled.[115] In an attempt to remedy this situation all-women party units were formed in a number of cities to increase their participation in party life. Composed mostly of housewives, many of whom had children, those units met during the day so as not to disrupt family life or raise objections from their husbands who, although possibly Communists as well, would not look favorably on their wives' absence in the evenings. While all-women units did not directly challenge the many sexist cultural traditions prevalent within the Party, they allowed women to engage in political activities and discussions without relying on men. These units helped draw and keep more women into the Party, many of whom then became leaders.[116]

The new branches tried to break the dreariness of internal party life marked by interminable meetings, tedious tasks, and constant requests for contributions to various causes. George Charney recalled how Communists happily threw out *Peter's Manual* that codified the elements of its organization; it was, he wrote, "so incredibly dull as to make the Army manuals seem melodramatic."[117] Members were no longer expected to devote to the Party their entire lives and demands on their leisure time were eased. At the Ninth Convention the decision was made to collect membership dues on a monthly rather than on a weekly basis: this change implicitly made Party participation less burdensome.[118] Despite all the changes, turnover, particularly among recruits, continued to be a major problem. Party leaders still blamed inner Party life ("we bore the newcomers!") and the excessive demands placed on the members' free time for driving recruits away from the CPUSA.[119] Evidently old habits were difficult to break.

The Communist party's new definition of the People's Front policy in the United States was endorsed by the majority of the leadership. There were some uncertainties: a number of Party leaders were still unsure of the precise nature of the Democratic Front, while others feared that the Party was both acting too independently and sliding towards reformism. This led to an outpouring of contradictory statements. Hathaway argued that the Democratic Front was not a revision of the Party's line. The Communist goal, he said, "still remains the building of a nationwide Farmer-Labor party" and the Democratic Front simply "an effort to advance a step closer to the People's Front."[120] A month later Gene Dennie said the exact opposite: the Farmer-Labor party was not the only form of People's Front in the United States. This view could only be supported by those for whom "Marxism has become a dogma and not a guide to action." In fact, he concluded, the Democratic Front could well have become the specific People's Front in the United States.[121] Others such as Bittelman, Gil Green, and again Dennis, resorted to extensive quotes from Marxist classics to justify the Party's defense of bourgeois democracy as consistent with its socialist objectives.[122]

Browder himself must have felt some misgivings about the changes of the previous months, during which the Party had traveled in unchartered territory. Reviewing a volume of articles and speeches by Dimitrov, he explicitly linked the Democratic Front with the International's Seventh Congress. At the Tenth Convention, he wrote, the CPUSA had "matured as an American party, standing fully on its own two feet, and sinking roots among the American masses." This process had begun with the Seventh Congress and was the expression of "the great traditions and teachings of Lenin and Stalin."[123]

While these contradictory statements represented attempts to provide an orthodox foundation for a new policy that the Party was pursuing eagerly, for Foster they were only attempts to rationalize a policy that he saw as leading the CPUSA down a dangerous road. Since his rise to general secretary of the CPUSA in 1934, Browder had eclipsed Foster as the Party's recognized leader and spokesman. After returning to active politics in 1935, having been on the sidelines recovering from his 1932 heart attack, Foster had been relegated to the role of respected elder statesman, limited to agitational writings on secondary matters, and he devoted much of his time to writing two autobiographies.[124] Foster's doctrinal views caused him to disagree with the Party's new course, but there were other problems as well. The relationship between Foster and Browder had been strained since Browder displaced him in the Party and Foster took every opportunity to tangle with his former lieutenant.

The first open clash had come in 1936 over the Communist party's position on the presidential elections; Foster's defeat must have been all the more painful due to the Comintern's decision to endorse his rival as the Party's standard bearer in 1936. Events since the elections increased Foster's opposition to Browder's policies. Foster believed that the new line was shadowing bourgeois-democratic forces, and, in so doing, soft-pedaling the Communist party's revolutionary program; "recently," he wrote, "there has been considerable slackness in this respect."[125] The Communist party "is not only a Party of the progressive immediate demands, but also the Party of proletarian revolution."[126] In applying their policy, Communists had been too soft in their attitude toward other progressive forces. According to Foster, within the labor movement the CPUSA had accepted a subaltern role trailing Lewis, and the *Daily Worker* had become the mouthpiece of the CIO. Foster complained of the tendency to "liquidate our Party into the mass trade union movement." There was "inadequate criticism of Roosevelt and Lewis" as well as a failure to "put forward our own program (including our revolutionary slogans) in the mass movements led by these men."[127] Foster's view of the Party's role remained that of channeling all mass movements toward the Party. The CPUSA was to place itself openly at the helm of the growing mass movement; he measured the Party's influence only in those terms and not by what it achieved as part of a broader movement. Foster believed that while in some cases it was acceptable to support candidates on the Democratic ticket, the Party had to go "much further." It was to assume the lead in placing "united front candidates independent of the old parties, for the crystallization of all the toilers' scattered political forces into a great national Farmer-Labor party."[128]

Foster was not the only leader concerned with the Party's new course. Sam Darcy, who in 1938 had become Party leader in Minnesota, felt that because of their activities within organizations, such as the MFLP, Communists were losing their identity as an independent political force. The leader least receptive to change was Bittelman who, because of his orthodox views, had a reputation of treating the writings of Marx and Lenin as sacred scriptures. While agreeing that there was no immediate prospect for the formation of a Farmer-Labor party, Bittelman insisted that such a party must remain the Communist objective.[129]

Browder and Foster once again had brought their differences to Moscow in April 1937 and in January 1938. On both occasions Browder prevailed, since the Comintern endorsed his changing definition of the People's Front policy in the United States.[130] Foster himself later related how he had been criticized by the leadership of the Comintern for his opposition to Browder's policies. Dimitrov himself had charged that Foster's opposition to the Party's role in the People's Front policy showed "certain sectarian remnants."[131]

The antagonism between Foster and Browder eventually required a special meeting of the Party's Political Committee at the end of March 1939. The complete minutes of this meeting—one of the few such documents available—provide a clear picture of Foster's isolation within the Party leadership. The meeting began with Foster's complaint that he had been relegated to a secondary role by Browder. Conceding his limited theoretical capacities, Foster spoke of his abilities as a leader of mass movements. The Party, he complained, "was not making use of my services." He protested bitterly that "every proposal of any importance" that he made Browder voted down or "waved aside." Foster accused Browder of having put "padlocks" on his hands.[132] Foster also complained that his ally, Sam Darcy, had been demoted from full to candidate member of the national committee.[133] Browder skillfully assumed a calm and conciliatory tone, and remained on the sidelines; no one stood up in defense of Foster as speaker after speaker lambasted him for his political views and personality while praising Browder's leadership.[134] Gene Dennis was the first to speak, and set the tone for subsequent speeches. He criticized Foster for having turned what was essentially a political difference with the political committee about overall policies into a personal matter against Browder. Dennis concluded by warning that "if there isn't a certain change, or better understanding on the part of WZF [Foster] in particular regarding EB [Browder], who is the leader of our Party, it will create serious difficulties for our Party and WZF."[135]

All the other members expressed similar views. Roy Hudson, union secretary, lavishly praised Browder: Communists measured "the growth of the Party in terms of the growth of EB." On the other hand, Foster had "the closest thing to a persecution complex of anybody that I ever saw."[136] Gil Green, head of the YCL, and the strongest supporter of Browder's policies within the Party's top leadership, called him "the greatest thinker in our midst" and gave him the credit for making the Party "more of an American Party, tied up with the masses."[137]

Browder's language and his traditional demeanor fit the Party's new image and the requirements of the People's Front policy and culture. Moscow was quick to recognize these attributes; at the end of the 1930s Browder's prestige in Moscow was such that Dimitrov praised him as "the foremost Marxist in the English-speaking world." At the same time it was suggested that Foster be removed from leadership positions.[138] Browder had a firm hold on the Party and in a Stalin-like fashion, he became the object of glorification. The *Daily Worker* carried greetings for Browder's birthday from leading Communists, praising him as "a sterling Bolshevik comrade," and at the Party's Tenth Convention all the speeches (with the exception of Foster's) greatly praised his leadership.[139]

Whatever the motivations, however, Foster's concerns over the new course Browder had impressed on the Communist party touched upon a real problem: could Communists blend defense of bourgeois democracy with revolutionary ideology? Since 1936 the Party had dropped its slogan "for a Soviet America," which, while questionable, had provided Communists with a coherent view of societal change. The slogan's disappearance was not accompanied by plausible theoretical explanation nor was an alternative offered up in its stead. As Al Richmond put it, Communists were left in "a vacuum," with the "lively ghost of the old slogan."[140]

Throughout the People's Front years, the CPUSA never concealed its ultimate objective, a socialist revolution based on the Soviet model—the only way American Communists were able to imagine it—in which gradual transition played no role. As Bittelman clearly stated, the People's Front policy was merely a way to "accelerate the maturing of the socialist revolution."[141] Increasingly however, the belief in the Bolshevik revolutionary model was in tension with the Party's emphasis on the struggle for progressive unions, on pushing the New Deal toward more left-wing policies, and particularly on the defense of democracy. For the time being the Party was unable to solve this dilemma. The result was that the CPUSA avoided the issue altogether and increased its support for Roosevelt, concentrating on short term objectives and accomplishments and downplaying its revolutionary ideology.[142] It postponed the issue of achieving socialism to an uncertain but presumably more favorable future; Communist leaders downplayed their radicalism to such a point that the *New Republic* noted that the struggle for socialism had been relegated so far to the background that "one needs a telescope to see it at all."[143]

Nevertheless, among Party leaders Browder certainly recognized the issues raised by the Party's new course since on various occasions he addressed the problem of the relationship between the Party's defense of democracy and its continued battle for socialism. The program of the Democratic Front was not a socialist one, Browder noted, but rather it was "the minimum of those measures necessary, under capitalism, to preserve and extend democracy, all those things which have been the heart of the American tradition in the past, ever since the revolutionary foundation of the United States."[144] Communists determined that socialism would not advance through vague slogans. Given that the majority of the population was "not yet prepared for socialism," the CPUSA presented a program not for the revolutionary overthrow of capitalism but one that could be realized within the framework of the existing economic system.[145] The Party's campaign for the extension of social legislation, higher living standards for workers, and limitation of the powers of the Supreme Court was a program "which the masses are ready to support, to point out the path along which the people can maintain and advance their fundamental interests and rights."[146] In a most significant statement, Browder said that Communists could not remain indifferent to how a defensive anti-fascist unity would eventually lead to the defeat of capitalism. This "transition" however, would not be the result of vague revolutionary slogans "disconnected from everyday life." It would not be "a discouraged, defeated and demoralized working class that will take up and realize the great program of socialism," but rather "the enthusiastic, victorious and organized workers who will move forward from victories in the defensive struggle to the offensive, and finally to socialism."[147]

Browder did not spell out what would be the forms of the transition to socialism. It was clear, however, that the Communist leader had abandoned the view that the Communist party would become a mass organization and eventually reach its revolutionary goals as an inevitable consequence of economic hardship. Rather Browder believed that workers were to achieve class consciousness through a long and gradual process, the result of the struggle for major reforms within the framework of bourgeois democratic institutions. Implicitly, then, the secretary of the CPUSA was setting the American experience apart from the Bolshevik revolutionary model.

6

COMMUNISTS AND LABOR

> This great mass movement [for industrial unionism] needed our still small Communist party in order to achieve these results, just as we needed this great mass movement to find scope for our program and energies, to bring us once and for all out of our isolation into the broad streams of the mass life of America.
>
> Earl Browder, 1936[1]

At the same time Communists sought to become accepted constituents of a broad based political coalition, they likewise approached the labor movement. The Party's activities within the labor movement, and especially its role in the formation of the CIO, were indeed the most conspicuous achievements of the People's Front period.

The growing demand within the AFL for industrial unionism, having gained momentum with the labor upheaval of 1933–1934, was strengthened further in 1935 by the approval of the Wagner Act, providing federal protection for organizing and collective bargaining that the NRA had failed to enforce. The upsurge of unionization created by this situation further widened the gulf between advocates of industrial and craft unions. At the AFL's Atlantic City convention in October 1935, the industrialists, led by John L. Lewis, were defeated in their attempt to place the federation's resources behind a campaign for industrial unionism. Despite this setback, the image of Lewis slugging "Big Bill" Hutcheson in the jaw and sending him sprawling among overturned chairs, represented for the advocates of industrial unionism a blow struck against craft unionism; Lewis' action gave him, as well as the new organization he was soon to found, the fighting image that appealed to advocates of industrial unionism. On November 9, 1935, three weeks after the end of the AFL convention Lewis, together with Sidney Hillman and David Dubinsky, founded the Committee for

Industrial Organization to promote the organization of mass-production workers into industrial unions within the AFL. For the next five years Lewis dominated this organization.[2]

Recalling his reaction to the founding of the CIO, Steve Nelson likened it to "when you fall in love, you don't notice the pimples."[3] Despite this new found love, the Party did not elope; its relationship with the CIO was instead a gradual courtship. Within the CPUSA there were strong reservations about joining the CIO, since Party leaders still mistrusted Lewis for his anti-Communist crusades and his exclusion of Party members from the UMW. At a Central Committee meeting at the end of May 1935, Browder referred to Lewis and his allies' campaign for industrial unionism as an attempt to "make use of the deep-going currents among the radicalized masses for their own reactionary needs."[4] Shortly before the historic 1935 AFL convention, Foster still listed the president of the miners' union as one of the mainstays of fascism in the United States.[5] As Jack Stachel reported after the convention, Communists, bearing in mind Lewis's past record, judged him on the basis of every proposal he made. "It was not possible," Stachel warned, "to predict with certainty what will be his role tomorrow."[6]

Despite misgivings the CPUSA moved closer to Lewis and eventually embraced the CIO as a consequence of events. In the Party's view new forces had taken up the battle for industrial unionism which Communists had advocated and practiced for years; the Party's commitment to these goals was such that it willingly set all other considerations aside to further them.

The first favorable mention of Lewis came during the AFL convention in an article in the *Daily Worker* by Carl Reeve; he commented on the miners' president's offensive against Matthew Woll and John Frey, the two ideological spokesmen for craft-unionism. The next laudatory report came two days later in an editorial commenting on Lewis's demand for industrial unionism: "Whatever may be the motives of these union officials [Lewis and Charles Howard, president of the Typographical workers union], whatever admissions they may have made, their stand for industrial unionism marks a new era in the history of the American Federation of Labor."[7] Among the top Communist leaders, Browder was one of the first to appreciate the importance of the CIO. Consequently, at the Central Committee meeting in November, he pledged support to Lewis and his allies.[8]

The Party's support was promoted by Lewis's decision to set aside his political differences with Communists in favor of strengthening industrial unionism. By launching a frontal assault on the open shop, Lewis set out to do battle with corporate giants, a momentous task which would determine the future of the CIO and of industrial unionism. The head of the UMW realized that to insure victory he could not rely exclusively on UMW organizers, whose chief characteristic was their loyalty to him rather than their organizing capacity. Hence, while placing men he trusted at the head of the various organizing campaigns, Lewis had to look elsewhere for experienced and dedicated unionists and give up political or ideological screening tests.

Setting aside old quarrels and antagonisms, Lewis turned to many of those old foes he had driven out of the UMW, such as John Brophy, Powers Hapgood, and Adolph Germer. He also drew on left-wingers from the garment unions such as Rose Pesotta and Leo Krzycki. The miners' president, while remaining firmly anti-Communist, needed the support and commitment of Communist organizers. At the end of October, in what certainly was a gesture of friendship toward Communists, Lewis gave Marguerite Young an exclusive interview for the *Daily Worker*.[9] Communists and Party sympathizers Len DeCaux and Lee Pressman were placed at the top of the new organization, one as editor of the *CIO News* and the other as the CIO's general counsel, becoming Lewis's close and trusted advisers. Shortly after being named CIO director of organization by Lewis, Brophy visited Browder in New York City and asked for the Party's cooperation in building the CIO, particularly by providing organizers. Browder readily accepted and pledged the CPUSA's full support. Initially the Party had made the end of red-baiting and the restoration of union democracy both in the UMW and in newly forming unions the conditions for its participation. But the Communists' eagerness to be part of the movement was such that they willingly joined even if it was clear that the official restrictions discriminating against Party members were not going to be lifted.[10]

Communist organizers were indisputably an essential asset and the leadership of the CIO went to considerable lengths to shield them from attack. At the first convention of the Steel Workers Organizing Committee, Philip Murray ruled out of order a motion condemning Communism.[11] Claiming ignorance Lewis brushed aside red-baiting attacks. "I do not turn my organizers and CIO members upside down and shake them," he said, "to see what kind of literature falls out of their pockets."[12] When pressed further on this issue by David

Dubinsky, Lewis gave his famous reply: "Who gets the bird—the hunter or the dog?"[13]

When Lewis became the moving force behind the drive to organize workers in mass production industries into industrial unions, Communists were reconciled to their former antagonist. Browder recalled, Lewis, "the nemesis of the Communists in the twenties, was transformed into their patron saint in the thirties."[14] In fact, in the eyes of Communists, Lewis competed with Roosevelt in praise worthiness. At the end of 1937, Browder told Canadian Communists that democracy could survive in the capitalist world only through adoption of programs similar to those "of John L. Lewis and the Committee for Industrial Organizations and the economic reforms and the peace program of President Roosevelt." Bittelman wrote that the programs of Roosevelt, Lewis, and the CIO formed the "basic program of the People's Front."[15]

As the trade-union civil war between the leaders of the CIO and those of the AFL raged, the Party walked a narrow line, on one hand identifying with the objectives of the CIO, while on the other opposing a break with the AFL. The Communist predicament is understandable. A split would not only have weakened organized labor but the CPUSA had just recently given up "dual unionism" to carry on the fight for industrial unionism inside the AFL. Within the federation Communists had become a sizable force and controlled a number of unions. Jack Stachel told the Party's Ninth Convention that the number of Communists in the AFL had grown from 2,000 to 15,000 in the period from 1934 to the summer of 1936. Party members sat as delegates at every AFL state convention and there were twenty at the national convention. Brown estimated that 39 percent of the Party's membership was in the AFL. In New York State alone, out of 16,000 Party members, 10,000 belonged to the AFL.[16] This was a difficult position to yield after having been for so long on the margins of organized labor.

Had a split occurred, Communist leaders feared that most workers would not have left the security of the AFL unions, condemning the CIO to the same fate of all the other unions which had previously attempted to challenge the AFL. Consequently, the CPUSA feared that it would find itself again isolated from the mainstream of the labor movement. As one historian pointedly remarked, Communists were afraid of going out on a limb as they "did not know how far and how determinedly Lewis, Hillman, and Dubinsky intended to proceed."[17]

Mindful of the failure of the TUUL, the Party at first believed that the fight for industrial unionism could be pursued within the AFL with CIO forces wresting the leadership of the federation away from the leaders of the craft unions, and to this end the Party adopted the slogan "For a Powerful, United A.F.L."[18] An editorial in the *Daily Worker* commented on Lewis's resignation as vice-president of the AFL, categorizing it as "ill advised." The editorial ended: "The workers in the A.F. of L. should be on guard against any tendency to carry these developments toward a split. They should fight for continued trade union unity, for industrial unionism, and for class struggle policies."[19]

The Party, however, had to work hard to keep its followers in line. Peggy Dennis described the mood among the rank-and-file and Party supporters in Wisconsin as strongly in favor of bolting from the AFL: the sentiment was "Screw the piecards, let's leave 'em cold." Eugene Dennis had to use all his influence to convince the supporters of industrial unionism of the importance of remaining within the AFL, a concern repeated in a number of speeches at the Ninth Convention. Roy Hudson criticized all left-wingers that harbored the illusion "that the quicker the progressive forces get out of the reactionary A.F. of L. the better it will be." If such a course were to be adopted, he added, it would only lead to "isolating the unions supporting the CIO movement from broad sections of workers in the unions still controlled and dominated by the craft unions."[20] In a Labor Day network broadcast in 1936, Browder declared that the response to the decision of the Executive Committee of the AFL to suspend the CIO unions was to be a "ringing cry for *unity* which will defeat all those who seek to weaken or destroy the labor movement."[21] Foster wrote that the Party's trade union policy was to revolutionize the AFL by "systematic work within its ranks."[22]

At first, then, Communists kept the unions they controlled in the AFL. In some notable cases, however, such as the United Electrical Workers (UE) and the Auto Workers Union, where Party members held a number of high leadership positions, but were not the majority, they followed the general sentiment into the CIO. Only in the spring of 1937, after the victories against General Motors and United States Steel, did most Party-led unions leave the AFL for the CIO. In May 1937, James Matles led fourteen lodges, totaling 14,000 members, of the Association of Machinists into the CIO where they merged with the UE. The Transport Workers Union affiliated to the CIO in the spring of 1937; and the Federation of Woodworkers in mid-July after which it took the name International Woodworkers of America. Harry Bridges led his Longshoremen's union into the CIO in August, consequently being named West Coast director of the CIO; and the Newspaper Guild whose affiliation to the AFL in July 1936 had been supported by its Communists members, switched to the CIO in June of the following year.[23] While the Party's influence was growing within the CIO, it also remained a factor within the AFL where Communists and their sympathizers were strong in the New York City locals of the Painters' Union, the Hotel and Restaurant Employees, and Local 5 of the Federation of Teachers, 500 of whom marched in the Communist parade on May Day 1936.[24]

The vigorous and militant CIO fired the imagination and hopes of Communists; in the words of an organizer it was "where the action was." Not very long after the formation of the CIO, Jack Stachel enthusiastically described it to a Communist audience as the "TUUL with muscle."[25] Party unionists were swept up by this situation and rushed into building the CIO; militant and devoted to the struggle for improved working conditions and for industrial unionism, Communists were in the front ranks and helped shape the union movement through the end of the decade.

Lewis could not have found better trained and more devoted unionists than the Communists for his drive to build the CIO. Browder estimated that one third to one fourth of the Party's membership had some degree of experience in union work, much of it acquired during the early struggles of the TUUL and from Communist activities among the unemployed. Always hardworking, Communists were experts in the various techniques of setting up cores of union members in plants without the company's knowledge; they knew how to write, print, and hand out leaflets and how to set up a newspaper and run an office. In a report to Stachel, the Party's trade union secretary, John Steuben, compared Communist organizers to those drawn from the UMW and commented on the latter's inadequacies. He was amazed "how people can be so long in the labor movement and know so little!"[26] In many of the industries that the CIO was trying to unionize, Communists counted on skeleton organizations and widespread contacts dating back to the TUUL activities which provided the first nucleus around which CIO unions would be formed. In certain cities, such as Memphis, Birmingham, and Tampa, notwithstanding very difficult local conditions and strong opposition by local authorities, Communists conducted the CIO's organizing activities and successfully promoted black and white labor unity. When faced with a particularly difficult plant to unionize CIO offices did not shy away from appealing directly to local Party organizers for help.[27]

In his biography of John L. Lewis, Saul Alinsky gave the following assessment of the Communists' role on building the CIO: "Communists worked indefatigably, with no job being too menial or unimportant. They literally poured themselves completely into their assignment . . . The fact is that the Communist party made a major contribution in the organization of the unorganized for the CIO."[28]

The CPUSA made available all its resources and turned over to the union some of its best people: the influx of Communists into the CIO reached such proportions that the CPUSA determined it was being stripped of its best cadres at the expense of Party activities and had to fight to retain at least some of them.[29] John Williamson, at the time the Party's Ohio state chairman, claimed that the entire state leadership of the Party as well as of the YCL's was absorbed into staff of the Steel Workers Organizing Committee (SWOC). This included, among others, Gus Hall in charge of Warren and Niles, and John Steuben, in charge of Youngstown.[30]

When Lewis made the unionization of steel the CIO's first priority, Communists became invaluable in organizing workers, particularly in areas where the power of the national steel companies was the strongest. Foster later wrote that of 200 full-time SWOC organizers, sixty were Party members. Communists were in the front lines of the organization of steel workers from the iron range of northern Minnesota to the steel areas of Ohio and Alabama.[31] The Party helped the organizing campaign by setting up its own steel organizing committee, led by Foster; it published a number of pamphlets for use by Communist organizers in steel that drew on the past experiences of the IWW, TUEL, and TUUL and outlined the most effective methods for organizing, running strikes, and setting up a union. The Party also ran special auto and steel inserts in the *Daily Worker*.[32]

Particularly valuable for SWOC was the Party's role in recruiting and ensuring the support of ethnic groups and fraternal organizations. The International Workers Order was crucial in this effort. William Gebert, the Party's district organizer in Pittsburgh and leader of the Polish section of the IWO, was put in charge of the SWOC's efforts to organize foreign-born fraternal organizations. As such Gebert chaired a conference of the organizations of the foreign born in Pittsburgh at the end of October 1936, attended by 447 representatives from Lithuanian, Polish, Croatian, Serbian, Slovenian, Ukranian, Russian, and other groups. The delegates were addressed by Philip Murray and greeted by Lewis.[33]

Communists also helped rally black support for the union movement through the National Negro Congress (NNC). Founded in February 1936 on the initiative of the Party, the NNC represented the convergence of Communists with a range of black personalities and organizations. While the organization campaigned in favor of a federal anti-lynching bill and against racial discrimination, the preponderance of its activities centered around bringing blacks into the labor movement. As the battle for the organization of steel unfolded, the NNC mobilized its resources and played an important role in assuring the support of black steel workers for SWOC. In early February 1937 the NNC sponsored a national conference of black organizations, attended by 186 delegates representing 110 organizations to rally support for SWOC. Chairman of the conference was Benjamin L. Careathers, SWOC organizer and a leading black Communist in Pittsburgh. The NNC's activities in favor of organized labor were very successful. Everywhere it brought large numbers of blacks into SWOC, in some areas they signed up even in greater proportion than whites.[34]

While the CIO was concentrating on organizing steel workers, major and more significant events took place in the auto industry where, again, Party members played a central role. Communists had been very prominent in the organization of auto workers and had established a presence and a nucleus of workers in that industry. In Detroit the *Party Organizer* reported that all of the Party's efforts "were centered on helping the organization of the auto workers."[35] In the early organizing stages of the United Auto Workers, which had to be carried out in the greatest secrecy, Wyndham Mortimer and Bob Travis relied on fellow Communists, the only people they could trust in a company town where spies and stooges were everywhere.[36]

Communists were at the forefront when, on December 30, 1936, workers at Fisher Body No. 1 in Flint refused to leave the plant at the end of the day shift, sparking the great sit-down movement of 1937[37]. Once the sit-down strike began, the Party's Central Committee called upon all Communists to "rally wholeheartedly and at once to the aid of the strikers."[38] The *Party Organizer* instructed Communists to place "themselves at the total disposal of the union and to do everything possible toward winning the strike." Weinstone, who since 1934 had been the Party's Michigan district organizer, and Williamson acted as close advisers to the strike leaders, meeting with some of them daily.[39] Communists were present at every stage and level of the confrontation: from its leadership down to the most menial tasks.[40] Bob Travis was the chief UAW organizer in Flint; Henry Kraus was in charge of the union's paper as well as of publicity. Bud Simons, the head of the strike committee inside Fisher 1, was a Communist as were most of the committee's members. Bob Travis played an essential role in devising the basically military strategy for the capture of the vital Chevrolet No. 4 engine plant in February. By enlarging the strike, this action helped bring General Motors to its knees.[41]

Outside the plant Communists also organized a network of support for the strikers. In Flint, Dorothy Kraus and Margaret Anderson formed a Women's Auxiliary of the UAW which organized a number of essential activities in support of the strike: it helped picket and provided material support for the strikers and their families, as well as coordinated community support. Dorothy Kraus also chaired the UAW food committee that ran the restaurant across the street from Fisher 1 that fed as many as 6,000 during the strike. After the first clashes with police a Women's Emergency Brigade was established to allow women to fight beside the men. Brigade members were noticeable for their red berets and ax handles.[42]

The autoworkers achieved victory because of their militancy and discipline, which inspired morale and enabled them to resist all attempts to dislodge them from the occupied factories. The sit-down movement was also successful because of the general political atmosphere at the local, state, and federal level which, if not prounion, was at least tolerant of its activities, effectively neutralizing the corporation's traditional arsenal of repressive methods against trade unionism. Eventually through the auspices of Governor Frank Murphy and the pressure from President Roosevelt, a negotiated settlement was reached: on February 11, General Motors agreed to recognize the UAW as the bargaining representative of its members and to end discrimination against union members.[43]

The victory over General Motors was not just a feat of the UAW. The CIO gained legitimacy as a national labor union, and unionism in mass-production industries was advanced. The fall of this citadel of the open shop led to agreements with all the major automobile and auto parts industries except Ford, and increased the pace of unionization and labor activities throughout the nation. In the wake of these successes, sit-down strikes spread across the nation. In 1937 over 400,000 workers engaged in similar forms of protest. Similar drives were launched in the rubber and textile industries and among radio and electrical workers.

The settlement of the auto strike, however, had paramount repercussions in the organization of steel. By January 1, 1937, Murray claimed a SWOC membership of 125,000. In early March 1937, U.S. Steel, the world's largest company and the bastion of the open shop, faced with this display of union strength, worker militancy, and uncooperative state and federal officials, coupled with fears of the effects of a prolonged strike, abruptly caved in without a struggle and signed a contract recognizing SWOC, granting a 10 percent wage increase, an eight-hour work day and forty-hour work week. Following the lead of U.S. Steel, a number of other independent steel companies signed similar agreements with the union. By May SWOC could claim a membership in excess of 300,000. By March, the CIO's victories over General Motors and U.S. Steel opened the union's flood gates as hundreds of thousands of workers poured into the CIO.[44]

In October 1937, the CIO held its first national conference in Atlantic City. The symbolic nature of this meeting was evident as delegates from industrial unions across the country met in the same hall from which two years earlier they had walked out on the AFL. The meeting was a celebration of the union's accomplishments. The CIO claimed a membership of 4 million members, and while it was possible that this figure was inflated, the fact remained that in less than two years the CIO had eclipsed the AFL. Among the major unions were the UMW with 600,000 members; UAW with 375,000; SWOC with 525,000; UE with 137,000; and the Textile Workers Organizing Committee with 450,000. Engulfed in the multitude of labor delegates from across the country, Communists could not help but feel proud of their contribution to the CIO's success.[45]

The Communist-CIO tie was a mutually beneficial arrangement. While the CIO had much to gain from the commitment and devotion of Communists to industrial unionism, so did the Party. In an unusually candid statement, Browder recognized that "we needed this great mass movement to find scope for our program and energies, to bring us once and for all out of our isolation into the broad streams of the mass life in America."[46] In order to preserve this alliance Communists were careful to prevent any domestic issue from disturbing good relations with the union leadership or undermining the struggle of CIO unions for recognition.

Communists were concerned with proving to their allies that they were a reliable force. Learning from their past experiences, particularly those of the 1920s when the "packing" of conventions had backfired, Communists willingly accepted lesser positions and refrained from taking power even in those situations where they were in a position to do so. During the strike at General Motors in Cleveland, the Party, in the name of "unity, consolidation, democracy," did not put forth any of its people to head the local union; instead it supported the election of those non-Communists whom Communists considered "good progressives." At a SWOC conference at the end of 1937, the Party's leadership enjoined its unionists to keep the number of Communist delegates from any one local at no more than 40 percent.[47] Foster told Communists not to "scramble" for union posts; they were to achieve leadership positions only by demonstrating "superior work in the class struggle."[48] Although the Party continued to criticize the lack of democracy within several CIO unions, it was not about to endanger its entry by raising this question forcefully.

In later years several Communist leaders reproached the Party's willingness to accept a secondary role within unions.[49] By far the most critical was Foster. In his history of the Party, Foster wrote that Communists "were in a strong enough position locally at the time to have insisted that representative steel workers be brought into the top leadership; but they failed to do so." He placed the blame for this situation on Browder's leadership. While serving his urge to denigrate his, by then, former rival, Foster's view had very little basis of fact.[50] In spite of their proven commitment and essential organizing capabilities Communists entered the CIO on Lewis's terms; within it they remained a closely watched minority. If at any time they had pushed for more power or for an official acknowledgment of their presence, they would have undoubtedly lost the acceptance and any position of influence they had gained.

Just as they had done in the TUUL days, Communists refrained from putting forward revolutionary slogans and socialist objectives. The decision to set aside the Party's long term objectives was not only the result of concern with jeopardizing their precarious situation within the trade-union movement, it was also motivated by a recognition of the nonrevolutionary character of the strike movement.

Despite the occupation of private property by workers taking physical possession of factories and of the machinery within them, the sit-down movement was not seen as leading to the expropriation of property or as a direct challenge to capitalism. A spokesman for the Fisher No. 2 strikers told reporters, "We're just here protecting our jobs. We don't aim to keep the plants or try to run them, but we want to see that nobody takes our jobs."[51] Weinstone wrote that "the workers were not motivated by revolutionary aims in occupying the plants but were limiting themselves to a form of pressure to achieve their immediate ends."[52] Most importantly, however, Communists did not raise revolutionary objectives because they recognized that effective union organizers were to fight above all for the workers' immediate needs. The degree to which Communists were successful in this regard determined the esteem and support they received.

The Party's eagerness to discard its conspiratorial image and refute charges of Communist "domination," may as well be seen in its decision to eliminate shop papers and to dissolve Party fractions within unions that acted as caucuses to coordinate the application of the Party's policy.[53] These changes also provided Communist union leaders with greater flexibility and increased their effectiveness: as long as they did not endanger the Left-Center alliance within the labor movement, Party unionists were free from constant higher supervision, or from having to clear all their policies with fractions.[54] According to Browder, Communist or sympathetic union leaders had only to read the *Daily Worker* to know what the correct line was.[55] However, even if the Party was relinquishing some of the supervision over the activities of unionists, Roy Hudson warned that it would continue to "reserve the right to decide who is worthy of membership in the Communist party."[56]

The Party's position during the long and bitter factional struggle within the UAW provides the best example of how unwilling the CPUSA was to endanger its ties with the leadership of the CIO. At the UAW's second convention held in South Bend, Indiana, in April 1936, Communists deliberately chose not to take advantage of the strong influence they had within that union to elect the popular Wyndham Mortimer as its first president. If Mortimer had decided to run, the Party was sure he would have easily won. Party leaders John Williamson and William Weinstone, however, advised Communist delegates not to risk possible divisions within the union and instead support the election of Homer Martin. This decision resulted from fear that Mortimer's close connection to the Communist party could split the delegates and alarm the leadership of the CIO, and possibly lead to the breakup of the young and still weak UAW. Consequently Mortimer withdrew his candidacy, he became the union's first vice president and was sent to supervise union activities in Michigan.[57]

By all accounts Homer Martin lacked the essential qualities to head a union. His initial popularity came from his evangelical background and his talents as an orator, important leadership assets that particularly appealed to workers from the fundamentalist South.[58] While impressive public speaking was a valuable asset in the formative stages of the new union, this sole characteristic was hardly adequate to the laborious task of leading the UAW. Martin's behavior has been described as erratic, impulsive, and unpredictable. Easily swayed, he lacked the patience necessary to conduct long negotiations and had a habit of disappearing at crucial times, leaving most of the responsibilities to his subordinates. Martin had become such a liability that during the settlement of the General Motors strike, Lewis and Mortimer convinced him to go on a speaking tour of a number of locals to build up morale. Martin readily accepted the assignment to get away from the tediousness of negotiating. Eventually, Martin began to resent the contempt with which he was treated by other union officials, and he feared he would eventually be replaced. He therefore struck back.

In 1936, Martin had already given some signs of his uneasiness with Communists when he replaced Mortimer as head of the union's organizing efforts in Flint. Martin was helped in his campaign by Jay Lovestone, the former Communist secretary who had many gripes with his former comrades. Lovestone became Martin's closest adviser and supplied a number of his supporters to fill vital union positions.

Soon after the conclusion of the General Motors strike, in an effort to strengthen his position, Martin began trying to dislodge Communists and Socialists from the union. This led to a protracted period of factional struggle that lasted until early 1939.[59] In March 1937, Martin accused Communists of having fomented opposition among Chrysler workers to the agreement he and Lewis had negotiated with the company in which the union was to evacuate plants in return for the company's promise not to resume production while talks were under way. Weinstone, the top Communist leader in Michigan, stepped in and praised the agreement as a "step forward."[60] While certainly a number of Communists were among the workers that protested the agreement, they received an immediate and public reprimand. Browder told Michigan Communists that some of them "were entirely in error in thinking they saw intolerable compromises and wrong methods in the settlement of the Chrysler strike." He added, "we are a fully responsible Party, and our sub-divisions and fractions do not independently take any actions which threaten to change our whole national relationship with a great and growing mass movement." Even if the fears of local Communists were legitimate, Browder said, "it was necessary to proceed with much more tact, foresight and consideration."[61]

As spontaneous and unauthorized "quickies" and wildcat strikes continued, Martin again accused the Communist party of being the instigator. In line with its policy of avoiding breaks with union leadership, once again the Party officially denounced such strikes. Communist unionists such as Mortimer, Kraus, and Travis repeatedly and publicly condemned the indiscriminate resort to strikes. William Weinstone released a statement in which he declared "unequivocally and emphatically that the Communists and the Communist party had never in the past and do not now in any shape, manner or form advocate or support unauthorized and wildcat action and regard such strikes as gravely injurious to the union's welfare."[62]

For the sake of unity the Party continued its policy of conciliation toward Martin. Bill Gebert gave the UAW president credit for the growth of the union and, in September 1937, Browder wrote Martin a letter in which he denied that the Communist party had any intention of taking over the union and blamed any "misunderstanding" on Jay Lovestone.[63] Communists failed to react strongly even after Martin dismissed Henry Kraus as editor of the *United Automobile Worker*, tried to exile Mortimer to St. Louis, and finally demoted Bob Travis, together with Victor and Roy Reuther. The Communist party resisted Martin's provocations and avoided confrontation, frequently to the discontent of many of its members. Communists went so far as to endorse Martin's reelection at the August 1937 UAW convention.[64] Despite this restraint, the Party failed in its intent to appease Martin.

Only in early January 1938 did the Party openly begin to oppose Martin when it became obvious that he had lost most of his support from the rank and file as well as from non-Communist union leaders. Martin's opposition to collective security and his endorsement of the Ludlow Amendment, calling for a national referendum before the Congress could commit the country to war, further encouraged the Communists to end an uneasy coexistence. Eventually even John L.

Lewis supported the anti-Martin forces, shifting the balance of power into their hands.[65]

Once Martin had been removed, however, the Communist party passed up yet another opportunity for leadership of the UAW. At the UAW convention in Cleveland in April 1939, Communists and their allies controlled about 85 percent of the delegates. The election of the new president, Mortimer wrote, was "a toss up" between himself and George F. Addes. A younger man with excellent organization talents, while not a Communist, Addes was close to the left-wing caucus within the union. So strong was the Communist influence that Sidney Hillman and Philip Murray arrived at the convention in the hope of preventing the election of either Mortimer or Addes. The two CIO leaders campaigned forcefully for the election of R. J. Thomas, the union's acting president, a relative unknown with limited experience, who had only recently defected from Martin's camp. Hillman and Murray found support for their pro-Thomas campaign among the Party's top leadership. Again faced with the choice between passing up the opportunity to place a close ally at the top of the UAW or possibly antagonizing the leadership of the CIO, the leadership of the Party backed the election of Thomas. Earl Browder, Louis Budenz, William Gebert, and Roy Hudson arrived at the convention to persuade reluctant Communist delegates to support Thomas' election. After much pressure, Addes withdrew from the race and Thomas was elected. To limit further the power of the left, Hillman and Murray also obtained the abolition of the vice presidency, thus eliminating from the UAW top leadership Wyndham Mortimer, who was then sent off to organize aircraft workers in California.[66] Communists had thus deliberately given up positions of power and influence, and in fact their position within the union became weaker than it had been before the convention.

Despite all their efforts and commitment, Communists never gained full acceptance within the CIO. Recruited when needed and closely watched at all times, the moment they finished organizing or gained a following they were quickly transferred or more often summarily dismissed. Consequently, Communist unionists had few opportunities either to establish strong ties with the organizations that they had created or to influence their policies. Eventually, to curb the left's influence, Lewis limited Harry Bridges' responsibilities from being regional director of the entire West Coast to being just director of California. Determined to be too close to the Left, John Brophy was removed from his position as CIO director and replaced with Allan Haywood from the UMW.[67]

Acknowledged Communists on SWOC payrolls were particularly vulnerable to Lewis and the CIO leadership, who could hire and fire organizers at will. Despite this situation, the Party continued to take a conciliatory stance, avoiding a break with Lewis and the Party's other liberal allies. In May 1937, as Communist organizers were being purged in greater numbers from SWOC, the Party leadership decided to do nothing; Communist organizers still in SWOC were told to avoid confrontation over the dismissals and to continue their work.[68] Similarly, the Party did not challenge the anti-Communist clause in the UMW constitution, and instead minimized its importance. In an attempt to justify such a position an editorial in the *Daily Worker* stated that it was not "opportune to raise the question at all . . . especially since it already has so little meaning in actual life." The editorial confidently added that Communists were certain "that miners who know the work of the Communists with whom they work shoulder to shoulder will soon find ways of eliminating the clause from the Constitution as they have eliminated it in life."[69]

Lewis, however, was not successful in removing Communists from positions of leadership in a number of important unions controlled by the rank and file. Workers respected and elected Communists and their allies because of their steadfast commitment to improving working conditions, to union recognition, and because they were recognized as the best organizers. Party members also achieved positions of leadership for their skills in parliamentary maneuvering. As Nathan Glazer wrote: their experience carried Communists "like corks in a flood to top positions in a number of new unions." Along the same lines, Len DeCaux wrote that Party members were elected to union office, not because they were Communists themselves, but because workers "just liked the reds as union leaders."[70] William Carney, CIO rubber organizer, expressed the same sentiment: "It doesn't make any difference if a man is a Communist, Socialist, Republican, or Democrat, as long as he is loyal to the union."[71] In Chicago, Communists led a number of local unions, district councils, and central labor bodies. Peggy Dennis estimated that in Wisconsin, out of a state-wide membership of 600, more that 100 Communists were union officials, and nearly 300 were active either in the CIO or in the AFL.[72] Some of the most prominent emerging labor leaders around the country had various degrees of alliance to the Party. Among them were "Red

Mike" Quill, of the Transit Workers; Joe Curran, of the Merchant Seamen; Ben Gold of the Fur and Leather Workers; Julius Emspak and James Matles, of the Electrical Workers; Harold Pritchett, president of the Woodworkers union; and Donald Henderson, head of the Cannery Workers. Browder later estimated that Communists and their allies led unions representing one-third of the CIO's membership and played significant roles in another third.[73] In addition to those above, the most important were the American Newspaper Guild, the Mine, Mill, and Smelters Workers, the Farm Equipment Workers, the Screen Writers Guild, the State, County, and Municipal Workers, and the Office and Professional Workers.[74]

Many years later, Browder recalled that Communist activities within the CIO were what really "built the Party to 100,000."[75] Due to the prestige Communists gained in the labor struggles of that period, the Party's influence and acceptance among workers grew as did the toleration of its activities. After the strike, Communists in Flint emerged from their underground existence and began acting as a visible force within the city, selling the *Daily Worker* at the plant gates and holding open meetings. At the second convention of the UAW in 1936, the delegates turned down a resolution to expel known Communists from the union, or, as amended, to forbid them from holding union office. Endorsing the Party line of the time, the Convention went as far as to call for the founding of a Farmer-Labor party and did not endorse Roosevelt.[76] During the sit-down strike at Fisher 1, the strike committee rejected a request to ban the *Daily Worker* from the plant. By a unanimous vote, the Communist paper was termed "the best paper that comes into the plant." Similarly the *Daily Worker* correspondent was the only reporter allowed to cover all the sessions at the 1937 convention of the International Woodworkers Union. At the union's 1939 convention a constitutional amendment barring Communists from membership was also defeated.[77]

The Party's role in the strike movement and in the organization of industrial unions translated into an increase in the number of workers who joined the Party. During the sit-down movement, the Cleveland Fisher Body Communist shop nucleus grew from approximately twelve members to over fifty. According to Williamson, after the sit-down strike hundreds joined the Party in Akron, among them many of the strike's leaders. Communist membership increased in a number of other auto plants.[78] In February 1938, a Party steel worker from western Pennsylvania reported how he and three others had recruited thirty-three new members, by putting themselves "in the front line to help build the union," and thus winning the confidence of workers.[79] In Seattle another organizer reported that, following a similar course, membership had grown from ninety-two to approximately 250 members.[80] In Detroit, during the period from 1934 to 1936 total membership increased from 600 to 1,600; following the sit-down strike the Party had twenty-eight shop nuclei. In the period from 1935 to 1939 the total number of Communists in the auto industry increased from 630 to 1,100. Of these, many held positions of leadership and responsibility at various levels of the UAW.[81]

In February 1938, Jack Stachel reported to the Party's leadership that during the previous year membership had jumped from 37,000 to approximately 60,000. Although the process of analyzing membership information had not yet been completed, he could report that over 50 percent of the new recruits belonged either to the AFL or the CIO. In basic industries the Party's recruitment was as follows: 603 marine workers, 552 steel workers, 474 miners, 415 metal workers, 426 autoworkers, 269 transportation workers.[82]

Despite this increase in membership and in the number of workers employed in basic industries, Communists accounted for a minuscule fraction of the total union membership.[83] By mid-1938, the Party's leadership complained that out of a total membership of approximately 75,000, only 27,000 were union members.[84] Understandably this situation of notable but unsubstantial membership was of great concern to the Party. Its press carried numerous articles trying to dissect the Party's activities to uncover shortcomings and failures of responsibility in recruiting. Expressing a general view, Foster found no reason "in the objective situation why our Party should not be numerically several times stronger than it is at the present time."[85] There were a number of real factors behind the scant numbers. Bud Simons recalled that while the leadership urged organizers not to neglect direct Party work and recruitment, most Communists gave priority to union activities. Weinstone wrote that during the Flint sit-down movement Party members were too busy with the strike to concentrate on Party activities.[86] In one case, a number of midwestern Party leaders went so far as to protest that their attendance at an important strategy meeting with Browder in Cleveland got in the way of what they considered more important union organizing activities.[87] Commenting on the disappointing number of recruits, an article in the *Party Organizer* asked, "What do our comrades say to this?" Their answer was: "Let us build the union first, and then we can start building the Party."[88]

Another problem of recruitment of workers was that while the Party's presence was certainly more conspicuous, essentially among labor it continued to be hidden. Denying membership had become a common practice among left-wing unionists, adopted in the 1920s to avoid expulsion from unions with restrictive amendments in their constitutions barring Communists. The Party vernacular for those unionists who concealed their Communist affiliation was "submarines." Communist unionists such as Wyndham Mortimer, Bob Travis, and Henry Kraus never openly proclaimed their political allegiance. When an AFL leader called Mortimer "ComMUNE-ist," his response was "I will not dignify the wild charges made against me . . . by either denying or admitting them. Red baiting is, and always has been, the employers' most potent weapon against those of us who believe in and fight for industrial unionism."[89]

Several of the Party's top leaders complained about this situation. John Williamson argued that the practice by "leading Communists who occupy strategic posts of trade union leadership," of concealing their membership resulted "in the real contribution of our Party not being made known publicly at this time."[90] Similar views were expressed by Foster, who warned Communist unionists that workers would not join a party which they did not see "definitely in action as a Party." To this he added that the practice of concealing membership was an "outgrowth from past persecution experiences and is out of place in the present broad united front mass movement."[91] Even stronger were Hudson's remarks: the time had past, he wrote, when "in order to maintain our positions, we have to hide." Concealing membership in the CPUSA "breeds distrust among workers. They cannot understand why we are ashamed; why we hide the fact that we are Communists."[92]

While Communist leaders thus expressed their resentment at not being able to "flex their muscles," statements such as these showed little concern for reality. The problems faced by "submarines" were real. American Communists were in a political dilemma. The Party was legal: as such it had offices, neighborhood branches, published newspapers, ran electoral campaigns, held public meetings and its leaders addressed public forums and spoke on the radio. However, legal and extralegal penalties against Communists often required concealment.

Communists had to take a number of factors into consideration before deciding whether or not to reveal their political views. The most obvious danger was of losing their jobs. As one Communist unionist put it: to "stand up shake your fist and say you were a Red was just plain stupid."[93] Communist unionists were also keen to undercut charges that the strike movement was a "Communist plot," and often in a tacit agreement with their non-Communist allies, deliberately played down their political affiliation and role in the strikes. Communist union members acted as inconspicuously as possible, speaking as union men, never as party members. During the Flint strike, no national Communist leader addressed the strikers or visited the strike headquarters.[94] Williamson held his daily meeting with the Fisher Body strike committee to discuss the conduct of the strike outside of the plant gates. "For me to meet them inside the plant," the Communist leader acknowledged, "would be stretching things too far."[95]

Finally, with few exceptions, if Communists active in trade union activities had disclosed their affiliation, they would have jeopardized the leadership they had achieved in areas the Party considered vital. Party members had to take into account the attitudes and values of union members. It was not unusual for Communists to head local unions that did not have any other Communists in them, and whose members, while militant on the shopfloor, were politically and socially conservative.[96] Many were recent immigrants from the South, possibly under the reactionary influence of organizations such as the Ku Klux Klan, while some ethnic groups were guided by the conservatism of the Catholic Church. Given such opposition to communism on principle, a false step bore serious consequences, including expulsion and futile isolation. Based on his own experience as Party organizer in Schenectady, Max Gordon recounted that after Communists gained control of the company union at General Electric in 1936, local priests began a campaign against them. Local workers, many of whom were Catholics, told the priests to "keep their hands off."[97] A Communist UE organizer remembered workers "would support individual Communists because they found them to be good leaders or because they liked them personally, but they tolerated party membership rather than accepting it and regarding it as something good. They thought it was a handicap."[98] So it was that Communist fears of rejection inspired notable extremes of behavior. For example, in the Transport Workers Union, Communists and Communist sympathizers led an Irish-Catholic, conservative, and often racist membership. In dealing with the privately owned transportation companies in New York, the union's leadership feared endangering their position of leadership. Hence, it was with reluctance that they called for the end of employment discrimination against blacks and only after pressure from the NAACP, the Urban League, black organizations, and local community leaders.[99]

Most Communist union leaders then chose to preserve their positions of influence rather than to reveal their political ideology. Therefore they were prevented from taking credit for their role and hence limited their effectiveness and possible source of recruitment. Consequently most recruitment occurred on a one-to-one basis: Party members would size up, cultivate the most militant workers and trade unionists, and in a gradual process introduce them into the Party.[100]

Communists were admitted into the movement for industrial unionism by virtue of their stalwart commitment to its objectives and their unsurpassed organizing skills. They were able to remain a part of it, however, and to broaden their influence as well as their relative acceptance within it, because they showed restraint and a willingness to accomodate an often hostile environment; ultimately, Communists placed the consideration of strengthening the union movement above their objective of bringing about fundamental changes in U.S. society.

7

"THEY SHALL NOT PASS!"

With rifle, bomb, and our machine guns
We'll exterminate the fascist plague,
Free all Spain of plunderers and pirates—
Spanish brothers, Spain belongs to you.
Show no mercy to the fascist rebels,
Nor to any traitor in our ranks.

> Song of the International Brigades, 1936

One may accept or reject the ideology of Hitlerism as well
as any other ideological system; that is a matter of political
opinion.

> Vyacheslav Molotov, October 1939[1]

Communists waged a struggle against fascism both on an international and a domestic plane. Just as the Communist movement had come to distinguish between fascist and democratic forces within each country, so did it come to discriminate among capitalist countries between fascist aggressive states, like Germany, Italy, and Japan, and nonaggressive states such as the United States, France and, to a lesser degree, Great Britain. In his report on the international situation at the Seventh Congress of the Communist International, the Italian Communist leader Palmiro Togliatti, emphasized the fascist threat to peace and how it polarized world politics.

> The policy of aggression of German fascism and Japanese militarism leads inevitably to a new accentuation of all international antagonisms, but at the same time to a differentiation in the policy of the great imperialist powers, some of which are interested in the defense of the *status quo* and in a temporary and conditional defense of peace.[2]

Consequently, while on the domestic front the Communists' strategy to stop fascism was the Popular Front, its international equivalent was collective security, a defensive alliance between capitalist democratic countries and the Soviet Union.

The Seventh Congress placed the dual objectives of struggle for peace and resistance to fascist aggression at the center of the strategy of the Communist movement. These objectives augmented in importance as the increased belligerence and military preparations of fascist nations failed to elicit from western powers a response that went beyond formal protests or outright appeasement.

In the United States, Communists contended with a growing isolationist sentiment fostered by the omen of another European war and reinforced by the Nye Committee's revelations that the munitions' industry had reaped enormous profits from World War I. Such revelations confirmed what many already suspected: involvement in World War I had been a mistake. Only strict neutrality, it would seem, could prevent a similar mistake. The sentiment in favor of isolationism cut across ideological lines. Millions of Americans, vowing "never again," rallied around midwestern progressives who mixed their traditional anti-imperialism with the disillusionment in war. Others listened to Father Coughlin and Huey Long lambaste the "plutocrats" and the international banking community. Isolationist feeling expressed itself in Congress with the election, year after year, of men like William E. Borah, Key Pittman, Burton Wheeler, Gerald P. Nye and young Robert LaFollette, and with the passage between 1935 and 1937 of Neutrality Acts aimed at preventing the United States from being drawn into another war for having aided one of the belligerent sides.[3]

As it urged collective security, the CPUSA pointed out that in a polarized world there was no room for neutrality, which could only nurture fascism. By a resolution adopted at its Ninth Convention, the CPUSA set as its chief goal to convince the country that to "Keep America Out of War" was to "Keep War Out of the World."[4] In May 1936, speaking at a rally at Madison Square Garden, Browder said it was "nonsense to talk about peace except insofar as we mobilize all peace forces in the world to place obstacles in the way of these fascist forces who are preparing war."[5]

The CPUSA offered collective security as being in the best interest of the United States. If democratic Spain fell, native fascists would be encouraged to plot against American democracy and "we would be a step nearer to facing the kind of horrors the Spanish people are enduring today."[6] In an attempt to strengthen his argument, Browder asserted that rejection of isolationism would be beneficial to capitalism itself: if the United States isolated itself economically from the rest of the world, this step "would precipitate an economic crisis," inevitably followed by a "sudden and drastic change in our system of government." Ironically, in the battle between "progress" and "reaction," the leader of the CPUSA seemed to display a remarkable solicitude for preserving the wealth as well as the political prominence of the bourgeoisie.[7]

The CPUSA particularly deplored the strength of isolationist feeling in the progressive movement, especially what the Communist party called the "left-wing" of the isolationist front as embodied by Congressman Maury Maverick and Senator LaFollette. Browder wrote that "by their stand on the question of peace and how to maintain it, they are decisively strengthening the hands of the reactionary forces which they fight against so admirably on domestic questions."[8] The Communist leader repeatedly pointed to the threat that isolationism posed for democratic institutions in the United States. Under the cover of isolation "to which great masses adhere as a peace sentiment, there is being broadcast a spirit of cynicism toward peace as a goal to be striven for, and as a consequence also toward the very idea of democracy."[9] To oppose domestic reaction entailed opposing international reaction as well; it was not possible to support advanced social and political reforms at home and at the same time "in foreign policy to be 'neutral' as between fascism and democracy, between warmaking and peace-seeking governments, to retreat before and surrender to the bandit governments."[10]

The Party wanted the United States to collaborate with the "peace forces" of the world, most prominent among them France and the Soviet Union. In opposition, as Bittelman wrote, Great Britain's Chamberlain government was leaving fascist nations a free hand in China and Latin America, to the point of endangering the national security of the United States. As a step in the right direction the CPUSA wanted the United States to support the measures of the League of Nations aimed at curbing fascist aggression and called for sanctions against the nations violating the Kellogg-Briand Pact.[11] The Party was also opposed to the Ludlow amendment, requiring a national referendum to declare war, as an impediment to the ability of peaceful powers to defend themselves. Recounting a conversation with an unnamed congressman, Clarence Hathaway summed up the party's opposition to the amendment as doing too little too late: He explained "the problem is not how war is declared. It is how war is to be prevented."[12]

The CPUSA, as we have seen, was initially very critical of Roosevelt's foreign policy. During the 1936 presidential campaign the Party pointed to the president's stance in foreign affairs to demonstrate that, just as in domestic policy, he was not an effective defense against international fascism and reaction. The Roosevelt administration was blamed for its rhetorical condemnation of aggressor nations that led to no concrete action to stop them.[13] The CPUSA claimed that Roosevelt's policies were similar to those of Woodrow Wilson in that they helped to pave the way "so that bankers can drag the United States into the next world war."[14] Although in early 1936 Roosevelt attempted to amend the Neutrality Act to gain some discretionary powers to help the victims of aggression, the Party's Central Committee dismissed this gesture of support as a futile attempt by the president to "satisfy both his own hesitant tendency to collaborate in a measure with other peace forces for the maintenance of peace as well as the aggressive pressure of the Hearsts and Du Ponts to help the war-mongers."[15]

As the presidential campaign progressed Communists toned down their criticism without altering its essential message that Roosevelt, despite his "many correct statements about the need for peace," had not identified the major threat as fascist aggression. Hence, he "hung on" to neutrality and isolation policies that "encouraged the fascist aggressors, instead of stopping them dead in their tracks."[16]

Communists were strongly critical of the Administration's request to Congress to extend the Neutrality Act to Spain in disregard of conventional practice that allowed arms sales to recognized governments. An editorial in the *Daily Worker* defined such an extension as a "blow to world peace and democracy." Addressing a public meeting on January 20, 1937, Browder called the Administration's position "a gratuitous act of war against a friendly nation, upon the hypocritical plea of 'neutrality' and the desire to keep out of war."[17] The Communist leader added, "our government actually performed an act of war against Spain, against Spanish democracy, and for the alien fascist hordes bombarding Madrid and slaughtering hundreds of thousands of men women and children."[18] Speaking at the Coney Island Velodrome on September 2, 1937, he warned, "The bombs on Madrid, and the bombs on Shanghai are surely going to bring bombs on New York and San Francisco, unless America changes this policy, and clasps hands with the peaceloving people of all the world, to remove this fascist, militarist menace from the world."[19]

Throughout 1937, as the Party moved closer to the New Deal in domestic policy, criticism of the president's stance on international affairs became less adamant. Congress rather than the administration was blamed for neutrality, while Roosevelt and Cordell Hull were praised for showing a sincere concern for peace.[20]

The news of Roosevelt's "quarantine" speech reached Browder in Canada where he was to address the Convention of the Canadian Communist party. In his speech, delivered on December 8, Browder planted the CPUSA squarely behind Roosevelt and adopted the "quarantine the war makers" formula. In the past, he said, Communists had been the president's "sharpest critics" for what they considered "his cowardly surrender to the reactionary neutrality policy." In contrast they now supported the president's statements as "the only course which can save the world from a terrible catastrophe." The Party's new responsibility, he said, was to enlist "the active support of the masses of the people" at home as well as throughout the western democracies in support of Roosevelt's policies as expressed in Chicago.[21] At a meeting of functionaries in early December, Browder stated that the president's "quarantine" policy had to be "worked out in deeds, it must be implemented, it is not enough merely to be pronounced." Browder once again called for the abrogation of the "infamous Neutrality Law."[22]

Encouraged by what it perceived as the president's embrace of collective security, the CPUSA now gave complete support to Roosevelt, and all subsequent Party declarations during the following months voiced the necessity of applying Roosevelt's proposals. Speaking at Madison Square Garden on May 4, 1938, Browder went so far as to propose that the United States assume the outright leadership of organizing the peace forces of the world.

The United States has the strongest selfish interest in peace, without which it cannot maintain world commerce so necessary to it under the present system . . . The United States holds in its hands the key to world peace.[23]

Despite the Party's hopes, Roosevelt's "quarantine" declaration did not translate into a policy shift away from isolation. Repeatedly Communists, while praising Roosevelt for his "splendid contribution

toward a change in policy," and for having "encouraged and strengthened the forces of peace everywhere," nevertheless lamented that he
lacked "the courage or the support necessary" to put his declared
policies into effect.[24] However, even as Communists criticized what
they viewed as the president's unwillingness to follow the Quarantine declaration with concrete actions, they still placed the blame on
isolationist circles which were "cleverly exploiting the peace and
democratic aspirations of the masses."[25]

The Communist position concerning the administration's requests
for increased military expenditures was contradictory. While no
longer opposing war, and even recognizing that a capitalist state
forced to defend its own sovereignty waged a just struggle, the
Party continued its campaign against increases in military expenditures. The CPUSA repeated that a consistent policy of collective
security, based to a great degree on the economic and political
isolation of aggressor nations, was sufficient to stop fascist expansion. When a reader of the *New Masses* questioned Browder about
the Party's putative stance in the case of war with Japan, he coun-
tered that "the cause of progress and democracy everywhere would
demand the defeat of Japan." In light of the Party's position on
military expenditures, it was difficult to see how such a victory
could be accomplished without endorsing the request for increased
naval appropriations.[26]

The CPUSA's policy in favor of action to stop fascism abroad paral-
leled the developing perceptions of growing numbers of politically
active liberals, noncommunist left-wingers and unionists. The fascist
menace was not a Moscow invention: Communists were not the only
ones to see in the invasion of Ethiopia, the militarization of the Rhine-
land, and the Japanese attack on China, portents of a global menace.
Reports and images coming out of Germany of book burnings, torch-
light parades, and pogroms strengthened the liberals' sense of alarm
and for many replaced their exclusive concerns for domestic issues of
the early depression years with international concerns for the defense
of democracy. Pacifists such as Albert Einstein renounced their long
held beliefs.

> Present-day world political conditions demand . . . a new attitude toward
> the problem of peace. The existence of two great powers with definitely
> aggressive tendencies (Germany and Japan) makes an immediate realiza-
> tion of movement toward disarmament . . . impracticable. The friends of

peace must concentrate their efforts rather on achieving an alliance of the military forces of the countries which have remained democratic.[27]

In particular, the struggle of the Spanish republic against enemies supported by Hitler and Mussolini symbolized for many the contrast of the decade: the forces of democracy and social reform battling fascist rebel generals. Scores of intellectuals traveled to Spain in a show of support for the Republic. Upon his return, Malcolm Cowley characterized the struggle as between on the one hand, the Church, the Army, and the landlords, who represented all "the old traditions of class intolerance"; and on the other hand, the workers, the peasants and the artists united in the fight for "more knowledge, more freedom, more everything."[28] The struggle against fascism was elevated to a superior art form: in reviewing Hemingway's *To Have and to Have Not*, Cowley wrote that the book had benefited from the author's anti-fascism. After visiting the front lines, Hemingway had rewritten part of the novel to reflect some of his new perceptions. This change could be seen in the dying words of the novel's protagonist, Harry Morgan: "No man alone now . . . No matter how, a man alone ain't got no bloody fucking chance." According to Cowley, this was the message Hemingway had brought back with him from Spain, his free translation of Marx's "Workers of the World Unite."[29]

For liberals the Spanish struggle became the symbol of the worldwide battle against fascism before which all other differences receded in importance. After initially favoring non-intervention the *Nation* and the *New Republic*, when it became clear that Germany and Italy were impudently helping Franco, shifted to opposing the embargo, a position also shared by Eleanor Roosevelt.[30] An editorial in the *New Republic* expressed a common view of the time that given current threats past ideological differences had to be set aside: now there was only one condition for participating in the united front: "are you for fascism (under that or some other name) or against it?" Being against it, the article concluded, was enough.[31]

As fascism or anti-fascism became the dividing lines, more liberals and left-wingers viewed with satisfaction the People's Front and supported the Soviet Union and the Communist party as the staunchest antagonists of fascism. Although remaining critical of the CPUSA, intellectuals, such as Archibald MacLeish, Lewis Mumford, and Reinhold Niebuhr, lent their names to front organizations and willingly worked with Communists.[32]

The Party adapted itself to these new circumstances. Concern with international events, and consequently the need to enlist illustrious intellectuals, had led in 1934 to the replacement of the John Reed Clubs with the League of American Writers. The emphasis on the need to defend democracy from reactionary forces was even more visible at the League's Second Congress convened in New York in June 1937. Open Communists, such as Joseph Freeman, Mike Gold and Granville Hicks, shared the limelight with prominent non-communists like Thornton Wilder, as well as Ernest Hemingway and Archibald MacLeish, who had once been criticized by Communists, but who were now symbols of the Party's success in its search for broad support for the antifascist front.[33] Browder's address at the opening session exemplified the new priorities of the movement. Communists extended "the hand of fellowship and co-operation to Republicans, Democrats and Socialists, as well as to those of no party at all" in the world-wide struggle to preserve democracy against fascism.[34] At the League's Third Congress in early June 1939, the broad People's Front coalition was even more impressive. At the opening session at Carnegie Hall an audience of 3,500 listened to Browder, but also to Louis Aragon, Thomas Mann, President Beneš of Czechoslovakia, and Fernando De Los Rios, the Spanish ambassador to the United States. The League's acceptance and prestige were such that when it extended honorary membership to Roosevelt, he readily accepted.[35]

The Spanish Civil War and the strong response that it generated among the country's intellectual and liberal left overshadowed emerging doubts concerning the Soviet Union and Stalinism as a result of the Moscow trials. From August 1936 to mid-1938 the Soviet Union was rocked by a series of show trials that led to the execution of thousands of Party and military leaders. Beginning with the trials of Grigori Zinoviev and Lev Kamenev, followed by those of Grigori Pyatakov, Karl Radek, and Grigori Sokolnikov, the most shocking trial was the last one that placed on the dock Nikolai Bukharin, Aleksei Rykov, Christian Rakovsky, and Nikolai Krestinsky, all members of the Bolshevik old guard, who in the past had been very popular within the international Communist movement. The accusations, all of which were fabricated and presented without a shred of evidence, were quite fantastic. In the early trials the accused were charged with terrorist activities in alliance with Trotsky and with planning to kill Party leaders, Stalin included, in an attempt to reestablish capitalism. In the later trials the charge was conspiracy (again supposedly under

"They Shall Not Pass!"

Trotsky's prodding) with Germany and Japan to overthrow the Soviet government and dismember the country.[36]

Out of faith in the Soviet party, Communists subscribed to the official version of the trials provided by Moscow, many like John Gates thought it inconceivable "that men of their stature could confess to these grave crimes unless they had committed them." A number of independent observers of the international press and the diplomatic corps also shared this view. After attending the Radek trial, the United States ambassador, Joseph Davies, reported back to Washington that he was convinced of the veracity of the confessions.[37] In March 1937 eighty-eight intellectuals signed a statement against the findings of a commission of inquiry chaired by John Dewey that had exonerated Trotsky. In May 1938, after the third trial, over 150 well-known novelists, performers, and literary critics, prominent among them Jack Conroy, Malcolm Cowley, John Garfield, Dashiell Hammett, Corliss Lamont, Lillian Hellman, Langston Hughes, Dorothy Parker, Henry Roth, Lionel Stander, and Irwing Shaw, signed a statement in support of the trials accepting that some of Lenin's closest associates were in fact saboteurs and fascists.[38]

Some, however, did express their doubts openly and questioned the Moscow trials. One who did was Waldo Frank, chairman of the League of American Writers and a close ally of the Party, and for this break of "discipline" he was fiercely attacked by Browder. In Browder's view Frank had shown bad political judgment and his doubts were inimical to the anti-fascist cause: "it is the requirement that when the democratic front is fighting the open enemy before us, it shall not be attacked from the rear by those who pretend to be part of it."[39]

Most took Browder's advice and, if they had any, kept their doubts to themselves, since their overriding concern was to maintain the alliance of the left in the face of world-wide fascist offensive. Granville Hicks, at the time literary editor of the *New Masses*, was a good example of such reticence. Looking back to the Moscow trials, many years after having left the Party, he wrote:

Again and again, between 1935 and 1939, I was troubled by events in Russia, especially the trials for treason of men who had been held up to us as heroes of the revolution. I felt that if the Old Bolsheviks were guilty, then corruption had gone deep in the Communist party of Russia; if they were innocent, the trials were outrageous. Yet it was true, I thought, that Russia

167

was the bulwark of anti-fascism in Europe and that the Communist party was leading the fight against fascism in America, and I convinced myself that I had no right to let my private doubts interfere with this great struggle against evil.[40]

The *Nation* and the *New Republic* shared similar views. Faced with mounting fascist aggression, even the *New Republic* decided not to question the latest Russian events out of fear of weakening the anti-fascist front. The magazine told its readers to "be content to let opinions differ and turn our attention to the matters nearer to home."[41] To counter claims issuing from the press, the Congress, and to a great degree from those liberals that had signed the statement of the Committee for Cultural Freedom associating the Soviet Union with fascist regimes, an impressive group of 400 intellectuals signed a letter carried by the press on August 19, 1939, denouncing the "fantastic falsehood" that the Soviet Union and Nazi Germany were alike. Among the signers were a number of prominent journalists such as Vincent Sheean and Max Lerner, as well as Matthew Josephson, Roger Baldwin, Ernest Hemingway, Clifford Odets, and William Carlos Williams.[42]

Support of collective security became the diviner's rod that determined friend from foe. While noting that a number of important unions had come out in favor of collective security, Browder even found something good to say about William Green for having expressed similar beliefs in an editorial in the February 1938 issue of *American Federationist*.[43] The Party, in contrast, had harsh words for Oswald Garrison Villard, Charles Beard, and Bruce Bliven.[44] The strongest criticism was directed at the Socialist party.

In line with their shift to the left in domestic policy, in foreign policy Socialists blended traditional pacifism with anti-capitalist and revolutionary rhetoric. Consequently, Socialists opposed all wars as imperialist. Since they also believed that war and democracy were incompatible, they therefore opposed collective security against fascist aggression. In the words of Norman Thomas, Socialists believed that there was no such thing as a "good war":

> Any world war no matter how high and holy the alleged end, will involve the most catastrophic destruction the world has seen . . . Its end may not be the victory of any belligerents, but a kind of chaos of misery, fear and hate. It cannot be fought without putting all the belligerent nations under the severest military control with a denial of all real civil liberty.

War, the Socialist leader concluded, "means inevitable fascism at home."[45] In early 1938, following its anti-war campaign, the Socialist party organized the "Keep America Out of War Congress" to oppose the repeal of neutrality legislation as well as any increase of appropriations for the country's military.[46]

The position of the Socialist party in foreign affairs widened the gap with the CPUSA which had developed over differences in domestic policy. Communists were persuaded that the Socialist party's unwillingness to distinguish between fascist and non-fascist capitalist countries strengthened fascism and "demoralized the struggle for peace."[47] According to Browder, while fascism was on the offensive, Socialists such as Norman Thomas blindly continued to offer socialism as the immediate objective: "they would demand in the United States that no one be admitted into the anti-fascist front unless he first commits himself to Socialism." Such a demand would only serve to weaken anti-fascist forces and strengthen their enemies.[48]

The CPUSA continued to launch appeals for united action with the Socialist party, their tone however became increasingly more rhetorical; on most important issues, domestic as well as foreign, there were no common grounds.[49] Progressively the split between the two parties grew wider and more bitter, and by the end of 1937, all attempts at reconciliation were over. While not mentioning the Socialist party directly, Browder made clear what the CPUSA though of Socialist policies: "The time has come to end the fascist menace to world peace. Everyone must line up on one side or the other. Whoever is opposed to collective action for peace, is an enemy of peace, an agent of the international bandits."[50]

The divergence between Communists and Socialists was felt the strongest within the youth and student movements. The Young Communist League and the Young People's Socialist League had worked together during the early stages of the American Youth Congress and the American Student Union. Nevertheless, the collaboration began to fall apart as soon as their different priorities in foreign affairs became irreconcilable. The Communists' effort to move both the AYC and the ASU toward embracing collective security engendered stiff opposition from young Socialists. However, Communists strengthened their influence within both organizations because from 1936 to 1938 many liberals and even a considerable number of Socialists were increasingly convinced by the course of international events of the need for a world-wide antifascist alliance.

The AYC had no individual members but acted as an umbrella for a broad spectrum of youth organizations claiming approximately five million members. With most liberal organizations supporting collective security, Socialists could put up only a weak opposition. By the Second American Youth Congress, held in 1935, a cleft resulted when, over Socialist opposition, Communists and their liberal allies had the Congress adopt a Declaration of Rights of American Youth that placed the American Youth Congress on the side of the Soviet Union's "struggle for peace."[51] Despite continued Socialist opposition, at the AYC's fourth convention held in Milwaukee in the summer of 1937, the Communist-liberal coalition endorsed collective security against fascism and came out in support of the New Deal.[52]

The position the Communist party achieved within the American Youth Congress was notable. The AYC devoted most of its efforts in favor of the passage of the American Youth Act that called on government to provide aid and vocational training for unemployed youths, a bill first introduced in Congress in 1936 by two farmer-laborites: Senator Benson of Minnesota and Congressman Amlie of Wisconsin.[53] Because of its broad nature, the AYC projected the image of being representative of a wide cross section of young Americans and as such became a bargaining agent of sorts with the administration and the officials of the National Youth Administration, on whose advisory committee the AYC was given a position. Mrs. Roosevelt, always very sensitive to the problems of youth, attended AYC events, met with its delegations, provided access to the White House, and was the guest of honor at a AYC banquet in New York City. Among the other guests were Mickey Rooney, Archibald MacLeish, A. A. Berle, Clare Booth Luce, James Farley, Archibald William Byrd, Orson Welles, Thomas Watson, Herbert Bayard Swope, Dorothy Canfield Fisher, Ernest Hemingway, Henry Morgenthau, and Mrs. Felix Frankfurter.[54] In 1937 the AYC mobilized 4,000 young people to converge on Washington, D.C., to lobby for the bill, and a delegation spoke with the president in a meeting arranged by Eleanor Roosevelt.[55]

In August 1938 the AYC played host to the Second World Youth Congress held at Vassar and attended by 500 delegates from fifty-four countries. The organizing committee included a number of Popular Front organizations together with the American Jewish Congress, the American Youth Hostel Association, the New York State Federation of Churches, the YMCA and YWCA, and the Girl Scouts. At the opening session, held at Randall's Island Stadium in New York, Mayor La

Guardia and Eleanor Roosevelt addressed the delegates. After the Congress had been moved up river to Poughkeepsie, it committed itself to collective security based on a "Peace Pact" presented by the AYC.[56] The AYC had reached the peak of its respectability. Its fifth convention in July 1939 was attended by Mrs. Roosevelt, President Beneš, and Harold Ickes. On that occasion the AYC shelved the youth act and instead joined several New Dealers in proposing a series of improvements of the National Youth Administration. The high point of the convention was the adoption of the resolution opposing "all forms of dictatorship, regardless of whether they be Communist, Fascist, Nazi or any other type." Young Communists who had a disproportionate number of delegates both as representatives of the YCL and of other organizations, could have easily defeated the motion. Yet, in order to preserve the internal unity of the Youth Congress as well as to deflect any accusation that it was dominated by the Communist party, Young Communists protested the phrasing but went along with the resolution, despite opposition among their ranks. They rationalized their position arguing that the issue was not worth fighting over because Communist dictatorships did not exist.[57]

Within the American Student Union the split between Communists and Socialists centered on the Oxford Pledge. When the organization was founded in 1935, Communists were already embracing collective security and no longer opposed war if it were to fight fascism. In these early stages of the People's Front they still did not want to jeopardize their relations with Socialists. Given this situation, the ASU's program was a compromise between various positions. Communists who wanted an endorsement of the Soviet Union's foreign policy settled for a statement acceptable to young Socialists that the USSR was an example of a "non-imperialist" country whose peace policy was to be supported. The issue of affiliation to the Communist-dominated American League Against War and Fascism was settled through a resolution not to join any such body without the consent of three-quarters of the national committee. The main dispute, however, took place over the issue of collective security. To preempt the shift of Communists and their supporters, Socialists attempted to tie the ASU to the Oxford Pledge. They presented a three-part resolution that challenged the concept of collective security; the resolution made the Oxford Pledge applicable if Japan invaded the United States, if the United States attacked Japan, and if the United States were to join with other nations in a war against fascism. The Socialist resolution

171

was narrowly defeated by a 193 to 155 vote in favor of a Communist motion that, while opposing support of any war undertaken by the country's government, designated Italy, Germany, and Japan as the threats to world peace. The vote, however, was so close that Communists decided not to push immediately for the abrogation of the Oxford Pledge; instead, they acquiesced in retaining it as the base of the ASU's peace program in order not to force a split with Socialists.[58]

The ASU reasserted the Oxford Pledge at its 1936 convention, but it was clear that the commitment was not as strong as in the past. Already on the brink of breaking with the Socialist party, Joseph Lash announced changes to come: "The Oxford Pledge is not for the ASU, although it may be for pacifists, an ethical absolute." Soon key Socialists in the ASU embraced collective security, altering the balance of power in the organization: aside from Lash, who made the shift upon his return from Spain in 1937, most important among them were Molly Yard, the ASU's treasurer, and Robert Spivack.[59] By the end of 1937, Communists were so eager to embrace Roosevelt's "quarantine" speech that they had few reservations about dumping Socialists, who by then had become a small and isolated organization. Early in December Browder had harsh words for those who were still, as he put it, "hysterically calling for the sanctity of the so-called 'Oxford Pledge.' " World events had shown that "the time has long passed when it was proper to boycott military training camps"; military science was no longer to be the exclusive knowledge of fascists and reactionaries.[60]

A message from President Roosevelt greeted the 500 delegates convened for the ASU's third convention also held at Vassar at the end of 1937. After the delegates had settled down for business and the Socialists had staged a last ditch fight, the forces in favor of collective security won the battle by a 282 to 108 margin and the Oxford Pledge was dropped. Lash declared that the Oxford Pledge was "too fantastic. . . . The United States must 'snap out of a dream world.' " From then on the ASU strongly supported Roosevelt's foreign policy, eventually even abandoning opposition to ROTC and to an increased military budget. Roosevelt rewarded the ASU for its support with a second letter of greeting to its 1938 convention. Mayor Fiorello LaGuardia, the president of CCNY, and the women's director of the Democratic National Committee also sent messages.[61] The ASU had become a respectable organization.

Reporting on the ASU's 1938 convention for the *New Republic*, Bruce Bliven described the changed atmosphere:

Their enthusiasm reached its peak at the jamboree in the huge jumbo jai-alai auditorium of the Hippodrome (seating capacity 4,500) which was filled to its loftiest tier. There were a quintet of white-flanneled cheer leaders; a swing band and shaggers doing the Campus Stomp (". . . everybody's doing it, ASUing it")—confetti. There were ASU feathers and buttons, a brief musical comedy by the Mob Theatre and pretty ushers in academic caps and gowns. All the trappings of a big-game rally were present and the difference was that they were cheering, not the Crimson to beat the Blue, but Democracy to beat Reaction.[62]

The major and possibly the most successful organization through which Communists advocated their foreign policy was the American League Against War and Fascism. The League was an offshoot of the Amsterdam-Pleyel Congress against imperialist war and fascism founded in late spring 1933 by Henri Barbusse and Romain Rolland.[63] On September 29, 1933, Barbusse presided over the founding congress of the American League Against War and Fascism in New York City. The Socialist party showed an initial interest in joining, but, after conflicts arose with the CPUSA, it decided to withdraw from the organization. The Communist party also showed its influence by refusing to allow "renegades," in this case Jay Lovestone, to sit on the Congress' Presiding Committee. Therefore, despite the League's "non-partisan" nature, it was thoroughly dominated by the Communist party, the only affiliated political organization.[64] Browder, who was the League's vice chairman, defined its program and policies as "politically satisfactory," since they were indeed indistinguishable from those of the CPUSA. At first the expansion of the activities and role of the organization, however, were severely limited by the Party's insistence on continuing its attacks on "social-fascists" and its unwillingness to compromise with other forces. This sectarian approach limited the organization's appeal to Communists and Communist-sympathizers. Consequently, until the mid-1930s the League's activities stagnated.[65]

Eventually, however, as the Party's policies evolved toward the People's Front so did the League's. At its second Congress held in Chicago at the end of September 1934, all references linking the battle against war and fascism to anti-capitalist struggle were dropped. In response to the CPUSA's call for a broad anti-fascist unity, a sizable number of AFL unionists, as well as forty-nine Socialist delegates, headed by Meta Berger, defied their party's threat to expel them.[66] At the League's Third Congress, held in Cleveland in January 1936, 2,300 delegates were officially welcomed by the city's mayor, Harold H. Burton, former national commander of the American Legion. At the following congress, in November 1937, in an attempt to dispel the image of a Communist-dominated group as well possibly to broaden the League's appeal, the CPUSA formally withdrew its affiliation. This move was merely cosmetic, and Communist influence remained strong. The League endorsed collective security, and, befitting its new more positive outlook and belief that anti-fascist wars were justified, the name of the organization was changed to American League for Peace and Democracy.[67]

By the end of the 1930s, with increased concern over fascist expansion, the League became an effective vehicle for collective security. While the League never reached the 7 million members Browder claimed for it, by including all the members of the groups affiliated with it, a more realistic figure of 20,000 dues-paying members was still respectable.[68] As usual the influence and power of the League went beyond its limited membership. It offered a platform for many personalities to express their anti-fascism and as such was an effective way to establish contacts with Congressmen and other influential people who would not otherwise have associated themselves directly with Communists. In 1935 Dr. Harry F. Ward, a Methodist minister who taught Christian Ethics at the Union Theological Seminary, became chairman. Among its leaders were Roger Baldwin; Meta Berger; Robert Morss Lovett; Dorothy McConnell, daughter of a Methodist bishop; Margaret Forsyte, of the International YWCA; James Waterman Wise, son of Rabbi Stephen S. Wise president of the American Jewish Congress; and Annie Gray, president of the Women's Peace Party. Two Congressmen, Jerry O'Connell, and John Bernard, sat on the National Committee of the League.[69] The League's activities were favorably reported by liberal journals. At one of its rallies in 1937, Governor Benson of Minnesota was the main speaker and several members of Roosevelt's cabinet lent their names as speakers or sponsors to several of the activities of the League.[70]

The League's influence reached its peak at its Fifth Congress held in Washington D.C. in January 1939. Delegates received a letter of welcome from Harold Ickes as well as from Representative Walter Judd, Judith Epstein, president of the Hadassah, and J. Finley Wilson of the Elks. Delegates represented a broad range of religious organizations and labor unions, including such non-communists as A. F. Whitney of the Trainmen's Brotherhood, Mayor Berry of the Pressmens Union, and A. Philip Randolph of the Sleeping Car Porters.[71]

By 1936, American Communists were not just fighting fascism on the political-agitational front in the United States, but also on the military front in Spain. As the Spanish Civil War catalyzed the battle against fascism worldwide, many in the Party decided that more was required of them than just raising money, picketing consulates or, as in the case of Communist seamen, smuggling literature into fascist countries. Steve Nelson, who left the Pennsylvania anthracite fields to become political commissar of the XV Brigade, recalled in his memoirs:

> When Franco, Hitler, and Mussolini, attacked Spain, the die was cast. No longer could our campaigns be confined to agitation. The tragedy of the Spanish struggle strained the nerves of every conscientious man and woman. . . . Many of us in the United States knew we had to move beyond passing resolutions that urged our government to aid Spain.[72]

Foreign volunteers had been going to Spain to help the Republic from the beginning of the war. At first small numbers, mostly German and Italian anti-fascist political refugees, saw this as an opportunity to make up for their defeats at home. They began by joining local militias, and, as their numbers increased, the first national units were formed. The flow of volunteers increased after the Comintern launched the campaign for the formation of the International Brigades in September 1936. Approximately 35,000 volunteers from fifty-two countries joined, a concrete sign of anti-fascist solidarity with the Spanish people.

In the late fall of 1936, the CPUSA began its own recruiting drive for the International Brigades.[73] The first organized group of volunteers from the United States sailed from New York on the *Normandie* on Christmas Day 1936. They were followed by approximately 3,000 others who crossed the Atlantic to join the Spanish Republican forces and become part of the XV Brigade, which became known as the Lincoln Brigade.[74] The Americans who went off to fight in Spain represented a cross section of United States society. There was a high percentage of Communists among them (higher in command positions), but the Brigade's variety of ideologies demonstrated how pervasive anti-fascism had become.[75] Most of the American volunteers were in their early twenties. Because of the extension of the Neutrality law to the Spanish war, they traveled as tourists or students on their way to

175

Europe, not declaring their real destination. Once in France, an underground railroad took them to Spain. For a few it was as easy as taking the bus from Perpignan to Figueras. For most, however, after the French government closed the border, it meant a voyage by boat or, most usually, a perilous night-time journey over the Pyrenees to reach their training center in Tarazona.

In the Jarama Valley in February 1937, the Lincolns, as they were soon called, underwent their trial of fire in their attempt to stop the rebels from severing the strategic road between Madrid and Valencia. Out of 450 that went into battle, 120 were killed and 175 were wounded.[76]

Americans took part in three of the four major offensives of the war: Brunete, Aragon, and the Ebro. Despite primitive armaments, scanty supplies of food, medicine, and ammunition, and little previous military experience, the American volunteers withstood the onslaught of Franco's better equipped troops and helped the Republic survive for almost three years. The Lincolns, who in the witch hunts of the 1950s were disparagingly referred to as "premature anti-fascists," paid a very high price for their commitment. By the time the Spanish government decided to withdraw and repatriate the International Brigades in the vain hope that Western democracies would pressure Franco to do the same with his Italian and German troops, fewer than half of all the Americans who had gone to Spain were still alive. Considering the small size of the CPUSA, as well as the sense of strong community that affected its members, the price paid had been high. Recalling dead comrades, George Charney stated that "From Brunete to the Ebro retreat, the death toll had mounted staggeringly; there was hardly a Communist family that did not have a relative or a friend on the casualty list."[77]

The International Brigades had gone to Spain to help gain time for the Republic. Their faith that Western democracies would eventually change their policy and help defeat Franco and his Italian and German allies remained alive despite the sham of the policy of nonintervention that denied any substantial aid to the Republican camp, but did not stop Mussolini's troops nor Hitler's planes from reaching the rebels. The capitulation of France and Great Britain at Munich dashed whatever hopes remained that the Western democracies would stand up to fascism and provide Republican Spain the help it so desperately needed.

By March 1938 Hitler's policy had escalated from violations of the treaty obligations imposed on Germany at Versailles to aggression against neighboring countries in the name of bringing all Germans into the Third Reich. Hitler's annexation of Austria, the *Anschluss* of March 1938, evoked little protest from the democracies and bolstered Germany for its invasion of Czechoslovakia. Despite the pact of mutual assistance, the French government was reluctant to come to Prague's aid, as was London. The British views are best summarized in Neville Chamberlain's often quoted remark that he was unwilling to sacrifice British lives "because of a quarrel in a far away country between people of whom we know nothing." At the quadripartite meeting held in Munich at the end of September 1938, Chamberlain and Édouard Daladier conceded to Hitler's demands on the Sudeten, a prelude to the occupation of the entire country, and thus traded away the sovereignty of a friendly nation for an uncertain peace due to last less than a year.

Moscow's advocacy of collective security did not end at Munich, but Soviet estimation of the French and British governments fell. As both the Spanish and Czech tragedies approached their dire climax in 1939, Stalin warned western democracies that the USSR would not be drawn into a war "to pull somebody else's chestnuts out of the fire."[78]

More immediate effects were felt in France where Munich destroyed the last ties that bound the Popular Front coalition together. Relations between the various parties that made up the Popular Front coalition were already strained over the government's failure to provide substantial aid to the Spanish Republic as well as over its undermining of social legislation in an attempt to revive industrial production. Daladier's role at Munich, however, became the superseding cause of the collapse of the Popular Front in France. Isolated by the general public's euphoria over the Munich agreement, the French Communist party defined it the "greatest treason a republican government had ever committed against peace." The PCF voted virtually alone against Daladier's request for ratification of the treaty in the National Assembly. In November the Radical delegate withdrew from the national committee of the *Rassemblement Populaire*, formally bringing the Popular Front to an end.[79] After Munich, the overthrow of the Daladier government became the chief objective of the French Communist party. On the twenty-first anniversary of the Bolshevik revolution, the Comintern issued a call to "replace the governments of national treachery and shame . . . by governments that are ready to repulse the fascist aggressor."[80]

The partition of Czechoslovakia virtually sealed the fate of Europe's most important Popular Front experiences in Spain and France. In the United States instead the CPUSA found itself able to use recent international developments to further what it considered its two most important objectives: the defense of the Soviet Union and support for Roosevelt.

At the end of September 1938, while on his way to Spain to visit the American volunteers, Browder was invited by the French Communist party to attend the meeting of the French National Assembly where the Munich accords were to be debated. Afterwards Browder flew to Moscow for two days where he discussed with the leadership of the Comintern his thesis on the effects of the agreement on the policy of the CPUSA. According to Browder, his views were accepted with minor modifications and published at the end of October in *World News and Views*, which had replaced the Comintern's *International Press Correspondence*, the Imprecor.[81] In his article, Browder asserted that Munich had radically altered the international balance of forces; France and Britain, in rejecting collective security, had become accomplices of Italy and Germany in their worldwide designs and had helped Japan strengthen its position in the Pacific. This new situation, he wrote, presented grave dangers for the United States: "the menace of fascism, hitherto considered by the United States as primarily a European problem, becomes world-wide and directly strikes against the national interests of the U.S.A.'"[82] According to the Communist leader, with the acquiescence of France and Great Britain, fascism was now in a position to leap across the Atlantic and directly threaten the United States with a pincer movement from Latin America and Canada.[83] Browder went so far as to insinuate that fascist expansion would take place with the help of the Royal Navy. The fascists' objective was to encircle the United States and then force it into "submission to the Munich bloc and into the service of its plans for world hegemony."[84]

From this scenario evolved what was to be the essence of the Party's new line until mid-September 1939. Pointing out the "antidemocratic" and consequently "anti-American" implications of the Munich agreements, the Communist party concluded that the United States and the Soviet Union now stood alone against the fascist offensive. It was therefore in their mutual national interest to join forces against the "common enemy."[85] A world-wide movement was taking shape against fascism and appeasement, within it

> there stand out before the peaceloving peoples of all the world two centers of resistance to the fascist flood, two points from which leadership and inspiration can be given to the majority of mankind struggling for democracy and peace, two rallying grounds for the hard-pressed forces of progress and culture—the Soviet Union and the United States.[86]

In its press and in the declarations of its leaders, the Party renewed its appeals for Roosevelt's "quarantine" declaration "to be made into a policy and to shake off isolationism."[87] The Party also applauded the president's attempts to develop closer military ties with Latin American countries for the defense of the hemisphere, a plan that Cordell Hull advanced at the eighth Pan-American Conference in Lima in 1938.[88] The CPUSA reiterated that if Moscow and Washington made it clear that neither would tolerate further aggression, there would be no need for "an army of Americans to march into Berlin," since Germans themselves would rise in arms against Nazis, while the French and British people would replace their leaders with new ones that would bring appeasement to an end.[89] On the other hand, however, once it became clear that France and Great Britain were unwilling to go to war to stop fascism, Browder could no longer exclude the possibility that "only American arms can preserve the Americas from conquest by the Rome-Berlin-Tokyo alliance. . . . An unarmed people stands today as helpless victims for fascist conquest."[90] This statement caused a reversal in the Party's stance on military appropriations and the expansion of the armed forces. The Party now supported Roosevelt's request for a $300 million increase in military spending and the formation of an Atlantic Squadron of the Navy.[91]

As pressure from international events increased and the link between foreign and domestic policy became stronger, Browder coined a new slogan for the CPUSA: "For Social and National Security." This slogan symbolized the Party's belief in the interdependence of protection from aggression and the social well-being of the population. Speaking on the eve of the 1938 mid-term elections, Browder defined those opposed to Roosevelt and the New Deal as "the same forces that brought us the 'peace' of Munich and all its consequences." Those who opposed Hitler were "the same who fight for fuller democracy and a better life for the American people in our domestic affairs, while those who advocate 'peace' through submission to Hitler are the same who would limit, choke and try to destroy American democracy, trade unionism and the American standard of living, in the interests of the economic royalists."[92]

The Congressional elections of 1938 dealt a sharp defeat to Roosevelt and the New Deal, raising the possibility of conservative Democrats nominating their candidate for the 1940 elections. Consequently, for the CPUSA the elections of 1940 represented a referendum on whether the country was going to adopt reactionary domestic policies and submit to fascist expansionism or to become "one of the chief centers of world progress" by continuing on the road of social reforms and strengthening the world anti-fascist front.[93] Bittelman wrote that Roosevelt was the symbol of the "progressive and liberal camp" against the Tory coalition of conservative Republicans and southern Democrats. The Party's stated objective for the election was to preserve and extend the New Deal "as a way to progress, democracy and peace."[94] Once again Browder renewed his analysis of the relative, purely nominal, character of the two-party system; the Communist leader explained that Roosevelt and the New Deal had successfully united the traditional Democratic electorate with the "progressive" and "radical" sections of the voting population. This coalition had given the president his victory in 1936, and it had to be preserved if Democrats wanted to win again in 1940.[95] The issue then was for the Democratic party to nominate a candidate of "the Roosevelt type." If such a candidate failed to appear, a possibility that the Party had already accepted, then it would have been "an anti-democratic stupidity to allow the tradition [against a third-term], however sanctified by age and progressive origin, to deny democracy the chosen leader necessary to victory in the most critical moment of national and world history."[96]

The CPUSA was accordingly among the first to come out in favor of Roosevelt's third term. Browder prefaced his pro-Roosevelt declaration with an apparently conflicting statement that the Communist party would not be "committed to any candidate except its own." The endorsement of Roosevelt was then formally intended for those who, while not voting Communist, still valued the Party's advice. In reality, however, even more openly than in 1936, the CPUSA was avoiding a Communist endorsement that could be used as a weapon against the president by his enemies.[97] Should the Democratic party nominate a right-winger, the Communist leader concluded, the forces favorable to "the New Deal democracy" would have no other choice but to launch their own party with the president as its standard bearer.[98]

In January 1939, in order to further its domestic and foreign program, the Party began publishing a new monthly, *National Issues*. Edited by Gene Dennis, who had left Wisconsin to become Party secretary for legislative affairs, the paper bore a striking resemblance to the format of the *New Republic* and the *Nation*. Its objective was to spread the CPUSA's views on legislative matters among supporters of the People's Front. During its brief existence, the monthly published articles opposing appropriations for the House Un-American Activities Committee, favoring tax reform, more money to expand WPA employment and relief activities, a Farm Bill, and higher Social Security payments to the aged. At the end of each issue could be found an abridged list of the most important Congressional proposals to be discussed as well as the Party's position on each one. When the first session of the 76th Congress ended, the magazine published the voting record of all Congressmen.[99] The magazine's main emphasis, however, was on foreign affairs, especially in favor of the repeal of the Neutrality Act and of appropriations for rearmament. Articles appeared supporting the president's requests for increased military appropriations on the basis that "an unarmed democracy is helpless in a world where fascist dictators are on the march."[100] The Republican attacks on the Administration's defense program were defined as "nothing less than sabotage in the interests of Hitler, Mussolini, and the Mikado."[101] In August the paper denounced the House's refusal to grant the president his request for a repeal of the arms embargo as the "go-ahead signal to Hitler and Mussolini. . . . And we know this too: and we know whom to blame and where to place the responsibility should another war break out between the first and second sessions of the 76th Congress."[102]

The Soviet leadership and the Comintern supported the CPUSA's pro-Roosevelt stance. Both had strong words of praise for the president's 1939 State of the Union message in which he warned of the dangers to democracy caused by passive acceptance of international lawlessness.[103] In April, Gabriel Peri, the foreign affairs editor of the French Communist daily *L'Humanité*, wrote that Roosevelt's message to Hitler and Mussolini asking them to refrain from aggression was the "most constructive initiative taken in the course of the present international crisis."[104] More cautious but very significant was

Dimitri Manuilsky's positive reference to the foreign policy of the Administration. As the Soviet representative to the Executive Committee of the Comintern, Manuilsky declared at the Eighteenth Congress of the CPSU that the United States was "stimulating resistance to the aggressive plans of the fascists in other parts of the world, including Europe."[105]

Speaking at the University of Virginia in the summer of 1939, Browder stated self-assuredly: "There is as much chance of a Russo-German agreement as of Earl Browder being elected president of the Chamber of Commerce."[106] Despite France's and Britain's policy of appeasement, the majority of the Party's leadership could not imagine the possibility of a radical veering in Soviet foreign policy away from anti-fascism.[107] Consequently the Communists were caught completely by surprise when they learned on August 22 that the German foreign minister, Joachim von Ribbentrop, was on his way to Moscow to sign a non-aggression pact with the Soviet Union. The switchboard at Party headquarters on 12th Street was flooded by phone calls from members as well as sympathizers anxious to have more information, if not a denial.[108] Much later a number of Communists described their response to the news as one of dismay, confusion, and personal trauma. Steve Nelson's reaction was undoubtedly typical: "I felt like I had been hit by a bolt of lighting."[109] United States Communists had become totally committed to anti-fascism, at the core of the Party's policies since 1934. The news issuing from Germany, the tragedy of the Spanish Republic, and Nazi expansion through Europe made Communists genuinely hate Nazi Germany as the embodiment of murderous oppression and criminal expansionism. Understandably then, they were devastated by the image on the front page of every newspaper of Ribbentrop and Stalin toasting to Hitler's health. Individual Communists had to face criticism from family, friends, and co-workers: George Charney recalled how party members "literally prayed for guidance" and clung to any justification of the pact coming from authoritative non-Communist sources.[110]

Once the first shock over the pact had been subdued, the main problem for Communists became "How to justify it?"[111] As events rapidly unfolded, the Communist party found itself in the difficult situation of having to provide immediate explanations for events of international significance while lacking any precise information or directives from Moscow. Left on its own the CPUSA's reaction was a strenuous attempt to minimize the significance and the implications of the pact by staunchly claiming that the pact did not represent a shift in Soviet policy away from antifascism. As the Party was trying to limit the consequences of the Moscow agreements, its main concern remained preserving its ties with Roosevelt and saving the Democratic Front in the United States.

The August 22 *Daily Worker* omitted any mention of the pact. Party members had to wait until the next day for the Party's first statement on the matter. A front page editorial in the *Daily Worker* described the pact as a major defeat for a Nazi Germany forced to come to terms with its Soviet arch enemy; the pact strengthened "the anti-fascist struggle for peace" and helped both Poland, "whose national independence is in imminent danger from the threats of fascist aggression," and the German people in their struggle against "fascism, for peace, freedom and democracy." In conclusion, the editorial even tried to show how the pact in no way contradicted the policy of collective security and even went as far as to predict that the pact would certainly include a provision making it void if one of the signers should invade a third-country—a proviso that, when the text of the pact was made public the next day, Communists realized did not exist.[112]

On August 24, Harry Gannes, the foreign affairs editor of the *Daily Worker*, wrote that the non-aggression pact was both the inevitable consequence of French and British refusals to adopt a policy of collective security, and the Soviets' answer to Chamberlain's and Daladier's attempt to direct Nazi expansion toward the Soviet Union.[113] Along the same lines the following day, the *Daily Worker* called the pact a "smashing blow at Munich treachery. . . . By compelling Germany to sign a nonaggression pact, the Soviet Union not only tremendously limited the direction of Nazi war aims, but thereby bolstered the possibilities for peace in the world."[114] The pact was even presented as an aid to the United States by helping to curb Japanese expansionist plans; in addition, it did not preclude the possibility of stronger ties between the United States and the Soviet Union, as the Party resolutely affirmed.[115] This interpretation of Moscow's action accompanied by attacks on French and British appeasement, constituted the essence of the Party's line through the end of the month.[116]

Upon receiving news of the pact, Browder cut short his vacation and immediately returned to New York where, on the evening of August 23, he met with a large group of journalists in his office on the ninth floor of Party headquarters. In contrast to his usual self assured calmness, Browder was nervous, rocking back and forth in his chair and chain smoking. Pressed by hostile questions, he defended Moscow's action, defining as "nonsense" charges that it represented a change in policy by the Soviets. The Communist leader even advocated the idea that it would be in the interest of peace if all world powers would follow the Soviet example and commit themselves not to attack other countries. Answering a reporter's question, the Communist leader stated that the pact "should strengthen Popular Front movements everywhere."[117] Two days later, in a radio interview on the NBC network, Browder tried to present the pact as a contribution to world peace and to democracy in the United States.

> The Soviet Union was finally forced to proceed to organize peace in its own way. That this way is effective is proved by the admitted smashing of the axis world alignment, which was the chief danger to American interests, the immediate lessening of international tensions, and the improved position in world affairs of the two greatest and most peaceful powers, the Soviet Union and the United States.

According to the Communist leader, the United States government should follow a similar policy and safeguard the peace by staying out of war. "If President Roosevelt's admirable appeals for peaceful settlements obtain any results, it can only be along the line of similar agreements by other nations."[118]

Once the Party's position had been established, it rallied its forces. On the evening of August 29, meetings were held to assure the support of the pact from the rank and file. The Party provided explanation and assurance that Moscow's move was consistent with the anti-fascist policy it had previously followed. At the end of these meetings, resolutions were passed endorsing the pact.[119] Communists committed themselves to an explanation of recent events that placed them in a continuity with previous policies the Party had followed. The crisis seemed to be under control; however, within a few hours the CPUSA was facing a new challenge.

As war broke out in Europe, the Party struggled to determine its stance. Communists had to bridge conflicting positions. The CPUSA renewed its criticism of Chamberlain and Daladier, who it believed could not be trusted to lead the fight against fascism; it opposed the United States' involvement in a war that some within its ranks already defined as imperialist; but in contradiction, reflecting a wide-spread view among Communists that at last the global fight against fascism had begun, the Party took an open anti-German and pro-Polish position, and its declarations continuing to reflect the People's Front policy.[120] Within hours of the Nazi attack on Poland, the *Daily Worker* hit the streets with an editorial in support of Poland and stating that Americans should give "every possible support to the heroic and beleaguered Polish people."[121] On September 4, the National Committee of the CPUSA declared that Communists were in favor of "Full moral, diplomatic and economic help for the Polish people and those who help Poland defend its national independence."[122] The CPUSA renewed its campaign for the repeal of the Neutrality Act and against isolationists in favor of the United States placing its "mighty influence on the side of peace, against the aggressor." The Party also wanted a total embargo against Germany and Japan to "defeat the fascist aggression."[123] During the following week the pages of the Communist daily were full of praise of the national unity both France and Great Britain had achieved in the face of fascist threat. The French Communist party's pledge to support the Daladier government's declaration of war, and the fact that Maurice Thorez, together with other leaders of the PCF, had joined their regiments, was approvingly reported by the *Daily Worker.*[124] As late as September 11, the *Daily Worker* published a front page appeal for "All aid to the heroic Polish people," whose plight an editorial in the *Freiheit* equated to those of Ethiopians, Spanish, and Chinese. Browder, while not sparing criticism for the Allies, still blamed Germany, Italy, and Japan, "the bloody fascist dictatorships," for having started the war.[125]

Browder's concern through this period was to preserve the Party's support of the president; in this he was indirectly helped by Roosevelt's stance during the early stages of the war. Although he expressed his opposition to the country's involvement in the war, in a Fireside Chat on September 3, Roosevelt clearly voiced his pro-Allied sentiment.[126] The Communist leadership was very pleased with the president's declaration, which the *Daily Worker* reprinted in its entirety.[127] At the beginning of September in Chicago, when the Party's National Committee met for a previously scheduled celebration of the twentieth anniversary of the founding of the CPUSA, Browder avoided the recent international events and instead devoted his speeches mostly to the 1940 elections and noted with satisfaction that the Party and the president saw eye to eye concerning the war. He consequently renewed the support for Roosevelt's third-term.[128] At the end of the meeting the National Committee issued a number of slogans that condensed the Party line. Significantly while retaining the slogan, "For jobs, security, democracy and peace," a new one was added: "Unite the American People around the New Deal and its progressive policies."[129] On the night of September 11, Browder once again renewed the Party support for Roosevelt in a speech at Madison Square Garden in front of a cheering crowd of 20,000. Browder defined the president as "the man who was chosen by a ten million majority, who promised the people that he would never let them down, that he had just begun to fight, who has tried to make good his promises sufficiently to earn the hatred of all the worst enemies of the people."[130] The same day, Browder and Foster sent the president an open letter to express the Communists' support for his declarations against American involvement in the war: "At this moment the hope for firm national unity lies in rallying all Americans in support of this policy, and in support of the president who has best expressed the hearts and minds of the people."[131]

Despite the drastic changes and events that had taken place since the end of August, Browder had been successful in avoiding any substantial change in the policy of the CPUSA. In this effort he had been favored by the lack of any statement from Moscow on the character of the war. All this changed within hours of the rally at Madison Square Garden, as the Party leadership received word from Moscow that drastic readjustments were necessary: the message was very critical of the Polish government and stated that, since the war was imperialist, Communists were to support neither side.[132] On the morning of September 13, the *Daily Worker* published a front page interview with Browder in which the Party's secretary illustrated the new line. Echoing the message from Moscow, and in sharp contrast with his speech of the 11th, Browder asserted that the Polish government was fascist and the war was an imperialist conflict "in which the rulers of both sides are equally guilty; it is not a war waged for the destruction of fascism, but is carried on to extend and perpetuate imperialist control over the world," and thus, he added, it had "nothing to offer the masses of any participating country except death and destruction, further miseries and burdens." Despite this radical departure from previously expressed positions, Browder continued to support Roosevelt. Concerning the president's September 13 announcement that he was convening a special session of Congress to discuss a revision of the Neutrality Act, Browder stated that this was not an attempt to draw the country into the war but rather to buttress "the position of the United States as a force making for the limitation of this war."[133]

Moscow's intervention forced a sweeping reassessment of the Party's policies and analysis. Foster and Bittelman saw the opportunity to force a complete redirection of all the policy the Party had followed under Browder, particularly its support for Roosevelt. Encouraged by the situations of uncertainty and fluidity within the CPUSA created by Moscow, Foster and Bittelman prepared to square off their differences with Browder at the meeting of the Political Committee that was called to discuss the Party's position concerning the events of the previous weeks.

The Party's top leaders met in New York on September 14 and 16. The minutes of the Political Committee provide a picture of the internal debate of the Party's leadership that was previously only partially known.[134] At the meeting two views concerning the conclusions and consequences of the previous weeks' events on the Party's policies confronted each other. On one side, Browder attempted to limit the possible consequences of Moscow's new line on the CPUSA's pro-Roosevelt stance. Specifically Browder wanted to salvage as much as possible of the alliances Communists had established with the labor and political forces that supported the president, alliances which had been the basis of the Party's political achievements during the previous years. On the other side, Foster and Bittelman wanted to take advantage of the new direction of Soviet policy and end the People's Front policy as Browder had defined it and bring the Party back to a policy of revolutionary agitation. More generally, however, the confrontation illustrated different views concerning the entire evolution of Communist policies during the 1930s.

For the first time since he had become secretary, Browder found himself on the defensive, isolated within the Party leadership. This isolation was demonstrated by the conduct of Gil Green, Roy Hudson, and Eugene Dennis who in the past had been among the secretary's most outspoken supporters. While at this time Green and Hudson refrained from taking definite positions during the debate, Dennis instead sided with Bittelman and Foster. Furthermore, contrary to common practice, the introductory speech was given by Bittelman, a further sign that he, rather than Browder, was considered more in tune with the new course the CPUSA was expected to take.

Bittelman based his report on the premise that the imperialist nature of the war forced a total revision of the Party's policies. The events since Munich, particularly the refusal by western powers, including the United States, to join with the Soviet Union in an anti-fascist front meant that "the old division between democratic and the fascist camp" had lost "its former meaning."[135] Given the new situation, the position toward the war, ("for the imperialist war or against the imperialist war,") constituted the discriminant that defined new alignments.[136] According to Bittelman, the war required a drastic change in the Party's tactics, despite the fact that the United States was officially neutral; Communists had to be ready "for rapid changes in the world situation, which may necessitate again a new tactic of the CP," in other words Communists had to be ready to abandon the People's Front policy.[137] In the course of the meeting both Bittelman and Foster maintained that within the belligerent nations there was a genuine possibility that the imperialist war would evolve into a civil war as it had in Russia in 1917. Although they were quick to add that revolution was not imminent in the United States, they still insisted that changed conditions made it imperative for the CPUSA to state openly that socialism was on the agenda in the country. As a first step Bittelman proposed to eliminate the word "peace" from the slogan "For Jobs, Security, Democracy, and Peace" and to replace it with "socialism."[138]

Concerning the issue of neutrality, Bittelman stated that if the Party continued to support Roosevelt's request that Congress abrogate the Neutrality Act the CPUSA would be seen as supporting the Allies. At first, he was in favor of abstaining from having any position at all on the issue. However, Foster and Eugene Dennis went even further: they opposed any revision of the Neutrality legislation, and, in the course of the proceedings, Bittelman moved to embrace their position. This position on the Neutrality Act was, of course, a radical departure from the policy the CPUSA had followed up to then. The major consequences of the changes put forth by Bittelman and Foster would have been a return to a policy based soley on anti-capitalist propaganda, the end of the Party's support for Roosevelt, and the severing of alliances with other liberal pro-New Deal groups.

Skillfully, Browder prefaced his remarks by expressing agreement with the report's overall analysis concerning changing international circumstances. However, in contrast with his opponents, Browder then argued that the Communists' definition of the war as "imperialist" did not necessarily entail a revision of the policy the Party had adopted after Munich of criticizing Chamberlain and Daladier but of supporting Roosevelt. Browder in fact insisted that Communists maintain the "continuity of our line before the masses through every change . . . We must completely disarm that angle of attack against our Party which is perhaps the most dangerous of all . . . [the] feeling that after all the Party makes its changes disconnectedly."[139] The proposal to add "socialism" to the Party's objectives was for him a "fundamental error of strategy." It was imperative for the CPUSA to maintain its "democratic slogans" for reforms within the existing system and not to isolate itself with slogans that few were willing to follow.[140]

In line with his attempt to assure continuity in the Party's policies, Browder believed that it was mandatory to maintain the Party's opposition to the Neutrality Act. To do otherwise, he said, would only create confusion, and most importantly, place Communists on the same side with the anti-Roosevelt and pro-neutrality forces. According to Browder, any break with the president was premature; Communists should give the benefit of the doubt to Roosevelt's promise to keep the country out of war. The Communist leader, therefore, concluded, at least for the time being, "our estimate of the role of the New Deal has to be substantially the same as it has been up to now."[141]

In the course of the sometimes quite heated discussion at the Political Committee, Browder was able to gain enough support to force Bittelman to abandon his proposal for the substitution of socialism for peace in the Party's slogan. On even the issue of the Party's stance on the Neutrality Act, the result was a compromise position not to take a position; given the situation, even inaction was a victory for Browder since it avoided an open split with the president.[142] The Political Committee, hence, ended favorably for Browder. Despite Moscow's new policy and pressure from within the Party, Browder had been able to limit the consequences of the new direction of Soviet policy on the CPUSA and had reasserted his authority over the Party.

In the eye of the storm, the French, the British, and the German Communist parties, like their comrades in the United States, had at first come out in support of the war. By the end of September, when they were apprised of the new course of Soviet foreign policy, however, they abandoned the definition of the war as anti-fascist and took on a strong anti-French and anti-British posture, demanded peace with Germany, and blamed the Allies for the continuation of the war.[143]

The course pursued by the CPUSA during the following month set it apart from the rest of the Communist movement. Through Browder's efforts, the CPUSA tried to keep international events and Moscow's new policy from modifying the Party's domestic policy and particularly its support of Roosevelt. In the weeks following the meeting of the Political Committee, the CPUSA, while stepping up both its attacks on Chamberlain and Daladier as well as its declarations against the war, avoided all criticism of the president, trusting in his pledge to keep the country out of war, a promise that appeared less convincing with every passing day. The Party did not alter its position even after Roosevelt's September 21 request that Congress reconvene to replace the Neutrality Act with a cash-and-carry provision to allow the Allies to buy war material in the United States. Speaking in Cleveland on the same evening, Browder praised Roosevelt without hesitation. Communists, he said,

> join wholeheartedly with the vast majority of the American people whose hearts and minds were well expressed today in President Roosevelt's unequivocal declaration that the best interests of world peace and of American demand that we keep out of this war and out of the rivalries from which it arose.[144]

Communists must have been among the few that accepted at face value Roosevelt's assurances that such a change was in the best interest of keeping the United States out of the war and would not modify the country's neutrality.

Despite the president's support of the Allies, the Party continued in its pro-Roosevelt course possibly in the hope that somehow events would make a break unnecessary. Browder persisted in this position even after he received at the end of September and in early October two short coded radio messages directly from Dimitrov giving the American leader the injunction to change course. The two messages summarized the main points of Dimitrov's article on the imperialist character of the war about to be published in the Comintern's press. The CPUSA, according to the head of the Comintern, was to "cease to trail in the wake of FDR"; Communists had to differentiate themselves from the neutrality of the American bourgeoisie whose objectives were not anti-imperialist but rather profit-oriented exploiting the sufferings of other nations. The second message, received in early October, was even more explicit.

The new situation changes our relation with FDR . . . FDR may want to help Chamberlain and Daladier. Big task to unmask fake neutrality which covers help to Japan against China, etc. Must stop imperialist bourgeoisie of USA from providing others, enriching itself, and later entering to save the crumbling capitalist system.[145]

The messages left no doubt about Moscow's opinion of Roosevelt. Nevertheless, Browder decided to ignore even this unequivocal directive and instead found the communications concerning Roosevelt sufficiently ambiguous to allow him to emphasize those elements in them closer to his own position and ignore the rest. Just in case, Browder decided not to disclose the existence of the messages to other Party leaders.[146]

During the following weeks while the anti-Allied tone of the Party's statements increased, all criticism of Roosevelt remained moderate and indirect. The Party continued to place much credence in any presidential statement promising to keep the country out of war. There was obviously some hope among Communists that they could fuse their opposition to war together with Roosevelt's promises of U.S. neutrality. In early October, Michael Gold still claimed that the Soviet Union was the "worst enemy" of Nazi Germany. A few days later an editorial in the *Daily Worker* maintained a conciliatory tone and suggested that the president mediate the end of the conflict: "Roosevelt can really win the ear of the world which is attuned to peace, if he correctly and fully voices the demands of the people and rejects the aims of the monopolists and profiteers."[147] While criticizing the Administration's foreign policy, even Foster directed his attacks against Undersecretary of State Sumner Welles, rather than against Roosevelt.[148]

Until mid-October, despite clear warning from Moscow and pressure from within the Party, Browder obstinately kept the CPUSA from breaking with Roosevelt. Browder could not have defied Moscow for much longer. Ironically, what finally brought Browder to conform completely to the Moscow line was not pressure from abroad but rather events in the United States. On October 23, Federal agents arrested the Communist leader on passport violation charges that stemmed from his testimony to the HUAC in early September. During questioning, Browder had carelessly admitted that during the 1920s he had traveled with passports obtained under assumed names. Following this admission, the Justice Department, which had known about the violation but declined to take action, came under increasing attack from conservative Republicans trying to embarrass the president. Within the Administration itself the indictment of the Communist leader eventually came to be viewed as a convenient, yet overall harmless, way to appease mounting anti-Communist sentiments. Because of the statute of limitations Browder could not be prosecuted for using a false identity. The Communist leader was instead indicted on a minor technicality: in 1937 when he had applied for renewal of his passport, this one under his own name, Browder had neglected to mention his earlier applications.[149]

Browder's arrest was not the first incident of intimidation against the Party. Since the beginning of the war, verbal and even physical attacks on Communists had escalated. In Congress the pressure to outlaw the Communist party increased, and a number of states began arresting Party members under the most diverse pretexts. In New York, Communist candidates were prevented from running for office. Without an immediate precedent, however, was the direct involvement of federal authorities. The Communist leadership interpreted this move as the Administration's involvement in the campaign to outlaw the Party because it opposed the war. Dennis observed that throughout the world the outlawing of Communist parties was the first step against democracy and toward fascism. Roosevelt, he said, was following the lead of the French government whose offensive against the PCF had been the final step before plunging France into the war and "establishing a more open reactionary dictatorship of finance capital." Along the same lines, Browder specified that in the United States the outlawing of the CPUSA would have represented one of the "first decisive steps on the road of American entrance into imperialist war."[150]

The Party's line changed overnight: on October 28 an editorial in the *Daily Worker* directly attacked Roosevelt, accusing him of having become an agent of big business in defense of British imperialism.[151] The strongest attack against the president came from Browder who had been recently released on bail. On November 5 in Boston he charged that

"democratic" America even while it is still technically neutral, forgets its liberal dreams about a "New Deal," and loses itself in a wave of reactionary sentiment. . . . The president and his Administration succumb more and more every day to this greed for profits by American monopoly capital, and

make use of its former prestige among the masses to secure their acceptance of the program of Wall Street.[152]

Using language not heard for years Browder stated that the country's
ruling class realized that the United States was "technically, objectively, the country which is the most ripe, the most prepared, for a
quick transition to socialism."[153] In a speech to 2,000 textile workers at
the end of November, Foster unleashed his sentiments: "The Roosevelt administration adopts a more and more warlike policy. The lifting
of the arms embargo was a long step toward getting us into war."[154]
The tone of the anti-Roosevelt rhetoric grew more biting after the
president condemned the Soviet attack on Finland; a December 9
editorial in the *Daily Worker* included Roosevelt in the anti-Soviet
front: "The Administration has become a leading world sponsor of the
imperialist puppets operating their provocative conspiracy on the bor-
ders of the Soviet Union."[155] The president was accused of having
become the "leader and organizer of all the reactionary forces in the
country," and Browder went so far as to state that the president's new
policy followed "the same direction which Hitler gave to Germany in
1933." The Party resuscitated language and accusations against the
president what went back to the third period of the early 1930s. Once
again Roosevelt was chided for his imperialist and anti-Soviet activities while serving as assistant secretary of the Navy and governor of
New York. The political division between the parties of the New Deal
and the anti-New Deal had disappeared: Roosevelt had instead become the head of the "War Party." According to the Party's new analysis the country had gone back to the pre-1936 division of the electorate
of "Tweedledum and Tweedledee," in which the only differences
were formalities based on how to limit best the liberties and living
standards of the working class.[156] If anyone wondered why the Party
had once been such an ardent supporter of the president, Browder's
answer was: "it is not we who have changed, but rather the Roosevelt
Administration."[157] Predictably, Foster took this one step further and
extended his criticism to the Administration's policies from 1937 to
August 1939. During that time, he said, the president had done nothing more than grant "very limited concessions to the rising labor and
democratic movement."[158]

It would be unrealistic to believe that the CPUSA would have openly
challenged Soviet foreign policy, ignored the clear admonitions from

the Comintern, and continued indefinitely to support Roosevelt. Considering the nature of the international communist movement and its links to the Soviet Union, Browder's arrest and Roosevelt's criticism of the Soviet Union only hastened a break that was inevitable. This fact, nonetheless, must not lead to an underestimation of the significance of the Party's position during the two months following the Nazi–Soviet pact. Browder tried to preserve a "continuity" of policy because on such stability depended the credibility of the CPUSA as an "American" organization. Within the general context of the history of the international communist movement the unwillingness of American Communists to accept the implications of the new course of Soviet policy is in itself an unequivocal refutation of any notion that United States Communists automatically aligned themselves to the "twists and turns" of Moscow's policies. The attempt to preserve support for Roosevelt reveals how ingrained, at least for some of its leaders, was the importance of the People's Front program of alliances with other forces and organizations.

PART THREE

8

"STANDING ON ITS OWN FEET"

For the first time we are meeting and solving problems for which there are no precedents in history and no formulas from the classics which give us the answer. Perhaps we could say that our party is fully standing on its own feet for the first time.

Earl Browder, 1944

Browder's analysis of capitalism in the United States is not distinguished by a judicious application of Marxism–Leninism.

Jacques Duclos, 1945[1]

Early on September 17, 1939, applying the provisions of the secret protocol that accompanied the Molotov–Ribbentrop pact, the Red Army moved into Poland and quickly occupied Western Ukraine and Western Byelo-Russia. Ten days later, motivated by Hitler's military strength and by the Allies' inactivity in the West, Stalin agreed to the transformation of the nonaggression pact into a Friendship Pact. As a first token of such the Soviet Union agreed to sign a joint statement with Germany recognizing the fall of Poland as a *fait accompli*, urging an end to the hostilities, and blaming France and Britain for any continuation of the war.[2]

The CPUSA aligned itself with the new course of Soviet foreign policy. All anti-fascist propaganda came to an end, criticism of Germany was muted. Britain and France were blamed for the continuation of the war; according the the CPUSA, the Allies' objective was to defeat Hitler and replace him with a government willing to transform the "imperialist war" into a counterrevolutionary war against the Soviet Union.[3]

As a result of the dramatic change in Soviet policy and the resulting new course of the CPUSA, membership, which had steadily climbed throughout the decade, fell. At the end of September, Browder tried to minimize the number of defectors; he told a rally of Philadelphia Communists that no more than "a dozen or so" had deserted the Party and predicted that in the coming weeks there would be only "a couple of dozen more who will run away from the fight."[4] While the Party suffered losses to a higher degree than Browder had predicted, defections were not numerous, a remarkable situation given the radical change in the Party's direction. Estimates on the Party's loss of membership vary. The CPUSA acknowledged a 15 percent drop between 1939 and 1940; more significant was the drop in recruitment from a monthly average of 3,000 in February and March of 1937 and 1938, to 700 for the same period in 1940.[5]

Except for some groups such as Finns, who in states such as Minnesota had always been the backbone of the Party and who left the CPUSA in droves, the majority of American Communists remained with the Party. Even among Jewish Communists the losses were limited.[6] Although Communists must have looked back with nostalgia to the Democratic Front period, they still could find a rationale for their present course. Their attachment to the Party, their faith in the USSR, and their strong sense of duty to defend the Workers' State were such that most Communists submerged their doubts and accepted their leaders' explanations virtually without debate either at a local or national level. Among those who had fought in Spain there was a particular sense of bitterness toward the French and British governments for having denied aid to the Spanish Loyalist cause. Now that the tables had turned and London and Paris were forced into the war, some Party members expressed the feeling that "the sons-of-bitches had it coming."[7] Finally, the Party's new policy was accepted without major splits because it seemed to find confirmation during the early months of "Phoney War" on the Western front, as well as in the planning by the French and British General Staffs of a strike against the Soviet Union after the Red army attacked Finland at the end of November.[8]

Although the Nazi–Soviet Pact and the "imperialist war" period may have had a limited impact on Communist membership, they devastated the alliances Communists had formed and carefully nurtured through the Popular Front years. The Nazi–Soviet pact tarnished the image of the Soviet Union as the anti-fascist bastion, and undermined the credibility of the CPUSA as an indigenous radical organization.

A reaction shared by many former supporters of the Soviet Union was not one of criticism of Stalin's *realpolitik,* but instead one of consternation that to act in its country's best interest the Soviet government was willing to give up the ideals of the Popular Front. Consequently, they concluded that, just like the Pact, anti-fascist collective security was a policy the Soviet Union had followed simply for its own national self-interest against Germany.

The major disillusionment, however, was with the CPUSA. In the 1930s many liberals and "fellow travelers" had supported United States Communists as committed fighters against fascism and for social change; now they questioned the Party's motives and sincerity. They felt betrayed by an organization that, despite declarations of being bound to United States' reality and professed democratic principles, had in a short period of time veered from advocating collective security against fascism to denying with equal vehemence that there was a moral distinction between Nazi Germany and the Allies. In his letter of resignation from the CPUSA, which appeared in the *New Republic* on October 4, Granville Hicks took issue with the Party's leadership for having embraced the pact with a deluge of statements "devoid of clarity and logic." From these statements, he wrote, only one conclusion could be drawn: "if the Party leaders could not defend the Soviet Union intelligently, they would defend it stupidly." The choice to embrace Moscow's new course spelled the end of the Democratic Front line and led Hicks to declare: "I cannot accept a change that is dictated by the exigencies of Soviet foreign policy."[9]

Fellow travelers and liberals who made anti-fascism their main concern were bound neither by a sense of Party discipline nor by the priority to defend the Soviet Union. This attitude made it impossible for them to follow the CPUSA's shift from advocating anti-fascism to opposing the "imperialist war." While the *Nation* called the nonagression pact, "The Moscow–Berlin axis," the *New Republic* described it as "Stalin's Munich," whose consequences would be the loss "of moral prestige of the Soviet government" among liberals and progressives.[10] As the terms of the secret protocol became clearer, granting Moscow a free hand in Eastern Poland against Finland and the Baltic states, the theme of the similarity between Hitler and Stalin began to appear. Following the partition of Poland, the Soviet Union was defined as "a member of the Fascist bloc," and after its attack on Finland, the *New*

Republic equated Moscow with Berlin as carrying out their foreign policy in "identical ways."[11] The *New Republic* and the *Nation* both ridiculed as "nonsense" the Party's attempt to show that the new direction of Soviet foreign policy helped peace and democracy. For the *New Republic*, the Communists' shift to a policy that contradicted previously touted beliefs proved that the Party's overriding concern was to defend the Soviet Union. This exclusive priority undermined the respect Communists had achieved, a prestige, the article concluded, that would "be hard to recover."[12]

As a consequence of these circumstances, liberals joined traditional anti-Communist circles in expressing the view that fascism and communism shared identical objectives and methods. Beginning in late 1939, an increasing number of liberal organizations and unions passed "Communazi" resolutions, barring Communists as well as members of fascist and Nazi organizations from membership.[13] Even the American Civil Liberties Union went so far as to expel Elizabeth Gurley Flynn, a charter member as well as a member of the board of directors.[14] Both the *Nation* and the *New Republic* supported the American Federation of Teachers in its expulsion of Communist-led locals in New York and Philadelphia and urged the Newspaper Guild to rid itself of Communist influence. The *New Republic* approved of the ACLU's ban on Communists and fascists as neither of them shared "the democratic belief in individual freedom."[15]

The plethora of organizations which had come to symbolize the Communist party's anti-fascist priority and concern with the defense of democracy, was devastated. Predictably the organization hardest hit was the American League for Peace and Democracy, whose main objective had been the campaign in favor of collective security. The signs of its crisis were immediately apparent. The League's yearly peace march, which in 1938 had attracted 20,000 people, now drew less than half that number; some estimated that out of 20,000 members in August, 1,000 members a month resigned until in early 1940 the league was disbanded.[16] Another casualty in the crumbling of the Popular Front was the League of American Writers. A third of the organization's officers resigned; 100 out of 800 members broke with the league publicly while many others just drifted away.[17]

The Nazi–Soviet Pact sheared the alliance between Communists and their allies within the American Student Union. The forces opposed to the Party's new line crystallized around Joseph Lash, who had publicly criticized the Pact and the invasion of Finland, urging instead support for the president and the repeal of the Neutrality Act. At the organization's Fifth Convention in December 1940, Communists were able to muster enough support to defeat the liberal pro-collective security forces. The Convention defeated a motion condemning the Soviet attack on Finland by a 322 to 49 majority and adopted instead a program calling the war "imperialist" and favoring neutrality. Following the defeat, Lash left the organization together with scores of lesser officials and most of its membership.[18]

A similar split took place within the American Youth Congress. Communists and their allies progressively moved the organization away from collective security toward an anti-war campaign. Long gone were the days of the Popular Front when the organization's support for the president was at its highest. In February 1940 in Washington, 4,500 delegates at a American Youth Congress meeting stood on the south lawn of the White House and defiantly booed and hissed Roosevelt's attacks on the Soviet Union; later the same day they cheered as John L. Lewis lambasted the president.[19] The UMW president had fallen out with Roosevelt, whom he blamed for declining to take the side of labor in 1937 during the fierce struggle between SWOC and "Little Steel" as well as for failing to push for more social reforms. With the start of the war, Lewis's isolationism added another dimension of difference.[20] Following its increasing realignment with the new Communist line, the AYC lost most of its support from liberal and religious groups and personalities.

The Party's position within New York's American Labor Party became tenuous, since the organization went on record in support of the Allies and Roosevelt. In early October an overwhelming majority of the ALP's executive committee voted to remove all known Communists and their sympathizers as "betrayers of the labor movement" and "antagonists of democracy." The meeting endorsed Roosevelt's demand for a revision of the arms embargo and expressed support for the Allies.[21]

Moreover, the Party's new policies had a negative impact on the traditionally sympathetic Jewish community. Coworkers, many of whom had relatives in Poland, greeted Jewish Communists with jeers and "Nazi salutes." Most of them found unconvincing both the Communist party's assertion that the occupation of Western Ukraine and Western Byelo-Russia saved Jews from the anti-Semitism of the Polish government and Browder's claims in a 1940 pamphlet that Jews had nothing to gain from an Allied victory.[22] A further indication of the Party's alienation from the Jewish community was the result of Browder's race for the vacant congressional seat in the predominently Jewish New York's Lower East Side, a Communist stronghold. While in 1938 the Communists candidate for City Council had received 7,000 votes, in January 1940 the Party secretary mustered a scant 3,000, approximately the number of Party members residing in the district.[23] This was a defeat that even Browder had to admit was "unchallengeable."[24]

As opposed to claims in recent historical accounts, the Nazi–Soviet Pact, the reversal of the Party's anti-fascist priority, and the subsequent loss of support from its former liberal allies, did not sound the death knell for the CPUSA. Counter to Harvey Klehr's affirmation, at no time during the "imperialist war" period was "the Party over," nor did the Communist party return to the revolutionary posturing of the "third period."[25] Quite to the contrary Party leaders displayed flexibility, and strove to maintain a degree of continuity in the Party's policies. This course was apparent in the case of organized labor.

The leadership of the AFL and the CIO shared the Party's opposition to United States involvement in war. However, the majority of the trade union movement supported Roosevelt as well as the Administration's policy of furnishing aid to the Allies and its program of national defense. Because of the Party's pro-Soviet and anti-Roosevelt stance, even here Communists became the victims of a powerful "anti-Communazi" sentiment. As mentioned earlier left-wingers lost their leadership positions in the American Newspaper Guild and the International Woodworkers of America, while four Communist-controlled locals of the American Federation of Teachers were expelled in New York City and Philadelphia.[26] The 1940 UAW convention in St. Louis exemplified the Communists' increasingly tenuous position within organized labor. Although all factions agreed to oppose United States intervention, Communists found themselves isolated on other matters even from their factional allies, since the convention went on record as equating Nazi Germany to the Soviet Union and as supporting Roosevelt's reelection.[27] In a similar vein, in November the CIO national convention in Atlantic City proscribed "Nazism, Communism, and Fascism," as "foreign ideologies" with "no place in this great modern labor movement."[28]

At the CIO convention the Party chose not to challenge anti-Communist and pro-Roosevelt resolutions that were introduced by

Lee Pressman and voted for by Communist delegates. This course denotated a more general posture: while the leadership of the CPUSA emphasized the importance of Communists' raising all aspects of the Party's program, on a more practical level the Party did not force left-wing unionists to choose between following the Party line and break-ing with their unions. Communist unionists were therefore able to avoid even greater isolation and possible expulsion. They retained, and in some cases even increased, significant influence within orga-nized labor.

Concerning the 1940 presidential election, in an attempt to insure some degree of continuity, the Party presented itself as the only orga-nization which still embodied the spirit of the New Deal.[29] Resurrect-ing the main theme of the early 1930s, the CPUSA pointed out repeat-edly the lack of any substantial difference between Roosevelt and Willkie: both expressed the views of the "War Party Coalition"; their differences in domestic and foreign policy were "only of method, and of degrees of demagogy," and of how better "to deceive the masses, and to prevent their independent political organization and strug-gles."[30] The issue for the CPUSA was no longer one of a "third term" but rather once again of a "third party": of a farmer-labor party that would unite opponents of the war and pro-New Dealers disen-chanted with Roosevelt. Eugene Dennis called it "an anti-imperialist party of peace" to fight against the war and for realizing "the social objectives of the New Deal as understood and fought for by labor and the people."[31] In mid-February 1940, the Party's national committee spelled out the program of the revived farmer-labor party: "Keep America Out of the Imperialist War!"; "Put America Back to Work; Curb the Monopolies; Jobs, Security for All!"; "Higher Wages, Shorter Hours—An American Standard of Living for All!" and "Protect and Extend Civil Liberties."[32]

At first Communists hoped that John L. Lewis would become the rallying point around which such a party would be formed.[33] Through most of 1940, Lewis spoke to different audiences about the need for a new political coalition independent of the two traditional parties. This new party, he said, was to be committed to social reforms at home and to nonintervention in foreign affairs.[34] However, Communist hopes that Lewis would emerge as the head of a progressive anti-war coali-tion were dashed since he refused to commit himself, associated openly with reactionary circles, and, eventually at the end of October

1940, endorsed the Republican candidate, Wendell Willkie. Isolated once again, the Communist party nominated Browder and Ford as its standard bearers.[35]

The Party could have no illusions as to the result of the elections. While Roosevelt's margin of victory was the closest since 1916, the president still retained the working class vote despite Lewis's deprecatory efforts. For his foreign policy, the president gained the support of pro-British groups, he also retained the goodwill of many who opposed the United States' intervention in the war but who chose to believe Roosevelt's last minute pledge to the mothers of America that their boys were "not going to be sent into any foreign war." The total vote for the Browder–Ford ticket was 48,548 votes, almost half of what it had been in 1936 when the Party had indirectly supported Roosevelt. Another reason for the Party's poor showing was that through technicalities and intimidation Communist candidates had been struck off the ballot in half the states, including such centers of Communist strength as New York, Ohio, and Illinois.[36]

The Party's loss of former liberal allies made it more vulnerable to the concerted campaign by state and federal authorities. On January 22, 1940, after a speedy trial, Browder was sentenced to four years in jail. In March 1941, after having exhausted his appeals all the way to the Supreme Court, he began to serve his time. Old charges that lay dormant for years were now resurrected. William Weiner and Harry Gannes were indicted on passport charges. In June 1940, William Schneiderman, the head of the Party in California, who had lived in the United States since the age of two, was stripped of his citizenship because of his Communist affiliation. On a local level Sam Darcy was extradited from Pennsylvania to California on charges of perjury for having provided a false name and birth date on his voter's registration in 1934. In West Virginia, Oscar Wheeler, Communist candidate for governor, was accused of soliciting signatures to put the Party on the ballot under false pretenses and was sentenced to fifteen years in jail. In Oklahoma eighteen Party activists were arrested while campaigning and were held at $100,000 each, accused of violating the state's criminal syndicalism laws.[37] Communists were barred from teaching at the University of California. In New York the state legislature set up the Rapp-Coudert Committee to uncover Communists in New York City's college system. Its activities led to the dismissal of twenty faculty and staff as well as the resignations of twenty more.[38] Formed in May 1938 and chaired by conservative Texas Democrat Martin Dies, the House Committee on Un-American Activities proceeded to investigate the American League for Peace and Democracy, the AYC, the ASU, the NMU, and the League of Women Shoppers. Eventually Committee investigators carried out a number of much publicized raids on Party offices throughout the Northeast and Midwest, culminating in the raid on the Philadelphia headquarters in May 1940.[39]

Reflecting the fear of foreigners and radicals typical in times of international trouble, in 1940 Congress passed the Smith Act, which made it a crime to advocate the overthrow of the United States government, and the Voorhis Registration Act, calling for the dissolution and arrest of the leaders of any organization with international affiliation considered a threat to national security at the discretion of the Attorney General.[40] In order to continue to operate, the provisions of the Voorhis Act required the Party to disaffiliate formally from the Comintern. The CPUSA reluctantly took this step on November 16-17, at a special congress called for this purpose. Having done so the delegates then defiantly proceeded to reaffirm that the Party was severing only formal ties and that it remained firmly committed to the principles of proletarian internationalism.[41]

Contrary to the events of August and September 1939, the CPUSA's shift back to anti-fascism after the Nazi invasion of the Soviet Union in June 1941 did not create hesitation or raise opposition among its ranks; the common reaction was one of concern for the future of the Socialist state but also one of relief. The enemy was again fascism, the force that events and sentiment had drawn Communists to oppose since 1933.[42] Once again the defense of the Soviet Union and the national interest of the United States coincided: internationalism and Americanism returned to being synonymous. The war went from "imperialist" to anti-fascist, for the defense of democracy. The Party became among the most vocal supporters of the war effort, of Roosevelt and, as Soviet losses increased, of the campaign in favor of a second front.

Communists saw the new situation as allowing them to return to the mainstream of the progressive movement from which they had been cut off during the "imperialist war" period. The old front organizations that had been either disbanded or discredited with the end of the Party's advocacy of collective security were replaced by new prowar ones, such as the Russian War Relief, the National Council of American-Soviet Friendship, and numerous others aimed at specific national groups, whose goal was to provide material support and promote lobbying efforts in favor of aid and cooperation. As such they attracted considerable support outside the Party.[43]

After the United States was drawn into the conflict, some 15,000 Communists joined the armed forces, while scores of Communists in the merchant marine helped supply armies in the field.[44] Communists, however, viewed as their most important contributions to victory ensuring the mobilization and full use of the country's industrial potential and solidifying a national consensus around Roosevelt's foreign policy of Soviet-American collaboration. The most far reaching consequence of the Party's wartime policy can be seen in its labor policy. Reversing its traditional militancy, the CPUSA supported the no strike pledge to which the leaders of the AFL and the CIO had agreed ten days after Pearl Harbor. To show its commitment to the war effort, the Party also proposed a system of "incentive pay," which would have provided pay hikes proportional to overall production increase in a given work place.[45] By 1943 the Party rigidly adhered to the no strike pledge even when opposition to it began to mount among labor as it became apparent that workers were making disproportionate sacrifices to the war effort, while their wages were not keeping up with the rising cost of living and with soaring profits.[46]

The popularity of the Soviet Union courageously repulsing the Nazis and the Party's return to anti-fascism and its support for Roosevelt combined to good effect. The Red scare against the CPUSA came to an end. In May 1942 Roosevelt commuted Browder's prison sentence to time served to "promote national unity." Wendell Willkie argued Schneiderman's case in front of the Supreme Court, which restored his citizenship on the basis that being a member of the Communist party was not sufficient reason to revoke it.[47] The CPUSA strengthened its position within the Democratic party in California and the Minnesota FLP. Communists regained lost ground within the American Labor Party, where they maintained their close ties with the ALP's Congressman Vito Marcantonio. In 1943, the Party won its most important electoral success with the election of two Communist councilmen, Pete Cacchione from Brooklyn and Benjamin Davis, Jr., from Manhattan.[48] New acceptance of the Party was such that Browder even met a number of times with Sumner Welles to discuss various aspects of State Department policy.[49] Despite the break with Lewis over his opposition to the no strike pledge, Communists within the labor movement forged new alliances and reconstituted old ones which had been strained by the "imperialist war," and they remained a considerable force within the CIO.

Communist membership increased during the war. Among new recruits there was a notable increase in the percentage of industrial workers, a phenomenon that perhaps indicated that many among them shared the Party's view that production was to be increased at all costs. The growth in membership was certainly also encouraged by new changed demands placed on Communists: participation at meetings was no longer required, reading the Communist press and involvement in community organizations was sufficient. Communist activities became synonymous with model and concerned citizenship. The Party also benefited from the prestige of the Soviet ally; the media, even the most conservative, projected an image of the USSR similar to that of the United States, a country endowed with the same goals, pragmatism, and enthusiasm.[50]

Soon after his release from jail, Browder wrote *Victory and After,* published in the fall of 1942. This work was an attempt to provide a coherent framework within which to place the Party's support for the policy of national unity and of class collaboration during the war. According to the Communist leader, victory over fascism was an absolute priority to which all other considerations were to be subordinate. National unity would be achieved only through compromise between the conflicting interests of capital and labor; it was up to workers to shoulder the greater burden; capitalists were to be guaranteed adequate profits so that they would not become "disaffected and sabotage the war." If capitalists did not support the war, he wrote, "the necessary measures to suppress their resistance would be more costly and damaging than the concessions that must be made to win them to a workable compromise."[51] Browder's view of national and international collaboration was not limited to the wartime emergency. In a momentous proposition, Browder transformed the alliance from a policy based on tactical necessities into a long term strategy extending to the postwar period. He expressed the view that the collaboration between the Allies and the preservation of national unity continue after the war to deal collectively with the economic and political challenges of reconstruction and guarantee of an orderly transition from a wartime to a peacetime economy.[52]

The Party's return to anti-fascism in June 1941 and its all out support for the war effort did not reestablish the close ties and credibility with liberals swept away by the nonaggression pact. In light of its obvious link to events in the Soviet Union, the Communists' return to the People's Front was met by most of the Party's former allies with continued suspicion and cynicism. The Party's changing course reinforced the image of an organization whose policies were shaped not in response to conditions in the United States but rather by the need to align itself with the new priorities of Soviet foreign policy. The Communists' unqualified support for national unity and their campaign for a second front appeared to be dictated by the priorities of Soviet-American relations. Once the coalition ended, there was no telling what the Communist party's next somersault would be.

While the heroic role of European Communists in the Resistance was able to erase, at least for the most part, the negative image of the 1939–1941 period, American Communists had to find different ways to redeem themselves from the legacy of the "imperialist war" period, to break their isolation, and mend relations with liberals. The need to regain the "American image" of an organization responsive to domestic circumstances as well as the support and relative acceptance they had lost in 1939 weighed heavily on the successive history of the CPUSA and specifically on Browder's proposals. As Maurice Isserman has pointedly shown, through a dramatic gesture the Communist leader wanted to impress on liberals that Communists were sincerely committed to democracy and to the best interests of the country but, at the same time, he did not want to criticize past policies and, by implication, the USSR.[53]

Browder saw such an opportunity following the meeting in Teheran in the late fall of 1943, where Stalin, Churchill, and Roosevelt pledged to collaborate for the defeat of Germany and to continue to work for peace after the war was over. In his report to the enlarged meeting of the National Committee on January 7-9, 1944, Browder described the Teheran agreement as a turning point in history; confirming his predictions in *Victory and After,* Teheran promised that the collaboration achieved among the Allies in the heat of battle would continue in the postwar world, and demonstrated that capitalism and socialism had "begun to find the way to peaceful coexistence and collaboration in the same world."[54] For the "promise of Teheran" to materialize, national support for Roosevelt's policies was essential. According to the Party's secretary, the goal of reinforcing such national unity took precedence over all other considerations. In light of this Communists were to recognize that "the American people are so ill-prepared subjectively, for any deep-going change in the direction of socialism that postwar plans with such an aim would not unite the nation but would further divide it." In the interest of national unity, Browder boldly stated that the task of the Communist party was to set aside its program for the establishment of socialism in the United States to dispel fears that could become a rationale for a swing to the right and a victory by the forces opposed to continued collaboration with the USSR.[55]

According to Browder, Communists were to do everything in their power to ensure continued Soviet-American collaboration and national unity. As he had done many times in the past, the Communist leader discussed the nature of the two-party system as encompassing an ideologically heterogenous coalition of groups expressing various geographical and social interests. He also emphasized its specific American character: within the two-party system, he stated, a third party was "regarded as a sect which has withdrawn itself from the practical political life of the nation."[56] Based on this premise, Browder went on to make a dramatic proposal. If Communists wanted to participate in preserving national unity as well as to become part of the mainstream of the country's political life there was only one solution: to dissolve the CPUSA as an autonomous political party and to replace it with the Communist Political Association (CPA) which would act as an organized pressure group within the existing political structure. By replacing the CPUSA with the CPA, Browder felt Communists adjusted their organizational name "to correspond more exactly to the American political tradition" and their "own practical political role."[57]

Throughout the years as leader of U.S. Communists, Browder had not shied away from innovation, but this was his boldest proposal. Browder could not miss the unorthodox character of the path he was charting for United States Communists. He interpreted the disbanding of the Communist International in May 1943 as the Soviet Union's authorization to Communist parties to elaborate independent political programs suited to specific national conditions. Top figures of the international Communist movement, including André Marty, Dimitrov, and Togliatti, whom Browder kept abreast of all the changes and inner debates within the CPUSA, reassured the American leader with signs of approval for his policy of national unity centering around Roosevelt.[58] Furthermore, Browder must have believed that he had proven himself as a leader: under his direction the Party had successfully molded its policies to accommodate the country's unique circumstances. He must have deemed that these accomplishments allowed him room for independence and innovation. Communists he said were finding solutions for problems for which there were "no precedents in history and no formulas from the classics to provide them with answers." In doing so, he concluded, the Party was "standing on its own feet for the first time."[59]

The only challenge to Browder came once again from Foster, supported by Sam Darcy. On January 20, 1944, Foster addressed a letter to the members of the national committee expressing his dissent and taking issue with Browder's view of the postwar perspective. Foster did not challenge the proposal to dissolve the Party, instead he took issue with Browder's predictions concerning the postwar world. According to Foster, Browder underestimated how the war would accelerate the economic and political crisis of capitalism, which in turn would intensify U.S. imperialist aggression. Furthermore, rather than believing that the decisive sectors of American capitalism would become partners in carrying forth the decisions of the Teheran conference, Communists should instead recognize that the postwar period would usher in a renewal of class conflict in the United States. During this conflict Communists needed to revitalize their efforts in the direction of socialist transformation of society.[60]

Once again, however, Foster was unable to muster support for his views. Knowledge of the existence and the contents of the letter was limited to the top leadership which voted down Foster's views on February 8.[61] On May 20, 1944, at a carefully choreographed convention the Party was formally dissolved and replaced with the Communist Political Association. The convention stressed unanimity within the Communist ranks, continuity with their history, and praise for Browder's leadership.[62]

The almost unanimous acceptance of Browder's Teheran policy is in part attributable to the highly centralized and undemocratic character of the Communist party, which allowed only limited debate at the top and none among the rank and file. Most importantly, however, Communists accepted the formation of the CPA because, while not a party by name, the new organization preserved Communists as a cohesive and organized force and enabled them to display greater flexibility as they pursued coalition politics in favor of social and economic reforms and of continued collaboration between the United States and the Soviet Union. Setting aside Browder's evaluation of the Teheran meeting, the dissolution of the CPUSA, while dramatic in form, in substance simply represented an adaptation of the Party's name to the analyses and policies which United States Communists had been shaping since the early 1930s.

Having made the transition from Party to Association, Communists maintained their support for Roosevelt and for the first time openly endorsed his reelection. They continued to promote maximum industrial production and all out aid for the embattled Soviet Union. The dissolution of the Communist party did not have an adverse effect on recruitment which continued to grow: by 1944 membership achieved the same level as before the nonaggression pact.[63]

Through the 1930s, Communists had been very careful to balance any new innovative policy they adopted with profuse proclamations of their firm commitment to Marxism-Leninism. In the case of the dissolution of the CPUSA no such claim was possible. Almost exactly a year after the founding of the Communist Political Association, the theoretical monthly of the French Communist party, *Cahiers du Communisme*, published the famous article by Jacques Duclos. Drawing extensively from Browder's speeches and Foster's letter to the national committee, the French Communist leader recounted the debates leading to the dissolution of the CPUSA. Duclos' views were extremely critical of Browder whom he accused of misinterpreting the significance of the Teheran meeting from which he had drawn conclusions "in no wise flowing from a Marxist analysis of the situation."[64] Domestically, Duclos took issue with the dissolution of the Party and with the predictions of harmonious relations between the classes in the United States after the war, and he branded Browder's views as a "notorious revision" of Marxism.[65] It was immediately apparent to United States Communists that the Duclos article was expressing a political judgment not peculiar to the French party but rather originating in Moscow. While in theory the dissolution of the Communist International freed parties from centralized control, Moscow's views were still accepted as higher wisdom.

Whatever may have been Moscow's motivations for this intervention, it was clearly not intended to bring about Browder's downfall nor a substantial change in the policies of Communists in the United States. Duclos' article criticized the dissolution of the Party and Browder's predictions of long term class peace in the United States; the French leader did not take issue with the tactics followed by the CPUSA during the previous decade. It is safe to assume that Moscow expected that Browder, having learned his lesson that political innovation should not lead to a challenge to orthodoxy, would have continued to lead in a reconstituted CPUSA.

The Duclos article, however, had a very different effect. Such an authoritative challenge confused United States Communists who had believed that their decisions of the previous year had the support of Moscow. Implicitly, Foster's position as the chief opponent of Browder's "revisionism" was strengthened by the article as well as by the deterioration of the Grand Alliance and the first indications of the great strike movement that was to rock the country after V.J. day. As a result, Foster emerged as the Party's outstanding leader. Starting at the end of May and through June, the top leadership of the CPA held three separate meetings to discuss the implications of the Duclos article.[66] While Browder's position had been undoubtedly shaken, he continued to enjoy considerable support, and most of the leaders of the CPA, including Foster, expected him to steer them through these dangerous waters. However, Browder undermined his own position. After over a decade as the unquestioned leader of Communists in the United States, he stubbornly refused to concede to criticism of his analysis of the Teheran agreements, and he held fast to his predictions of improved U.S.–Soviet relations even in the face of growing strains between the two countries. Browder's unwillingness to accept any compromise eventually steered him toward an arrogant refusal to take part in the debate that followed the Duclos article, and he irreversibly isolated himself from the rest of the Communist leadership. Foster and his supporters were quick to seize the opportunity presented by Browder's intransigence to openly turn against him and to transform the entire issue into an indictment of all the courses followed under Browder. Consequently by the end of June, within two months of the Duclos article, Browder had been removed from leadership (a first step toward his subsequent expulsion). A date had also been set for a special convention to reconstitute the CPUSA. Foster had ascended as the political and ideological leader of Communists in the United States and the experiment to attune the Party to the country's realities came to an end. These changes would have fatal implications for the Communist party.

CONCLUSION

During the years of the depression and World War II the increase in Communist strength, broadened influence, relative acceptance, and their ability to make significant contributions to the labor and social struggles of the time, were direct consequences of their search for policies, language, and organizational forms which reflected the country's circumstances, culture, and singular political system as Communists understood and articulated them. This process, sometimes termed "Americanization," transformed the Party into the leading left-wing organization in the country; moreover, it was initiated and defined, in its various phases, by United States Communists. The new directions of the Comintern and Soviet foreign policy of the Popular Front period provided new opportunities and more room to maneuver for those within the Party who were pushing for a revision of past sectarian policies in favor of the adoption of a new line that would enable them to deal with the challenges that had emerged from the complex political and economic situation that had developed during the depression.

Futhermore, the experiences they accumulated in the labor and political movements of the 1930s and their dedicated antifascism made it imperative that Communists join in coalition with a wide range of political and labor organizations for common objectives of social reform and in defense of democracy. Under Browder the preservation and the strengthening of these ties became the centerpiece of the Party's strategy.

New tactics forced Communists to consider the relationship between the defense of democracy and socialism: of how to transform a defensive policy of broad democratic unity against fascism and for limited reforms into a program for social change. During the late 1930s Browder addressed the implicit contrast between the Communists' Americanization with the Bolshevik revolutionary model by

213

presenting socialism as a distant objective. Looking at the circumstances leading to the dissolution of the CPUSA, it is hard not to avoid a parallel between this event and a contemporary recognition within a number of European Communist parties that the diversity of national historical experiences might require new "national roads" to building socialism very different from the one followed by the Soviet Union. Palmiro Togliatti, the most attentive among Communist leaders in the search for policies better reflecting national environments, did not overlook this parallel. After the war he angrily confronted two leading Italian Communists, Giuseppe Berti and Ambrogio Donini, who while in exile in the United States had openly sided with Moscow in condemning the dissolution of the CPUSA. Togliatti accused them not only of having partaken in what he described as the Soviets' inadmissible interference into the affairs of United States Communists but also of having given support to what he perceived as Moscow's warning not to go too far to other Communist parties who were raising new political and theoretical questions.[1]

In 1944, however, in proposing the replacement of the Party with the Communist Political Association, Browder did not raise the socialist perspective. While stating that Communists were setting their course "to realize the possibilities inherent in the present situation of what would have been described in the past as an evolutionary development of the transition period," he acknowledged in a disarmingly candid statement the major inadequacy of his analysis: "We are not prepared to give any broad theoretical generalizations for this period."[2]

Browder's failure to address such a fundamental question was possibly a reflection of a theoretical weakness or of an unwillingness to venture too far down the path of political innovation. In addition, however, it is important to consider the weight of objective domestic conditions on Browder's thought. In Europe a number of Communist parties that had achieved considerable strength and prestige because of their wartime activities, chief among them Togliatti's PCI, were part of the new coalition postwar governments. For these parties the transformation of wartime objectives expressing national and democratic themes into a program of economic and social change raised the issue of national roads to socialism.

In the United States, however, Communists had not emerged from the war as a political force on par with their Italian and French comrades, nor, consequently, was socialism realistically an immediate option. These were realities that weighed heavily on Browder's strategy and possibly on his decision not to address the forms of the transition to socialism. Browder's silence on this issue, therefore, could be viewed as a recognition on his part of the specific national reality that confronted United States Communists. Whatever the reasons, Browder's silence did not preclude the possibility of future theoretical evolution or, as Isserman has argued, " 'Browderism' held the potential for leading to something other than itself—sheltering and lending legitimacy to the efforts of those American Communists who had the capacity for and commitment to finding what would later be described as the 'American Road to Socialism.' "[3]

Communists had withstood the traumatic experience of the "imperialist war" period and forseeably it would have been possible for the reconstituted CPUSA to do the same after 1945. The Party retained a significant membership and its alliances with the mainstream of labor and with left-wing and liberal organizations remained intact. However, contrary to the 1939–1941 period, the Communist party did not endeavor to preserve a constancy in its policies as well as its recognition of distictive U.S. circumstances.

Browder's downfall in June 1945 effectively brought to an end the long and complex experience of United States' Communists during the depression and the war years. While the reconstituted Communist party preserved the coalition policies adopted under Browder's leadership, for Foster these were only momentary tactical expedients, necessary instruments of the Party's broader strategy that would ultimately lead to a Bolshevik-style revolution, alliances made all the more questionable because they fostered the illusion that the system could be made to work.

The cold war climate undoubtedly was a major factor in the weakening of the CPUSA but the Party's break up was induced by its return to a cataclysmic view of social change. This irreparably isolated the CPUSA during the red scare of the postwar years.

The impact of the shift of 1945 became apparent once the tolerance of the war years turned into the repressive atmosphere of cold war. Once the Party came under attack, rather than attempting to ensure continuity in its policy and saving its alliances as it had done during the red scare of 1940, the CPUSA tried to shield itself behind revolutionary orthodoxy. The Communist party predicted an impending cataclysmic economic crisis followed by domestic fascism and war against the Soviet Union all leading to a radical domestic upheaval. As a consequence the Party forced a showdown over the Marshall plan and over support for Henry Wallace's 1948 presidential campaign; these decisions had the result of rupturing alliances with New Deal liberals and provided the opportunity for the expulsion of left-wing led unions from the CIO as well as the break with union leaders who had been close to the Party, thus eradicating the ties which Communists had carefully built and labored to preserve since the 1930s. The Party's isolation coincided with a reinvigorated anti-Communist hysteria and persecution. While congressional committees were busily searching for Communist infiltration in Hollywood, government, and universities, over 100 Communist leaders were arrested nationwide and tried for conspiracy to "teach and advocate" the violent overthrow of the US government. The Party responded to these attacks with its own brand of hysteria: an internal witch hunt was launched in the unsuccessful attempt to weed out stool pigeons, inactive but faithful members were dropped, and scores of Party cadres were sent underground removing them from their day-to-day activities.[4] These measures served only to weaken further the CPUSA. By the time the cold war deescalated in the mid-1950s, it was obvious that none of the forecasts upon which Communists had based their policies since 1945 had materialized. The Communist party was again a small and critically isolated organization: in 1956 the crisis brought about by Khrushchev's revelations of Stalin's crimes followed by the Red Army's bloody repression of the Hungarian uprising, delivered the final blow and ushered the Party from the country's political scene.

NOTES

Introduction

1. Harvey Klehr, *The Heyday of American Communism* (New York: Basic Books, 1984), 415.
2. Theodore Draper, *Roots of American Communism* (New York: Viking, 1957), 395.
3. Daniel Bell, "Marxian Socialism in the United States," in Donald Drew Egbert and Stow Persons, eds., *Socialism and American Life* (Princeton, New Jersey: Princeton University Press, 1952), 350; Irving Howe and Lewis Coser, *The American Communist Party, A Critical History: 1919–1957* (Boston: Beacon Press, 1957), 506.
4. James Weinstein, *Ambiguous Legacy* (New York: New Viewpoints, 1975), chs. 3, 5, and 6; Stanley Aronowitz, *False Promises* (New York: McGraw-Hill, 1973). Also see Staughton Lynd, "The Possibility of Radicalism in the Early 1930s: The Case of Steel," *Radical America* (November–December 1972), 37–64; Phyllis Jacobson, " 'Americanizing' the Communist Party," *New Politics* (Summer 1985), 152–171. For a critique of New Left historiography see Max Gordon, "The Communist Party of the Nineteen-Thirties and the New Left," *Socialist Revolution* (January–March 1976, 11–48).
5. Among these works the most important are Paul Buhle, "Jews and American Communism: The Cultural Question," *Radical History Review* (December 1980), 9–33; "Historians and American Communism: An Agenda," *International Labor and Working Class History* (Fall 1981), 38–45; George Charney, *A Long Journey* (Chicago: Quadrangle, 1968); Peggy Dennis, *The Autobiography of an American Communist* (Berkeley: Creative Arts, 1977); Maurice Isserman, "The 1956 Generation: An Alternative Approach to the History of American Communism," *Radical America* (March–April 1980), 43–51; "The Half-Swept House, American Communism in 1956," *Socialist Review* (January–February 1982), 71–101; *Which Side Were You On?* (Middletown: Wesleyan University Press, 1982); Roger Keeran, *The Communist Party and the Auto Workers Unions* (Bloomington: Indiana University Press, 1980); Paul Lyons, *Philadelphia Communists, 1936–1956* (Philadelphia: Temple University Press, 1982); Mark Naison, "The Communist Party in Har-

217

lem in the Early Depression Years: A Case Study in the Reinterpretation of American Communism," *Radical History Review* (Fall 1976), 68–95; "Historical Notes on Blacks and American Communism: The Harlem Experience," *Science and Society* (Fall 1978), 324–343; "Harlem Communists and the Politics of Black Protest," *Marxist Perspectives* (Fall 1978), 20–50; "Lefties and Righties: The Communist Party and Sports During the Great Depression," *Radical America* (July–August 1979), 47–59; "Communism and Harlem Intellectuals in the Popular Front: Anti-Fascism and the Politics of Black Culture," *Journal of Ethnic Studies* (Spring 1981), 1–25; *Communists in Harlem during the Depression* (Urbana: University of Illinois Press, 1983); Bruce Nelson, " 'Pentecost' on the Pacific: Maritime Workers and Working-Class Consciousness in the 1930s," in Maurice Zetlin, ed., *Political Power and Social Theory* (Greenwich, Connecticut: Jai Press, 1984), 141–182; Steve Nelson, James Barrett, and Rob Ruck, *Steve Nelson, American Radical* (Pittsburgh: University of Pittsburgh Press, 1981); Nell Irvin Painter, *The Narrative of Hosea Hudson* (Cambridge: Harvard University Press, 1979); Al Richmond, *A Long View From the Left* (Boston: Houghton Mifflin, 1972); Roy Rosenzweig, "Organizing the Unemployed: The Early Years of the Great Depression, 1929–1933," *Radical America* (July–August 1976), 47–60; Irving Junius Scales, *Cause at Heart: A Former Communist Remembers* (Athens: University of Georgia Press, 1987); Robert Shaffer, "Women and the Communist Party, U.S.A., 1930–1940," *Socialist Review* (May–June 1979), 73–118; Joseph R. Starobin, *American Communism in Crisis, 1943–1957* (Berkeley: University of California Press, 1972); Kenneth Waltzer, "The Party and the Polling Place: American Communism and the American Labor Party in the 1930s," *Radical History Review* (Spring 1980), 104–129.

6. Theodore Draper, "The Popular Front Revisited," *The New York Review of Books* (30 May 1985), 46.
7. Isserman, *Which Side Were You On?*, 17.

Chapter 1: Difficult Beginnings, 1919–1929

1. James Cannon, *The First Ten Years of American Communism* (New York: Pathfinder Press, 1973), 16–19.
2. The best overall guides through the intricacies of the history of the Party are Theodore Draper's two volumes: *The Roots of American Communism*, and *American Communism and Soviet Russia* (New York: Viking Press, 1960).
3. For the revival of the left wing of the Socialist party from 1915 to 1919, see Draper, *Roots of American Communism*, 50–147; David A. Shannon, *The Socialist Party of America* (New York: Macmillan, 1955), 95–98; James Wein-

stein, *The Decline of Socialism in America, 1912–1925* (New York: Vintage, 1969), 125–127, 177–181.

4. Draper, *Roots of American Communism*, 164–190, 197–199; Weinstein, *Decline of Socialism in America*, 201–205; Cannon, *First Ten Years of American Communism*, 42.

5. Weinstein, *Decline of Socialism in America*, 249–250.

6. Jane Degras, ed., *The Communist International* vol. 1 (London: Oxford University Press, 1956), 101–103; Draper, *Roots of American Communism*, 267–272, 272–273.

7. Draper, *Roots of American Communism*, 341–343, 353–362, 381–390; W. Z. Foster, *From Bryan to Stalin* (New York: International Publishers, 1937), 295.

8. Kermit E. McKenzie, *Comintern and World Revolution, 1928–1943* (New York: Columbia University Press, 1964), 51; Degras, *Communist International* vol. 1, 241–256.

9. Draper, *Roots of American Communism*, 277–278.

10. Foster, *From Bryan to Stalin*, 11–38. On Foster's activities before he joined the Communist party see also Edward Johanningsmeier, "William Z. Foster and the Syndicalist League of North America," *Labor History* (Summer 1989), 329–353.

11. Foster, *From Bryan to Stalin*, 48–51, 55–57, 59–60, 73, and 86–104; and Bert Cochran, *Labor and Communism* (Princeton, N.J.: Princeton University Press, 1977), 24.

12. Foster, *From Bryan to Stalin*, 134–136; Draper, *Roots of American Communism*, 313.

13. Foster, *From Bryan to Stalin*, 138–142, 163; Draper, *The Roots of American Communism*, 322.

14. Cochran, *Labor and Communism*, 24; Draper, *American Communism and Soviet Russia*, 71–72.

15. Draper, *American Communism and Soviet Russia*, 71–72; Foster, *From Bryan to Stalin*, 168–171; Roger Keeran, *The Communist Party and the Auto Workers Unions* (Bloomington: Indiana University Press, 1980), 35–37.

16. Foster, the Communist standard-bearer in the 1924 elections, polled a scant 33,300 votes. Draper, *American Communism and Soviet Russia*, 35–51; Foster, *History of the Communist Party of the United States* (New York: International Publishers, 1952), 222. On the Party's role in the 1924 presidential campaign see Draper, Ibid, 96–126; Weinstein, *Decline of Socialism in America*, 290–313.

17. Foster, *From Bryan to Stalin*, 181–184; Draper, *American Communism and Soviet Russia*, 117–119; Earl Browder, "The American Communist Party in the Thirties," in Rita James Simon, ed., *As We Saw the Thirties* (Urbana: University of Illinois Press, 1967), 218.

18. Draper, *American Communism and Soviet Russia*, 127–247.

19. Draper, *American Communism and Soviet Russia*, 275–278, 377–429; Degras, *Communist International* vol. 3, 8–16.

20. Following the removal of Lovestone a secretariat of four was created to lead the Party. Its members were Robert Minor, William Weinstone, Max Bedacht, and Foster. A year later, at the Seventh Convention, the secretariat was reorganized: Minor and Bedacht stepped down, and the latter was put in charge of the IWO. The new secretariat retained Weinstone and Foster, and Earl Browder was added as a new member. Weinstone was in Moscow as Party representative to the Comintern where he was to remain for another year, and Foster was in jail for his role in the March 6 unemployed demonstration in New York City; consequently Browder found himself alone at the head of the Party. Foster, *History of the Communist Party*, 274–275, 292; *Daily Worker*, 11 September 1930.

21. James Gilbert Ryan, "The Making of a Native Marxist: The Early Career of Earl Browder," *The Review of Politics* (July 1977), 341. In describing Browder's physical appearance Ryan relied on the records of the Atlanta Federal penitentiary where Browder was confined in the early 1940s. Also see Bella Dodd, *School of Darkness* (New York: J. Kennedy and Sons, 1954), 68; Malcolm Cowley, *The Dream of the Golden Mountains* (New York: Penguin Books, 1981), 273.

22. Ryan, "The Early Career of Earl Browder," 343–346; Browder, "The Reminiscences of Earl Browder," Oral History Collection, Columbia University, 8–91, 107–115. Browder briefly described his family background going back to the 1600s in an article in the *Daily Worker*, 6 November 1939.

23. Ryan, "The Early Career of Earl Browder," 350–352; Interview with Earl Browder, 19 May 1953, Draper Papers, I, 1:3, 1; All references citing the Draper Papers are in the Theodore Draper Papers, Special Collection Department, Robert W. Woodruff Library, Emory University, Atlanta, Georgia. Also see Browder, "Reminiscences," 117–127.

24. Browder, "Reminiscences," 162. On Browder's experience in China see 194–197.

25. Ryan, "The Early Career of Earl Browder," 361; Joseph R. Starobin, *American Communism in Crisis, 1943–1957* (Berkeley: University of California Press, 1972) 53; Interview with Earl Browder, 19 May 1953, Draper papers, I, 1:3, 2–3.

26. Jack Stachel, "Organization Report to the Sixth Convention of the CPUSA," *Communist* (April 1929), 180–186; Browder, *Report of the Central Committee to the Eighth Convention of the CPUSA* (New York: Workers Library Publishers, 1934), 181; Draper, *Roots of American Communism*, 189–190; Robert Jay Alperin, "Organization in the Communist Party, U.S.A., 1931–1938," (Ph.D. diss., Northwestern University, 1959), 53.

Chapter 2: To the Masses! 1929–1933

1. W. Z. Foster, *Toward Soviet America*, (New York: International Publishers, 1932), 269; Earl Browder, "Next Tasks of the Communist Party of the U.S.," *Communist* (November–December, 1930), 975.
2. The Workers party had been renamed Workers (Communist) party in 1925. Its present name was adopted at the Sixth Convention in 1929. Theodore Draper, *American Communism and Soviet Russia* (New York: Viking Press, 1960) 160.
3. *Daily Worker*, 21 June 1930; *New York Times*, 21 June 1930.
4. Al Richmond, *A Long View From the Left* (Boston: Houghton Mifflin, 1972) 73.
5. The essential characteristics of the third period are described in "Extracts From the Theses of the Sixth Comintern Congress on the International Situation and the Tasks of the Communist International," in Jane Degras, *The Communist International* vol. 2 (London: Oxford University Press, 1956), 455–464; Kermit E. McKenzie, *Comintern and World Revolution, 1928–1943* (New York: Columbia University Press, 1964) 113–139. On the proceedings of the Sixth Congress of the Communist International see Degras, *Communist International* vol. 2, 446–548.
6. On the Tenth Plenum of the E.C.C.I see Degras, *The Communist International* vol. 3, 36–52; McKenzie, *Comintern and World Revolution*, 122–124.
7. Tom Tippett, *When Southern Labor Stirs* (New York: Jonathan Cape & Harrison Smith, 1931), 23–26.
8. Irving Bernstein, *The Lean Years* (Boston: Houghton Mifflin, 1960), 128, 360–381.
9. Ibid., 300, 319.
10. Foster, *Toward Soviet America*, 241–242, 244.
11. Ibid., 252.
12. Ibid., 269, 270–271.
13. Ibid., 271–272.
14. Ibid., 277–280, 280–281, 288–291, 296–300.
15. "Extracts From The Theses Of The Tenth ECCI Plenum On The Economic Struggle And The Tasks Of The Communist Parties," in Degras, *The Communist International* vol. 3, 52–64, 142–143; McKenzie, *Comintern and World Revolution*, 133–134.
15. Draper, *American Communism and Soviet Russia*, 284–296.
17. *Report of the Fourth Congress of the Red International of Trade Unions*, (London 1928), 136–137, cited in Irving Howe and Lewis Coser, *The American Communist Party, A Critical History: 1919–1957* (Boston: Beacon Press, 1957), 253.
18. Howe and Coser, *The American Communist Party*, 253–255; W. Z. Foster, *From Bryan to Stalin* (New York: International Publishers, 1937) 195–220;

On anti-communism within trade unions during the 1920s, see Stanley Nadel, "Reds Versus Pinks: A Civil War in the International Ladies Garment Workers Union, *New York History* (January 1985), 49–72. James R. Prickett also provides a brief description of the genesis of red unionism from 1920 to 1928 in his essay "New Perspectives on American Communism and the Labor Movement," in Maurice Zeitlin, ed., *Political Power and Social Theory* (Greenwich, Conn.: JAI Press, 1984), 8–11; and David Montgomery, "Thinking about American Workers in the 1920s," *International Labor and Working-Class History* (Fall 1987), 17. On Profintern's Fourth Congress see Draper, *American Communism and Soviet Russia*, 287–289. On controversy within CPUSA over new policy, ibid., 291–299. Foster, who consistently through his career had opposed dual-unionism, was the main opponent of the new course. But soon, unwilling to challenge Moscow, even his opposition came to an end. In later years, after the Communist party had abandoned this policy, Foster made repeated references to his disagreement with adopting the dual-union stand in the first place. Foster, *From Bryan to Stalin*, 215 and *History of the Communist Party of the United States*, (New York: International Publishers, 1952), 258.

19. John J. Watt, "Launching the National Miners Union," *Labor Unity* (October 1928), 2–6; Sam Weiseman, "The Textile Workers Organize their Union," ibid. 10–12; and "Needle Workers Organize New Union," ibid. (January 1929), 4. Foster, *From Bryan to Stalin*, 216–218. Foster claimed that upon their foundation the membership of the NMU was 15,000 and in the textile and needle trades it was a combined total of 27,000. In his history of the CPUSA (257) he wrote that in 1929 the combined membership of these unions had reached 57,000. These figures appear to be exaggerated. On the TUUL see *The Trade Union Unity League: Its Program, Structure, Methods and History* (New York: Trade Union Unity League, 1930).

20. Cited in Foster, *From Bryan to Stalin*, 218.

21. Bernstein, *The Lean Years*, 84, 335–338, 341–342; John I. Griffin, *Strikes: A Study in Quantitative Economics* (New York: Columbia University Press, 1939), 91.

22. On concentration see "Comintern Documents," *Communist* (May 1931), 402–407.

23. Interview with Earl Browder, 15 June 1955, Draper Papers, I, 1:4, 5.

24. On the Passaic strike see Foster, *From Bryan to Stalin*, 201–203; Bert Cochran, *Labor and Communism: The Conflict that Shaped American Unions* (Princeton, N.J.: Princeton University Press, 1977), 31–32. On the New Bedford strike, see Albert Weisbord, "The New Bedford Textile Strike," *Labor Unity* (June 1928), 3–4; "The Present Situation in New Bedford," ibid. (July 1928), 14; Fred E. Beal, *Proletarian Journey* (New York: Hillman-Curl, 1937), 98–106; Michael W. Santos, "Community and Communism: The 1928

New Bedford Textile Strike," *Labor History* (Spring 1985), 230–249; and Foster, *History of the Communist Party*, 251.

25. Foster, *History of the Communist Party*, 255–257; Melvyn Dubofsky and Warren Van Tine, *John L. Lewis* (New York: Quadrangle, 1977), 127–128.

26. Stachel, "Organization Report to the Sixth Convention of the Communist Party of the U.S.A.," *Communist* (May 1929), 244.

27. For the activities of the Communist party in the auto industry during the 1920s see Roger Keeran, *The Communist Party and the Auto Workers Unions* (Bloomington: Indiana University Press, 1980), 35–59. For the number of Communists employed in the auto industry see Nathan Glazer, *The Social Basis of American Communism* (New York: Harcourt, Brace & World, Inc., 1961) 115; "Organization Work in Detroit," *Party Organizer* (March–April 1928), 9.

28. Foster, *From Bryan to Stalin*, 241.

29. Fred Beal, *Proletarian Journey*, 123–129. On the strike movement of 1929–1930 through the Piedmont, see Tippett, *When Southern Labor Stirs.*

30. Foster, *From Bryan to Stalin*, 229; Frankfeld, "The Struggle in the Anthracite," *Daily Worker* (3 July 1930); Draper, "The Communists and the Miners," *Dissent* (Spring 1972), 378; Keeran, *The Communist Party and the Auto Workers Unions*, 79–80. For a critique by one of its leaders of the Party's shortcomings in leading strikes see: Jack Stachel, "Coming Struggles and Lessons in Strike Strategy," *Communist* (March 1931), 204–213.

31. Cletus E. Daniel, *Bitter Harvest* (Ithaca: Cornell University Press, 1981), 111–113; John W. Hevener, *Which Side Are You On? The Harlan County Coal Miners, 1931–39* (Urbana: University of Illinois Press, 1978), chs. 2–4; Draper, "The Communists and the Miners," 380–381.

32. On the cotton pickers' strike, see Daniel, *Bitter Harvest*, 179–221.

33. National Committee for the Defense of Political Prisoners, *Harlan Miners Speak* (New York: Harcourt, Brace and Co., 1932), *passim.*

34. On the Gastonia strike see Albert Weisbord, "Passaic-New Bedford-North Carolina," *Communist* (June 1929), 319–323; Bill Dunne, "Gastonia—The Center of the Class Struggle in 'The New South'," ibid. (July 1929), 375–383; Beal, *Proletarian Journey*, 123–214; Foster, *From Bryan to Stalin*, 233–235. Vera Buch Weisbord who was sent to Gastonia by the NTWU provided an eyewitness account of the strike and the trials in her book *A Radical Life* (Bloomington: Indiana University Press, 1977), 173–289. See also Bernstein, *The Lean Years*, 20–27; Blanshard, "Communism in Southern Textile Mills," *The Nation*, 24 April 1929, 500–501; "One-hundred Per Cent Americans on Strike," ibid. (8 May 1929), 554–556.

35. Keeran, *The Communist Party and the Auto Workers Unions*, 79–80.

36. *Daily Worker* (23 January, 23 May, 17, 27 June 1930); John Dos Passos, "Back

to Red Hysteria!" *New Republic* (2 July 1930), 168–169; Peggy Dennis, *The Autobiography of an American Communist: A Personal View of a Political Life, 1925–1975* (Berkeley, Calif.: Creative Arts, 1977), 42–46; and Daniel, *Bitter Harvest*, 111–128.

37. Daniel, *Bitter Harvest*, 127–129, 135–138; Foster, *From Bryan to Stalin*, 241–242.
38. "10,000 Strike in Lawrence Led by NTWU," *Labor Unity* (28 February 1931), 1, 3; "Fight Not Over in Lawrence," ibid. (7 March 1931), 1, 7; Martin Russack, "Building a Union in Lawrence," ibid. (June 1932), 7–8; Jack Stachel, "Some Lessons of the Lawrence Strike," *Communist* (May 1931), 433–443.
39. Robert Ingalls, *Urban Vigilantes in the New South: Tampa, 1882–1936* (Knoxville: The University of Tennessee Press, 1988), 150–157.
40. Nelson et al., *Steve Nelson, American Radical* (Pittsburgh: University of Pittsburgh Press, 1981), 89.
41. Foster, *From Bryan to Stalin*, 229–233; *Daily Worker* (28 May 1931). For a contemporary assessment of the accomplishments and goals of the 1931 miners' strike see Foster, "The Coal Strike," *Communist* (July 1931), 595–599. The entire August 1931 issue of the Party's internal publication, *Party Organizer*, was devoted to the mine strike. On the Harlan strike see Stachel, "Lessons of Two Recent Strikes," *Communist* (June 1932), 527–542; Harry Gannes, *Kentucky Miners Fight* ([NY]: Workers International Relief, 1932); Hevener, *Which Side Are You On?*, chs. 2–4; Draper, "The Communists and the Miners," 380–389. Foster mistakenly recalled the Kentucky general strike as being called for 1 January 1931. See also Herbert Abel, "Gun-Rule in Kentucky," *The Nation* (23 September 1931), 306–308; and John Dos Passos, "Harlan: Working Under the Gun," *New Republic* (2 December 1931), 62–67.
42. Robin Davis Gibran Kelly, " 'Hammer n' Hoe,' Black Radicalism and the Communist Party in Alabama, 1929–1941" (Ph.D. diss., UCLA 1987), 118–119.
43. Foster, *From Bryan to Stalin*, 230–231; Bernstein, *The Lean Years*, 387.
44. Tom Johnson, "The Fight Against Sectarianism in the National Miners Union," *Communist* (August 1932), 697; Foster, *From Bryan to Stalin*, 231.
45. On the Briggs strike see "Developing Shop Work in Detroit," *Party Organizer* (July 1933), 12; Jack Stachel, "The Strikes in the Auto Industry," *Labor Unity* (March 1933), 3–7; Robert Gray, "The A.F. of L. and the Briggs Strike," ibid., 8–9; Keeran, *The Communisty Party and the Auto Workers Unions*, 83–95; and Sidney Fine, *The Automobile Under the Blue Eagle* (Ann Arbor: University of Michigan Press, 1963), 27–29.
46. Foster, *From Bryan to Stalin*, 241–242; Sam Darcy, "Not Reliance on Spontaneity But Organization is Needed," *Party Organizer* (September–October 1931), 23; "Agricultural Strikes," ibid. (August–September, 1933), 82–83;

Western Worker (21, 28 August 1933); Ella Winter, "California's Little Hitlers," *New Republic* (27 December 1933), 188–190; Joe Evans, "15,000 Cotton Pickers on Strike, *Labor Unity* (December 1933), 8–9. The Agricultural Workers Industrial Union changed its name in 1931 after it led the cannery workers' strike in the Santa Clara Valley.

47. *Western Worker* (15, 22, 29 January 1934); Chester Williams, "Imperial Valley Mob," *New Republic* (21 February 1934), 39–41; and Daniel, *Bitter Harvest*, 223–230.

48. Foster, *Toward Soviet America*, 233.

49. Robert N. Nathan, "Estimates of Unemployment in the United States, 1929–1935," *International Labour Review* (January 1936), 49–73.

50. "Notes of the Month," *Communist* (March 1930), 198.

51. Steve Nelson, "How the Unemployment Councils Were Built in Lackwana County," *Party Organizer* (March 1934), 7–9.

52. Irving Seid interviewed by Danny Czitrom, Oral History of the American Left, Tamiment Institute, New York City (hereafter OHAL.)

53. Steve Nelson provides a very informative day-to-day description of the organization of the unemployed on a local level both in Chicago and in Eastern Pennsylvania anthracite region in his *American Radical*, 73–81, 94–124. See also Edmund Wilson, "Detroit Motors," *New Republic* (25 March 1931), 149. For Communist activities among the unemployed in Birmingham, Alabama, see Kelly, "Hammer n' Hoe," 105–114. Through the 1930s Army Intelligence kept detailed files on countless instances of Communist led unemployed protests and demonstrations, *U.S. Military Intelligence Reports: Surveillance of Radicals in the United States, 1917–1941* (Frederick, MD: University Publications of America, 1984), reel 24, series 2661–2662.

54. Studs Terkel, *Hard Times: An Oral History of The Great Depression* (New York: Pantheon, 1970), 466; and St. Clair Drake and Horace R. Cayton, *Black Metropolis* (New York: Harcourt, Brace and Co., 1945), 87.

55. Jose Alvarez interviewed by Paul Buhle, OHAL; *Daily Worker* (12, 15, 22, 28 February 1930).

56. J. W., "Recruiting Party Members During 3–8th Aug. Events in Chicago," *Party Organizer* (September–October 1931), 16; *Daily Worker* (4, 5 August 1931).

57. Anna Taffler interviewed by Jon Bloom, OHAL.

58. Nelson, *American Radical*, 77.

59. *Daily Worker* (27 January, 17 February 1930); Daniel J. Leab, "United We Eat," *Labor History* (Fall 1967), 305–307; Foster, *History of the Communist Party*, 281.

60. *New York Times* (6 March 1930).

61. Interview with Earl Browder, 15 June 1955, Draper Papers, I, 1:4, 1. According to the *Daily Worker* there were 100,000 demonstrators in Detroit; 50,000 respectively in Chicago and Boston; 40,000 in Milwaukee; 30,000 in

Philadelphia; 25,000 in Cleveland; 20,000 in Youngstown; and 10,000 in Washington, D.C. *Daily Worker* (7 March 1930).

62. Dennis, *Autobiography of an American Communist*, 48; Keeran, *The Communist Party and the Auto Workers Unions*, 67; Nelson, *American Radical*, 81–84; *Daily Worker* (26 January, 28 February, 3, 7 March 1930); *New York Times* (26 January, 28 February, 2, 7 March 1930); Karl Yoneda, interview by Paul Buhle, OHAL. The *Daily Worker* estimated the crowd in Union Square at 110,000, the *Times* set the figure at 35,000.

63. Moissaye J. Olgin, "From March Sixth to May First," *Communist* (May 1930), 417. Also see "Notes of the Month," ibid. (April 1930), 291–295. In an ironic twist, the demonstration led Republican Representative Hamilton Fish, Jr. of New York to introduce in Congress on 6 March, a resolution to create a special committee to investigate Communist activities. Passed by the House the Committee was the predecessor of the HUAC; *New York Times* (7 March 1930).

64. *Daily Worker* (5, 6, 7 July 1930); Foster, *Toward Soviet America*, 232.

65. Leab, "United We Eat," 313; Keeran, *The Communist Party and the Auto Workers Unions*, 69.

66. *Fight! Don't Starve! Organize!* (New York: Trade Union Unity League, 1931), 3–5. This pamphlet also contains the text of the Workers' Unemployment Insurance Bill. Years later Browder claimed to have been the author of the bill; Browder, "The American Communist Party in the Thirties," in Rita James Simon, ed., *As We Saw the Thirties* (Urbana: University of Illinois Press, 1967), 220–221.

67. *Daily Worker* (8 December 1931); John Dos Passos, "Red Day on Capitol Hill," *New Republic* (23 December 1931), 153–155; John Gates, *The Story of an American Communist* (New York: Thomas Nelson and Sons, 1958), 23–25.

68. Foster, *From Bryan to Stalin*, 228; John Williamson, *Dangerous Scot* (New York: International Publishers, 1969), 82–85; "Hoover Ignores Hunger Marches," *Daily Worker* (8 December 1931); Amter, "The National Hunger March—A Political Victory," *Labor Unity* (January 1933), 18–21; "Red Day in Washington," *New Republic* (21 December 1932), 153–155. For accounts of local hunger marches and unemployed demonstrations see Steve Nelson's description of the hunger march on Harrisburg, *American Radical*, 153–160; on marches in New York, Los Angeles, and Akron see *Daily Worker* (20, 21, 22, 23 January 1931); Edmund Wilson, "Communists and Cops," *New Republic* (11 February 1931), 345–347. Also see, "Uniting the Struggle of Employed and Unemployed—Briggs Hunger March, *Party Organizer* (January 1932), 3–7; E. T. C., "Education Through Stuggle—The Experience of the State Hunger Marches to Columbia, Ohio," ibid. (July 1933), 27–29.

69. *Daily Worker* (8, 9, 10, 11 March 1932); Oakley Johnson, "After the Dear-

born Massacre," *New Republic* (30 March 1932), 172–174; Keeran, *The Communist Party and the Auto Workers Unions,* 71–74; Alex Baskin, "The Ford Hunger March," *Labor History* (Summer 1972), 331–360.

70. The Party claimed a participation of 400,000 and 500,000 respectively. Foster, *From Bryan to Stalin,* 228.

71. Clarence Hathaway, "An Examination of Our Failure to Organize the Unemployed," *Communist* (September 1930), 789, 791–792. Similar views were expressed in a resolution of the 13th Plenum of the Central Committee of the CPUSA in August 1931: "Resolution on Work Among the Unemployed," *Communist* (October 1931), 838–850.

72. Herbert Benjamin, "Unity on the Unemployment Field," *Communist* (April 1936), 333.

73. For the text of the bill see Earl Browder, *Unemployment Insurance: The Burning Issue of the Day* (New York: Workers Library Publishers, 1935), 23–24; *Daily Worker* (3, 4, 5, 6 February 1934). The bill was first introduced as H.R. 7598 then as 2827. For Browder's address to the meeting see, Earl Browder, "The Workers' Bill Belongs to the Whole Working Class" in *Unemployment Insurance,* 2–9; Amter, "The National Congress for Unemployment and Social Insurance—And After," *Communist* (January 1935), 33–34; "Results of the Washington Congress," *Labor Unity* (January 1935), 5–7; and Jonathan Mitchell, "The Left Revives," *New Republic* (23 January 1935), 300–301.

74. Earl Browder, "Only the Workers' Bill Meets the Immediate Needs of the Masses," in *Unemployment Insurance,* 10, 12–13. On February 19, Browder read a statement to the Senate Finance Committee considering the Wagner-Lewis Bill which was to provide the basis for the Social Security Act. Browder criticized the bill as being inadequate; see "The Wagner-Lewis Bill Cannot Still the Demand For Real Unemployment Insurance," in *Unemployment Insurance,* 14–22.

75. Leab, "United We Eat," 310, 313–314. Howe and Coser also concluded that the Party "politicized" the struggle of the unemployed raising issues not directly pertaining to the plight of jobless workers. Howe and Coser, *The American Communist Party,* 193–194.

76. *Daily Worker* (8, 10, 12 April 1936).

77. Interview with Earl Browder, 15 June 1955, Draper Papers, I, 1:4, 1.

78. On the unemployed movement also see Roy Rosenzweig, "Organizing the Unemployed: The Early Years of the Great Depression, 1929–1933," *Radical America* (July–August, 1976), 47–60 and John A. Garraty, "Unemployment During the Great Depression," *Labor History* (Spring 1976), 133–159.

79. James Weinstein, *The Decline of Socialism in America, 1912–1925* (New York: Vintage, 1969), 65–73; David Shannon, *The Socialist Party of America: A History* (New York: Macmillan, 1955), 50–53; Harry Haywood,

Black Bolshevik: Autobiography of an Afro-American Communist (Chicago: Liberator Press, 1978), 122–125, 174; Draper, *American Communism and Soviet Russia*, 319–332.

80. The Executive Committee of the Communist International first voiced its views on the "Negro Question" in a resolution adopted in October 1928. The text of the resolution was published by the *Daily Worker* on 12 February 1929. In 1930 the Comintern expressed its positions in more detail in an effort to clear up "all *lack of clarity* on the Negro question"; see "Resolution on the Negro Question in the United States," *Communist* (February 1931), 153–167; Draper, *American Communism and Soviet Russia*, 345–353; and Haywood, *Black Bolshevik*, 227–235, 259–269.
81. Naison, *Communists in Harlem*, 31–36. Cyril Briggs as quoted in Rosenzweig, "Organizing the Unemployed," 51.
82. *Daily Worker* (16 February, 2 March 1931); *New York Times* (2 March 1931); Haywood, *Black Bolshevik*, 352–357. The proceedings of the "trial" were published in a pamphlet, *Race Hatred On Trial* (New York: Workers Library Publishers, 1931).
83. "Resolutions on the Negro Question in the United States," 52. For an account of the relations between Communists and UNIA through the 1920s and 1930s, see Tony Martin, *Race First* (Westport, Conn.: Greenwood Press, 1976), 221–265.
84. Cyril Briggs, "The Decline of the Garvey Movement," *Communist* (June 1931), 547.
85. Naison, *Communists in Harlem*, 39.
86. Charles H. Martin, *The Angelo Herndon Case and Southern Justice* (Baton Rouge: Louisiana State University Press, 1976), 5–6; Bruce Nelson, *Workers on the Waterfront* (Urbana: University of Illinois Press, 1988), 84. On the Party's activities in Birmingham during the early 1930s see Nat Ross, "The Communist Party in the Birmingham Strikes," *Communist* (July 1934), 687–699; Kelly, "Hammer n' Hoe," 53–89; "A New War in Dixie: Communists and the Unemployed in Birmingham, Alabama," *Labor History* (Summer 1989), 367–384; and Nell Painter, *The Narrative of Hosea Hudson, His Life as a Negro Communist in the South* (Cambridge, Mass: Harvard University Press, 1979), 75–156; for the text of the leaflet see, 373–374.
87. Murphy, "The Share Croppers Union Grows and Fights," *Party Organizer* (May–June 1934), 45; "What Happened in Tallapoosa County," *Labor Defender* (February 1933), 4; Haywood, *Black Bolshevik*, 395–400; Kelly, "Hammer n' Hoe," 233–247. On the structure and objectives of the Sharecroppers Union, see "Negro Share Croppers Building Their Union," *Party Organizer* (January 1933), 14–16; Comrade M, *Achievements and Tasks of Sharecroppers Union*, Speech at the Extraordinary Conference of the Communist Party, 7–10 July 1933 (New York: Workers Library Publishers, 1933).

88. Browder, "Reminiscences," Oral History Collection, Columbia University, 282.
89. William Weinstone, "The Economic Crisis in the United States and the Tasks of the Communist Party," *The Communist International* (15 February 1930), 1230. See also Beal, *Proletarian Journey*, 140; Briggs, "The Negro Question in the Southern Textile Strikes," *Communist* (June 1929), 324–328; Briggs, "Further Notes on the Negro Question in Southern Textile Strikes," ibid. (July 1929), 391–394; Weisbord, *A Radical Life*, 175.
90. Earl Browder, *Build The United People's Front* (New York: Workers Library Publishers, 1936), 60.
91. Very important was the defense of Angelo Herndon, a young black Communist organizer of the unemployed movement. Herndon was arrested in Atlanta, following the June 1932 unemployed demonstration, charged under the state's anti-insurrection law, and convicted to eighteen to twenty years in jail. After a long legal battle the conviction was thrown out by the Supreme Court on grounds that the Georgia anti-insurrection law was unconstitutional. The ILD was involved in numerous other cases in defense of black defendants. Among its major efforts were the defense of the Atlanta Six, of Euel Lee, and several members of the Sharecroppers Union. For an overview of the activities of the ILD in defense of blacks and the Herndon case, see Angelo Herndon, "That Demonstration in Atlanta," *Daily Worker* (15 November 1935); Benjamin J. Davis, *Communist Councilman from Harlem* (New York: International Publishers, 1969), 53–81; and Charles H. Martin's work on the subject, "The International Labor Defense and Black Americans," *Labor History* (Spring 1985), 165–194; *Angelo Herndon*, 6–7, 61, 182.
92. For the Party's attitude toward the Scottsboro case I have relied on Dan T. Carter's definitive work *Scottsboro: A Tragedy of the American South*, rev. ed. (Baton Rouge: Louisiana State University Press, 1979).
93. This statement was one of many giving a positive black assessment of the activities of the CPUSA published in *The Crisis*. See "Negro Editors on Communism: A Symposium of the American Negro Press," *The Crisis* (April–May, 1932), 156.
94. Carter, *Scottsboro*, ch. 3; Naison, *Communists in Harlem*, ch. 3; Painter, *The Narrative of Hosea Hudson*, 127–130; Browder, "Reminiscences," 278.
95. *Daily Worker* (5 May 1931).
96. Carter, *Scottsboro*, 330–335; Browder, "Reminiscences," 277–278.
97. William Weinstone, "The XI Plenum of the Executive Committee of the Comintern. Extracts from Reports to the 13th Plenum of the Central Committee CPUSA," *Communist* (October 1931), 792–793; Earl Browder, "Why an Open Letter to Our Party Membership—Report for the Political Buro to the Extraordinary Party Conference, New York City, 7 July 1933," ibid.

(August 1933), 740; Foster, *History of the Communist Party,* 269; Glazer, *Social Basis,* 174–176. In Harlem in 1934 the Party had only 200 black members. Louis Sass, "On Some Problems of the Harlem Section," *Party Organizer,* March 1934, 19–20.

98. Glazer, *Social Basis,* 174–175; Jack Stachel, "Organizational Report to the Sixth Convention," *Communist* (April 1929), 245; Painter, *Narrative of Hosea Hudson,* 114; C. Smith, "The Problems of Cadres in the Party," *Communist* (February 1932), 113–114; Max Steinberg, "Achievements and Tasks of the New York District," ibid. (May 1935), 449; "Problems of Party Growth in the New York District," ibid. (July 1936), 645.

99. For the interpretation of the effects and consequences of the Party's activity on the black community I have relied on Mark Naison's exhaustive work on the subject, "The Communist Party in Harlem in the Early Depression Years: A Case Study in the Reinterpretation of American Communism," *Radical History* (Fall 1976), 68–95; "Harlem Communists and The Politics of Black Protest," *Marxist Perspectives* (Fall 1978), 20–50; Communism and Harlem Intellectuals in the Popular Front: Anti-Fascism and the Politics of Black Culture," *The Journal of Ethnic Studies* (Spring 1981), 1–25; and *Communists in Harlem.*

100. *Daily Worker* (25 April 1932). In 1934, Browder recalled that the Party had "distributed over a million pamphlets, over seven million political leaflets and spoke directly in meetings to more than a million workers." Earl Browder, "Approaching the Seventh World Congress and the Fifteenth Anniversary of the Founding of the CPUSA," *Communist* (September 1934), 841.

101. *Communist Election Platform* (New York: Communist Party National Campaign Committee, 1932), 10–11. For the Communist and Socialist vote see *Congressional Quarterly's Guide to U.S. Elections* (Washington, D.C.: Congressional Quarterly, 1975), 289. For examples of anti-Socialist rhetoric during the campaign, see Moissaye Olgin, *The Socialist Party: Last Bulwark of Capitalism* (New York: Workers Library Publishers, 1932); I. Amter, *Is the Socialist Party a Party of the Workers?* (New York: Communist Party, U.S.A., 1932).

102. Earl Browder, "Next Tasks of the Communist Party of the U.S.," 975.

103. Among European Communist parties the major blow was in 1933 Hitler's crushing of the German party which, with its 360,000 members, had been the largest Communist party in the West. Between 1928 and 1933, the French Communist party dropped from 50,000 to 29,000 members; the Czech Party declined from 81,500 members in 1929 to 55,000 five years later. Daniel R. Brower, *The New Jacobins* (Ithaca: Cornell University Press, 1968), 15; Degras, *The Communist International* vol. 3, 38, 316. Browder, *Report to the Eighth Convention,* 82, 87. In 1930 the leadership of the CPUSA, betraying an ill-destined optimism, set the goal of recruiting by

year's end 25,000 new members into the Party, and 50,000 into the TUUL. Earl Browder, "The Bolshevization of the Communist Party," *Communist* (August 1930), 693.

104. Browder, *Report to the Eighth Convention*, 87; J. P., "Building Party into Mass Proletarian Party," *Party Organizer* (August–September 1933), 28; Jack Stachel, "Organizational Problems of the Party," *Communist* (July 1935), 625–626; "Facts and Materials on Organizational Status, Problems and Organizational Tasks of the Party," *Party Organizer* (May–June 1934), 7, 9, 12–18; *An Open Letter to All Members of the Communist Party, Adopted by the Extraordinary National Conference of the CPUSA, New York, 7–10 July 1933* (New York: Communist Party, 1933), 6; Glazer, *The Social Basis of American Communism*, 101. Communists who were not politically active in recruiting fellow workers in their shops were a source of constant concern, they were referred to as "6 P.M. Communists." *Party Organizer* (March 1931), 21. Throughout the third period countless articles and statements dealt with the question of the Party's failure to expand its working class presence.

105. Browder, *Report to the Eighth Convention*, 91.

106. "Experiences in Keeping New Members," *Party Organizer* (June–July 1930), 13. The *Party Organizer* printed a letter by a farmer who, with seven others, had applied four times to join the Party, each time they had been blocked by red tape; "Blocking the Door of the Party," *Party Organizer* (March 1931), 16–18. In another case, the *Party Organizer* reported that in Kansas City a worker had filled out twelve applications before he was "finally noticed"; *Party Organizer* (January 1933), 18. In 1933 the New York District issued more than 500 membership cards that were never delivered. "Facts and Materials on Organizational Status, Problems and Organizational Tasks of the Party," 12.

107. C. A. Hathaway, "On the Use of 'Transmission Belts' In Our Struggle for the Masses," *Communist* (May 1931), 417.

108. Albina Delfino interviewed by Ruth F. Prago, OHAL.

109. For a description of the demands of Party life see Jose Alvarez interviewed by Paul Buhle, Bertha Bazell interviewed by Bill Schecter, Otis Hood interviewed by Bill Schecter, Anna Taffler interviewed by Jon Bloom, OHAL; George Charney, *A Long Journey* (Chicago: Quadrangle, 1968), 30–31. The Party's press printed countless articles dealing with the causes and proposing solutions to the problem of membership turnover. This was particularly the case with the Party's internal organizational bulletin, the *Party Organizer*, in which virtually every issue included at least one article on this topic. One article even made fun of the habit of many Communists of employing language and abbreviations that were incomprehensible to new members. Eventually however the *Party Organizer* had to publish a dictionary of the most commonly used

abbreviations within the Party. "Shall We Issue a Dictionary?" *Party Organizer* (May 1931), 24–25.

110. S. Mingulin, "The Crisis in the United States and the Problems of the Communist Party," *Communist* (June 1930), 500–518; Resolution of the XIII Plenum of the Central Committee, "Tasks in the Struggle Against Hunger, Repression and War," *Daily Worker* (17 September 1931); C. Smith, "The Problem of Cadres in the Party," *Communist* (February 1932), 110–123; S. Willner, "Organizational Problems in Our Unemployed Work," ibid. (March 1932), 215–229; John Steuben, "Shop Politics and Organization," ibid. (April 1932), 338–349; Hathaway, "For a Complete Mobilization of the Party for Real Mass Work in the Election Campaign," ibid. (May 1932), 419–420.

111. Earl Browder, "Fewer High-Falutin' Phrases, More Simple Every-Day Deeds," *Communist* (January 1931), 13–15; Tom Johnson, "The Fight Against Sectarianism in the National Miners Union," ibid. (August 1932), 697–704; Jack Stachel, "Lessons of Two Recent Strikes," ibid. (June 1932), 527–542; Nathaniel Honig, "Miners Discuss their Problems," *Labor Unity* (April 1932), 19–21; and "The TUUL Board Meeting," ibid. (May 1932), 19.

112. Browder "Why an Open Letter," 726. Mario Alpi wrote that regardless of failures and setbacks Communists could not *"have the perspective that capitalism can overcome its own contradictions, can stabilize itself"*; Alpi, "Resolution of the Sixth Session of the E.C. of the Profintern," *Communist* (March 1930), 271. Alpi, also known as Fred Brown, was a refugee from Fascist Italy. Close to Browder he was national organizational secretary.

113. The letter had been drawn up a few weeks earlier in Moscow by Foster, Clarence Hathaway, and Browder together with Otto Kuusinen representing the Comintern; Browder, "Reminiscences," 269, 271. The Party was so concerned with its poor showing among labor that, to make sure that all Communists read the "Open Letter," Browder wanted notations made on membership books showing that every Communist had received and presumably read the document. Browder, "Why an Open Letter," 768; *An Open Letter to All Members of the Communist Party*, 7. The entire August–September 1933 issue of the *Party Organizer* was dedicated to the "Open Letter" conference with excerpts of reports on the Party's activities in basic industries.

114. Draper, "Communists and Miners," 380; Howe and Coser, *The American Communist Party*, 193, 262; Weinstein, *Ambiguous Legacy*. 43–44, 55, 61; Klehr, *The Heyday of American Communism*, 85, 86.

115. Klehr, *The Heyday of American Communism*, 37, 86.

116. Maurice Isserman, "The 1956 Generation: An Alternative Approach to

the History of American Communism," *Radical America* (March–April 1980), 43–51.

Chapter 3: The Origins of the People's Front, 1933–1935

1. Michael Gold, "Against Fascist Terror in Germany," *New Masses* (April 1933), 11; Earl Browder, "The Situation in the United States," in *Communism in the United States* (New York: International Publishers, 1935), 178.
2. John Griffin, *Strikes: A Study in Quantitative Economics* (New York: Columbia University Press, 1939), 39, 44; Irving Bernstein, *Turbulent Years* (Boston: Houghton Mifflin Co., 1970), 217–298. The AFL's timid attempt to organize auto workers failed once the union's opposition to strikes, and more generally to industrial unionism, led it to acquiesce to an unfavorable NRA code. Sidney Fine, *The Automobile Under the Blue Eagle* (Ann Arbor: University of Michigan Press, 1969), 142–163. In the steel industry the AFL's dormant Amalgamated Association of Iron, Steel and Tin Workers, found itself at the center of a spontaneous unionization drive carried out by the rank-and-file and jumped from 4,801 members in 1933 to 50,000 in early 1934. The resistance of the union leadership, backed by Green, to launching a strike in the industry destroyed the rank-and-file movement and eliminated the AFL from the steel industry; see Bernstein, *Turbulent Years*, 92–94, 197–203.
3. For an account of the growth of the UMW, see Melvyn Dubofsky and Warren Van Tine, *John L. Lewis* (New York: Quadrangle, 1977), 185–200.
4. Bernstein, *Turbulent Years*, 75–77.
5. Ibid., 84, 89.
6. W. Z. Foster, *From Bryan to Stalin* (New York: International Publishers, 1937), 254–257; Earl Browder, "Why an Open Letter to Our Party Membership—Report for the Political Buro to the Extraordinary Party Conference, New York City, July 7, 1933," *Communist* (August 1933), 718–719. Stachel, who had replaced Foster at the head of the TUUL in 1933, wrote that 100,000 workers had joined in 1933, adding to the 35,000 existing members. The number of permanent members stabilized at 100,000 showing a fluctuation of almost one third. Jack Stachel, "Recent Developments in the Trade Union Movement," *Communist* (December 1933), 1155–1168. Also on the League's failure to recruit, see Stachel, "Some Problems In Our Trade Union Work," *Communist* (June 1934), 524–535; John Williamson, "The Lessons of the Toledo Strike," *Communist* (July 1934), 639–654; B. Frank, "Party Functioned Poorly in Mining Strike District," *Party Organizer* (November 1933), 8–9; John Williamson, "Main Points of Concentration Forgotten," ibid., 15–16.

7. The best account on the Party's activities among maritime workers during the third period is Bruce Nelson, *Workers on the Waterfront: Seamen, Longshoremen, and Unionism in the 1930s* (Urbana: University of Illinois Press, 1988), 75–102. On the events leading to the strike and on the strike itself see Mike Quin, *The Big Strike* (Olema, California: Olema Publishing House, 1949), 38–62, 71–198; Foster, *From Bryan to Stalin*, 260–264; "The Communist Program . . . Only Way Out for Labor NOW," statement by Earl Browder and Sam Darcy in the *Western Worker* (1 August 1934); William F. Dunne, "San Francisco General Strike," *Labor Unity* (August 1934), 29–30; Earl Browder, "The Struggle for the United Front," *Communist* (October 1934), 940–955; "New Developments and New Tasks in the U.S.A.," ibid. (February 1935), 107; Darcy, "The Great West Coast Maritime Strike," ibid. (July 1934), 664–686; "The San Francisco Bay Area General Strike," ibid. (October 1934), 985–1004; Ella Winter, "Stevedores on Strike," *New Republic* (13 June 1934), 120–122; Robert Cantwell, "San Francisco: Act One," ibid. (25 July 1934), 280–282; Miriam Allen De Ford, "Riot Guns in San Francisco," *The Nation* (18 July 1934), 65–66; "San Francisco: An Autopsy On the General Strike," ibid. (1 August 1934), 121–122; Iris Hamilton, "Longshoremen on the Pacific," *New Masses* (5 June 1934), 12–15; " 'Shoot to Kill' on the Coast," ibid. (17 July 1934), 10–12; "General Strike," ibid. (24 July 1934), 9–11; William F. Dunne, "Fascism in the Pacific Coast Strike," ibid. (31 July 1934), 9–11; and Nelson, *Workers on the Waterfront*, 103–155.

8. Browder, "New Developments and New Tasks in the U.S.A.," *Communist* (February 1934), 107.

9. Ibid.

10. Browder, "For a Mass Revolutionary Trade Union Movement in the U.S.A.," 2. The text of Browder's speech was forwarded to military intelligence by the U.S. legation in Riga, which at this time was very active in monitoring U.S. Communist activities in the Soviet Union. *U.S. Military Intelligence Reports*, "Communist Activities within U.S. Armed Forces, December 1934–March 1935," Reel 22, Ser. 10110–2452, Pt. 24, 655; CPUSA Political Buro, "Directives on Work within the AFL and Independent Trade Unions," *Communist* (January 1934), 113–115. (All emphasis in the original).

11. R. D. G. Kelly, " 'Hammer n' Hoe', Black Radicalism and the Communist Party in Alabama, 1929–1941" (Ph.D. diss., UCLA 1987), 118–119; Nelson et al., *Steve Nelson, American Radical* (Pittsburgh: University of Pittsburgh Press, 1981), 90–92, 116; Steve Nelson, interview with author, 3 August 1984, personal holding; Foster, *From Bryan to Stalin*, 232–233.

12. Browder, "For a Mass Revolutionary Trade Union Movement in the United States," 56.

13. Wyndham Mortimer, *Organize! My Life as a Union Man* (Boston: Beacon Press, 1971), 54–61.
14. Roger Keeran, *The Communist Party and the Auto Workers Unions* (Bloomington: Indiana University Press, 1980), 103–107.
15. Fine, *The Automobile Under the Blue Eagle*, 293–299; Keeran, *The Communist Party and the Auto Workers Unions*, 121–125; Mortimer, *Organize!*, 69–71.
16. Fine, *The Automobile Under the Blue Eagle*, 178–181.
17. Bernstein, *Turbulent Years*, 93–94; Bert Cochran, *Labor and Communism: The Conflict that Shaped American Unions* (Princeton, N.J.: Princeton University Press, 1977), 75; Foster, *From Bryan to Stalin*, 239–240. Staughton Lynd describes the first failed attempt by the leaders of the rank-and-file movement within the Amalgamated to establish an alliance with the Communist union in "The Possibility of Radicalism in the Early 1930s: The Case of Steel," *Radical America* (November–December 1972), 18–19.
18. "Organizational Status of the Party, 1934," Browder Papers II, 3:36. All references citing the Browder Papers are in the Earl Browder Papers, Arents Research Library, Syracuse University, Syracuse New York. Also see Browder, *Report of the Central Committee to the Eighth Convention of the Communist Party of the U.S.A.* (New York: Workers Library Publishers, 1934), 35.
19. Browder, *Report to the Eighth Convention*, 34.
20. In the summation, Browder condemned those Party members who resisted relinquishing sectarian policies and were particularly adamant in their opposition to joining the AFL. Referring to Joe Zack, Party unionist, and the only delegate to vote against the new trade union policy, Browder said that his insistence on dual unionism had absolutely nothing "in common with the line of our Party," ibid., 106. For the convention's final resolutions see "Lessons of Economic Struggles, Tasks of the Communists in the Trade Unions," in *The Way Out, A Program for American Labor* (New York: Workers Library Publishers, 1934), 76–81.
21. Browder, *Report to the Eighth Convention*, 33, 35, 37–38. The Party's assessment of independent unions as well as its proposal for the Independent Federation of Labor (IFL) were further outlined by Jack Stachel in "The Independent Unions and the Fight for Unity in the Trade Unions," *Labor Unity* (June 1934), 26–30.
22. For the text of the letter, see "For the Unification of the Trade Union Movement," *Labor Unity* (October 1934), 27–30.
23. Foster, *From Bryan to Stalin*, 272–273.
24. Ibid., 272–273; "Communists and the Trade Unions," *Labor Unity* (January 1935), 3–4; Roy Hudson, "For One Marine Workers Union," ibid., 9–10; James Matles, "Toward Unity in the Metal Trades," ibid., 18.
25. Browder, "New Developments and New Tasks in the U.S.A.," 109; Cen-

tral Committee of the CPSU, *Outline History of the Communist International* (Moscow: Progress Publishers, 1971), 363–364.

26. "On the Main Immediate Tasks of the C.P.U.S.A, Resolution Adopted by the Central Committee Plenum, 15–18 January 1935," *Communist* (February 1935), 118–120. For a brief account of the TUUL final convention see Foster, *From Bryan to Stalin*, 274.

27. Kermit E. McKenzie, *Comintern and World Revolution, 1928–1943* (New York: Columbia University Press, 1964), 121, 131–135; "Extracts From The Theses Of The Tenth ECCI Plenum On The International Situation And the Tasks Of The Communist International," in Jane Degras, *The Communist International, 1919–1943*, vol. 3 (London: Oxford University Press, 1956), 39–52.

28. The persistence of the analysis and policies of the third period can be clearly seen in the debate and resolutions of the XIII Plenum of the Executive Committee of the Comintern held in November–December 1933. Most of the speeches repeated the view concerning the link between crisis of capitalism, "fascization" of bourgeois rule, and the growth of the revolutionary movement. The Plenum renewed its attacks on Socialist organizations: the theses stated that social-democracy, continued to "play the role of the main social prop of the bourgeoisie also in the countries of open fascist dictatorship." Obviously the International had remained bound to its policies of the past. There was no attempt at self-criticism or revision of its tactics in light of the events of the previous years. For a discussion of the XIII Plenum, see Degras, *The Communist International* vol. 3, 285–306; E. H. Carr, *Twilight of the Comintern, 1930–1935* (New York: Pantheon Books, 1982), 104–116.

29. W. Z. Foster, *Toward Soviet America* (New York: Coward-McCann, Inc., 1932), 177.

30. Ibid., 196–200, 239.

31. Moissaye Olgin, *The Socialist Party: Last Bulwark of Capitalism* (New York: Workers Library Publishers, 1932), 28. These were common themes of Communist propaganda in this period. Similar views were expressed by Israel Amter in *Is the Socialist Party a Party of the Workers?* (New York: Communist Party, U.S.A., 1932).

32. Foster, *Toward Soviet America*, 240–241.

33. *Daily Worker* (15, 17 February 1934); *New York Times* (17 February 1934); *New Republic* (28 February 1934), 58–59; Daniel Aaron, *Writers on the Left* (New York: Harcourt, Brace and World, 1961), 350. The six were Mary Fox, William Pickens, Devere Allen, Tucker Smith, David Lasser, and Francis A. Henson. "American League Against War and Fascism," Browder Papers II, 1:7.

34. Browder, *Report to the Eighth Convention*, 15–16.

35. Ibid., 17–18.

36. Matthew Josephson, *Infidel in the Temple* (New York: Alfred A. Knopf, 1967), 365.
37. *New Masses* published letters written by Newton Arvin, Roger N. Baldwin, Heywood Broun, Lewis Corey, Waldo Frank, Michael Gold, Horace Gregory, Granville Hicks, Sidney Hook, H. M. Kallen, Scott Nearing, James Rorty, Isidor Schneider, and Edwin Seaver. "Against the Fascist Terror in Germany," *New Masses* (April 1933), 10–13. Freeman's manifesto, "The Background of German Fascism," ibid., 3–9.
38. Ibid., 11.
39. *Harper's* (July 1931), 129–136.
40. George P. Rawick, "The New Deal and Youth: The Civil Conservation Corps, The National Youth Administration and the American Youth Congress" (Ph.D. diss., University of Wisconsin, 1957), 275; Eileen Eagan, *Class, Culture, and the Classroom* (Philadelphia: Temple University Press, 1981), 38; Hal Draper, "The Student Movement in the Thirties: A Political History," in Rita James Simon, ed., *As We Saw the Thirties* (Urbana: University of Illinois Press, 1967), 157–158.
41. Rawick, "The New Deal and Youth," 276–277; Eagan, *Class, Culture and the Classroom*, 114. For an account of the trip of the NSL's delegation to Harlan County, see Joseph Lash, "Students in Kentucky," *New Republic* (20 April 1932), 267–269; and James Wechsler, *Revolt on the Campus* (New York: Covici, Friede, 1935), 99–105.
42. Eagan, *Class, Culture and the Classroom*, 90–91.
43. Wechsler, *Revolt on the Campus*, 170–171; Eunice Clark, "Lo, the Poor Student," *New Republic* (17 January 1934), 8–9; Rawick, "The New Deal and Youth," 278–281.
44. The poll was conducted by the Brown University *Daily Herald*; see *The Nation* (24 May 1933), 571.
45. Rawick, "The New Deal and Youth," 282; Eagan, *Class, Culture and the Classroom*, 58–59.
46. Wechsler, *Revolt on the Campus*, 174; Draper, "The Student Movement in the Thirties," 169–170.
47. Wechsler, *Revolt on the Campus*, 142–143.
48. Rawick, "The New Deal and Youth," 283–284; Wechsler, *Revolt on the Campus*, 171. For an account of the strike in various campuses, see Eagan, *Class, Culture and the Classroom*, 116–118.
49. Wechsler, "The Student Union Begins," *New Republic* (19 January 1936), 279–280; and Wechsler, *Revolt on the Campus*, 452–454, for quote 453. Draper, "The Student Movement in the Thirties," 173–175; Eagan, *Class, Culture and the Classroom*, 136–137; Rawick, "The New Deal and Youth," 300–306.
50. Eagan, *Class, Culture and the Classroom*, 134; Rawick, "The New Deal and Youth," 299–301.

51. For the proceedings of the first congress of the American Youth Congress, see *Daily Worker* (18, 20 August 1934); "Youth Divides," *New Republic* (29 August 1934), 62–63; Rawick, "The New Deal and Youth," 284–285, 289–291. On the Communist party's accusations against Viola Ilma, see Browder, "New Developments and New Tasks in the U.S.A.," 111; John L. Spivack, "Plotting the American Pogroms: Who Paid Viola Ilma's Way to Nazi Germany?" *New Masses* (13 November 1934), 8–11. In later years Joseph Lash downplayed Viola Ilma's Nazi connection; *Eleanor and Franklin* (New York: Norton, 1971), 543–544.

52. Gil Green to author, 19 November 1987; and Gil Green, interview with author, 21 December 1987.

53. Quoted in Aaron, *Writers on the Left*, 281. See also *Daily Worker* (11 October 1934); Orrick Johns, "The John Reed Clubs Meet," *New Masses* (30 October 1934), 25–26.

54. Richard Wright, *American Hunger* (New York: Harper & Row, 1944), 91–93; Aaron, *Writers on the Left*, 281–282.

55. "Call for an American Writers' Congress," *New Masses* (22 January 1935), 20. Also on the Congress see Henry Hart, ed., *American Writers' Congress* (New York: International Publishers, 1935); Granville Hicks, *Part of the Truth* (New York: Harcourt, Brace and World, 1965), 129–130.

56. Earl Browder, "Communism and Literature," in Hart, ed., *American Writers' Congress*, 68.

57. Ibid., 69.

58. Ibid., 70.

59. Foster, *Toward Soviet America*, 236–237.

60. William E. Leuchtenburg, *Franklin D. Roosevelt and the New Deal* (New York: Harper & Row, 1963), 9.

61. James MacGregor Burns, *Roosevelt: The Lion and the Fox* (New York: Harcourt, Brace and World, 1956), 142–144.

62. National Election Campaign Committee of the CPUSA, *The Democratic Twin of the Hoover Hunger Government* (New York: Workers Library Publishers, 1932), 4.

63. Ibid., 8.

64. Grace Hutchins, "Roosevelt and Labor," *Labor Unity* (September 1932), 16–17; W. Z. Foster, *The Words and Deeds of Franklin D. Roosevelt* (New York: Workers Library Publishers, 1932), 5.

65. The National Election Campaign Committee of the CPUSA, *Will Beer Bring Back Prosperity?* (New York: Workers Library Publishers, 1932), 4–5.

66. "The Roosevelt Program—An Attack Upon the Toiling Masses," *Communist* (May 1933), 420–422.

67. Ibid., 423. The Party was not alone in charging the military character of the CCC; the War Department played an important role in the program.

This situation was eyed with great concern by many liberals including Eleanor Roosevelt; see Rawick, "The New Deal and Youth," 112; Lash, *Eleanor and Franklin,* 536.

68. Military intelligence files contain numerous confidential reports together with an assortment of Communist leaflets, pamphlets, and papers confiscated either from YCL members or found in the camps. *U.S. Military Intelligence Reports,* Reel 22, Ser. 10100–2452, Pt. 23; Reel 24, Ser. 2661–34 through 80; and Reel 25.

69. "The Roosevelt Program," 424.

70. Ibid.

71. Earl Browder, "Why An Open Letter to Our Party Membership," *Communist* (August 1933), 713.

72. Ibid., 715–716.

73. I. Amter, *Industrial Slavery—Roosevelt's New Deal* (New York: Workers Library Publishers, 1933), 12–13.

74. Ibid., 16.

75. Earl Browder, "Why An Open Letter," 711–712; see also "The Open Letter and the Struggle Against the N.R.A.," *Communist* (October 1933), 267.

76. *Daily Worker* (6, 17, 23 January; 10, 27 February; 6, 7, 28 March; 7 April; 5, 18 May; 26 June; 24, 26 July; 18 August; 28, 29 September; 15, 20 October; 19 November; 22 December 1934). See also "Through May Day to a Soviet America," *Communist* (May 1934), 423; Browder, *Report to the Eighth Convention,* 20–21; Communist Party, *The Way Out,* 21, 36. This pamphlet also contained the manifesto and principal resolutions adopted by the Party's convention.

77. Alexander Bittelman, "The New Deal and the Old Deal," *Communist* (January 1934), 81.

78. *New Masses* (2 January 1934).

79. *Rundschau* (13 January 1934), 23.

80. Palmiro Togliatti, *Opere,* vol. 3, tome 2 (Rome: Editori Riuniti, 1973), 288. Rajani Palme Dutt said that all the measures adopted by the Roosevelt administration demonstrated more than elsewhere the development toward fascism: "extreme violence against the workers and intensified war preparations, all under a cover of extreme social demagogy. Here is the classic type of the most modern process of fascization within the Western imperialists, still nominally bourgeois democratic states." Quotes in Degras, *The Communist International* vol. 3, 286.

81. Browder, "The Situation in the United States," 178; Weinstone, *Rundschau* (30 January 1934), 393.

82. The *New Republic* made its concerns explicit through a series of editorials: "General Johnson Goes Fascist" (25 October 1933), 294–295; "A Labor Model for General Johnson" (20 December 1933), 155–156; "Mr. Roose-

velt's First Year" (14 March 1934), 116; and "Will Roosevelt Back Up Labor" (9 May 1934), 351. See also John P. Diggins, *Mussolini and Fascism: The View From America* (Princeton, N.J.: Princeton University Press, 1972), 164–165, 280.

83. Browder, "Why An Open Letter," 728.

84. Earl Browder, *What Every Worker Should Know About the NRA* (New York: Workers Library Publishers, 1933), 8.

85. Ibid., 18.

86. *An Open Letter to All Members of the Communist Party,* 8.

87. "Resolution of the 17th Central Committee Meeting of the Communist Party, U.S.A.," *Communist* (October 1933), 1090.

88. Browder, *Report to the Eighth Convention,* 21.

89. Ibid., 22.

90. *Daily Worker* (31 January 1934).

91. "Results and Lessons of the Elections," *Communist* (December 1934), 1187.

92. Quoted in Leuchtenburg, *Roosevelt and the New Deal,* 91–92.

93. Browder, "The Struggle for the United Front," 935–936.

94. Ibid., 937.

95. Ibid., 936.

96. Browder, "Recent Political Developments and Some Problems of the United Front," Report to Meeting of the Central Committee, CPUSA, 25–26 May 1935, *Communist* (July 1935), 609–610.

97. Earl Browder, "The Seventeenth Anniversary of the October Revolution," *Communist* (November 1934), 1065–1074; "On the Main Immediate Tasks of the CPUSA," Resolution adopted by the Central Committee Plenum, 15–18 January 1935, *Communist* (February 1935), 125–126.

98. For examples of the Party's failure to distinguish between Roosevelt and his right-wing opposition see Alexander Bittelman, "The Supreme Court, the New Deal and the Class Struggle," *Communist* (July 1935), 588; Editorials in the *Daily Worker* (6, 16, 19 March 1935); William F. Dunne, *Why Hearst Lies About Roosevelt* (New York: Workers Library Publishers, 1935); I. Amter, *Working Class Unity or Fascism?* (New York: Workers Library Publishers, 1935); Brown, "Toward the Study of Fascization in the United States," *Communist* (June 1935), 558–568.

99. W. Z. Foster, "Fascist Tendencies in the United States," *Communist* (October 1935), 886.

100. "Forge a Mighty United Front for May Day!" Manifesto of the Central Committee, CPUSA *Communist* (April 1935), 294; Bittelman, "The Supreme Court, the New Deal and the Class Struggle," 581.

101. David Ramsey, "The AAA—And After," *Communist* (February 1936), 133. As in the case of the NRA the Party's attack on the Supreme Court did not imply a defense of the AAA. In the same article Ramsey de-

scribed the objectives of the AAA as follows: "to raise farm prices, to regulate agricultural surpluses by restricting production, to keep the poor farmers in check by giving them some meager cash relief, and to drive farmers off so-called submarginal lands," ibid., 132. See also Bittelman, "Review of the Month," ibid. (February 1936), 100.

102. Earl Browder, "Abe Lincoln—Champion of the People," *Sunday Worker* (16 February 1936).

103. Ibid. See also Earl Browder, "The Farmer-Labor Party—The People's Front in the U.S.A," *Communist International* (September 1936), 1118–1126.

104. Bittelman, "The Supreme Court, the New Deal and the Class Struggle," 589, 593; Bittelman's introduction in Earl Browder, *Communism in the United States* (New York: International Publishers, 1935) viii–ix.

105. *Daily Worker* (1, 28 May 1935); Robert Minor, "May Day Under the Guns," *Communist* (May 1935), 387–410; "The 'Security' Bill," *New Masses* (30 April 1935), 8; "Two Kinds of Social Security," ibid. (9 July 1935), 6–7.

106. "Approaching the Seventh World Congress of the Communist International," *Communist* (June 1935), 523 , 524. See also Brown, "Toward the Study of Fascization in the United States," 567.

107. Arthur M. Schlesinger, Jr., *The Politics of Upheaval* (Boston: Houghton Mifflin Company, 1960), 109–124.

108. Millard L. Gieske, *Minnesota Farmer-Laborism: The Third-Party Alternative* (Minneapolis: University of Minnesota Press, 1979), 187–188.

109. Browder, "The Struggle for the United Front," 938.

110. *An Open Letter to All Members of the Communist Party*, 9. Similar views were expressed by Browder in "Why an Open Letter," 734–735; and in "What About This Labor Party Talk?" *Daily Worker* (9 September 1933).

111. "The Present Situation and the Tasks of the Communist Party of the U.S.A.," in *The Way Out*, 40; Browder, "The Struggle for the United Front," 963.

112. "Results and Lessons of the Elections," 1190. For the Party's position on Upton Sinclair's EPIC, see Robert Minor, "The 'EPIC' Mass Movement in California," *Communist* (December 1934), 1214–1233. For the Communist position on Huey Long's "Share the Wealth" program, see Alexander Bittelman, *How Can We Share the Wealth? The Communist Way Versus Huey Long* (New York: Workers Library Publishers, 1935).

113. "Results and Lessons of the Elections," 1190–1191.

114. Ibid., 1194.

115. Browder, "New Developments and New Tasks in the United States," 101.

116. Ibid., 102.

117. Ibid., 114.

118. CCCPSU, *Outline History of the Communist Party*, 364; Interview with Earl Browder, 23 June 1955, Draper Papers, I, 1:5. 3; Browder, "The Workers'

Bill Belongs to the Whole Working Class," in *Unemployment Insurance* (New York: Workers Library Publishers, 1935), 5–9.

119. *Daily Worker* (31 January 1934).

120. Jack Stachel, "The Problem of a Labor Party," in *How Do We Raise the Question of a Labor Party?* (New York: Workers Library Publishers, 1935), 12.

121. Ibid., 16. The final resolution adopted by the central committee at the end of January also illustrated the Party's views on the Labor party, see "On the Main Immediate Tasks of the CPUSA," 123–125.

122. Foster, *Daily Worker* (22 June 1935).

123. For Communist activities in favor of the Labor party during this period, see Morris Childs, "Our Tasks in the Light of Changed Conditions," *Communist* (April 1935), 299–311; Ralph Shaw, "Initiating Labor Party Tickets," ibid. (June 1935), 548–557; Browder, "Recent Political Developments and Some Problems of the United Front," 623.

124. Gil Green, interview with author, 21 December 1987.

125. On events in France in February 1934, and during the following months, see Daniel Brower, *The New Jacobins* (Ithaca: Cornell University Press, 1968), 31–67. On the new position taken by the Communist International see Carr, *Twilight of the Comintern*, 124–146.

126. James Weinstein, *Ambiguous Legacy: The Left in American Politics* (New York: New Viewpoints, 1975), 57; Harvey E. Klehr, *The Heyday of American Communism: The Depression Decade* (New York: Basic Books, 1984), 171. Howe and Coser attribute the Party's abandonment of revolutionary unions to instruction from Moscow in the Spring of 1934, *The American Communist Party: A Critical History* (Boston: Beacon Press, 1957), 269–270.

Chapter 4: The People's Front

1. Georgi Dimitrov, *Working Class Unity—Bulwark Against Fascism* (New York: Workers Library Publishers, 1935), 10.

2. Jane Degras, *The Communist International, 1919–1943*, vol. 3 (London: Oxford University Press, 1956). For my interpretation of the Seventh Congress I have relied on several sources, amongst them Kermit E. McKenzie, *Comintern and World Revolution, 1928–1943* (New York: Columbia University Press, 1964); Franco De Felice, *Fascismo Democrazia Fronte Popolare* (Bari: De Donato, 1973); E. H. Carr, *Twilight of the Comintern* (New York: Pantheon Books, 1982). For an interesting view of recent Soviet historiography on the congress and its antecedents also see V. M. Lejbzon and K. K. Sirinja, *Povorot v Politike Kominterna* (Moscow: Mysl, 1965).

3. The report was delivered on 2 August 1935.

4. Dimitrov, *Working Class Unity*, 17 and 22.
5. Ibid., 31.
6. Ibid., 39.
7. McKenzie, *Comintern and World Revolution*, 154; Dimitrov, *Working Class Unity*, 70.
8. Dimitrov, *Working Class Unity*, 71 and 75.
9. McKenzie, *Comintern and World Revolution*, 155.
10. Dimitrov, *Working Class Unity*, 76.
11. Ibid., 77.
12. Browder addressed the Congress twice: the first time on July 27 following Wilhelm Piek's report on the activities of the ECCI, the second on August 21 following Dimitrov's address. In both his speeches Browder described the Party's activities and dealt with tactical matters such as the importance of building the Farmer-Labor party movement as well as the need to build strong ties with the Socialist party. Browder in Communist International, *VII Congress of the Communist International* (Abridged stenographic report of the proceedings) (Moscow: Foreign Language Publishing House, 1939), 83–88; "For Working Class Unity!" *Communist* (September 1935), 789.
13. Foster's speech was read on August 5 by another delegate as the American leader was sick. That Rajani Palme Dutt was referring to Foster in his criticism is mentioned in Lejbzon and Sirinja, *Povorot v Politike Kominterna* as well as by Browder in "For Working Class Unity!" 792. See also *Daily Worker* (7 August 1935). Palme Dutt's quote is in Degras, *The Communist International* vol. 3, 57.
14. Dimitrov's summation in *VII Congress of the Communist International*, 361. Dimitrov's reply was delivered on August 13.
15. Dimitrov, *Working Class Unity*, 42.
16. W. Z. Foster, "Fascist Tendencies in the United States," *Communist* (October 1935), 893.
17. *New York Times* (19 September 1935); *Daily Worker* (17, 19 September 1935).
18. Browder, "New Steps in the United Front," *Communist* (November 1935), 988.
19. Earl Browder, *Build the United People's Front* (New York: Workers Library Publishers, 1935), 23–24.
20. Ibid., 24.
21. Statement by the Party's Central Committee in the *Daily Worker* (28 March 1936) and Hathaway, "Why a Farmer-Labor Party?" *Daily Worker* (12 April 1936). Also see Alexander Bittelman, "Review of the Month," *Communist* (February 1936), 102. In April Bittelman wrote "Roosevelt is already moving to the Right, has been for some time, except that he continued to cover it up with 'Left' gestures." The Party's immediate problem then was "to win away the masses from the capitalist parties."

Failure to do so would have meant "helping Roosevelt, helping the Republicans, helping reaction." *Communist* (April 1936), 302. Bittelman expressed similar views of Roosevelt's dependency on "reactionary" forces in the following issue of the *Communist* (May 1936), 398. A central committee statement issued for May Day called upon workers not to "rely upon Roosevelt who uses high-sounding words against reactionaries but who on every issue retreats before them and carries out their dictates"; "For a United May Day!" *Communist* (May 1936), 408. Roosevelt was also accused of "returning to the unvarnished hunger program of Hoover"; Herbert Benjamin, "Unity on the Unemployment Field," *Communist* (April 1936), 329.

22. Browder, "The Party of Lenin and the People's Front," *Communist* (February 1936), 129.

23. Richard H. Pells, *Radical Vision and American Dreams: Culture and Social Thought in the Depression Years* (New York: Harper & Row, 1973), 299–300; Arthur M. Schlesinger, *The Politics of Upheaval* (Boston: Houghton Mifflin, Co., 1960), 548–550; Frank Warren, *Liberals and Communism* (Bloomington: Indiana University Press, 1966), 39–50. For an example of liberal criticism of the New Deal, see "Balance Sheet of the New Deal," *New Republic* (10 June 1936), 141–157.

24. Earl Browder to Norman Thomas, 17 August 1934; Norman Thomas to Earl Browder, 21 August 1934, Norman Thomas Papers, New York Public Library, ser. I, reel 3; *Daily Worker* (5 September 1934). The correspondence between the two leaders was also printed in the *Daily Worker* (20, 25 August 1934). Also see Earl Browder, "The Struggle for the United Front," *Communist* (October 1934), 955; Sam Brown, "The Proposals of the Communist Party for a United Front With the Socialist Party in the U.S.A.," *Communist International* (5 November 1934), 740–742. The Thomas papers contain letters and copies of letters appealing for unity sent by Browder from the end of August 1934 to April 1935, addressed to the Socialist leader as well as to the Socialist party's National Executive Committee and its secretary, Clarence Senior.

25. Browder, "New Steps in the United Front," 1004.

26. Alexander Bittelman, "Developments in the United Front," *Communist* (December 1934), 1201–1213.

27. Thomas Papers, ser. I, reel 4.

28. Norman Thomas, *After the New Deal, What?* (New York: Macmillan, 1936), 218–219.

29. David A. Shannon, *The Socialist Party of America: A History* (New York: Macmillan, 1955), 211–218, 235–240; John Herling, "The Socialist Convention," *New Republic* (20 June 1934), 152–153.

30. "Declaration of Principles of the Socialist Party: As Adopted in Conven-

tion at Detroit and Approved by Referendum," in Frank A. Warren, *An Alternative Vision* (Bloomington: Indiana University Press, 1974), 193–194.

31. Thomas, *After the New Deal, What?*, 7, 214.
32. *New York Times* (28 November 1935). The 14 December 1935 issue of the *Daily Worker* was entirely devoted to the debate.
33. *Which Road for American Workers, Socialist or Communist, Norman Thomas v. Earl Browder* (New York: Socialist Call, 1936), 11, 14.
34. Ibid., 20.
35. Earl Browder, "New Developments and New Tasks in the U.S.A.," *Communist* (February 1935), 103; "The Struggle for the United Front," 957–958.
36. John Dean, "The Socialist Administration in Reading and Our United Front Tasks," *Communist* (January 1936), 84; C. A. Hathaway, "Problems in Our Farmer-Labor Party Activities," *Communist* (May 1936), 430–431; *Daily Worker* (29 November 1936); "Mrs Berger Endorses Unity in Fight on War and Fascism," *Daily Worker* (14 October 1935).
37. *Daily Worker* on May Day. Alexander Bittelman, "Review of the Month," *Communist* (June 1936), 491. The Communist party addressed a letter to the Socialist party's convention in which again it called for unity and a joint ticket. Browder Papers, II, 18:140. See also "Letter of the Central Committee of the CPUSA to the NEC of the Socialist Party," *Daily Worker* (31 May 1936); Joseph Freeman, "The Socialists Hesitate," *New Masses* (9 June 1936), 11–12.
38. *Daily Worker* (26 February, 16 April 1936).
39. *Daily Worker* (8 August 1936); Earl Browder, *The People's Front in America* (New York: Workers Library Publishers, 1936), 8–11; Alexander Bittelman, "Review of the Month," *Communist* (August 1936), 678–680 and (October 1936), 907–908; W. Z. Foster, *From Bryan to Stalin* (New York: International Publishers, 1937), 303–312.
40. James P. Cannon, *The History of American Trotskyism* (New York: Pioneer Publishers, 1944), 216–233; Constance Ashton Myers, *The Prophet's Army* (Westport, Conn.: Greenwood Press, 1977), 112–122.
41. Earl Browder, *The People's Front* (New York: International Publishers, 1938), 27.
42. William Mangold, "On the Labor Front," *New Republic* (9 October 1935), 245; *New York Times* (1, 2 February 1936).
43. Quoted in Schlesinger, *The Politics of Upheaval*, 593.
44. Irving Bernstein, *Turbulent Years* (Boston: Houghton Mifflin Co., 1970), 449–450; Melvyn Dubofsky and Warren Van Tine, *John L. Lewis* (New York, Quadrangle, 1977), 216–217; 248–252; William E. Leuchtenburg, *Roosevelt and the New Deal* (New York: Harper & Row, 1963), 188–189; C. K. McFarland, "Coalition of Convenience: Lewis and Roosevelt, 1933–1940," *Labor History* (Summer 1972), 401–404.

45. John Earl Haynes, *Dubious Alliance: The Making of Minnesota's DFL Party* (Minneapolis: University of Minnesota Press, 1984), 13–14; Millard L. Gieske, *Minnesota Farmer-Laborism: The Third-Party Alternative* (Minneapolis: University of Minnesota Press, 1979), 217–218, 220–222.

46. In his interviews with Theodore Draper, Browder gave conflicting accounts that would have placed him in Minneapolis either in December 1935 or January 1936. Interviews with Earl Browder by Theodore Draper on 23 June and 10 October 1955. Draper Papers, I, 1:5, 1:8. In fact Browder was in Minneapolis on 20 October 1935. *Daily Worker* (27 October 1935).

47. "Proceedings Farmer-Labor Association of Minnesota," Browder Papers, III, 22, 9; Gieske, *Minnesota Farmer-Laborism*, 222. Noticeably absent was the Socialist party which criticized the conference's platform as reformist. This was a reflection of the Socialist party's leftward swing. Thomas, *After the New Deal What?*, 205–207.

48. "Proceedings Farmer-Labor Association of Minnesota," 2.

49. Ibid., 3.

50. Ibid., 4.

51. Ibid., *passim*.

52. Ibid., 60–74.

53. Browder, *Build the United People's Front*, 30; "The Farmer-Labor Party and the Struggle Against Reaction," Resolution adopted at the November plenum of the Central Committee of the CPUSA, *Communist* (December 1935), 1189; CC of CPUSA, "Communists Call for Building of Farmer-Labor Party Now," *Daily Worker* (26 December 1935); Alexander Bittelman, "Farmer-Labor Demands Spring from the People," *Daily Worker* (28 December 1935); "Support of Roosevelt Plays into Hands of Reaction," *Daily Worker* (1 January 1936); W. Z. Foster, "The Farmer-Labor Party and Roosevelt," *Daily Worker* (12 January 1936).

54. Browder in later years said he had received this information from someone within the Roosevelt administration who had with all probability spoken to Maxim Litvinov, Soviet Commissar for Foreign Relations; Interview with Earl Browder, 23 June 1955, Draper Papers, I, 1:5, 5–6. Sam Darcy, at the time the Party's representative in Moscow, later claimed to have been the one to have convinced the Soviet leadership to abandon the Farmer-Labor ticket and in its place openly support Roosevelt. Interview with Sam Darcy, 15 May 1957, Draper Papers, III, 53.

55. The details of the meeting are taken from Interview with Earl Browder, 23 June 1955, Draper Papers, I, 1:5, 5–7; Earl Browder, "The Reminiscences of Earl Browder," Oral History Collection, Columbia University, 246–249, 354–355. There is a question of whether Eugene Dennis took part at the meeting. According to Browder, both he and Foster were met in Moscow by Dennis. In her biography Peggy Dennis wrote that by January 1936,

both of them were back in the United States; Peggy Dennis, *Autobiography of an American Communist* (Berkeley Calif.: Creative Arts, 1977), 86–88.

56. Interview with Earl Browder, 23 June 1955, Draper Papers, 5–7; Browder, "Reminiscences," 246–249, 354–355.

57. Harvey Klehr, *The Heyday of American Communism: The Depression Decade* (New York: Basic Books, 1984), 185, 189–190.

58. Farmer Labor Association of Minnesota to Earl Browder, Browder Papers, I, 1:3; Browder, "The American Communist Party in the Thirties," in Rita James Simon, ed., *As We Saw the Thirties* (Urbana: University of Illinois Press, 1967), 233.

59. "Speech of Earl Browder, at first session of Farmer-Labor Party Conference, Morrison Hotel, Chicago, 30 May 1936," Browder Papers, III, 22:207. Speech also appeared in the *Daily Worker* (4 June 1936).

60. Ibid.

61. Earl Browder, "We Choose Our Path," *Worker* (24 May 1936).

62. Browder, *Build the United People's Front*, 48–49; and *What is Communism?* (New York: Workers Library Publishers, 1936), 93–94; Jack Stachel, "A New Page for American Labor. The Communist evaluation of the 55th Convention of the A.F. of L.," *Communist* (November 1935), 1017–1020; *Daily Worker* (10, 11 October 1935).

63. For examples of the Party's criticism of the CIO's endorsement of Roosevelt see Michael Gold, "No Blank Check for Roosevelt," *New Masses* (21 January 1936), 6; *Daily Worker* (9 March 1936); Earl Browder, "The United Front—The Key to Our New Tactical Orientation," *Communist* (December 1935), 1093. Also see Editorials in the *Daily Worker* (1 January, 9 February, and 3 April 1936).

64. B. K. Gebert, "The United Mine Workers' Union Convention," *Communist* (March 1936), 217–218.

65. Browder, *The People's Front in America*, 13; and "Farmer-Labor Party—The People's Front in the U.S.A.," *Communist International* (September 1936), 1120. On the Party's support for the formation of the American Labor Party, *Daily Worker* (17 July, 8, 15 August 1936).

66. Browder's speech before the New York *Herald Tribune*'s Annual Forum on 23 September in the *Daily Worker* (27 September); Browder, *The People's Front in America*, 13–14; Kenneth Waltzer, "The Party at the Polling Place: American Communism and the American Labor Party in the 1930s," *Radical History Review* (Spring 1980), 109.

67. *Daily Worker* (15 June 1936).

68. George Charney, *A Long Journey* (Chicago: Quadrangle, 1968), 75; Browder's speech to the American Youth Congress in Chicago on 4 July, *Daily Worker* (6 July 1936); Alexander Bittelman, "Review of the Month," *Communist* (August 1936), 677.

69. Earl Browder, "Democracy or Fascism," in *The People's Front* (New York: International Publishers, 1938), 30.

70. Robert Dallek, *Franklin D. Roosevelt and American Foreign Policy, 1932–1945* (New York: Oxford University Press, 1979), 128–129; Browder, *Worker* (6 September 1936); Bittelman, "Review of the Month," *Communist* (September 1936), 803.

71. Alexander Bittelman, "Review of the Month," *Communist* (July 1936), 579.

72. Earl Browder, *Daily Worker* (6 July 1936); "Democracy or Fascism," 30.

73. Browder, "Democracy or Fascism," 30.

74. Ibid., 32.

75. Browder, *The People's Front in America*, 5. The Party had to explain the reasons for strong conservative opposition to Roosevelt. In an attempt to do so Foster wrote during the summer that finance capital had supported the New Deal when they saw capitalism in danger. Now they opposed it because "they believe they are over the worst of the crisis, that the New Deal has exhausted its benefits for them, and that fresh polices of a more reactionary character are necessary. They want to take away even Roosevelt's few concessions to the impoverished masses of workers, farmers and lower middle class." See Foster, *From Bryan to Stalin*, 247.

76. *Daily Worker* (25 June 1936); William Mangold, "The Communist Convention," *New Republic* (15 July 1936), 292; *Daily Worker* (29 June 1936).

77. *Daily Worker* (29 June 1936). For the Party's electoral program see also "The 1936 Election Program of the Communist Party of the United States," *Daily Worker* (19 July 1936).

78. Alexander Bittelman, *Daily Worker* (28 July 1936); see also Bittelman, "Review of the Month," *Communist* (August 1936), 682–683.

79. *Worker* (19 January 1936).

80. *Daily Worker* (17 July 1936). For other examples of the Communist party's campaign against demagogues see Alexander Bittelman, "Coughlin Speaks for the Bankers—Not the People," *Daily Worker* (29 July 1936). Bittelman, *Townsend Plan: What It Is and What It Isn't* (New York: Workers Library Publishers, 1936), 21–22; Bittelman, *How to Win Social Justice: Can Coughlin and Lemke Do It?* (New York: Workers Library Publishers, 1936). The Party also issued a statement for the members and supporters of the National Union for Social Justice in which the same arguments were used. The purpose of it was to expose the demagoguery of the organization's leaders who used legitimate demands and grievances to further the reactionary interests; "Editorial," *Daily Worker* (15 August 1936).

81. Schlesinger, *Politics of Upheaval*, 518–519, 526.

82. Ibid., 619–620.

83. U.S. Congress, House Special Committee on Un-American Activities, 76th Cong., 1st sess., 1939, H. Res. 282, 4293–4299.

84. Browder, "The Main Issues," in *The People's Front*, 102–103.

85. *Congressional Quarterly's Guide to U.S. Elections* (Washington, D.C.: Con-

gressional Quarterly, 1975), 304, 783; I. Amter, "The Elections in New York," *Communist* (December 1936), 1150–1151.

86. *Congressional Quarterly's Guide to U.S. Elections*, 290; Amter, "The Elections in New York," 1150–1151; *Daily Worker* (14 December 1936); Dennis, "The Wisconsin Elections and the Farmer-Labor Party Movement," *Communist* (December 1936) 1138.

87. Schlesinger, *Politics of Upheaval*, 643.

88. Bernstein, *Turbulent Years*, 449–450.

89. *Daily Worker* (18 July, 31 August, 27 September 1936); Steve Nelson, interview with author, 3 August 1984; and Steve Nelson et al., *Steve Nelson, American Radical* (Pittsburgh: University of Pittsburgh Press, 1981), 174.

90. Robert P. Ingalls, *Urban Vigilantes in the New South: Tampa, 1882–1936* (Knoxville: University of Tennessee Press, 1988), 200–202; *Daily Worker* (14 July, 27 August, 12 September, 9 October 1935); Interview with Earl Browder, 23 June 1955, Draper Papers, I:5, 7.

91. *Daily Worker* (31 August 1936).

Chapter 5: The Democratic Front

1. George Charney, *A Long Journey* (Chicago: Quadrangle, 1968), 60–61.

2. "The Communist Party on the Results of the Elections," *Communist* (December 1936), 1104.

3. Ibid.

4. Ibid.

5. Ibid., 1105.

6. Earl Browder, "Results of the Elections and the Popular Front," in *The People's Front* (New York: International Publishers, 1938), 129, 133–135.

7. "The Communist Party on the Results of the Elections," 1106.

8. Alexander Bittelman, "Review of the Month," *Communist* (December 1936), 1094.

9. Ibid., 1098–1099.

10. Browder, "Results of the Elections and the Popular Front," 131.

11. Ibid., 122–123.

12. Ibid., 132.

13. Leuchtenburg, *Franklin D. Roosevelt and the New Deal* (New York: Harper & Row, 1963), 231–239; MacGregor Burns, *Roosevelt: The Lion and the Fox* (New York: Harcourt, Brace and World, 1956), 297–303.

14. *Daily Worker* (9 February 1937). During the following weeks almost every issue of the *Daily Worker* contained an editorial or a major article praising Roosevelt and urging support for his proposal.

15. Alexander Bittelman, "Review of the Month," *Communist* (April 1937), 295.

16. C. A. Hathaway, "The People vs. the Supreme Court," *Communist* (April

1937), 310–311. A further sign of confusion was that less than two months later Hathaway reversed himself calling again for a Farmer-Labor party. "Broad People's United Front Needed to Defeat Fascism," *Daily Worker* (1 May 1937).

17. William Weinstone, "The Great Auto Strike," *Communist* (March 1937), 212; "Building the Party in the Struggle For Proletarian Unity and the People's Front," Resolution adopted at the Central Committee meeting of 17–20 June, *Communist* (August 1937), 738. The Party was very critical of Roosevelt's decision to reduce WPA jobs in an attempt to curb inflation through cuts in government spending. *Daily Worker* (21 April, 4 May 1937); and Alexander Bittelman, "Review of the Month," *Communist* (March 1937), 202.

18. Central Committee of the CPSU, *Outline History of the Communist International* (Moscow: Progress Publishers, 1971), 421.

19. For a radically different assessment of Browder's trip to Moscow see Harvey Klehr, *The Heyday of American Communism* (New York: Basic Books, 1984), 200.

20. Browder, *The People's Front*, 231.

21. Ibid., 231, 232.

22. Browder, "The Communists in the People's Front," in *The People's Front*, 155.

23. Ibid., 156.

24. Ibid., 159.

25. Ibid., 160.

26. Ibid., 161.

27. Ibid., 161–162.

28. Ibid., 163.

29. Alexander Bittelman, "Review of the Month," *Communist* (August 1937), 720; ibid. (September 1937), 780.

30. Robert Dallek, *Franklin D. Roosevelt and American Foreign Policy* (New York: Oxford University Press, 1979), 135–136; John Earl Haynes, *Dubious Alliance: The Making of Minnesota's DFL Party* (Minneapolis: University of Minnesota Press, 1984), 29–30.

31. W. Z. Foster, *Party Building and Political Leadership* (New York: Workers Library Publishers, 1937), 53.

32. Earl Browder, *The People's Front*, 165.

33. Browder, "The Communists in the People's Front," 183–184. Browder's placing of the blame for "neutrality" on Congress was repeated in the Central Committee's resolution: "Building the Party in the Struggle For Proletarian Unity," 744. See also Browder, "China and America" (speech delivered at the Coney Island Velodrome, 2 September 1937), in *The People's Front*, 313.

34. Browder, "Democracy and the Constitution," *Daily Worker* (20 September 1937).

35. Leuchtenburg, *Roosevelt and the New Deal*, 226–227; Dallek, *Roosevelt and American Foreign Policy*, 148–149; *Socialist Call* (16 October 1937).
36. *Daily Worker* (6, 7 October 1937); Alexander Bittelman, "Review of the Month," *Communist* (November 1937), 981.
37. Earl Browder, "The People's Front Moves Forward," *Communist* (December 1937), 1083, 1093; "Draft Convention Resolution," *Communist* (April 1938), 352–353.
38. C. A. Hathaway, "The 1938 Elections and Our Tasks," *Communist* (March 1938), 208–219.
39. Central Committee of the CPSU, *Outline History of the Communist International*, 422.
40. *Daily Worker* (27 May 1938); *New York Times* (27 May 1938); Joseph R. Starobin, *American Communism in Crisis, 1943–1957* (Cambridge, Mass.: Harvard University Press, 1972), 45, 260–261.
41. Earl Browder, *The Democratic Front for Jobs, Security, Democracy and Peace* (New York: Workers Library Publishers, 1938), 16.
42. Ibid., 17.
43. See Jack Stachel, "The United Front and the Socialist Party," *Daily Worker* (20 April 1938).
44. "The Offensive of Reaction and the Building of the Democratic Front," *Communist* (April 1938), 356.
45. Hathaway, "The 1938 Elections and Our Tasks," 208–219.
46. Eugene Dennis, "Some Questions Concerning the Democratic Front," *Communist* (June 1938), 535.
47. Browder, *The Democratic Front*, 32–37.
48. Browder, "The People's Front Moves Forward," 1088–1089; Roy Hudson, "Leninism Shows the Way to Democracy, Peace and Prosperity," *Daily Worker* (21 January 1938).
49. "Jackson Speech and Anti-Monopoly," in "Polburo Meeting held 31 December 1937," Draper Papers, I, 7:17, 1–2. See also Hudson, "Leninism Shows the Way"; Leuchtenburg, *Roosevelt and the New Deal*, 247; and Ferdinand Lundberg, *America's 60 Families* (New York: The Citadel Press, 1937).
50. "Get Behind the President's Job and Recovery Program," *Daily Worker* (16 April 1938).
51. Earl Browder, "America Must Help Organize World Peace," *Daily Worker* (27 August 1938).
52. *Communist Election Platform 1938* (New York: Workers Library Publishers, 1938), 3. See also Earl Browder "Rise of the Democratic Front in the U.S.A.," *Daily Worker* (19 April 1938); "Draft Convention Resolution," *Communist* (April 1938), 351.
53. Quoted in Norman Markowitz, "A View From the Left," in Robert Griffith and Athan Theoharis, eds., *The Spectre* (New York: New Viewpoints, 1974), 8.

Notes to Pages 118–120

54. Hudson, "Leninism Shows the Way."
55. W. Z. Foster, "Win the Western Hemisphere for Democracy and Peace!" *Communist* (July 1938), 610.
56. *Worker* (26 March 1939). See also *Daily Worker* (13 July 1937; 14, 27 May 1938).
57. "The 1938 Elections Draft Convention Resolution," *Daily Worker* (22 March 1938).
58. Klehr, *Heyday of American Communism*, 270–273; William Schneiderman, *Dissent on Trial: The Story of a Political Life* (Minneapolis: MEP Publications, 1983), 62.
59. Morris Childs, "Building the Democratic Front in Illinois," *Communist* (September 1938), 812.
60. Haynes, *Dubious Alliance*, 12–13.
61. Earl Browder interviewed by Theodore Draper, 23 June and 10 October 1955, Draper Papers, I, 1:5 and 1:8.
62. Haynes, *Dubious Alliance*, 15–16; Gieske, *Minnesota Farmer-Laborism*, 211; Waltzer, "The Party and the Polling Place," 109. For the Party's presence at the Minnesota F.L. Convention see C. A. Hathaway, "The Minnesota Farmer-Labor Victory," *Communist* (December 1936), 1117; William Williamson, "The 1936 Elections and the Problems of a Labor Party in Ohio," *Daily Worker* (31 March 1936).
63. Haynes, *Dubious Alliance*, 16–19.
64. Earl Browder, "A Great Victory," *Daily Worker* (4 November 1937); "The Offensive of Reaction and the Building of the Democratic Front," 355; Simon W. Gerson, *Pete: The Story of Peter V. Cacchione New York's First Communist Councilman* (New York: International Publishers, 1976), 67. Kenneth Waltzer in his article "The Party and the Polling Place," provides a good analysis of the evolution of the Party's electoral politics. The article analyzes the contributions this policy made to the growth of the CIO, to the extension of reforms as well as the major theoretical problems it raised. On the Communist party and the ALP see also his "The American Labor Party: Third-Party Politics in New Deal-Cold War New York, 1936–1954" (Ph.D. dissertation, Harvard, 1977).
65. Earl Browder, "The Elections and the International Situation," in *Fighting for Peace* (New York: International Publishers, 1939), 176; Max Gordon to the author, 9 July 1985; *Congressional Quarterly's Guide to U.S. Elections* (Washington, D.C.: Congressional Quarterly, 1975), 789; *Daily Worker* (November 12, 1938).
66. Klehr, *The Heyday of American Communism*, 253–257.
67. For the CPUSA's activities in Wisconsin see Gene Dennis, "The Wisconsin Elections and the Farmer-Labor Party Movement," *Communist* (December 1936), 1125–1140; Peggy Dennis, *The Autobiography of an American Communist* (Berkeley, Calif.: Creative Arts, 1977), 104–105.

68. For an overview of the Party's involvement in local politics see John Earl Haynes, "The New History of the Communist Party in State Politics: The Implications for Mainstream Political History," *Labor History* (Fall 1986), 549–563.

69. "Not Further Division, But Greater Unity," *Daily Worker* (11 May 1938); see also Browder, *The Democratic Front*, 18 and 21.

70. Starobin, *American Communism in Crisis*, 37; Dennis, *The Autobiography of an American Communist*, 128; Schneiderman, *Dissent on Trial*, 63.

71. Browder, "Rise of the Democratic Front"; Haynes, *Dubious Alliance*, 36–42.

72. Charney, *A Long Journey*, 65, 67.

73. Joseph Figueredo, interview by Paul Buhle, OHAL; John Williamson, *Dangerous Scott: The Life and Work of an American "Undesirable"* (New York: International Publishers, 1969), 137; R. G. D. Kelly, " 'Hammer 'n' Hoe,' Black Radicalism and the Communist Party in Alabama, 1929–1941" (Ph.D diss., University of California at Los Angeles, 1987), 586; and *Time* (30 May 1938).

74. On the 1925 reorganization of the Party's structure see Theodore Draper, *American Communism and Soviet Russia: The Formative Period* (New York: Viking Press, 1960), 153–163.

75. Charney, *A Long Journey*, 53, 332; Robert Jay Alperin, "Organization in the Communist Party, U.S.A., 1931–1938" (Ph.D. diss., Northwestern University, 1959), 45.

76. Charney, *A Long Journey*, 94–95, 332; Alperin, "Organization in the Communist Party," 45; *Constitution and By-Laws of the Communist Party, U.S.A.* adopted by the Tenth National Convention of the CPUSA (New York: Workers Library Publishers, 1938), 13–18.

77. Charney, *A Long Journey*, 95.

78. Cited in Alperin, "Organization of the Communist Party," 112.

79. V. I. Lenin, *A Letter to American Workers* (New York: International Publishers, 1934), 9, 16.

80. Bertram D. Wolfe, Jay Lovestone, William F. Dunne, *Our Heritage from 1776: A Working Class View of the First American Revolution* (New York: The Workers School, [1926]); Robert Minor, "An Old Prison Speaks," *The Workers Monthly* (February 1925), 155–158.

81. W. Z. Foster, *Daily Worker* (7 November 1932).

82. "Against the 'New Deal' of Hunger, Fascism and War! For the Revolutionary Solution of the Crisis," in *The Way Out, A Program for American Labor* (New York: Workers Library Publishers, 1934), 27.

83. Richmond, *A Long View From the Left* (Boston: Houghton Mifflin, 1972), 254–255; Bertram Wolfe's review was in the *Communist* (November 1927), 459–462; Earl Browder, *Communism in the United States* (New York: International Publishers, 1935), 174. During the 1930s Communists might

have been hard pressed to acknowledge any influence by Charles Beard given his isolationism and criticism of the Soviet Union.

84. Browder, *What is Communism?* (New York: Workers Library Publishers, 1936), 17.
85. *Constitution and By-Laws of the Communist Party, U.S.A.*, 5–6. The preamble was drafted by Browder, "The Reminiscences of Earl Browder," Oral History Collection, Columbia University, 364.
86. Alexander Bittelman, "Review of the Month," *Communist* (August 1937), 694; "Party Building" delivered at "Polburo Meeting, held 23 December 1937," Draper Papers, I, 7:16, 1.
87. Earl Browder, "Lessons of the Moscow Trials," in *Fighting for Peace* (New York: International Publishers, 1939), 119.
88. Browder, *What Is Communism?*, 17–23; "Reminiscences," 263; and "Concerning American Revolutionary Traditions," *Communist* (December 1938), 1079–1085.
89. Browder, "The Constitutional Crisis," "Democracy and the Constitution," and "Revolutionary Background of the United States Government," in *The People's Front*, 217–269.
90. Browder, "What Spain Means to America," in *The People's Front*, 97–98; "Lenin and Spain," in *The People's Front*, 285–296.
91. Granville Hicks, *I Like America* (New York: Modern Age Books, 1938), 146–154.
92. Irving Howe and Lewis Coser, *The American Communist Party: A Critical History* (Boston: Beacon Press, 1957), 340–341.
93. Browder, *Fighting for Peace*, 131, 185.
94. *Daily Worker* (30 June 1938).
95. Ibid. These principles were incorporated at the Party's Tenth Convention into its constitution. See the preamble and Article VI, Section 1, of *The Constitution and By-Laws of the Communist Party.*
96. *Daily Worker* (20 September 1936); *Constitution and By-Laws of the Communist Party*, 21.
97. Arthur Liebman, *Jews and the Left* (New York: John Wiley and Sons, 1979), 348–349, 492–497.
98. On the cultural and political dimension of the CPUSA's relationship with the Jewish community see Paul Buhle, "Jews and American Communism: The Cultural Question," *Radical History Review* (Spring 1980), 9–36.
99. Kelly, "Hammer n' Hoe," 301–303.
100. "Hitler and the Catholics," *Daily Worker* (24 March 1937); Earl Browder, *A Message to Catholics* (New York: Workers Library Publishers, 1938). Selections from this pamphlet were quoted during a sermon in St. Patricks Cathedral, *New Masses* (2 August 1938). See also Phil Frankfeld, "Work

Among Catholics—A Key Question in Massachusetts," *Communist* (July 1938), 659–662; and Sigmund G. Eisenscher, "Some Experiences in Work Among Catholics," *Party Organizer* (May 1938), 14–17.

101. Charney, *A Long Journey*, 74.
102. *Daily Worker* (7 December 1937); *Daily Worker* (16 February 1936).
103. John Gates, *The Story of an American Communist* (New York: Thomas Nelson, 1958), 69.
104. Karl Yoneda, interviewed by Paul Buhle, OHAL.
105. Mark Naison, "Communism and Harlem Intellectuals in the Popular Front," *The Journal of Ethnic Studies* (Spring 1981), 14–15.
106. Cited by Mark Naison in "Lefties and Righties," *Radical America* (July–August 1979), 54.
107. Jack Stachel, "Organizational Problems of the Party," *Communist* (July 1935), 625; Browder, *The Democratic Front*, 60; and "Summation Speech at the Tenth National Convention," *Communist* (July 1938), 598.
108. "National Membership Report—January 1 to June 30, 1937," Draper Papers, I, 7:12; Max Steinberg, "Rooting the Party Among the Masses in New York," *Communist* (September 1938), 829–838.
109. "Building the Party During the Election Campaign," *Communist* (October 1936), 966; Stachel, "Build the Party for Peace, Democracy and Socialism," *Communist* (March 1938), 223.
110. *Daily Worker* (8 July 1936); Otis Hood, interview by Bill Schecter, OHAL.
111. Org-Education Commission, C.C. "The January 1938 Registration—An Analysis and Conclusion," *Party Organizer* (June 1938), 1–2.
112. Stachel, "Build the Party 223–225; Foster, "The Communist Party and the Professionals," *Communist* (September 1938), 805.
113. "The January 1938 Registration," 1–2.
114. "The January 1938 Registration," 2; Alperin, "Organization in the Communist Party," 60, 65. Robert Shaffer estimates that from 1933 to the end of the decade the percentage of women party members more than doubled from 16 to between 30–40 percent. Shaffer, "Women and the Communist Party, U.S.A., 1930–1940," *Socialist Review* (May–June 1979), 90, 97.
115. Vivian Gornick, *The Romance of American Communism* (New York: Basic Books, 1977) 78; Anna Taffler, interview by Jon Bloom, and Otis Hood, interview by Bill Schecter, OHAL.
116. Shaffer, "Women and the Communist Party," 97, 90.
117. Charney, *A Long Journey*, 31, 94. *Peter's Manual* was exhumed by government prosecutors during the Smith Act trials of the post-war years as proof of the CPUSA conspiratorial character.
118. "New Party Dues Payments," *Party Organizer* (December 1936), 12–13.
119. Mike Gold, "The Great Task of Being a Unit Organizer," *Daily Worker* (27 November 1937); A. W. Mills, "Personal Contact Is the Key to Re-

cruiting and the 'Sunday Worker' Campaign," *Party Organizer* (January 1936), 5. In 1936 turnover among recruits was 72 percent, the following year it had been reduced to 46 percent. "The January 1938 Registration," 5.

120. C. A. Hathaway, "Building the Democratic Front," *Communist* (May 1938), 404.
121. Eugene Dennis, "Some Questions Concerning the Democratic Front," *Communist* (June 1938), 534.
122. Alexander Bittelman, "Review of the Month," *Communist* (May 1938), 393–394; Eugene Dennis and Gil Green, "Notes on the Defense of American Democracy," ibid., 410–418.
123. Earl Browder, "Three Years Application of the Program of the Seventh World Congress," *Communist* (August 1938), 699–670.
124. On 11 November 1935 the *Daily Worker* announced that Foster was coming back to active work.
125. Foster, *Party Building and Political Leadership*, 56.
126. Ibid., 57.
127. Ibid., 65, 66–67.
128. Ibid., 52.
129. Haynes, *Dubious Alliance*, 19–20; Gil Green, interview with author, 21 December 1987; Alexander Bittelman, "The Party and the People's Front," *Communist* (August 1937), 711. See also, "Review of the Month," ibid. (June 1937), 483; (September 1937), 780.
130. The Soviet account of the first meeting, while recording that "William Foster passed critical remarks about Earl Browder . . . who idealized the policy of the Roosevelt Government and considered that the forces supporting Roosevelt would act as one of the main factors of the popular front," implies Moscow's support for Browder's policies. In January 1938, the leadership of the Comintern did tell Browder to moderate his enthusiasm for Roosevelt. Dimitrov specifically warned that it would have been "wrong to create an apology of Roosevelt." This criticism did not have any effect since, if anything, Browder's praises for the President increased. See Central Committee of the CPSU, *Outline History of the Communist International*, 421–422. In an interview with Theodore Draper, Browder described his April 1937 trip to Moscow. Mistakenly he did not recall though that the Party's attitude toward the New Deal and the Farmer-Labor party issue were among the topics discussed with the International's leadership; Interview with Earl Browder, 10 October 1955, Draper Papers, I, 1:8, 25–27. In the same interview he also discussed the January 1938 trip, 29–32. See also Dennis, *American Communist*, 120–124.
131. "Pre-plenum meeting of the national committee, March 23, 1939," Philip

J. Jaffe Papers, VII, 35:4, 3. All references citing the Jaffe Papers are in the Philip J. Jaffe Papers, Special Collections Department, Robert W. Woodruff Library, Emory University.

132. Ibid., 2.
133. Ibid., 4.
134. The political committee members in 1939 included Earl Browder, W. Z. Foster, Jack Stachel, James W. Ford, Alexander Bittelman, Charles Krumbein, Clarence Hathaway, Rose Wortis, Henry Winston, Roy Hudson, Robert Minor, Eugene Dennis, and Gil Green. All of them spoke with the exception of Bittelman who was either absent or chose to remain silent.
135. Ibid., 9.
136. Ibid., 22.
137. Ibid., 24.
138. Starobin, *American Communism in Crisis*, 268; Earl Browder, "How Stalin Ruined the American Communist Party," *Harper's* (March 1960), 48.
139. *Daily Worker* (20 May 1938).
140. Richmond, *A Long View From the Left*, 247.
141. "Review of the Month," *Communist* (January 1936), 5.
142. Repeatedly Party leaders declared that "socialism was not on the agenda." Browder even stated that "proletarian dictatorship," would become a viable issue only if Roosevelt's promise for a "higher standard of living under the present system is defeated or betrayed." The assumption then was that class consciousness would result only as a consequence of the betrayal by "progressive and democratic" leaders of their promises. Browder, "Democracy and the Constitution," 239.
143. *New Republic* (15 June 1938), 144–145.
144. Browder, *The Democratic Front*, 87.
145. Browder, *The People's Front*, 24.
146. Browder, *The People's Front*, 24. On the issue of "transition," see also: Browder, *Daily Worker* (8 August 1936); "What Spain Means to America," in *People's Front*, 100; "Results of the Elections," 145–149; "Democracy and the Constitution," 244 and "Communism in Theory and Practice" (speech delivered on 24 March 1938), Browder Papers, III, 22:207, 10–11.
147. Browder, "The Communists in the People's Front," 169–170.

Chapter 6: Communists and Labor

1. Earl Browder, *Report of the Central Committee to the Ninth Convention of the Communist Party of the U.S.A.* (New York: Workers Library Publishers, 1934), 28.

2. Irving Bernstein, *Turbulent Years* (Boston: Houghton Mifflin Co., 1970), 386–398, and chapter 9; Melvyn Dubofsky and Warren Van Tine, *John L. Lewis* (New York: Quadrangle, 1977), 222–223.
3. Steve Nelson, interview with author, 3 August 1984.
4. Earl Browder, "Recent Political Developments and Some Problems of the United Front," *Communist* (July 1935), 611–612.
5. W. Z. Foster, "Fascist Tendencies in the United States," *Communist* (October 1935), 897.
6. Jack Stachel, "A New Page for American Labor: The Communist Evaluation of the 55th Convention of the AFL," *Communist* (November 1935), 1031.
7. *Daily Worker* (16 October 1935) and "10,924 Industrial Union Votes! A New Era Opens in the AFL," *Daily Worker* (18 October 1935).
8. Earl Browder, *Build the United People's Front* (New York: Workers Library Publishers), 51.
9. *Daily Worker* (28 October 1935).
10. Earl Browder, "The United Front—The Key to Our New Tactical Orientation," *Communist* (December 1935), 1110–1117; Interview with Earl Browder, 23 June 1955, Draper Papers, I, 1:5, 11–12.
11. Walter Galenson, *The CIO Challenge to the AFL* (Cambridge, Mass.: Harvard University Press, 1960), 111.
12. Quoted in Bert Cochran, *Labor and Communism, The Conflict that Shaped American Unions* (Princeton, N.J.: Princeton University Press, 1977), 97.
13. Bernstein, *Turbulent Years*, 783.
14. Earl Browder, "The American Communist Party in the Thirties," in Rita James Simon, ed., *As We Saw the Thirties* (Urbana: University of Illinois Press, 1967), 231.
15. Earl Browder, "Twenty Years of Soviet Power," in *The People's Front* (New York: International Publishers, 1938), 345; Alexander Bittelman, "Review of the Month," *Communist* (December 1937), 1068.
16. "Communists Fight For Strengthening And Unity of AFL," *Daily Worker* (27 June 1936); Brown, "New Forms of Party Organization Help Us to Win the Masses," *Party Organizer* (July–August, 1936), 9; I. Amter, "The Elections in New York," *Communist* (December 1936), 1141.
17. Cochran, *Labor and Communism*, 345.
18. "Statement of the Central Committee," *Daily Worker* (12 February 1936).
19. The Communist party continued to campaign for a united labor movement following the transformation of the CIO into an independent union. See *Daily Worker* (12, 25 November 1935); "Prevent the AFL Split from Spreading; Re-Unite the Trade Union Movement," ibid. (26 November 1936); Foster, "Regarding Trade Union Unity," ibid. (20 October 1937); Roy Hudson, "Leninism Shows the Way to Democracy, Peace and Prosperity," ibid. (21 January 1938); Jack Stachel, "Problems Before the 56th

Annual Convention of the AFL," *Communist* (November 1936), 1046–
1055; "Building the Party in the Struggle for Proletarian Unity and the
People's Front," ibid. (August 1937), 742–744; W. Z. Foster, "The American Federation of Labor and Trade Union Progress," ibid. (August 1938),
697; Earl Browder, *The Results of the Elections and the People's Front* (New
York: Workers Library Publishers, 1936). Years later, when the Party's
relations with Lewis were considerably cooler, Foster dug up past criticism: "inasmuch as Lewis had 40 percent of the A.F. of L. unions behind
him and a vast following among the rest of the labor movement, it would
have been possible for him to beat the Green machine by a resolute fight."
W. Z. Foster, *The History of the Communist Party of the United States* (New
York: International Publishers, 1952), 307.
20. Peggy Dennis, *The Autobiography of an American Communist* (Berkeley, Calif.: Creative Arts, 1977), 94–95; *Daily Worker* (29 July 1936).
21. Earl Browder, "Labor vs. Landon," *Worker* (13 September 1936).
22. W. Z. Foster, *From Bryan to Stalin* (New York: International Publishers,
1937), 275.
23. Ronald L. Filippelli, "UE: The Formative Years, 1933–1937," *Labor History*
(Summer 1976), 370; Galenson, *The CIO Challenge to the AFL*, 439, 554;
Jerry Lembcke and William M. Tattam, *One Union in Wood: A Political
History of the International Woodworkers of America* (New York: International
Publishers, 1984), 52–54; and Daniel J. Leab, *A Union of Individuals: The
Formation of the American Newspaper Guild* (New York: Columbia University
Press, 1970), 265–275. The finest account on the part played by Commu-
nists in the founding and the building of the Transit Workers Union is
Joshua B. Freeman's, "Catholics, Communists, and Republicans: Irish
Workers and the Organization of the Transport Workers Union," in Michael H. Frish and Daniel J. Walkowitz, eds., *Working Class America: Essays
on Labor, Community, and American Society* (Urbana: University of Illinois
Press, 1983), 256–277.
24. Harvey Klehr, *The Heyday of American Communism* (New York: Basic Books,
1984), 239; Bella V. Dodd, *School of Darkness* (New York: P.J. Kennedy,
1954), 85.
25. Steve Nelson, interview with author, 3 August 1984; George Charney,
Long Journey (Chicago: Quadrangle, 1968), 62.
26. Steuben's letter to Stachel provides a clear summary of some the techniques used to organize and recruit workers, tactics of concentration, as
well as how to infiltrate company unions to turn them to the workers'
advantage. Letter cited in Max Gordon, "The Communists and the Drive
to Organize Steel," *Labor History* (Spring 1982), 261, 262.
27. Michael Honey, "The Popular Front in the American South: The View
from Memphis," *International Labor and Working Class History* (Fall 1986),

44–55; R. D. G. Kelly, "Hammer n' Hoe" (Ph.D. diss., University of Calif., Los Angeles, 1987), 475–485; Jose Alvarez, interview by Paul Buhle, and Joseph Figueredo, interview by Paul Buhle, OHAL.

28. Saul Alinsky, *John L. Lewis* (New York: G. P. Putnam's Sons, 1949), 153.

29. Browder, "The American Communist Party," 230; Interview with Earl Browder, 16 June 1953, Draper Papers, I, 1:3, 2.

30. John Williamson, *Dangerous Scot: The Life and Work of an American Undesirable* (New York: International Publishers, 1969), 125–126.

31. Foster, *History of the Communist Party*, 349; Kelly, "Hammer n' Hoe," 477.

32. W. Z. Foster, *Unionizing Steel, Outline of Organizing Methods in the Steel Campaign,* and *Industrial Unionism,* issued in 1936 by Workers Library Publishers. These and other pamphlets were eventually combined in a book: *Organizing the Mass Production Industries* (New York: International Publishers, 1937); "Auto Strike Section," *Daily Worker* (16, 20, 27 January, 3 February 1937); Foster, *History of the Communist Party,* 347.

33. Foster, *History of the Communist Party,* 349–350; *Daily Worker* (26 October 1936); Bill Gebert, "The Steel Drive and the Tasks of Communists in Mass Organizations," *Party Organizer* (September 1936), 14; Roger Keeran, "The International Workers Order and the Origins of the CIO," *Labor History* (Summer 1989), 385–400.

34. Foster, *History of the Communist Party,* 349–350; On the National Negro Congress and its activities in support of organized labor see James W. Ford, "The National Negro Congress," *Communist* (April 1936), 325–327; "Build the National Negro Congress," ibid. (June 1936), 552–501; Lawrence Wittner, "The National Negro Congress: A Reassessment," *American Quarterly* (Winter 1970), 883–901; and John Baxter Streater, Jr., "The National Negro Congress, 1936–1947" (Ph.D. diss., University of Cincinnati, 1981), 190–235.

35. A. Allen, "Party Building in Auto," *Party Organizer* (June 1937), 10.

36. Henry Kraus, *The Many and the Few,* 2nd ed. (Urbana: University of Illinois Press, 1985), 1–69; and Wyndham Mortimer, *Organize! My Life as a Union Man* (Boston: Beacon Press, 1971), ch. 8. Kraus and Mortimer both provide a compelling picture of the difficulties and resourcefulness of Communist unionists in organizing autoworkers in Flint before the sit-down strike.

37. This sit-down received much publicity during its successful test in France in May and June 1936. In the United States, the sit-down had been used by rubber workers to protest layoffs and reduction in rates in Akron. Beginning against Firestone, the sit-down movement quickly spread to Goodrich and Goodyear. The sit-down captured the fancy of workers and union leaders, but its use in the auto industry was to be its crucial test. On the origins of the sit-down movement see Daniel Nelson, "Origins of the Sit-Down Era: Worker Militancy and Innovation in the Rubber Industry,"

Labor History (Spring 1982), 198–225. John Williamson provided accounts of the strikes at Firestone and Goodyear that highlighted the contribution of Communists. "Akron: a New Chapter in American Labor History," *Communist* (May 1936), 423; and *Dangerous Scot*, 110–122.

38. *Daily Worker* (16 January 1937).
39. "The Work of the Party During Strike Struggles," *Party Organizer* (February 1937), 3; Williamson, *Dangerous Scot*, 108.
40. Mortimer, *Organize!*, 142–145.
41. William Weinstone, *The Great Sit-Down Strike* (New York: Workers Library Publishers, 1937); Mortimer, *Organize!*, ch. 9; Roger Keeran, *The Communist Party and the Auto Workers Unions* (Bloomington: Indiana University Press, 1980), ch. 7; Kraus, *The Many and the Few*, chs. 5–13.
42. Sidney Fine, *Sit-Down* (Ann Arbor: University of Michigan Press, 1979), 161, 200–201.
43. Bernstein, *Turbulent Years*, 499–554.
44. Bernstein, *Turbulent Years*, ch. 10; Dubofsky and Van Tine, *John L. Lewis*, 272–277.
45. Bernstein, *Turbulent Years*, 684–685; Len DeCaux, *Labor Radical: From the Wobblies to the CIO* (Boston: Beacon Press, 1970), 296–302.
46. Browder, *Report to the Ninth Convention*, 28.
47. John Williamson, "A General Motors Shop Branch: Before and After the Strike," *Party Organizer* (June 1937), 17; Harvey Levenstein, *Communism, Anticommunism and the CIO* (Westport, Connecticut: Greenwood Press, 1981), 50–51.
48. W. Z. Foster, et al., *Party Building and Political Leadership* (New York: Workers Library Publishers, 1937), 70–71.
49. DeCaux, *Labor Radical*, 315–318; Mortimer, *Organize!*, 162–164; and Al Richmond, *A Long View from the Left* (Boston: Houghton Mifflin Co., 1972), 243–245.
50. Foster, *History of the Communist Party*, 351, 353.
51. Cited in Fine, *Sit-Down*, 174. Similar appraisal of the strike's nonrevolutionary goals is offered by Kraus in *The Many and the Few*, 96–97.
52. William Weinstone, "The Great Auto Strike," *Communist* (March 1937), 221.
53. On the role and scope of fractions see Peters, *The Communist Party: A Manual On Organization* (New York: Workers Library Publishers, 1935), 99–102.
54. Jack Stachel, "Build the Party for Peace, Democracy and Socialism!" *Communist* (March 1938), 233–234;
55. Interview with Earl Browder, 10 January 1956, Draper Papers, I, 1:4, 6.
56. Roy Hudson, "The Path of Labor's United Action," *Communist* (October 1939), 936.
57. Williamson, *Dangerous Scot*, 101–103; Bernstein, *Turbulent Years*, 508.

58. Martin was a former Baptist minister from Leeds, Missouri, who after working briefly as an autoworker had turned to unionism.
59. On the factional strife within the UAW see Bernstein, *Turbulent Years*, 554–566; Keeran, *The Communist Party and the Auto Workers Unions*, ch. 8; Mortimer, *Organize!*, ch. 10.
60. "Chrysler Pact Step Forward in Union Advance Says Weinstone," *Daily Worker* (8 April 1937).
61. Earl Browder, *The Communists in the People's Front* (New York: Workers Library Publishers, 1937), 64–65.
62. *Daily Worker* (2 December 1937). The Party's top leadership frequently discussed the dangers of local Communists jeopardizing the CPUSA's broader policies. In December the Party's Politburo criticized Detroit Communists for their "weakness in the application of our People's Front policy." "Polburo Meeting held 23 December 1937," Draper Papers, I, 7:16.
63. "Unity in Auto Workers Union Stressed as Convention Nears," *Daily Worker* (22 July, 16 September 1937).
64. Keeran, *The Communist Party and the Auto Workers Unions*, 190–192.
65. "Homer Martin—For Whom Does He Speak," *Daily Worker* (5 February 1938); Mortimer, *Organize!*, 150–162; "Polburo Meeting held 28 January 1938," Draper Papers, I, 7:20.
66. Mortimer, *Organize!*, 162–165.
67. Dubofsky and Van Tine, *John L. Lewis*, 322.
68. Levenstein, *Communism, Anticommunism and the CIO*, 38–39.
69. *Daily Worker* (3 February 1938).
70. Nathan Glazer, *The Social Basis of American Communism* (New York: Harcourt, Brace and World, Inc., 1961), 107; DeCaux, *Labor Radical*, 245.
71. *Daily Worker* (4 December 1936).
72. Morris Childs, "Forging Unity Against Reaction in Illinois," *Communist* (August 1936), 769; Dennis, *The Autobiography of an American Communist*, 93.
73. Browder, "The American Communist Party in the Thirties," 231.
74. Foster, *History of the Communist Party*, 354.
75. Interview with Earl Browder, 16 June 1953, Draper Papers, I, 1:3, 2.
76. The decision not to endorse the president's reelection was challenged by Adolph Germer, who was attending as the CIO representative. He obtained a reversal of this position after he convinced Martin that failure to support Roosevelt was playing into the hands of the Liberty League. Fine, *Sit-Down*, 90–91.
77. A. Allen, "Party Building in Auto," *Party Organizer* (June 1937), 11; Galenson, *The CIO Challenge to the AFL*, 390; Lembcke and Tattam, *One Union in Wood*, 62, 67–68.
78. Keeran, *The Communist Party and the Auto Workers Unions*, 161; Williamson, "A General Motors Shop Branch," 15–16; *Dangerous Scot*, 122.

79. "We Helped Build the Union," *Party Organizer* (April 1938), 28–29.
80. "We Made a Bold Attack Against Red-Baiting," *Party Organizer* (April 1938), 41.
81. William Weinstone, "Advancing Against Reaction in the Center of the Motor Industry," *Communist* (August 1936), 747; "Recruiting Among Trade Unionists," *Party Organizer* (August 1937), 15–18; Allen, "Party Building in Auto," 14; and Glazer, *The Social Basis of American Communism*, 115.
82. The figures concerning union membership were based on an analysis of 16,973 recruits, those on specific industries on 17,292. Stachel, "Build the Party," 220–221, 223–224.
83. Ibid., 224–226.
84. "The January 1938 Registration—An Analysis and Conclusion," *Party Organizer* (June 1938), 3.
85. Foster, *Party Building and Political Leadership*, 10–11.
86. Bud Simons, interview with author, 19 February 1989; Stachel, *Daily Worker*, (27 June 1936); Weinstone, "Recruiting Among Trade Unionists," *Party Organizer* (August 1937), 17. The Party even issued a pamphlet on the problems of recruiting within mass movements with articles by W. Z. Foster, Alexander Bittelman, James Ford, and Charles Krumbein, *Party Building and Political Leadership*.
87. Gordon, "The Communists and the Drive to Organize Steel, 1936," *Labor History* (Spring 1982), 265.
88. L. J. Braverman, "Some Good Union Organizers Poor Builders of the Party," *Party Organizer* (January 1937), 28.
89. Mortimer, *Organize!*, 81–82. Some like Lee Pressman, a Party member in 1935–1936, dropped out because he feared that public revelation could be used as an excuse to remove him from his position close to Lewis as well as a charge to discredit the union.
90. Williamson, "Party Mobilization in Ohio," *Communist* (March 1937), 256.
91. Foster, *Party Building and Political Leadership*, 61–62.
92. Hudson, "Building the Party in Marine," *Party Organizer* (August 1937), 9–10.
93. Bud Simons, interview with author.
94. Keeran, *The Communist Party and the Auto Workers Unions*, 162.
95. Williamson, *Dangerous Scot*, 108.
96. *Daily Worker* (27 June 1936).
97. Max Gordon, "The Party and the Polling Place: A Response," *Radical History Review* (Spring 1980), 131–132.
98. Quoted in Levenstein, *Communism, Anticommunism and the CIO*, 44.
99. August Meier and Elliot Rudwick, "Communist Unions and the Black Community: The Case of the Transport Workers Union, 1934–1944," *Labor History* (Spring 1982), 167–181; Mark Naison, *Communists in Harlem during the Depression* (Urbana: University of Illinois Press, 1983), 265–266.

100. Bud Simons, interview with author; George Edwards, interview by Paul Buhle, OHAL; Williamson, "Strengthening the Trade Union Backbone of the Farmer-Labor Party Movement in Ohio," *Communist* (August 1936), 791–793.

Chapter 7: "They Shall Not Pass!"

1. "Songs of the Spanish Civil War," Folkway Records FH 5436; Degras, *The Communist International* vol. 3 (London: Oxford University Press, 1956), 443.
2. Ercoli [Togliatti], "The Preparations for Imperialist War and the Tasks of the Communists International," in Communist International, *VII Congress of the Communist International* (Moscow: Foreign Language Publishing House, 1939), 409.
3. Alan Brinkley, *Voices of Protest* (New York: Alfred A. Knopf, 1982), 150–153; Robert Dallek, *Franklin D. Roosevelt and American Foreign Policy, 1932–1945* (New York: Oxford, 1979), 101–110.
4. "The Struggle for Peace," in *Resolutions of the Ninth Convention of the Communist Party of the U.S.A.* (New York: Workers Library Publishers, 1936), 39–40.
5. *Daily Worker* (25 May 1936).
6. Earl Browder, "What Spain Means to America," in *The People's Front* (New York: International Publishers, 1938), 98–99.
7. Earl Browder in *Fighting for Peace* (New York: International Publishers, 1939), 49. This book, published during the summer of 1939, is a collection of articles, speeches, and reports by Browder all dealing with foreign policy.
8. Earl Browder, "The Naval Bill and a Peace Program," *New Masses* (29 March 1938), 3.
9. Browder, "The 'Haves' and the 'Have-Nots'," in *Fighting for Peace*, 43.
10. Ibid., 44.
11. Alexander Bittelman, "Review of the Month," *Communist* (March 1938), 195–198; and "The Struggle for Peace," 45–46.
12. See *Resolutions Ninth Convention of the CPUSA*, 43; Browder, "The 'Haves' and 'Have-Nots'," 45–46; *Daily Worker* (6 January 1938).
13. Browder, "The United Front—The Key to Our New Tactical Orientation," *Communist* (December 1935), 1083.
14. "For a United Front May Day!" *Communist* (May 1936), 408.
15. "The Struggle for Peace," 44.
16. Earl Browder (radio speech broadcast 28 August 1936), in *The People's Front*, 72.

17. *Daily Worker* (7 January 1937); Browder, "Lenin and Spain," in *The People's Front*, 285.
18. Browder, "Lenin and Spain," 285.
19. Earl Browder, *China and the United States* (New York: Workers Library Publishers, 1937), 6–8.
20. Ibid., 6, 13.
21. Browder, "For a Common Front Against the War-Makers," in *The People's Front*, 332–333.
22. Earl Browder, *Next Steps to Win the War in Spain* (New York: Workers Library Publishers, 1938), 10.
23. Browder was debating Frederick J. Libby, Executive Secretary of the National Council for Prevention of War. Browder in *Fighting for Peace*, 86.
24. Browder, "The Naval Bill and a Peace Program," 4; "A Long Term Policy," *New Masses* (5 April 1938), 7–8; and "Unity for Peace," ibid. (20 September 1938), 5.
25. Alexander Bittelman, "Review of the Month," *Communist* (March 1938), 198. See also "A Dangerous Policy for the Peace of the U.S.," *Daily Worker* (14 May 1938); and Bittelman, "Review of the Month," *Communist* (July 1939), 585.
26. Browder, "Questions and Answers," *New Masses* (29 March 1938), 4.
27. Quoted in Lawrence S. Wittner, *Rebels Against War* (Philadelphia: Temple University Press, 1984), 16.
28. Malcolm Cowley, "To Madrid: V International Brigade," *New Republic* (6 October 1937), 237.
29. Malcolm Cowley, "Review of *To Have and Have Not*," *New Republic* (20 October 1937), 53.
30. Frank A. Warren, *Liberals and Communism: The "Red Decade" Revisited* (Bloomington: Indiana University Press, 1966), 128–130; Joseph P. Lash, *Eleanor and Franklin* (New York: Norton, 1971), 569.
31. "A People's Front for America," *New Republic* (8 January 1936), 24.
32. Warren, *Liberals and Communism*, 147–150.
33. Daniel Aaron, *Writers on the Left* (New York: Harcourt, Brace and World, 1961), 359–361. The proceedings of the Congress were published in Henry Hart, ed., *The Writer in the Changing World* (London: Lawrence and Wishart, 1937).
34. Browder, "Writers and the Communist Party," in *The People's Front*, 281.
35. *Daily Worker* (2, 3, 5 June 1939); Samuel Sillen, "American Writers: 1935 to 1939," *New Masses* (20 June 1939), 22.
36. On the purges see Robert Conquest, *The Great Terror: Stalin's Purge of the Thirties* (New York: Macmillan, 1968).
37. John Gates, *The Story of an American Communist* (New York: Thomas

Nelson, 1958), 55; Joseph E. Davies, *Mission to Moscow* (New York: Simon and Schuster, 1941), 42–46.

38. "An Open Letter to American Liberals," *Soviet Russia Today* (March 1937), 14–15; and "The Moscow Trials: A Statement by American Progressives," *New Masses* (3 May 1938), 19.

39. Browder, "Writers and the Communist Party," 278–279. For Waldo Frank's positions see "Communications," *New Republic* (12 May 1937), 19–20; for Browder's reply ibid. (26 May 1937), 76.

40. Granville Hicks, *Where We Came Out* (New York: Viking Press, 1954), 48. On liberal response to the Moscow trials, see Warren, *Liberals and Communism,* ch. 9.

41. "Russian Politics in America," *New Republic* (17 February 1937), 33–34.

42. Warren, *Liberals and Communism,* 182–184.

43. Earl Browder, "The Trade Unions and Peace," *New Masses* (22 March 1938), 5.

44. See Browder, "Concerted Action or Isolation?" *New Masses* (1 March 1938), 7–9; "The Isolationist United Front," *New Masses* (8 March 1938), 7–10; and "The Naval Bill and a Peace Program."

45. Norman Thomas, *After the New Deal What?* (New York: Macmillan, 1936), 131–132, 134.

46. Frank A. Warren, *An Alternative Vision* (Bloomington: Indiana University Press, 1974), 159.

47. *Daily Worker* (25 May 1936).

48. Earl Browder, *The Communists in the People's Front* (New York: Workers Library Publishers, 1937), 41–49.

49. Jack Stachel, "The United Front and the Socialist Party," *Daily Worker* (20 April 1938).

50. Browder, *The People's Front,* 333. As Norman Thomas associated himself with Jay Lovestone in the campaign against collective security, Communist attacks on the Socialist leader grew stronger, see "Review of the Month," *Communist* (July 1938), 591.

51. George P. Rawick, "The New Deal and Youth: The Civil Conservation Corps, the National Youth Administration and the American Youth Congress" (Ph.D diss., University of Wisconsin, 1957), 294–299.

52. Rawick, "The New Deal and Youth," 331–337; and *Daily Worker* (6, 7 July 1937).

53. The following years the bill was sponsored by Senator Lundeen, Benson's successor, and representatives Maury Maverick, James Coffee, and Jerry Voorhis. Rawick, "The New Deal and Youth," 325–329.

54. Rawick, "The New Deal and Youth," 319–325, 348.

55. Lash, *Eleanor and Franklin,* 544–547.

56. The first World Youth Congress was held in Geneva, Switzerland in August 1936 under the auspices of the Association of League of Nations

Societies. Rawick, "The New Deal and Youth," 341–345. See also Lash, *Eleanor and Franklin*, 549–550.

57. Rawick, "The New Deal and Youth," 354–355; *Daily Worker* (5, 9 July 1939); Gates, *The Story of an American Communist*, 70–71.

58. Rawick, "The New Deal and Youth," 301–308.

59. Rawick, "The New Deal and Youth," 314–317. On the impact of the Spanish Civil War on the student movement, see Eileen Eagan, *Class, Culture and the Classroom. :The Student Peace Movement of the 1930s* (Philadelphia: Temple University Press, 1981), ch. 8, 183–185.

60. Browder, *Next Steps to Win the War in Spain*, 13.

61. Eagan, *Class, Culture and the Classroom*, 195–196; Rawick, "The New Deal and Youth," 315–322, 345–346.

62. Rawick, "The New Deal and Youth," 350–353.

63. For an account of the formation of the Amsterdam-Pleyel congress see E. H. Carr, *Twilight of the Comintern, 1930–1935* (New York: Pantheon Books, 1982), 388–399.

64. For an account of the congress, see *Daily Worker* (30 September; 2, 3 October 1933); and "The United Front Against War," *New Republic* (11 October 1935), 227–228. Browder openly recognized that from the beginning the League was "led by our Party quite openly without in any way infringing upon its broad non-Party character." Browder, *Communism in the United States*, 184.

65. The manifesto and program of the American League Against War and Fascism are in Browder, "The Role of the Socialist Party Leaders in the Struggle Against War and Fascism," *Communist* (April 1934), 326–330.

66. *Daily Worker* (1, 2, 3 October 1934); Joseph North, "Warring on War," *New Masses* (16 October 1934), 12–13; and Robert Morss Lovett, "The Congress on War and Fascism," *New Republic* (17 October 1934), 263–264.

67. William Mangold, "Forming the People's Front," *New Republic* (22 January 1936), 310–311; *Daily Worker* (29, 30 November 1937); and Browder, "The People's Front Moves Forward!" *Communist* (December 1937), 1098.

68. Earl Browder, "The American Communist Party," in Rita James Simon, ed., *As We Saw the Thirties* (Urbana: University of Illinois Press, 1967), 221. During Browder's testimony to the Committee on Un-American Activities on 27 March 1937, the attorney for the committee, Rhea Whitley, asked the Communist leader to identify the most important or successful front organizations. Browder answered: "I would say the broadest and most successful of these is the American League for Peace and Democracy." The League, he added, "answered to our conception of what was needed for the broadest masses in this particular field." A copy of the transcript is in the Draper Papers, I, 2:51, 22.

69. Browder, "The American Communist Party," 222.

70. According to Earl Browder, following Munich, when Winston Churchill

was criticizing Chamberlain for appeasing Hitler, he asked the League to sponsor his tour in the United States. See Earl Browder, "How Stalin Ruined the American Communist Party," *Harpers Magazine* (March 1960), 48. See also Browder, "The American Communist Party," 222; John Earl Haynes, *Dubious Alliance: The Making of Minnesota's DFL Party* (Minneapolis: University of Minnesota Press, 1984), 21.

71. *Daily Worker* (7 January 1939).
72. Nelson et al., *Steve Nelson, American Radical,* (Pittsburgh: University of Pittsburgh Press, 1981), 185–186.
73. The process of recruiting was formally sanctioned by Earl Browder in his report to the Central Committee on 4 December 1936. Browder, "Results of the Elections," in *The People's Front,* 119.
74. As their numbers grew the Washington and the joint U.S.-Canadian MacKenzie-Papineau battalions were also formed, but the name Lincoln was the one that stuck.
75. Robert A. Rosenstone provides a general overview of the social, ethnic, geographic, and cultural origin and background of many volunteers in his *Crusade on the Left* (New York: Pegasus, 1969), ch. 4. Browder told the delegates at the Party's 10th Convention in 1938 that out of the 3,700 volunteers over 2,000 were Communists. Browder, "The Democratic Front," 81. John Gates, the *New York Times* correspondent Herbert Matthews, and Robert Rosenstone give higher figures. See Rosenstone, *Crusade on the Left,* 113.
76. Hugh Thomas, *The Spanish Civil War* (New York: Harper and Row, 1977), 595.
77. Charney, *A Long Journey,* 84. My account on the United States volunteers is based on Rosenstone, *Crusade on the Left,* and on a number of memoirs: Alvah Bessie, *Men in Battle: A Story of Americans in Spain* (San Francisco: Chandler and Sharp, 1975); Gates, *The Story of an American Communist,* ch. 4; and Nelson, *American Radical,* ch. 7.
78. Joseph Stalin, "Report on the Work of the Central Committee to the Eighteenth Congress of the Communist Party of the Soviet Union (B)" in *The Land of Socialism Today and Tomorrow* (Moscow: Foreign Languages Publishing House, 1939). Adam Ulam has written that Stalin's speech at the XVIII Congress of the Soviet Communist Party in March 1939 "through taunts, expressions of self-confidence, and insinuations of an as yet nonexistent *rapprochement* with Germany, it was intended to draw out the Western Powers. 'We don't need you, but you may need us; if so, better hurry up' is the most sensible translation of what Stalin was saying." Ulam, *Expansion & Coexistence* (New York: Praeger, 1968), 263–264. For the development of Soviet foreign policy from Munich up to August 1939, ibid., 258–273.
79. Quote from Daniel Brower, *The New Jacobins* (Ithaca: Cornell University Press, 1968), 224. The most detailed account of the crisis of the Popular

Front in France is Guy Bourdé, *La défaite du front populaire* (Paris: Maspero, 1977). On the same topic see also Brower, *The New Jacobins*, 191–232.

80. Quoted in Degras, *The Communist International* vol. 3, 432.
81. Interview with Earl Browder, 10 October 1955, Draper Papers, I, 1:8, 42–44.
82. Browder, "The United States and the New International Situation" in *Fighting for Peace*, 167–168.
83. The fear of fascist presence in the Western hemisphere cannot be dismissed as a ploy of Party propaganda. By 1938 Italy and Germany had managed to become major political, economic, and military factors in Latin America. In addition to this the belief that Germany possessed airplanes with sufficient range to strike at the Americas from the west coast of Africa seriously concerned Roosevelt and his advisors and led the president to declare that "the United States must be prepared to resist attack on the western hemisphere from the North Pole to the South Pole, including all of North America and South America." Quoted in Dallek, *Roosevelt and American Foreign Policy*, 175.
84. Browder, "The United States and the New International Situation," 168. See also "The Munich Betrayal," in *Fighting for Peace*, 179–189.
85. Browder, "The United States and the New International Situation," 168.
86. Earl Browder, *Social and National Security* (New York: Workers Library Publishers, 1938), 5.
87. "Review of the Month," *Communist* (November 1938), 974.
88. "Review of the Month," *Communist* (November 1938), 976; Browder, *Fighting for Peace*, 197.
89. Browder, "The Munich Betrayal," in *Fighting for Peace*, 183.
90. Browder, *Social and National Security*, 38.
91. Ibid., 42–43.
92. Browder, "The Elections and the International Situation," in *Fighting for Peace*, 174–175.
93. Browder, *Social and National Security*, 18.
94. "Review of the Month," *Communist* (July 1939), 584.
95. Earl Browder, *The 1940 Elections* (New York: Workers Library Publishers, 1939), 14–15.
96. Ibid., 18, 20.
97. Ibid., 18.
98. Ibid., 20–21.
99. Milton Howard, "The Un-American Dies Committee"; John Page, "A Progressive Tax Proposal," January 1939; Roger Bacon, "Tory Politics and Relief," February 1939; Roger Bacon, "Social Security for the Aged," April 1939; "How Your Congressman Voted," September 1939. The magazine's full title was *National Issues: A Survey of Politics and Legislation*.
100. Adam Lapin, "National Defense," *National Issues* (February 1939), 11.
101. John Page, "Planes and Plain Talk," *National Issues* (March 1939), 6.

102. Adam Lapin, "Congress Embargoes Peace," *National Issues* (August 1939), 9.
103. *Pravda* (6 January 1939); and Gabriel Peri, "Le message de Roosevelt," in *La Correspondence Internationale* (14 January 1939), 21–22.
104. Peri, "Les conditions de la résistance au fascisme," in *La Correspondence Internationale* (22 April 1939), 429.
105. Manuilsky in *The Land of Socialism Today and Tomorrow*, 65.
106. *Daily Worker* (6 July 1939).
107. Charney, *A Long Journey*, 123. According to Browder both Bittelman and Foster had already expressed the belief that an agreement was in the making. Earl Browder, "Reminiscences," Oral History Collection, Columbia University, 371.
108. Melech Epstein, *The Jew and Communism, 1919–1941* (New York: Trade Union Sponsoring Committee, 1959), 350.
109. Nelson, *American Radical*, 247; Richmond, *A Long View*, 283; Gates, *The Story of an American Communist*, 74; Dennis, *The Autobiography of an American Communist*, 133–135; Junius Irving Scales and Richard Nickson, *Cause at Heart: A Former Communist Remembers* (Athens: University of Georgia Press, 1987), 75–76.
110. Charney, *A Long Journey*, 124.
111. Nelson, *American Radical*, 248.
112. *Daily Worker* (23 August 1939).
113. *Daily Worker* (24 August 1939).
114. *Daily Worker* (25 August 1939).
115. *Worker* (27 August 1939).
116. See "Foster Tells How Pact is Aid to Peace," *Daily Worker* (29 August); Browder, "U.S. and World Peace Aided by Soviet Blow to Axis," *Daily Worker* (30 August 1939).
117. *New York Times* (24 August 1939); *Daily Worker* (24 August 1939); Browder in *As We Saw the Thirties*, 242–243; Epstein, *The Jew and Communism*, 350. In answering a reporter who asked if he had been in touch with Moscow, Browder was possibly voicing his frustration for being left in the dark: "All my connections with Moscow are through the news associations. I have exactly the same information that you gentlemen have." *Daily Worker* (24 August 1939).
118. Browder, "The German-Soviet Non-Aggression Pact," in *The Second Imperialist War* (New York: International Publishers, 1940), 36–37.
119. *Daily Worker* (30 August 1939).
120. Years later both Browder and Gil Green stated that by early September the leadership of the CPUSA had concluded that the war was imperialist. Interview with Earl Browder, 12 October 1955, Draper Papers, I, 1:9, 249; and Interview with Gil Green, 21 December 1987. These recollections are confirmed by the fact that references to the imperialist nature of

the war first appeared, although not prominently, in early September. See "America's Decision in the Face of War" editorial in the *Daily Worker* (2 September 1939); Milton Howard, *Worker* (10 September 1939) Browder's speech on 11 September in *Daily Worker* (13 September 1939).

121. *Daily Worker* (2 September 1939).
122. *Daily Worker* (5 September 1939).
123. *Daily Worker* (4, 5 September 1939).
124. *Daily Worker* (5, 11, 12 September 1939).
125. *Daily Worker* (11, 13 September 1939); Epstein, *The Jew and Communism*, 352–353.
126. *New York Times* (4 September 1939).
127. *Daily Worker* (4 September 1939).
128. Browder, *Unity for Peace and Democracy* (New York: Workers Library Publishers, 1939), 5–95.
129. *Daily Worker* (5 September 1939).
130. *Daily Worker* (13 September 1939).
131. *Daily Worker* (12 September 1939).
132. There is a certain confusion concerning both the exact contents of the message as well as the date it was received. Melech Epstein, who at the time was the editor of the pro-Communist *Freiheit*, later wrote in his memoirs that the message was the text of an article to appear on *Pravda* the following day. Epstein, *The Jew and Communism*, 353. According to Browder the message came instead in the form of a radio message summing up Dimitrov's article that was published by the Comintern's press in October. It is certain that Browder was confusing this with a radio message that he did receive at the end of September. Interview with Earl Browder, 12 October 1955, Draper Papers, I, 1:9, 247–248. Among the Browder Papers there is a telegram from Moscow dated 14 September that was reprinted in the *Daily Worker* on 15 September, that contains the essence of the Party's shift. Based on the fact that the change in policy took place between the evening of 11 or 12 September at the latest, it is possible that the Party either received advance notice of the contents of the telegram or that it was misdated. Browder Papers, I, 2:15.
133. *Daily Worker* (13 September 1939).
134. Browder gave his copy of the verbatim transcript of the minutes that he had kept after being expelled from the Party, to Philip J. Jaffe his confidant and benefactor. Throughout the years Jaffe placed many restrictions on the consultation of these documents by historians. This material has become accessible only recently and is deposited at the Robert W. Woodruff Library, Emory University, Atlanta, Georgia. The minutes have been erroneously labeled as being of the National Committee, but the names of the participants as well as internal evidence prove otherwise.

135. "Discussion by CP national committee on the international situation, 14 and 16 September 1939 (stenogram)," Philip J. Jaffe Papers, VII, 35:5, 1.
136. Ibid., 5.
137. Ibid., 8.
138. Ibid., 15–16.
139. Ibid., 56.
140. Ibid., 58
141. Ibid., 97.
142. The final statement of the meeting: "Keep American Out of the Imperialist War," appeared in the *Daily Worker* (19 September 1939).
143. Degras, *The Communist International* vol. 3, 439–443; Edward Mortimer, *The Rise of the French Communist Party: 1920–1947* (London: Faber and Faber, 1984), 284–285.
144. *Daily Worker* (22 September 1939).
145. The two messages are in Philip J. Jaffe, *The Rise and Fall of American Communism* (New York: Horizon Press, 1975), 44–47. Years later Browder told Jaffe that during his short trip to Moscow in September (it was really October) 1938, on instructions from Dimitrov, he had been provided with a short wave radio to keep in contact with the Comintern should events shut off the more conventional channel. The only messages Browder received were these (see p. 40). For Dimitrov's article, see "The War and the Working Class of the Capitalist Countries," *Communist International* (November 1939), 1100–1110.
146. Interview with Earl Browder, 12 October 1955, Draper Papers, I, 1:9, 246; and Jaffe, *The Rise and Fall of American Communism*, 40.
147. Michael Gold, "What Side Are You On?" *New Masses* (3 October 1939), 19; *Daily Worker* (10 October 1939). See also *Daily Worker* (30 September 1939); "Review of the Month," *Communist* (October 1939), 912–913; and "America and the International Situation," *Communist* (November 1939), 995–1001 and "Review of the Month," ibid., 1010–1011.
148. *Daily Worker* (22 October 1939).
149. *New York Times* (24 October 1939); Maurice Isserman, *Which Side Were You On? The American Communist Party during the Second World War* (Middletown, Conn.: Wesleyan University Press, 1982), 47–50; James G. Ryan, "Earl Browder and American Communism at High Tide: 1934–1945" (Ph. D. diss., University of Notre Dame, 1981), 319–325.
150. Eugene Dennis, "Roosevelt, the War and the New Deal," *Communist* (January 1940), 27; and Browder, *Whose War is It?*, 10.
151. *Daily Worker* (28 October 1939).
152. *Daily Worker* (6 November 1939).
153. Ibid.
154. *Daily Worker* (29 November 1939).
155. *Daily Worker* (1, 2, 9 December 1939).

156. Browder, "The People Against the War Makers," in *The Second Imperialist War*, 101; *The People's Road to Peace* (New York: Workers Library Publishers, 1940), 27, 44; *Campaign Book: Presidential Elections 1940* (New York: Workers Library Publishers, 1940), 17–18.
157. Earl Browder, "The Most Peculiar Election Campaign in the History of the Republic," *Communist* (October 1940), 885.
158. Browder, "The Most Pecular Election Campaign," 885; Foster, "Seven Years of Roosevelt," *Communist* (March 1940), 236–241.

Chapter 8: "Standing on Its Own Feet"

1. Browder, *Teheran and America* (New York: Workers Library Publishers, 1944), 43; Jacques Duclos, "A propos de la dissolution du Parti Communiste americain," *Cahiers du Communisme* (April 1945), 37.
2. For a discussion of the rapprochement between Moscow and Berlin see Adam Ulam, *Expansion and Coexistence* (New York: Praeger, 1968), 282–285.
3. "America and the International Situation," *Communist* (November 1939), 995. See also V. J. Jerome, "Then—And Now," *Communist* (November 1939), 1035–1036; "Review of the Month," *Communist* (December 1939), 1097–1113; W. Z. Foster, "The Soviet Union and the War," *Daily Worker* (1 December 1939); Earl Browder, *The People Against the War Makers* (New York: Workers Library Publishers, 1940), 5; W. Z. Foster, "World Socialism and the War," *Communist* (June 1940), 507–509; Gil Green, "Imperialist War and 'Democratic' Demagogy," ibid., 525–527.
4. Earl Browder, *Whose War is It?* (New York: Workers Library Publishers, [1939?]), 15. In May 1940 Browder's estimate of the number of "deserters" was still a few dozen, he categorized them as "the type we are well rid of—dry leaves only waiting for the first stiff breeze to blow them away, or decaying bureaucrats looking for some office chairs." Earl Browder, *The People's Road to Peace* (New York: Workers Library Publishers, 1940), 57.
5. Irving Howe and Lewis Coser, *The American Communist Party: A Critical History* (Boston: Beacon Press, 1957), 404; Roy Hudson, "For a Greater Vote and a Stronger Party," *Communist* (August 1940), 709.
6. John Earl Haynes, *Dubious Alliance* (Minneapolis: University of Minnesota Press, 1984), 51–52; Arthur Liebman, *Jews and the Left* (New York: John Wiley & Sons), 508–510; Melech Epstein, *The Jew and Communism* (New York: Trade Union Sponsoring Committee, 1959), 365–370.
7. Steve Nelson et. al, *Steve Nelson, American Radical* (Pittsburgh: University of Pittsburgh Press, 1981), 248.

8. Ulam, *Expansion and Coexistence*, 286, 291.
9. Granville Hicks, "On Leaving the Communist Party," *The New Republic* (4 October 1939), 244–245.
10. Freda Kirchway, "Communists and Democracy," *Nation* (14 October 1939), 400; *New Republic* (30 August 1939), 88–89.
11. *New Republic* (27 September 1939), 201; ibid. (13 December 1939) 221.
12. *New Republic* (13 September 1939), 143.
13. Les K. Adler and Thomas G. Paterson, "Red Fascism: The Merger of Nazi Germany and Soviet Russia in the American Image of Totalitarianism, 1930s–1959s," *American Historical Review* (April 1970), 1046–1051.
14. Corliss Lamont, ed., *The Trial of Elizabeth Gurley Flynn by the American Civil Liberties Union* (New York: Horizon, 1968), 45.
15. Frank A. Warren, *Liberals and Communism: The "Red Decade" Revisited* (Bloomington: Indiana University Press, 1966), 202 and 207.
16. " 'Red' Peace Parade," *New York Times* (27 August 1939); Maurice Isserman, *Which Side Were You On?* (Middletown, Conn.: Wesleyan University Press, 1982), 37–38.
17. Howe and Coser, *The American Communist Party*, 315. "Communications," *New Republic* (26 August 1940), 279–280.
18. George P. Rawick, "The New Deal and Youth: The Civil Conservation Corps, the National Youth Administration and the American Youth Congress," (Ph.D. diss., University of Wisconsin, 1957), 360–362; Eileen Eagan, *Class, Culture and the Classroom* (Philadelphia: Temple University Press, 1981), 209.
19. On the AYC's move away from collective-security, see Rawick, "The New Deal and Youth," 362–365; Joseph P. Lash, *Eleanor and Franklin* (New York: Norton, 1971), 597–605.
20. On the break between Lewis and Roosevelt see C. K. McFarland, "Coalition of Convenience: Lewis and Roosevelt, 1933–1940," *Labor History* (Summer 1972), 405–414; Melvyn Dubofsky and Warren Van Tine, *John L. Lewis* (New York: Quadrangle, 1977), 323–334; and Len DeCaux, *Labor Radical* (Boston: Beacon Press, 1970), 356–361.
21. Kenneth Waltzer, "The American Labor Party, Third Party Politics in New Deal–Cold War New York, 1936–1954" (Ph.D. diss., Harvard University, 1978), 228.
22. Epstein, *The Jew and Communism*, 351; Browder, *The Jewish People and the War* (New York: Workers Library Publisher, 1940).
23. Isserman, *Which Side Were You On?*, 56–57; Epstein, *The Jew and Communism*, 359.
24. Browder, *The People Against the War-Makers*, 21.
25. Harvey Klehr, *The Heyday of American Communism* (New York: Basic Books, 1984), 410–416.
26. Isserman, *Which Side Were You On?*, 76; Jerry Lembcke and William M. Tat-

tam, *One Union in Wood* (New York: International Publishers, 1984), 75–79; and Bella V. Dodd, *School of Darkness* (New York: P.J. Kennedy, 1954), 128.

27. Roger Keeran, *The Communist Party and the Auto Workers' Unions* (Bloomington: Indiana University Press, 1980), 210–211.

28. DeCaux, *Labor Radical*, 378–382.

29. See *Election Platform of the Communist Party, 1940* (New York: Workers Library Publishers, 1940); Browder, *The People's Road to Peace*, 55.

30. "Break the Grip of Wall Street's Twin War-Party," *Communist* (September 1940), 772–773; Browder, "The Most Peculiar Election Campaign in the History of the Republic," *Communist* (October 1940), 886–887; "To the Millions Who *Are* America," ibid., 96–101, and "Shall it be War?" ibid., 153. See also "The Wall Street Twins," in *Campaign Book: Presidential Elections, 1940* (New York: Workers Library Publishers, 1940), 17–27.

31. Earl Browder, *The People Against the War-Makers* (New York: Workers Library Publishers, 1940), 17; Eugene Dennis, "Roosevelt, the War and the New Deal," *Communist* (January 1940), 36.

32. "Resolutions Adopted by the National Committee of the CPUSA," *Communist* (March 1940), 215–216.

33. "Review of the Month," *Communist* (March 1940), 200–201.

34. Dubofsky and Van Tine, *John L. Lewis*, 348–353; and McFarland, "Coalition of Convenience," 409.

35. "Resolutions Adopted by the National Committee of the CPUSA," *Communist* (March 1940), 217.

36. *Congressional Quarterly's Guide to U.S. Elections* (Washington, D.C.: Congressional Quarterly, 1975), 304.

37. *New York Times* (23 January 1940); William Schneiderman, *Dissent on Trial* (Minneapolis: MEP Publications, 1983), 73–76, 85–93; Foster, *History of the Communist Party of the United States* (New York: International Publishers, 1952), 391–393; *Daily Worker* (11 November 1939).

38. Ellen W. Schrecker, *No Ivory Tower: McCarthyism and the Universities* (New York: Oxford University Press, 1986), 75–82.

39. Rawick, "The New Deal and Youth," 358–359; Walter Goodman, *The Committee* (New York: Farrar, Straus and Giroux, 1968), 95–96.

40. Michael R. Belknap, *Cold War Political Justice* (Westport, Conn.: Greenwood Press, 1977), 25–27.

41. *Daily Worker* (17, 18 November 1940); Foster, *History of the Communist Party*, 392–393; C.C.C.P.S.U., *Outline History of the Communist International* (Moscow: Progress Publishers, 1971), 467–468. For the Party's revised constitution, see *Communist* (December 1940), 1086–1092.

42. George Charney, *A Long Journey* (Chicago: Quadrangle, 1968), 126; Al Richmond, *A Long View from the Left* (Boston: Houghton Mifflin, 1972), 285–286; Nelson et al., *American Radical*, 253.

43. Isserman, *Which Side Were You On?*, 111–112.

44. John Gates, *The Story of an American Communist* (New York: Thomas Nelson, 1958), 82.
45. The concept of "incentive pay" was expressed by Earl Browder in a speech to the National Conference of the CPUSA, held on 29–30 November 1942, reprinted as a pamphlet with the title *Production for Victory* (New York: Workers Library Publishers, 1942).
46. Bert Cochran, *Labor and Communism* (Princeton, N.J.: Princeton University Press, 1977) 200.
47. Schneiderman, *Dissent on Trial*, 94–103.
48. Joseph R. Starobin, *American Communism in Crisis* (Cambridge, Mass.: Harvard University Press, 1972), 60–61; Waltzer, "The American Labor Party," 226–246; Benjamin Davis, *Communist Councilman from Harlem* (New York: International Publishers, 1969), 103–114; Simon W. Gerson, *Pete: The Story of Peter V. Cacchione, New York's First Communist Councilman* (New York: International Publishers, 1976), 153–155.
49. Isserman, *Which Side Were You On?*, 147–148.
50. John Williamson, "The Organizational and Educational Tasks of Our Party," *Communist* (October 1943), 922–933; and "Perspectives on the Functioning of the Communist Political Association," *Communist* (June 1944), 521–531.
51. Earl Browder, *Victory and After* (New York: International Library Publishers, 1942), 87–88.
52. Ibid., 132.
53. Isserman, *Which Side Were You On?*, 176–177.
54. Browder, *Teheran and America*, 14.
55. Ibid., 19.
56. Ibid., 39–40.
57. Ibid., 41.
58. Starobin, *American Communism in Crisis*, 74–76; Philip J. Jaffe, *The Rise and Fall of American Communism* (New York: Horizon Press, 1975), 62–63. In April 1944, Browder received a letter from André Marty, high ranking leader of the French Communist party, congratulating him on his address to the national committee in January 1944, as well as a cable from Dimitrov indirectly expressing support for his course. André Marty to Earl Browder, 3 April 1944, Browder Papers, I, 5:44; and Memorandum of Conversation with Earl Browder, 16 April 1959, Draper Papers 1:10. At the end of 1944 Togliatti also had words of praise for the dissolution of the CPUSA, a step, he commented, that was in the best interest of the United States and of the cause of democracy. Sergio Bertelli, *Il Gruppo: la formazione del gruppo dirigente del PCI, 1936–1948* (Milan: Rizzoli, 1980), 208.
59. Browder, *Teheran and America*, 43.
60. The membership first learned of the letter over a year later in the Duclos

article. Foster's letter was published in *Political Affairs* (July 1945), 640–654.

61. On the discussion of Foster's letter see "Stenogram of national board meeting, 8 February 1944," Jaffe Papers.

62. For the Convention's proceedings see *The Path to Peace, Progress and Prosperity* (New York: Communist Political Association, 1945).

63. Williamson, *Daily Worker* (1 July 1945).

64. Duclos, "A propos de la dissolution du Parti Communiste americain," 21. Article published in the *Daily Worker* (24 May 1945). For a detailed analysis of the article see Starobin, *American Communism in Crisis*, 78–82.

65. Duclos, "A propos de la dissolution du Parti Communiste americain," 36–38.

66. The national board of the CPA met on 22–23 May and again on 2 June 1945. The national committee convened on 18–20 June. The stenograms of the 22–23 May and 18–20 June meetings are in the Jaffe Papers. On the 2 June meeting see Starobin, *American Communism in Crisis*, 86–92.

Conclusion

1. Ambrogio Donini, interview with author, 20 July 1979. Following the reconstitution of the CPUSA in 1945, Togliatti made sure that neither the Italian Communist party, nor magazines and personalities supporting its policies, pass any political judgement on this event. See Sergio Bertelli, *Il Gruppo* (Milan: Rizzoli, 1980), 207–208, 317; and Riccardo Gori, *Storia di "Societa' " (1945–1959)* (Povegliano: Gutenberg, 1981), 61, 83.

2. Earl Browder, *Teheran and America* (New York: Workers Library Publishers, 1944), 45.

3. Maurice Isserman, *Which Side Were You On? The American Communist Party during the Second World War* (Middletown, Conn.: Wesleyan University Press, 1982), 242.

4. Joseph R. Starobin, *American Communism in Crisis, 1943–1957* (Cambridge, Mass.: Harvard University Press, 1972), 155–194; Maurice Isserman, "The Half-Swept House: American Communism in 1956," *Socialist Review* (January–February 1982), 71–101.

BIBLIOGRAPHY

Oral Sources

INTERVIEWS CONDUCTED BY THE AUTHOR:

Ambrogio Donini, 20 July 1979.
Max Gordon, 13 June 1985.
Gil Green, 21 December 1987.
Steve Nelson, 4 August 1984.
Bud Simmons, 19 February 1989.
Saul Wellman, 27 February 1988.

INTERVIEWS CONDUCTED BY OTHERS:

Jose A. Alvarez, interview by Paul Buhle, 15 March 1983.
Walter Barry, interview by Ruth F. Prago, 4 February and 12 October 1980.
Bertha Bazell, interview by Bill Schecter, 10 March 1981.
Fred Blair, interview by Paul Buhle, 26 July 1983.
Harold Christoffel, interview by Roger Keeran, 27 June 1974.
Rose Cohen, interview by Debby Cohen, 12 April 1976.
Albina Delfino, interview by Ruth F. Prago, 8 January 1981.
Dora, interview by Bea Lemisch, 25 March 1982.
George Edwards, interview by Paul Buhle, 4 November 1983.
Joseph Figueredo, interview by Paul Buhle, 8 November 1983.
Joseph Giganti, interview by Paul Buhle, 26 July 1983.
Ruth Glassman, interview by Ruth F. Prago, 1 February 1979.
Nina Goldstein, interview by Bea Lemisch, 19 March 1980.
Oive Halonen, interview by Jon Bloom, 7 February 1978.
Otis Hood, interview by Bill Schecter, 24 March 1981.
James Lustig, interview by Paul Buhle, 20 October 1982.
I. E. Ronch, interview by Paul Buhle, 14 April 1981.
Irving Seid, interview by Danny Czitrom, 4 June 1976.
Anna Taffler, interview by Jon Bloom, 5 January 1978.
Karl Yoneda, interview by Paul Buhle, 7 January 1983.
The preceding interviews are part of the Oral History of the American Left

Bibliography

collection at Tamiment Institute, Elmer Homes Bobst Library, New York University, New York.
Earl Browder, interview by Theodor Draper, Draper Research Files, The Robert W. Woodruff Library for Advanced Studies, Emory University, Atlanta, Georgia.
"The Reminiscences of Earl Browder," Columbia University Oral History Collection, Butler Library, Columbia University, New York.

Archival Collections

Earl Browder Papers, George Arents Research Library, Syracuse University, Syracuse, New York.
Philip J. Jaffe Papers, The Robert W. Woodruff Library for Advanced Studies, Emory University, Atlanta, Georgia.
Norman Thomas Papers, New York Public Library, New York.
Tamiment Collection, Elmer Holmes Bobst Library, New York University, New York.

Government Documents

U.S. Military Intelligence Reports: Surveillance of Radicals in the United States, 1917–1941 microfilm. Frederick, Maryland: University Publications of America, 1984.

Newspapers and Periodicals

Communist and its successor *Political Affairs.*
Communist International.
Daily Worker and its Sunday edition the *Worker.*
International Press Correspondence.
La Correspondance Internationale.
Labor Defender.
Labor Unity.
Nation.
National Issues.
New Masses.
New Republic.
New York Times.
Party Organizer.

Rundschau.
Western Worker.

Pamphlets

American League Against War and Fascism. *Fascism.* New York: American League Against War and Fascism, [1935?].

Amter, I. *Is the Socialist Party a Party of the Workers?* New York: Communist Party U.S.A., 1932.

————. *Industrial Slavery-Roosevelt's "New Deal."* New York: Workers Library Publishers, 1933.

Bittelman, Alexander. *From Left-Socialism to Communism.* New York: Workers Library Publishers, 1933.

————, and V. J. Jerome. *Leninism The Only Marxism Today: A Discussion of the Characteristics of Declining Capitalism.* New York: Workers Library Publishers, 1934.

————. *How Can We Share the Wealth? The Communist Way Versus Huey Long.* New York: Workers Library Publishers, 1935.

Bloor, Ella Reeve. *We Are Many.* New York: International Publishers, 1940.

Browder, Earl. *The Fight for Bread.* New York: Workers Library Publishers, 1932.

————. *What Is the New Deal?* New York: Workers Library Publishers, 1933.

————. *What Every Worker Should Know About the N.R.A.* New York: Workers Library Publishers, 1933.

————. *Is Planning Possible Under Capitalism?* New York: Workers Library Publishers, 1933.

————. *Report of the Central Committee to the Eighth Convention of the Communist Party of the U.S.A.* New York: Workers Library Publishers, 1934.

————. *Unemployment Insurance: The Burning Issue of the Day.* New York: Workers Library Publishers, 1935.

————. *New Steps in the United Front.* New York: Workers Library Publishers, 1935.

————. *Build the United People's Front.* New York: Workers Library Publishers, 1935.

————. *Religion and Communism.* New York: Workers Library Publishers, 1935.

————. *How Do We Raise the Question of a Labor Party?* New York: Workers Library Publishers, 1935.

————. *Norman Thomas vs. Earl Browder: Which Road for American Workers, Socialist or Communist?* New York: Socialist Call, 1936.

————. *Democracy or Fascism.* New York: Workers Library Publishers, 1936.

————. *Who Are the Real Americans?* New York: Workers Library Publishers, 1936.

Bibliography

————. *Build the United People's Front.* New York: Workers Library Publishers, 1936.

————. *Lincoln and the Communists.* New York: Workers Library Publishers, 1936.

————. *The Results of the Elections and the People's Front.* New York: Workers Library Publishers, 1936.

————. *Hearst's "Secret" Document.* New York: Workers Library Publishers, 1936.

————. *The People's Front in America.* New York: Workers Library Publishers, 1936.

————. *The Communist Position in 1936.* New York: CPUSA, 1936.

————. *Talks to America.* New York: Workers Library Publishers, 1937.

————. *The Communists in the People's Front.* New York: Workers Library Publishers, 1937.

————. *China and the U.S.A.* New York: Workers Library Publishers, 1937.

————. *North America and the Soviet Union.* New York: Workers Library Publishers, 1937.

————. *Next Steps to Win the War in Spain.* New York: Workers Library Publishers, 1938.

————. *Concerted Action or Isolation: Which is the Road to Peace?* New York: Workers Library Publishers, 1938.

————. *The Democratic Front For Jobs, Security, Democracy and Peace.* New York: Workers Library Publishers, 1938.

————. *Attitude of the Communist Party on the Subject of Public Order.* [s.l.]: Chevrolet Branch of the Communist Party, [1938?].

————. *Social and National Security.* New York: Workers Library Publishers, 1938.

————. *A Message to Catholics.* New York: Workers Library Publishers, 1938.

————. *The Nazi Pogrom.* New York: New York State Committee of the Communist Party, [1938?].

————. *Religion and Communism.* New York: Workers Library Publishers, 1939.

————. *The Economics of Communism.* New York: Workers Library Publishers, 1939.

————. *Theory As a Guide to Action.* New York: Workers Library Publishers, 1939.

————. *Whose War is It?* New York: Workers Library Publishers, 1939.

————. *Socialism War and America.* New York: Workers Library Publishers, 1939.

————. *The 1940 Elections: How the People Can Win.* New York: Workers Library Publishers, 1939.

————. *Stop the War.* New York: Workers Library Publishers, 1939.

————. *Unity for Peace and Democracy.* New York: Workers Library Publishers, 1939.

———. *America and the Second Imperialist War.* New York: New York State Committee of the Communist Party, [1939?].

———. *Finding the Road to Peace.* New York: New York State Commmittee of the Communist Party, [1939?].

———. *Earl Browder Takes his Case to the People.* New York: Workers Library Publishers, 1940.

———. *The Most Peculiar Election: The Campaign Speeches of Earl Browder.* New York: Workers Library Publishers, 1940.

———. *Internationalism, Results of the 1940 Elections: Two Reports by Earl Browder.* New York: Workers Library Publishers, 1940.

———. *The People Against the War-Makers.* New York: Workers Library Publishers, 1940.

———. *The Jewish People and the War.* New York: Workers Library Publishers, 1940.

———. *The People's Road to Peace.* New York: Workers Library Publishers, 1940.

———. *The Way Out of the Imperialist War.* New York: Workers Library Publishers, 1941.

———. *Earl Browder Says.* New York: Workers Library Publishers, 1941.

———. *The Road to Victory.* New York: Workers Library Publishers, 1941.

———. *The Communist Party of the U.S.A.: Its History, Role and Organization.* New York: Workers Library Publishers, [1941?].

———. *Production for Victory.* New York: Workers Library Publishers, 1942.

———. *Earl Browder on the Soviet Union.* New York: Workers Library Publishers, 1942.

———. *"Is Communism a Menace?" A Debate Between Earl Browder and George E. Sokolsky.* New York: New Masses, 1943.

———. *Wage Policy in War Production.* New York: Workers Library Publishers, 1943.

———. *Policy For Victory.* New York: Workers Library Publishers, 1943.

———. *Teheran: History's Greatest Turning Point.* [s.l.; s.d.].

———. *The Future of the Anglo-Soviet-American Coalition.* New York: Workers Library Publishers, 1943.

———. *A Talk About the Communist Party.* New York: Workers Library Publishers, 1943.

———. *Teheran and America.* New York: Workers Library Publishers, 1944.

———. *Moscow, Cairo, Teheran.* New York: Workers Library Publishers, 1944.

———. *The Road Ahead to Victory and Lasting Peace.* New York: Workers Library Publishers, 1944.

———. Eugene Dennis; Roy Hudson; and John Williamson. *Shall the Communist Party Change Its Name?* New York: CPUSA, 1944.

———. *The Meaning of the Elections.* New York: Workers Library Publishers, 1944.

———. *America's Decisive Battle.* New York: New Century Publishers, 1945.

Bibliography

——. *Why America Is Interested in the Chinese Communists*. New York: Workers Library Publishers, 1945.

——. *The Writings and Speeches of Earl Browder From May 24, 1945 to July 26, 1945*. [s.l; 1945?].

Communist Party. *Shop Paper Manual: A Handbook for Comrades Active in Shop Paper Work*. [s.l.]: Central Committee Communist Party, U.S.A., [1931?]

——. *Where do the Communists Stand? Communist Election Pamphlets—1932*. New York: Workers Library Publishers, 1932.

——. *Culture in Crisis: An Open Letter to the Writers, Artists, Teachers, Physicians, Engineers, Scientists and Other Professional Workers of America*. New York: Workers Library Publishers, 1932.

——. *Communist Election Platform: Against Imperialist War—For Jobs and Bread*. New York: Workers Library Publishers, 1932.

——. *The Democratic Twin of the Hoover Hunger Government*. New York: Workers Library Publishers, 1932.

——. *Hoover: The Great Engineer After Four Years*. New York: Workers Library Publishers, 1932.

——. *The Farmers' Way Out: The Position of the Communist Party on the Problems of the Farmers*. New York: Workers Library Publishers, 1932.

——. *Will Beer Bring Back Prosperity? The Communist Position on the Repeal of the Eighteenth Amendment*. New York: Workers Library Publishers, 1932.

——. *Working Women and the Elections*. New York: Workers Library Publishers, 1932.

——. *An Open Letter to All Members of the Communist Party*. New York: Central Committee, Communisty Party U.S.A., [1933?]

——. *The Communist Position on the Farmers' Movement*. New York: Workers Library Publishers, 1933.

——. *The Way Out-A Program For American Labor*. New York: Workers Library Publishers, 1934.

——. *Resolutions of the Ninth Convention of the Communist Party of the U.S.A.* New York: Workers Library Publishers, 1936.

——. *The Communist Election Platform*. New York: Workers Library Publishers, 1936.

——. *Resolutions of the 10th Convention of the Communist Party U.S.A.* New York: Workers Library Publishers, 1938.

——. *The Constitution and By-Laws of the Communist Party of the United States of America*. New York: Workers Library Publishers, 1938.

——. *Communist Election Platform 1938: For Jobs, Security, Democracy and Peace*. New York: Workers Library Publishers, 1938.

——. *The Smithy of the Revolution*. [s.l.]: National Training School, 1938.

——. *Political Almanac: 8th Assembly District, New York County 1938*. New York: Communist Party, 1938.

———. *Election Platform of the Communist Party, 1940*. New York: Workers Library Publishers, 1940.

———. *Campaign Book: Presidential Elections, 1940*. New York: Workers Library Publishers, 1940.

———. *Constitution of the Communist Party U.S.A.* New York: Workers Library Publishers, [1942?].

———. *Stages in the History of the Communist Party: A Political Review*. New York: Communist Party, U.S.A., [1943]

———. *Manual For Community Club Leaders*. New York: Organization Department, Communist National Committee, 1944.

———. *The Present Situation and the Next Tasks*. New York: New Century Publishers, 1945.

Dennis Eugene. *The Elections and the Outlook for National Unity*. New York: Workers Library Publishers, 1944.

———. *America at the Crossroads: Postwar Problems and Communist Policy*. New York: New Century Publishers, 1945.

Dimitrov, Georgi. *Working Class Unity—Bulwark Against Fascism*. New York: Workers Library Publishers, 1935.

Doran, David. *The Highway of Hunger: Story of America's Homeless Youth*. New York: Workers Library Publishers, 1933.

Foster, William Z., and James W. Ford. *Foster and Ford for Food and Freedom*. New York: Workers Library Publishers, 1932.

———. *The Words and Deeds of Franklin D. Roosevelt*. New York: Workers Library Publishers, 1932.

———. Alexander Bittelman, James W. Ford, and Charles Krumbein. *Party Building and Political Leadership*. New York: Workers Library Publishers, 1937.

———. Robert Minor, James W. Ford, Earl Browder, and others. *The Path of Browder and Foster*. New York: Workers Library Publishers, 1941.

———. *American Democracy and the War*. New York: Workers Library Publishers, 1942.

———. *Labor and the War*. New York: Workers Library Publishers, 1942.

———. Introduction to *America at the Crossroads: Postwar Problems and Communist Policy*. New York: New Century Publishers, 1945.

[Friends of the Abraham Lincoln Battalion.] *The Story of the Abraham Lincoln Battalion*. New York: Friends of the Abraham Lincoln Battalion, [1937].

Gannes, Harry. *Kentucky Miners Fight*. [NY]: Workers International Relief, 1932.

Gates, John. *On Guard Against Browderism, Titoism, Trotskyism*. New York: New Century Publishers, 1951.

Hathaway, C. A. *Communists in the Textile Strike: An Answer to Gorman, Green and Co.* New York: Communist Party, U.S.A., 1934.

Bibliography

Hutchins, Grace. *Women Who Work*. New York: International Publishers, 1934.
Minor, Robert. *Free Earl Browder*. New York: Workers Library Publishers, 1941.
———. *The Heritage of the Communist Political Association*. New York: Workers Library Publishers, 1944.
Olgin, Moissaye J. *The Socialist Party: Last Bulwark of Capitalism*. New York: Workers Library Publishers, 1932.
———. *Capitalism Defends Itself Through the Socialist Labor Party*. New York: Workers Library Publishers, 1932.
Peters, J. *The Communist Party: A Manual on Organization*. New York: Workers Library Publishers, 1935.
Stachel, Jack. "The Problem of a Labor Party" in *How Do We Raise the Question of a Labor Party?* New York: Workers Library Publishers, 1935.
Thompson, Robert. *The Path of a Renegade: Why Earl Browder Was Expelled From the Communist Party*. New York: New Century Publishers, 1946.
Trade Union Unity League. *Fight! Don't Starve! Organize*. New York: Trade Union Unity League, 1931.
Young Communist League. *Foster-Ford: The Candidates of the Working Youth*. New York: Youth Publishers, 1932.

Books

Aaron, Daniel. *Writers On the Left*. New York: Harcourt, Brace and World, 1961.
Alexander, Robert J. *The Right Opposition: The Lovestonites and the International Communist Opposition of the 1930s*. Westport, Conn.: Greenwood Press, 1982.
Aronowitz, Stanley. *False Promises: The Shaping of American Working Class Consciousness*. New York: McGraw-Hill, 1974.
Bart, Philip. *Highlights of a Fighting History: 60 Years of the Communist Party, U.S.A.* New York: International Publishers, 1979.
Beal, Fred E. *Proletarian Journey*. New York: Hillman-Curl, 1937.
Bell, Daniel. *The End Of Ideology* rev. ed. New York: The Free Press, 1967.
Bernstein, Irving. *The Lean Years*. Boston: Houghton Mifflin Company, 1960.
———. *Turbulent Years*. Boston: Houghton Mifflin Co., 1970.
Bessie, Alvah. *Men in Battle*. San Francisco: Chandler & Sharp Publishers, 1975.
Bloor, Ella Reeve. *We Are Many*. New York: International Publishers, 1940.
Browder, Earl. *Communism in the United States*. New York: International Publishers, 1935.
———. *What Is Communism?* New York: Workers Library Publishers, 1936.
———. *The People's Front*. New York: International Publishers, 1938.
———. *Fighting for Peace*. New York: International Publishers, 1939.

————. *The Second Imperialist War*. New York: International Publishers, 1940.

————. *The Way Out*. New York: International Publishers, 1941.

————. *Victory and After*. New York: International Publishers, 1942.

————. *Teheran: Our Path in War and In Peace*. New York: International Publishers, 1944.

Brower, Daniel. *The New Jacobins: The French Communist Party and the Popular Front*. Ithaca: Cornell University Press, 1968.

Buhle, Paul. *Marxism in the U.S.A.: Remapping the History of the American Left*. London: Verso, 1987.

Burns, MacGregor, James. *Roosevelt: The Lion and the Fox, 1882–1940*. New York: Harcourt, Brace and World, 1956.

————. *Roosevelt: The Soldier of Freedom*. New York: Harcourt Brace Jovanovich, 1970.

Cannon, James P. *The History of American Trotskyism*. New York: Pioneer Publishers, 1944.

————. *The First Ten Years of American Communism: Report of a Participant*. New York: Pathfinder Press, 1973.

————. *The Socialist Workers Party in World War II*. New York: Pathfinder Press, 1975.

Cantor, Milton. *The Divided Left: American Radicalism, 1900–1975*. New York: Hill and Wang, 1978.

Carr, E. H. *Twilight of the Comintern, 1930–1935*. New York: Pantheon Books, 1982.

Carter, Dan T. *Scottsboro: A Tragedy of the American South*. Baton Rouge: Louisiana State University Press, 1969.

Central Committee of the C.P.S.U. *Outline History of the Communist International*. Moscow: Progress Publishers, 1971.

Charney, George. *A Long Journey*. Chicago: Quadrangle, 1968.

Cochran, Bert. *Labor and Communism: The Conflict that Shaped American Unions*. Princeton, N.J.: Princeton University Press, 1977.

Communist International. *Seventh Congress of the Communist International*. Moscow: Foreign Languages Publishing House, 1939.

Communist Party of the Soviet Union (Bolshevik). *The Land of Socialism Today and Tomorrow*. Moscow: Foreign Languages Publishing House, 1939.

Communist Political Association. *The Path to Peace, Progress and Prosperity*. New York: Communist Political Association, 1944.

Dallek, Robert. *Franklin D. Roosevelt and American Foreign Policy, 1932–1945*. New York: Oxford University Press, 1979.

Daniel, Cletus E. *Bitter Harvest: A History of California Farmworkers, 1870–1941*. Ithaca: Cornell University Press, 1981.

Davies, Joseph E. *Mission to Moscow*. New York: Simon and Schuster, 1941.

Davis, Benjamin J. *Communist Councilman From Harlem*. New York: International Publishers, 1969.

Bibliography

DeCaux, Len. *Labor Radical: From the Wobblies to the CIO*, Boston: Beacon Press, 1970.

Degras, Jane. *The Communist International, 1919–1943*, 3 vols. London: Oxford University Press, 1956.

Dennis, Peggy. *The Autobiography of an American Communist: A Personal View of a Political Life, 1925–1975*. Berkeley, Calif.: Creative Arts, 1977.

Dodd, Bella V. *School of Darkness*. New York: P.J. Kennedy, 1954.

Draper, Theodore. *The Roots of American Communism*. New York: Viking, 1957.

———. *American Communism and Soviet Russia: The Formative Period*. New York: Viking Press, 1960.

Drew Egbert Donald and Persons Stow. *Socialism and American Life*. Princeton, N.J.: Princeton University Press, 1952.

Dubofsky, Melvyn, and Warren Van Tine. *John L. Lewis*. New York: Quadrangle, 1977.

Dyson, Lowell K. *Red Harvest: The Communist Party and American Farmers*. Lincoln: University of Nebraska Press, 1982.

Eagan, Eileen. *Class, Culture, and the Classroom: The Student Peace Movement of the 1930s*. Philadelphia: Temple University Press, 1981.

Epstein, Melech. *The Jew and Communism, 1919–1941*. New York: Trade Union Sponsoring Committee, 1959.

Fine, Sidney. *The Automobile Under the Blue Eagle*. Ann Arbor: University of Michigan Press, 1963.

———. *Sit-Down: The General Motors Strike of 1936–1937*. Ann Arbor: University of Michigan Press, 1969.

Flynn, Elizabeth Gurley. *The Rebel Girl, An Autobiography: My First Life (1906–1926)* rev. ed. New York: International Publishers, 1973.

Foner, Philip. *The Fur and Leather Workers Union: A History of Dramatic Struggles and Achievements*. Newark, N.J.: Worden Press, 1950.

Foster, William Z. *Toward Soviet America*. New York: Coward-McCann, Inc., 1932.

———. *From Bryan to Stalin*. New York: International Publishers, 1937.

———. *Pages From a Worker's Life*. New York: International Publishers, 1939.

———. *American Trade Unionism: Principles and Organization Strategy and Tactics*. New York: International Publishers, 1947.

———. *The Twilight of World Capitalism*. New York: International Publishers, 1949.

———. *History of the Communist Party of the United States*. New York: International Publishers, 1952.

Galenson, Walter. *The CIO Challenge to the AFL*. Cambridge, Mass.: Harvard University Press, 1960.

Gates, John. *The Story of an American Communist*. New York: Thomas Nelson, 1958.

Gerson, Simon W. *Pete: The Story of Peter V. Cacchione, New York's First Communist Councilman*. New York: International Publishers, 1976.

Gieske, Millard L. *Minnesota Farmer-Laborism: The Third-Party Alternative*. Minneapolis: University of Minnesota Press, 1979.

Glazer, Nathan. *The Social Basis of American Communism*. New York: Harcourt, Brace and World, Inc., 1961.

Goodman, Walter. *The Committee: The Extraordinary Career of the House Committee on Un-American Activities*. New York: Farrar, Straus and Giroux, 1968.

Gornick, Vivian. *The Romance of American Communism*. New York: Basic Books, 1977.

Griffith, Robert and Athan Theoharis, eds. *The Specter: Original Essays on the Cold War and the Origins of McCarthyism*. New York: New Viewpoints, 1974.

Hart, Henry, ed. *American Writers Congress*. New York: International Publishers, 1935.

———, ed. *The Writer in a Changing World*. London: Lawrence and Wishart, 1937.

Haynes, John Earl. *Dubious Alliance: The Making of Minnesota's DFL Party*. Minneapolis: University of Minnesota Press, 1984.

Haywood, Harry. *Black Bolshevik: Autobiography of an Afro-American Communist*. Chicago: Liberator Press, 1978.

Hicks, Granville. *I Like America*. New York: Modern Age Books, 1938.

———. *Part of the Truth*. New York: Harcourt, Brace and World, 1965.

Howe, Irving, and Lewis Coser. *The American Communist Party: A Critical History*. Boston: Beacon Press, 1957.

Howe, Irving. *Socialism in America*. New York: Harcourt Brace Jovanovich, 1985.

Ingalls, Robert P. *Urban Vigilantes in the New South: Tampa, 1882–1936*. Knoxville: University of Tennessee Press, 1988.

Isserman, Maurice. *Which Side Were You On? The American Communist Party during the Second World War*. Middletown, Conn.: Wesleyan University Press, 1982.

Jaffe, Philip J. *The Rise and Fall of American Communism*. New York: Horizon Press, 1975.

Josephson, Matthew. *Infidel in the Temple*. New York: Alfred A. Knopf, 1967.

Keeran, Roger. *The Communist Party and the Auto Workers Unions*. Bloomington: Indiana University Press, 1980.

Klehr, Harvey. *Communist Cadre: The Social Background of the American Communist Party Elite*. Stanford: Hoover Institution Press, 1978.

———. *The Heyday of American Communism: The Depression Decade*. New York: Basic Books, 1984.

Bibliography

Kraus, Henry, *The Many and the Few,* 2nd ed. Urbana: University of Illinois Press, 1985.

Lash, Joseph P. *Eleanor and Franklin.* New York: Norton, 1971.

Laslett, John H. M., and Seymour Martin Lipset, eds. *Failure of a Dream? Essays in the History of American Socialism.* Garden City, New York: Anchor Press, 1974.

Latham, Earl. *The Communist Controversy in Washington: From the New Deal to McCarthy.* Cambridge, Mass.: Harvard University Press, 1966.

Leab, Daniel. *A Union of Individuals: The Formation of the American Newpaper Guild, 1933–1936.* New York: Columbia University Press, 1970.

Lembcke, Jerry and William M. Tattam. *One Union in Wood: A Political History of the International Woodworkers of America.* New York: International Publishers, 1984.

Lenin, V. I. *A Letter to American Workers.* New York: International Publishers, 1934.

———. *"Left-Wing" Communism, an Infantile Disorder.* New York: International Publishers, 1940.

Leuchtenburg, William E. *Franklin D. Roosevelt and the New Deal.* New York: Harper & Row, 1963.

Levenstein, Harvey A. *Communism, Anticommunism, and the CIO.* Westport, Connecticut: Greenwood Press, 1981.

Liebman, Arthur. *Jews and the Left.* New York: John Wiley & Sons, 1979.

Lynd, Alice and Staughton. *Rank and File: Personal Histories by Working-Class Organizers.* Boston: Beacon Press, 1973.

Lyons, Paul. *Philadelphia Communists, 1936–1956.* Philadelphia: Temple University Press, 1982.

Martin, Charles H. *The Angelo Herndon Case and Southern Justice.* Baton Rouge: Louisiana State University Press, 1976.

Matles, James J. and James Higgins. *Them and Us: Struggles of a Rank-and-File Union.* Englewood Cliffs, N.J.: Prentice Hall, 1974.

McKenzie, Kermit, E. *Comintern and World Revolution, 1928–1943.* New York: Columbia University Press, 1964.

Mortimer, Wyndham. *Organize! My Life as a Union Man.* Boston: Beacon Press, 1971.

Myers, Constance Ashton. *The Prophet's Army: Trotskyists in America, 1928–1941.* Westport, Conn.: Greenwood Press, 1977.

Naison, Mark. *Communists in Harlem during the Depression.* Urbana: University of Illinois Press, 1983.

Nelson, Bruce. *Workers on the Waterfront: Seamen, Longshoremen, and Unionism in the 1930s.* Urbana: University of Illinois Press, 1988.

Nelson, Steve, James R. Barrett, and Rob Ruck. *Steve Nelson, American Radical.* Pittsburgh: University of Pittsburgh Press, 1981.

Painter, Nell. *The Narrative of Hosea Hudson, His Life as a Negro Communist in the South.* Cambridge, Mass.: Harvard University Press, 1979.

Pells, Richard H. *Radical Vision and American Dreams: Culture and Social Thought in the Depression Years.* New York: Harper and Row, 1973.

Quin, Mike. *The Big Strike.* Olema, California: Olema Publishing House, 1949.

Richmond, Al. *A Long View From the Left: Memoirs of an American Revolutionary.* Boston: Houghton Mifflin Co., 1972.

Robinson, Jo Ann Ooiman. *Abraham Went Out: A Biography of A. J. Muste.* Philadelphia: Temple University Press, 1981.

Rosenstone, Robert A. *Crusade on the Left, The Lincoln Battalion in the Spanish Civil War.* New York: Pegasus, 1969.

Scales, Irving Junius and Richard Nickson. *Cause at Heart: A Former Communist Remembers.* Athens: University of Georgia Press, 1987.

Schatz, Ronald W. *The Electrical Workers: A History of Labor at General Electric and Westinghouse, 1923–1960.* Urbana: University of Illinois Press, 1983.

Schrecker, Ellen W. *No Ivory Tower: McCarthyism and the Universities.* New York: Oxford University Press, 1986.

Schneiderman, William. *Dissent on Trial: The Story of a Political Life.* Minneapolis: MEP Publications, 1983.

Shannon, David A. *The Socialist Party of America: A History.* New York: Macmillan, 1955.

Simon, Rita James, ed. *As We Saw the Thirties: Essays on Social and Political Movements of a Decade.* Urbana: University of Illinois Press, 1967.

Starobin, Joseph R. *American Communism in Crisis, 1943–1957.* Cambridge, Mass.: Harvard University Press, 1972.

Thomas, Norman. *After the New Deal, What?* New York: Macmillan, 1936.

Tippett, Tom. *When Southern Labor Stirs.* New York: Jonathan Cape & Harrison Smith, 1931.

Warren, Frank A. *Liberals and Communism: The "Red Decade" Revisited.* Bloomington: Indiana University Press, 1966.

———. *An Alternative Vision: The Socialist Party in the 1930s.* Bloomington: Indiana University Press, 1974.

Wechsler, James. *Revolt on the Campus.* New York: Covici, Friede Publishers, 1935.

Weinstein, James. *The Decline of Socialism in America, 1912–1925.* New York: Vintage, 1969.

———. *Ambiguous Legacy: The Left in American Politics.* New York: New Viewpoints, 1975.

Weisbord, Vera Buch. *A Radical Life.* Bloomington: Indiana University Press, 1977.

Williamson, John. *Dangerous Scott: The Life and Work of an American "Undesirable."* New York: International Publishers, 1969.

Bibliography

Articles

Aaron Daniel, Malcolm Cowley, Kenneth Burke, Granville Hicks, and William Phillips. "Thirty Years Later: Memories of the First American Writers' Congress." *The American Scholar* 35 (Summer 1966):495–516.

Bellush, Bernard and Jewel Bellush. "A Radical Response to the Roosevelt Presidency: The Communist Party, 1933–1945." *Presidential Study Quarterly* 10(Fall 1980):545–561.

Baskin, Alex. "The Ford Hunger March—1932." *Labor History* 13(Summer 1972):331–360.

Brody, David. "Labor and the Great Depression: The Interpretative Prospects." *Labor History* 13(Spring 1972):231–244.

Browder, Earl. "How Stalin Ruined the American Communist Party." *Harper's Magazine* 220(March 1960):45–51.

Buhle, Paul. "Jews and American Communism: The Cultural Question." *Radical History Review* 23(Spring 1980):9–33.

Davin, Eric Leif and Staughton Lynd. "Picket Line and Ballot Box: The Forgotten Legacy of the Local Labor Party Movement, 1932–1936." *Radical History Review* 22(Winter 1979–1980):43–63.

Dennis, Peggy. "A Response to Ellen Kay Trimberger's Essay, 'Women in the Old and New Left.' " *Feminist Studies* 5(Fall 1979):451–461.

———. "On Learning From History." *Socialist Revolution* 6(July–September 1976):125–143.

Dowd, Hall Jacquelyn. "Disorderly Women: Gender and Labor Militancy in the Appalachian South." *Journal of American History* 73(September 1986):354–382.

Draper, Theodore. "Communists and Miners: 1928–1933." *Dissent* (Spring 1972):371–392.

Filippelli, Ronald L. "UE: The Formative Years, 1933–1937." *Labor History* 17(Summer 1976):351–371.

Dyson, Lowell K. "The Red Peasant International in America." *Journal of American History* 58(March 1972):958–973.

Freeman, Joshua. "Delivering The Goods: Industrial Unionism During World War II." *Labor History* 19(Fall 1978):570–593.

———. "Catholics, Communists, and Republicans: Irish Workers and the Organization of the Transport Workers Union," in Michael H. Frisch and Daniel J. Walkowitz, eds., *Working Class America: Essays on Labor, Community, and American Society.* Urbana: University of Illinois Press, 1983.

Garraty, John A. "Unemployment During the Great Depression." *Labor History* 17(Spring 1976):133–159.

Gordon, Max. "The Communist Party of the Nineteen-thirties and the New Left." With a response by James Weinstein and a reply by Max Gordon. *Socialist Revolution* 27(January–March 1976): 11–65.

————. "The Communists and the Drive to Organize Steel, 1936." *Labor History* 23(Spring 1982):254–265.

Haynes, John Earl. "The New History of the Communist Party in State Politics: The Implications for Mainstream Political Theory." *Labor History* 27(Fall 1986):549–563.

Homberger, Eric. "Proletarian Literature and the John Reed Clubs, 1929–1935." *Journal of American Studies* 13(August 1979):221–244.

Honey, Michael. "The Popular Front in the American South: The View From Memphis." *International Labor and Working-Class History* 30(Fall 1986):44–58.

Isserman, Maurice. "The 1956 Generation: An Alternative Approach to the History of American Communism." *Radical America* 14(March–April 1980):43–51.

————. "The Half-Swept House: American Communism in 1956." *Socialist Review* 12(January–February 1982):71–101.

————. "Three Generations: Historians View American Communism." *Labor History* 26(Fall 1985):517–545.

Johanningsmeier, Edward P. "William Z. Foster and the Syndicalist League of North America." *Labor History* 30(Summer 1989):329–353.

Keeran, Roger R. "Everything For Victory: Communist Influence in the Auto Industry During World War II." *Science & Society* 43(Spring 1979):1–28.

————. "The International Workers Order and the Origins of the CIO." *Labor History* 30(Summer 1979):385–408.

Kelley, Robin D. G. "A New War in Dixie: Communists and the Unemployed in Birmingham, Alabama, 1930–1933." *Labor History* 30(Summer 1989):367–385.

Leab, Daniel J. "United We Eat: The Creation and Organization of the Unemployed Councils in 1930." *Labor History* 8(Fall 1967):300–315.

Levenstein, Harvey. "Defending the No-Strike Pledge: CIO Politics during World War II." *Radical America* 9(July–August 1975):49–75.

————. "Leninists Undone By Leninism: Communism and Unionism in the United States and Mexico, 1935–1939." *Labor History* 22(Spring 1981):237–261.

Lichtenstein, Nelson. "Ambiguous Legacy: The Union Security Problem During World War II." *Labor History* 18(Spring 1977):214–238.

————. "The Communist Experience in American Trade Unions." (With replies by Robert H. Zieger and Roger Keeran.) *Industrial Relations* 19(Spring 1980):119–139.

Lynd, Staughton. "The United Front in America: A Note." *Radical America* 5(July–August 1974):29–38.

————. "The Possibility of Radicalism in the Early 1930s: The Case of Steel." *Radical America* 6(November–December 1972):37–64.

McFarland, C. K. "Coalition of Convenience: Lewis and Roosevelt, 1933–1940." *Labor History* 13(Summer 1972):400–414.

Martin, Charles H. "The International Labor Defense and Black America." *Labor History* 26(Spring 1985):165–194.

Meier, August and Elliot Rudwick. "Communist Unions and the Black Community: The Case of the Transport Workers Union, 1934–1944." *Labor History* 23(Spring 1982):165–197.

Monroy, Douglass. "Anarquismo y Comunismo: Mexican Radicalism and the Communist Party in Los Angeles during the 1930s." *Labor History* 24(Winter 1983):34:59.

Nadel, Stanley. "Reds Versus Pinks: A Civil War in the International Ladies Garment Workers Union." *New York History* (January 1985):49–72.

Naison, Mark. "Harlem Communists and the Politics of Black Protest." *Marxist Perspectives* 1(Fall 1978):20–50.

———. "Historical Notes on Blacks and American Communism: The Harlem Experience." *Science & Society* XLII(Fall 1978): 324–343.

———. "Lefties & Righties: The Communist Party and Sports During the Great Depression." *Radical America* 13(July–August 1979):47–59.

———. "Communism and Harlem Intellectuals in the Popular Front: Anti-Fascism and the Politics of Black Culture." *The Journal of Ethnic Studies* 9(Spring 1981):1–25.

Nelson, Bruce. "Unions and the Popular Front: The West Coast Waterfront in the 1930s." *International Labor and Working-Class History* 30(Fall 1986):59–78.

Nelson, Daniel. "Origins of the Sit-Down Era: Worker Militancy and Innovation in the Rubber Industry, 1934–38." *Labor History* 23(Spring 1982):198–225.

———. "The CIO at Bay: Labor Militancy and Politics in Akron." *Journal of American History* 71(December 1984):565–586.

Pahl, Thomas L. "The G-String Conspiracy: Political Reprisal or Armed Revolt?" *Labor History* 8(Winter 1967):30–51.

Peck, David. "The Tradition of American Revolutionary Literature: The Monthly *New Masses*, 1926–1933." *Science & Society* 42(Winter 1978–1979):385–409.

Peterson, Joyce Shaw. "Auto Workers and Their Work, 1900–1933." *Labor History* 22(Spring 1981):213–236.

Rosenzsweig, Roy. "Radicals and the Jobless: The Musteites and the Unemployed Leagues, 1932–1936." *Labor History* 16(Winter 1975):52–77.

———. "Organizing the Unemployed: The Early Years of the Great Depression, 1929–1933." *Radical America* 10(July–August 1976):47–60.

———. "Oral History and the Old Left." *International Labor and Working Class History* 24(Fall 1983):27–38.

Ross, Hugh. "John L. Lewis and the Election of 1940." *Labor History* 17(Spring 1976):160–190.

Ryan, James Gilbert. "The Making of a Native Marxist: The Early Career of Earl Browder." *The Review of Politics* 39(July 1977):332–362.

Santos, Michael W. "Community and Communism: The 1928 New Bedford Textile Strike." *Labor History* 26(Spring 1985):230–249.

Shaffer, Robert. "Women and the Communist Party, U.S.A., 1930–1940." *Socialist Review* 9(May–June 1979):73–118.

Trimberger, Ellen Kay. "Women in the Old and New Left: The Evolution of a Politics of Personal Life." *Feminist Studies* 5(Fall 1979):432–450.

Waltzer, Kenneth. "The Party and the Polling Place: American Communism and the American Labor Party in the 1930s." *Radical History Review* 23(Spring 1980):104–129.

Wittner, Lawrence S. "The National Negro Congress: A Reassessment." *American Quarterly* 22(Winter 1970):883–901.

Dissertations

Alperin, Robert Jay. "Organization in the Communist Party, U.S.A., 1931–1938." Ph.D. dissertation, Northwestern University, 1959.

Belknap, Michael R. "The Smith Act and the Communist Party: A Study in Political Justice." Ph.D. dissertation, University of Wisconsin, 1973.

Dixler, Elsa Jane. "The Woman Question: Women and the American Communist Party, 1929–1941." Ph.D. dissertation, Yale University, 1974.

Kelly, Robin Davis Gibran. " 'Hammer n' Hoe,' Black Radicalism and the Communist Party in Alabama, 1929–1941" Ph.D. dissertation, University of California at Los Angeles, 1987.

Lichtenstein, Nelson. "Industrial Unionism Under the No Strike Pledge: A Study of the CIO during the Second World War." Ph.D. dissertation, University of California at Berkeley, 1974.

Ottanelli, Fraser M. " 'What the Hell Is These Reds Anyways?' The Americanization of the Communist Party of the United States, 1930–1945." Ph.D. dissertation, Syracuse University, 1987.

Prickett, James R. "Communists and the Communist Issue in the American Labor Movement, 1920–1950." Ph.D. dissertation, University of California at Los Angeles, 1975.

Rawick, George P. "The New Deal and Youth: The Civil Conservation Corps, the National Youth Administration and the American Youth Congress." Ph.D. dissertation, University of Wisconsin, 1957.

Ryan, James G. "Earl Browder and American Communism at High Tide: 1934–1945." Ph.D. dissertation, University of Notre Dame, 1981.

Bibliography

Streater, John Baxter Jr. "The National Negro Congress, 1936–1947." Ph.D. dissertation, University of Cincinnati, 1981.

Urmann, Michael F. "Rank and File Communists and the CIO (Committee for Industrial Organization) Unions." Ph.D. dissertation, University of Utah, 1981.

Waltzer, Kenneth A. "The American Labor Party: Third Party Politics in New Deal-Cold War New York, 1936–1954." Ph.D. dissertation, Harvard, 1978.

Index